A 1960 Census Monograph

EDUCATION
of the
American Population

by

JOHN K. FOLGER

Florida State University

and

CHARLES B. NAM

Florida State University

Prepared in cooperation with the
Social Science Research Council

U.S. DEPARTMENT OF COMMERCE
Alexander B. Trowbridge, Secretary
William H. Shaw, Asst. Secy., Economic Affairs

BUREAU OF THE CENSUS
A. Ross Eckler, Director

BUREAU OF THE CENSUS

A. Ross Eckler, Director

Howard C. Grieves, Deputy Director

Conrad Taeuber, Assistant Director
for Demographic Fields

Library of Congress Catalog No. A66–7677

Suggested Citation:

U.S. Bureau of the Census, *Education of the American Population,* by John K. Folger and Charles B. Nam (A 1960 Census Monograph). U.S. Government Printing Office, Washington, D.C., 1967.

For sale by the Superintendent of Documents, U.S. Government Printing Office
Washington, D.C. 20402 - Price $2.25

FOREWORD

The Decennial Census of Population is the most important single source of information about social trends in the United States. Its data on the people and families who make up the population give an insight into the major social changes occurring in our country. Data on age, sex, color, and national origin provide the essential basis for determining the changes occurring in the composition of our population. The census results make it possible to learn much about the family organization, settlement patterns, education, work relationships, income, and other important characteristics of our people. Relationships such as that of age and education to occupation and industry, or of race and education to occupation and income, tell a great deal about how our society functions. The census provides an unequaled set of statistics to meet national and local needs. The advent of electronic computers has increased the availability of census results and the exploration of interrelationships which defied analysis previously.

The regular statistical reports resulting from a decennial census can supply only a fraction of the information and insights that are available from this important source. These reports present only those results which are believed to meet the general public needs. Comprehensive analyses of the results, and comparisons with other current data and with past censuses, open the door to many illuminating findings.

It has long been recognized that the public would reap additional benefits from its investment in the censuses if some of the analyses that are readily possible could be provided along with the basic data. A series of Census monographs was issued by the Bureau of the Census after the 1920 Census results had been published. A series of Census monographs followed the 1950 Census, through the cooperation of the Social Science Research Council. These monographs filled a real need and were so well received that it was felt desirable to initiate plans for a similar series following the 1960 Census.

The Council again took the lead in the formulation of these plans in 1958 when it appointed a Committee on Population Census Monographs. This Committee included:

Dudley Kirk, Population Council, Chairman
Robert W. Burgess, Bureau of the Census
John D. Durand, Population Branch, United Nations
Ronald Freedman, University of Michigan
Daniel O. Price, University of North Carolina
John W. Riley, Jr., Equitable Life Assurance
   Society of the United States
George J. Stolnitz, Indiana University.

Paul Webbink, of the Social Science Research Council, and Conrad Taeuber, of the Census Bureau staff, met regularly with the Committee, which reviewed proposals for Census monographs and aided in the selection of authors for specific publications.

The Council gratefully acknowledges a grant of funds from the Russell Sage Foundation for the planning and initiation of the program. The Foundation had provided similar assistance in the 1950 program.

In 1960, the Equitable Life Assurance Society of the United States, because of its concern with the expansion in knowledge of the ever-changing structure and functioning of the larger society of the United States, began a program of basic social research. As one of the first steps in this development, it has joined in encouraging and supporting a series of studies of which this monograph is a part.

The assistance from the sources named above made it possible to arrange for the time of some of the authors and to provide special tabulations and statistical and research services which were essential to the preparation of the monographs.

The program has received the active encouragement of scholars in the Federal Government and a number of universities, and we are glad to acknowledge the debt to these individuals and the institutions they represent. This cooperation was essential for the preparation of the monographs.

The monograph authors were asked to provide interpretations of census and related statistics that would illuminate major current problem areas. The authors were also asked to take a critical look at the data and to make any recommendations which in their opinion would contribute to better development and use of the data.

The views expressed in the monograph series are those of the individual authors, each of whom has been given the freedom to interpret available materials in the light of his technical knowledge and competence. These views are not necessarily those of the Bureau of the Census or the Social Science Research Council.

A. ROSS ECKLER, *Director*
Bureau of the Census

PENDLETON HERRING, *President*
Social Science Research Council

PREFACE

This study has as its purposes the description of the educational status of the American population over time, as revealed in Census data and other statistical materials, and the analysis of the relation of school enrollment and educational attainment to other social and economic characteristics of the population. In general, the monograph deals with the following questions: What has been the historical trend in extension of schooling in the United States? To what extent have different categories of the population shared in this educational achievement? How have social and economic forces affected the pace at which educational change has taken place? What have been some of the important consequences of educational improvement for American social institutions?

The large amount of information about education that is available in the decennial censuses of population and in the current population surveys conducted by the Bureau of the Census makes a balanced selection and presentation difficult, even for a full-length monograph. We have limited this monograph to three major aspects of education: enrollment of students, the characteristics of teachers, and the educational attainments of the adult population. On each topic we have presented both historical materials and analyses of educational differences among important groups of the population. Because we have tried to indicate the range and variety of relevant census data, the treatment of many topics is brief. For the reader who may want to examine particular topics in further detail, there is a topical index to published census data on education. There is also a summary chapter which presents the major findings and conclusions of our analysis, and appendixes concerned with the quality of census education data.

The detailed tabulations of the 1960 Census of Population that relate to education were made possible, in part, by funds granted to the authors by the U.S. Office of Education Cooperative Research Branch. As indicated in the foreword, the 1960 Census monograph program was sponsored by the Social Science Research Council and the Bureau of the Census. We want to express our appreciation to all of these organizations, without whose support the study could not have been accomplished.

We received a great deal of assistance in the preparation of this monograph from numerous individuals. Lois Ivey, Lois Queen, Edna Stoddard, Evelyn Hoffman, and Ruth Garrett of the Census Bureau staff were involved in performing computations, checking tabular materials, and typing drafts of chapters. Betty Stevens typed the final drafts of the entire manuscript, Leah

Anderson capably supervised the preparation of the final copy for the printer, and Hennie Schneider compiled the index.

Myron Blee, Edward Hallenback, L. J. Lins, and Donald Moyer assisted in the collection of comparative enrollment data for the study described in appendix A, and were largely responsible for the excellent response to that survey.

Allan Cartter, Paul Glick, Henry Shryock, Conrad Taeuber, and James Cowhig all contributed useful suggestions and ideas from their reading of all or part of the manuscript. We are particularly grateful to C. Arnold Anderson, who read the entire manuscript and offered numerous helpful criticisms and suggestions.

Norman Lawrence and Josephine Hemphill edited the manuscript, and helped to correct errors of substance, as well as to greatly improve the clarity and readability of many sections.

For the errors that remain, and the difficulties in style and clarity, the authors alone are responsible; we had good advice, but we may not have always heeded it.

Washington, D.C. JOHN K. FOLGER
May 1967 CHARLES B. NAM

CONTENTS

Chapter   Page

CHAPTER I

THE GROWTH OF ENROLLMENT IN AMERICA

Introduction

The new American Nation was fertile ground for the growth of universal education. The ideal of schooling for everyone found ready acceptance in egalitarian society unhampered by aristocratic traditions. Americans today so widely accept universal education as "natural" that it is hard to realize that in the world of 1800, outside the United States, it was an uncommon ideal.

In the Southern States the general American emphasis on universal schooling was lacking, and education was more aristocratic in its orientation. It was designed for the sons and daughters of the planters, and it served to indentify membership in the landowning class rather than to provide an education for all people. Much of the history of educational growth in the United States in the 19th and 20th centuries reflects the difference in educational philosophy between North and South.

The first part of this chapter traces enrollment trends in the Nation up to the present, and projects these into the future. The second part describes trends by age, sex, color, and region, and also examines some specific influences on enrollment trends.

The early origins of the American public school system cannot be presented statistically. The first statistical information on schooling for the Nation as a whole was provided by the 1840 Census, when school systems, except in the New England and Middle Atlantic States, were fairly rudimentary. The act governing the taking of the 1840 Census, provided that "the marshals and assistants should 'collect and return in statistical tables . . . all such information in relation to mines, agriculture, commerce, manufactures, and schools, as will exhibit a full view of the pursuits, industry, education, and resources of the country' . . . "[1] This first effort to collect national statistics about education resulted in a series of reports based on data gathered from school systems rather than from individuals. Slightly over 2 million persons were reported as enrolled in 1840. This was almost 40 percent of the population 5 to 19 years old. The census returns were severely criticized by a committee of

1

the American Statistical Association, which pointed out numerous errors, omissions, and inconsistencies. For example, in several States the number of students reported as enrolled exceeded the school-age population. The committee asked that the results be set aside and a new census be taken.[2]

The 1850 Census employed a different procedure for collecting educational statistics. Individuals were asked whether they had "attended school at any time during the year preceding the census." This question remained essentially unchanged until 1890. (See appendix C for the precise question wording used in each census.) Enrollment data from school systems were also collected in each census. The Censuses of 1850, 1860, 1870, and 1890 contained figures from both schools and individuals, but in the Census of 1880 only the data from schools were tabulated and published. As can readily be seen from table I–1, the data collected from individuals do not agree with the data collected from schools, nor is there a consistent relationship between them. This may be an indication of serious defects in each set of data. Instructions to the marshals were not very detailed, and there is internal evidence to indicate a highly variable quality of enumeration. These figures can be used for identifying gross trends in enrollment, provided they are interpreted with care.

Table I–1.—School Enrollment Statistics from Population Censuses, Bureau of the Census Reports Based on School Records, and U.S. Office of Education Reports from School Systems: 1850 to 1890

[Numbers in millions]

Source of data	1890	1880	1870	1860	1850
1. Census population statistics..................	11.7	(NA)	6.6	5.7	4.1
2. Census institutional statistics..............	14.4	10.0	7.2	5.5	3.6
3. Report of the Commissioner of Education (institutional statistics).................	14.6	9.9	6.9	(NA)	(NA)
4. Line 2 as a percent of line 1[1]..............	123	(NA)	109	96	88
5. Line 3 as a percent of line 1[1]..............	125	(NA)	105	(NA)	(NA)

NA Not available.

[1] The variable relationship between institutional and population statistics probably indicates major defects in reporting in both series. U.S. Bureau of the Census and Commissioner of Education reports are directly comparable only in 1890. Commissioner's reports are for public schools only in 1870 and 1880.

Source: Census data from tables I–2 and I–3. Data compiled by Commissioner of Education from U.S. Bureau of the Census, *Historical Statistics of the United States, Colonial Times to 1957*, Series H–223 and H–224.

The trends dealt with here will be considered mainly in two parts, one dealing with the less adequate data of the 19th century, and the other and more detailed analysis covering the 20th century, when the data were of more consistent quality.

The rise of universal education, 1840–1900

By 1840 the schools of the country had already been developed to the point where they served approximately 40 percent of the youth 5 to 19 years old for at least some of the time.[3] Enrollment in American schools grew rapidly during the period from 1840 to 1900. Between 1840 and 1860, enrollment grew by more than 50 percent each decade. Growth slowed to about 30 percent during the decade of the Civil War and increased to about 40 percent during each of the next two decades.

Much of the growth in school enrollment between 1840 and 1890 can be attributed to population growth. Data for these 50 years on the size of the population aged 6 to 19 or 7 to 19 are not available; hence the group aged 5 to 19 has been used to approximate the population of school age. Between 1840 and 1890 the school-age population increased about fourfold, from about 5½ million to 22½ million, and in the same period the enrollment indicated in institutional reports (that is, reports collected from school systems) increased about seven times. (See table I–2.) Enrollment figures based on reports by in-

Table I–2.—School Enrollment and Enrollment Rates of the School-Age Population According to School Records Compiled by the Bureau of the Census, by Geographic Division: 1840 to 1890

[Numbers in thousands]

Geographic division[1]	1890	1880[2]	1870	1860	1850	1840
NUMBER ENROLLED						
United States..............	14,374	9,952	7,210	5,477	3,643	2,026
North Atlantic....................	3,632	2,950	2,495	2,223	1,932	1,413
South Atlantic....................	1,954	1,239	496	392	323	142
North Central.....................	5,619	4,090	3,408	2,256	1,068	366
South Central.....................	2,576	1,374	655	560	318	104
Western[3]........................	592	299	157	46	2	(NA)
ENROLLMENT AS A PERCENT OF SCHOOL-AGE POPULATION						
United States..............	64.0	57.8	59.8	48.7	42.1	37.5
North Atlantic....................	66.3	65.6	71.7	63.8	65.1	58.8
South Atlantic....................	54.6	44.7	25.7	19.0	17.7	15.2
North Central.....................	70.7	67.1	81.0	67.8	50.4	28.8
South Central.....................	56.9	41.3	30.0	25.0	18.6	13.1
Western[3]........................	64.9	58.4	62.1	34.1	4.9	(NA)

NA Not available.

[1] Division of States and territories used in the Census of 1890.

[2] Enrollment was reported for "common" schools only; these are about the same as public elementary schools. There were approximately 1 million persons in other schools in 1870, 1.7 million by 1890. The 1880 Census figures probably exclude about 1.2 million pupils.

[3] Western division was unsettled territory not reported in the Census of 1840.

Source: *Eleventh Census of the United States: 1890, Report on Education in the United States,* tables 1–6.

dividuals increased only slightly more rapidly than the population in the period from 1850 to 1890.[4] (See table I–3.)

If some adjustments are made in the data collected from individuals (see preceding footnote)[5] it appears that about three-fourths of the growth in school enrollment between 1850 and 1890 was a result of population increase and one-fourth was due to increased enrollment rates.[6] On the basis of institutional enrollment figures, about 55 percent of the growth may be attributed to population increase and 45 percent to increases in enrollment rates.

Table I–3.—SCHOOL ENROLLMENT AND ENROLLMENT RATES OF THE SCHOOL-AGE POPULATION ACCORDING TO POPULATION CENSUS RETURNS, BY GEOGRAPHIC DIVISION: 1850 TO 1890

[Numbers in thousands]

Geographic division[1]	1890	1870	1860	1850
NUMBER ENROLLED				
United States.........................	11,489	6,596	5,693	4,090
North Atlantic.........................	2,958	2,443	2,317	1,991
South Atlantic.........................	1,428	496	529	416
North Central.........................	4,731	2,924	2,134	1,211
South Central.........................	1,882	597	665	466
Western.........................	488	137	47	5
ENROLLMENT AS A PERCENT OF SCHOOL-AGE POPULATION				
United States.........................	51.2	54.7	50.6	47.2
North Atlantic.........................	54.0	70.2	66.5	67.1
South Atlantic.........................	39.9	25.6	25.6	22.7
North Central.........................	59.5	69.5	64.1	57.2
South Central.........................	41.6	27.4	29.7	27.3
Western.........................	53.6	54.0	35.1	13.1

[1] Enumeration data recorded on population form for each person by the marshal's assistants.

Source: *Eleventh Census of the United States: 1890, Population*, Vol. I, Part 2, p. 138, following table 10; and *Ninth Census of the United States: 1870, Population and Social Statistics*, table IX, p. 394.

It appears that enrollment rates have increased about twice as much in the 60 years since 1900 as in the 60 years from 1840 to 1900. Although enrollment increased more than sixfold between 1840 and 1900, only about 55 percent of persons 5 to 19 years old were enrolled in 1900. This represents an improvement of 15 percentage points in 60 years. In the 60 years since 1900, enrollments have increased more than threefold, and there has been an increase of 30 percentage points in the enrollment of this age group.

Enrollment from 1900 to 1960

The beginning of the 20th century found the ideal of some education for everyone accepted in all parts of the country, and for most groups the norm of an elementary education was well established. But only a little more than one-half of the youths 5 to 20 years old were enrolled in school,[7] and the average teacher in 1900 had 40 percent more pupils than her counterpart in 1960.

During the period from 1900 to 1940, there was a tremendous expansion of enrollment at the secondary school level, a further increase in enrollment rates at the elementary school level, and a steady and rapid growth of college enrollment. By 1940, the educational goal of American citizens had expanded to include a high school education for virtually everyone, and substantial progress had been made toward this goal.[8] In fact, about 79 percent of the youths 14 to 17 years old were attending school by 1940. This was slightly more than the percentage of persons 10 to 14 years old who were enrolled at the turn of the century.

Since 1940, our educational system has continued to expand; by 1960, the goal of some college (or post high school education) for nearly everyone was being advocated by educational and other interest groups in the Nation.[9] The United States, with 36 percent of the population 18 to 21 years old attending school, was still a long way from this goal. Eighty-eight percent of the youths aged 14 to 17, and 98 percent of those aged 7 to 13, were enrolled in school in 1960. Education at the high school level had been attained by most groups in the population. Public concern with the problem of dropouts from elementary and high schools was greater in 1960 than ever before, even though the dropout rate was far smaller than it had ever been in the past.

The number of persons who drop out before completing high school is still substantial. A Bureau of the Census survey in 1962 indicated that there were 2.3 million persons 18 to 21 years old who were not enrolled in school and who had not completed high school.[10] The 1960 Census reported 3.1 million persons 21 to 24 years old who had not completed high school. A few of this number were still enrolled in school or would complete high school at some later date.

Estimates of the number of male high school dropouts have been prepared by Beverly Duncan from census data on educational attainment for 5-year periods from 1902 to 1956. She has also computed cohort retention rates for high school ages (i.e., the ratio of the part of an age group completing high school to the number of that same age group who had earlier started in high school) from enrollment data of the Current Population Survey of the U.S. Bureau of the Census for the period from 1946 to 1962.[11] For the earlier decades, students who dropped out before completing elementary school, or in the transition from elementary to high school, were more numerous than dropouts during the high school years. Improved retention in the earlier school years was more important than improved high school retention in accounting for the increasing size of high school graduating classes. The continuation of the trend toward improvement in school retention by the group 16 and 17 years old which occurred during the 1950's would mean that by 1970 there would be no more dropouts below age 18. While this appears unlikely, the number who drop out before completing high school will probably amount to only a small fraction of the number that dropped out just 5 to 10 years ago.

Enrollment by grade level. Censuses prior to 1940 do not provide direct information about the grade level of enrollment. While it is possible to make inferences concerning grade levels from the ages of persons enrolled in school, and to identify trends in the proportion of an age group which is enrolled, these trends give a very different picture than do the trends in elementary and high school enrollment recorded by the U.S. Office of Education. In the early part of the 20th century, many persons of high school age were retarded in school (that is, over age in grade), and remained in elementary school rather than proceeding to high school. The figures in table I–4 give estimates of the level (elementary or secondary) of enrollment by age. With the exception of the 1920 to 1930 decade, there has been a steady decline in the number and percent of elementary pupils above the "normal" elementary school age, and a corresponding decline in the number and percent of secondary pupils above normal high school age. (See footnote, table I–4.)

Table I–4.—ESTIMATED PERCENT OF ENROLLMENT IN ELEMENTARY AND SECONDARY SCHOOLS COMPRISED OF OVERAGE PUPILS: 1910 TO 1960

[Numbers in thousands]

Year	Adjusted[1] elementary enrollment	Estimated[2] elementary pupils over 13 years old	Percent overage col. 2 / col. 1	Adjusted[1] secondary enrollment	Estimated[2] elementary and secondary pupils 18 years old and over	Percent overage col. 5 / col. 4
1960	29,859	719	2.4	9,473	398	4.2
1950	20,290	1,171	5.8	6,225	316	5.1
1940	18,827	1,987	10.6	6,559	836	12.7
1930	22,173	3,606	16.3	4,648	1,428	30.7
1920	18,862	3,071	16.3	2,306	608	26.4
1910	16,617	4,065	24.5	1,019	834	81.8

[1] The percent distribution of enrollment by grade level as compiled by the U.S. Office of Education was applied to the enumerated population enrolled in schools below the college level. The adjustments ranged from 2 to 10 percent downward.

[2] Estimates are residuals and reflect errors and inconsistencies in the data as well as the number of overage pupils. Although individual estimates may have substantial errors, the trend and general magnitude of the figures are probably reliable.

Source: U.S. Bureau of the Census, *Historical Statistics of the United States, Colonial Times to 1957; Continuation to 1962 and Revisions,* Series H–226 and H–227.

Figures from the Office of Education on growth of enrollment by level show that between 1910 and 1960 elementary enrollment had expanded from 18 million to 30 million, or about 67 percent. On the other hand, census figures on enrollment growth of the group 5 to 13 years old, during the same period, show an expansion of enrollment at these ages from 12.5 million to 29 million, or about 130 percent. These two trends appear to be inconsistent, but the divergence may be explained in part by the decline in the number of older children in elementary school. See table I–4.

There is an even greater difference between the growth of secondary school enrollment and the increase in the number of persons 14 to 17 years old enrolled in school. Secondary school enrollment increased almost ninefold between 1910 and 1960—from 1.1 million to 9.6 million. In contrast, enrollment of the population 14 to 17 years old slightly more than doubled, rising from 4.2 million to 9.8 million, or at about the same rate as the enrollment of persons 5 to 13 years old. In 1910, the youths aged 14 to 17 enrolled in school were predominantly elementary pupils; by 1960 they were predominantly secondary pupils. In the census statistics on enrollment by age, the reduction in grade retardation which occurred between 1910 and 1960 masks the tremendous expansion of secondary education.

The number of persons completing each of the three major levels of the school system for each decade since 1900 is shown in table I–5. During the six decades of the 20th century, the number of high school graduates increased nearly twelvefold and the number of college graduates almost elevenfold.

Table I–5.—ESTIMATED OUTPUT OF THE EDUCATIONAL SYSTEM AT THE ELEMENTARY, SECONDARY, AND COLLEGIATE LEVELS: 1900 TO 1960

[Numbers in thousands]

Decade	Eighth grade enrollment	High school graduates	College graduates with bachelor's or first professional degree	Ratio of— High school graduates to eighth grade enrollment	Ratio of— College graduates to high school graduates
1900 to 1909	(NA)	1,151	314	(NA)	.27
1910 to 1919	12,581	2,278	413	.18	.18
1920 to 1929	16,017	4,817	840	.30	.17
1930 to 1939	18,891	9,364	1,441	.50	.15
1940 to 1949	18,888	11,490	1,946	.61	.17
1950 to 1959	24,763	13,464	3,422	.54	.25

NA Not available.

Source: Eighth grade enrollment from U.S. Office of Education, *Biennial Survey of Education, Statistics of State School Systems,* 1921–1922, 1929–1930, 1935–1936, 1947–1948, 1955–1956, and 1959–1960. Figures are for the number enrolled, not the number of graduates. Reports cover only public school enrollment. Private school eighth grade enrollment was estimated from the total private school elementary enrollment, and added to the reported public school figures.

High school graduates and college graduates from U.S. Bureau of the Census, *Historical Statistics of the United States, Colonial Times to 1957; Continuation to 1962 and Revisions,* Series H–232 and H–330.

In the 50-year period between 1910 and 1960, enrollment in the eighth grade (which is a close approximation to elementary school completion) about doubled.

From 1900 to 1940, the number of high school graduates grew slightly more rapidly than the number of college graduates. The proportion of high school graduates going on to college probably declined also. World War II reduced the number of college graduates more than the number of high school graduates, but in the postwar period, colleges replaced high schools as the fastest growing part of the American educational system.

Population growth as a factor in enrollment increases. Population growth was a major factor in the enrollment increases recorded between 1910 and 1960. Almost 70 percent of the increase in enrollment among persons 5 to 13 years old was attributable to population growth. The remaining 30 percent reflected higher enrollment rates. Among persons 14 to 17 years old, population increase accounted for 42 percent of the growth in enrollment, and for ages 18 and 19, only 15 percent. For the 5 to 19 age group as a whole, slightly more than one-half (55 percent) of the enrollment increase was attributable to population growth.

More than half of the total growth in enrollment during the period from 1910 to 1960 (about 13 million out of the 23.6 million increase) occurred between 1950 and 1960. About two-thirds of the enrollment growth between 1950 and 1960 was the result of population growth. For the period from 1910 to 1950, increased enrollment rates played a somewhat more important part in enrollment increases than did the growth of population.

Trends in grade retardation. The figures in table I–4 show very substantial grade retardation during the early part of the 20th century. The census provides no direct evidence on this point prior to 1940, but interest in the extent of grade retardation in the early years of the century led the Office of Education to conduct several surveys of the problem. In 1908, 319 cities were surveyed by George Strayer,[12] who reported that 38 percent of boys and 34 percent of girls were overage for their grade of enrollment. Although at that time most persons remained in school for the first four grades, the number of children who were retarded one or more grades increased very rapidly. According to Strayer, nearly half the dropouts were between the ages of 13 and 15, and in all the upper elementary grades and in high school the number of dropouts increased faster than the number overage in grade.[13]

A similar study was conducted in 1927 by Frank Phillips of the Office of Education.[14] Because Phillips' study, like Strayer's, was limited to urban school systems, both studies probably understate the amount of retardation in the Nation as a whole, since retardation in rural areas is typically greater than in urban areas. Phillips found that about 25 percent of boys and 20 percent of girls were retarded one or more grades at age 10, and about 40 percent of boys and 32 percent of girls were retarded at age 15. These two studies indicate that retardation in urban areas was very substantial in 1908 and in 1927, and they suggest that it did not decline very much during these years.[15]

The 1940 Census provided tabulations of age by highest grade of school completed. For enrolled persons, it was assumed that they were attending the grade above the highest grade completed. This assumption turned out to be inadequate, and introduced such large biases into the data that they are not comparable with 1950 or 1960 statistics. (See discussion in appendix A.)[16] Reliable national data on grade retardation from census materials are therefore limited to the 1950 and 1960 Censuses, but even in this short period, dramatic changes have occurred in grade retardation.[17]

If the Phillips study previously cited provided a reasonable sample of retardation in urban areas in 1927, then retardation in these areas was reduced by approximately 50 percent between 1927 and 1950. In 1950, about 18 percent of boys and 13 percent of girls were retarded one or more grades by age 10, and about 31 percent of boys and 21 percent of girls were retarded by age 15. Between 1950 and 1960, grade retardation in the precollege years was reduced another 40 percent. Table I-6 shows the percent of grade retardation at age 15 in both 1950 and 1960 for selected subgroups of the population. Fifteen is an age when retardation is near a maximum for the precollege years; above age 15, dropouts from the retarded student group reduce the size of the group and, consequently, the proportion of all students who are retarded. The distribution of retardation by age is similar for most groups, with retardation rising steadily to age 15 or 16 and declining slightly to age 18, when it rises sharply and erratically during the college years. At the college level, "retardation" changes its meaning as a concept because of the large number of part-time students and students who have deferred entry into college. (See figure I-1.)

At the precollege years, the percent of persons who were severely retarded (more than one year) was reduced much more rapidly between 1950 and 1960 than the percent who were retarded only one year (53 percent reduction compared with 32 percent, respectively). Retardation among nonwhites, both male and female, was approximately double the retardation for whites in both 1950 and 1960, and the percentage of reduction in retardation during this decade was greater for whites than nonwhites.

Although all subgroups of the population had lower percentages of retardation in 1960 than in 1950, the relative size of many differentials was increasing, because the greatest percentage decline in retardation was registered among the groups with the least retardation in 1950. Even though differentials persisted, all groups shared in the very substantial decline in retardation.

It seems unlikely that grade retardation in the American school system will be reduced much below 5 to 10 percent, which is the current rate for girls in urban areas. Future declines are likely to be concentrated among youth in rural areas and among nonwhites. For both groups, retardation is still substantial. Future decreases in retardation will reduce the differentials that existed in 1960.

Figure I–1.—GRADE RETARDATION OF PERSONS 8 TO 18 YEARS OLD ENROLLED IN SCHOOL: 1950 AND 1960

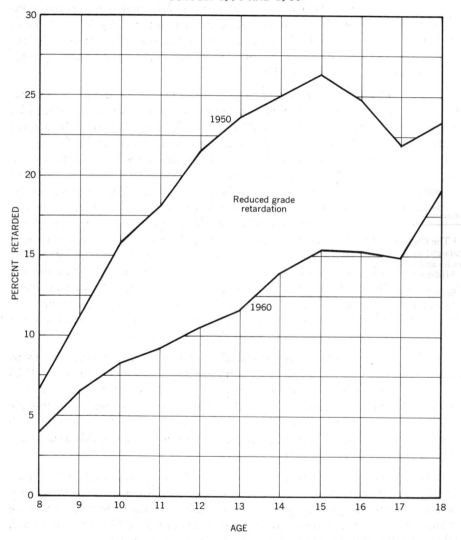

Source: *1950 Census of Population*, Vol. II, *Characteristics of the Population; 1960 Census of Population*, Vol. I, *Characteristics of the Population*, Part 1, U.S. Summary. Computed from Single Grade and Single Years of Age tables.

Table I–6.—PERCENT OF RETARDATION IN SCHOOL OF ALL PERSONS 15 YEARS OLD ENROLLED IN SCHOOL, BY URBAN AND RURAL RESIDENCE, COLOR, AND SEX: 1960 AND 1950

Area, color, and sex	Percent retarded[1]						Percent of decrease, 1950 to 1960		
	1960			1950					
	Total	1 year	More than 1 year	Total	1 year	More than 1 year	Total	1 year	More than 1 year
UNITED STATES									
Total	15.3	9.3	6.0	26.3	13.6	12.7	41.8	31.6	52.8
Male	18.8	11.3	7.5	31.3	15.8	15.5	39.9	28.5	51.6
White	16.3	10.4	5.9	27.8	15.4	12.4	41.4	32.5	52.4
Nonwhite	36.8	17.7	19.1	59.5	19.0	40.5	38.2	6.8	-52.8
Female	11.7	7.2	4.5	21.2	11.4	9.8	44.8	36.8	54.1
White	9.8	6.3	3.5	17.7	10.4	7.3	44.6	39.4	52.1
Nonwhite	26.0	14.2	11.8	47.1	19.0	28.1	44.8	25.3	58.0
URBAN									
Total	12.9	8.3	4.6	20.4	11.7	8.7	36.8	29.1	47.1
Nonwhite	24.3	14.3	10.0	39.0	18.6	20.4	37.7	23.1	51.0
RURAL NONFARM									
Total	20.6	11.9	8.7	31.3	15.9	15.4	34.2	25.2	43.5
RURAL FARM									
Total	18.3	9.7	8.6	37.0	16.4	20.6	50.5	40.9	58.3
Nonwhite	49.9	19.6	30.3	74.1	18.6	55.5	32.7	(2)	45.4

[1] The Census definition of "normal" progress in school includes 2 years; thus persons 7 and 8 years old in the second grade are "normal," 8 and 9 in the third grade, 9 and 10 in the fourth grade, and so on. Any one older than normal in grade is defined as retarded.

[2] Increase of 5.4 percent.

Source: *1960 Census of Population*, Vol. I, *Characteristics of the Population*, Part 1, U.S. Summary. Computed from Single Grade and Single Years of Age tables. *1950 Census of Population*, Vol. II, *Characteristics of the Population.*

Projections of future enrollment growth

In the 13-year period between 1950 and 1963, enrollment increased about 20 million: in elementary schools, about 12 million; in high schools, almost 6 million; and in colleges, about 2 million. By 1980, enrollment will probably have grown 10 to 23 million more, depending on whether the low or high projections are achieved. In the 17 years ending in 1980, the annual growth rate will probably be lower, and the total amount of growth may be less, than in the 13 years since 1950.[18]

This will be especially true if the lower enrollment projection, based on a smaller population projection, proves to be accurate. A growth of only 10 million in the next 17 years would represent less than one-half of the annual enrollment increase experienced by the Nation in the last decade.

In the period from 1963 to 1985, the largest amount of increase in enrollment (but not the greatest percent) will occur at the elementary level. Almost all of this increase will be a result of population growth. Only at the kindergarten level is any increase in enrollment rates projected, and even at this level 75 to 85 percent of the total increase will be due to population growth and only 15 to 25 percent to increases in enrollment rates. Enrollment growth at the high school level will also be due primarily to population changes, and the anticipated growth will be at about the same rate as growth at the elementary level. The rate of population growth at the college-age level will be higher and enrollment-rate increases will also be greater; the combined effect will produce projections for 1985 from two to almost three times the 1963 fall college enrollment. In the high college enrollment projection, about 60 percent of the growth will occur because of increased enrollment rates, while for the low projection only 30 percent of the growth will occur because of enrollment-rate increases. (See figure I–2.)

Almost all of the variation in projections of enrollment at the elementary and secondary levels is associated with the projections of population growth. The different assumptions about population growth result in enrollment projections ranging from a growth, by 1985, of 9 million in the low projection to 19 million in the high projection. (See table I–7.) At the secondary level the range of projections by 1985 is from 3 to 6 million. A sharp change in birth rates, always possible, would produce enrollments outside these fairly wide ranges. The important point is that future enrollments at both elementary and secondary levels will be almost entirely determined by the future trend in births.

Table I–7.—Projections of Fall Enrollment, by Level of School, for the Population 5 to 34 Years Old: 1963 to 1985

[In thousands]

Year and projection	Total	Level of school		
		Elementary	Secondary	College
HIGH PROJECTION				
1963	50,356	33,587	12,433	4,336
1970	58,757	37,034	14,796	6,927
1980	73,517	46,079	16,988	10,450
1985	84,008	52,117	19,583	12,308
LOW PROJECTION				
1963	50,356	33,587	12,433	4,336
1970	56,572	36,005	14,487	6,080
1980	60,511	37,405	15,047	8,059
1985	66,019	42,362	15,569	8,088

Source: Projections specially prepared for this monograph. See appendix B for description of method. Similar projections are contained in U.S. Bureau of Census, *Current Population Reports—Illustrative Projections to 1980 of School and College Enrollment in the United States,* Series P–25, No. 232 (June 1961).

Figure I–2.—Projected Percent Increase in Enrollment After 1963 for the Population 18 to 21 Years Old, by Sex and Component: 1970 to 1985

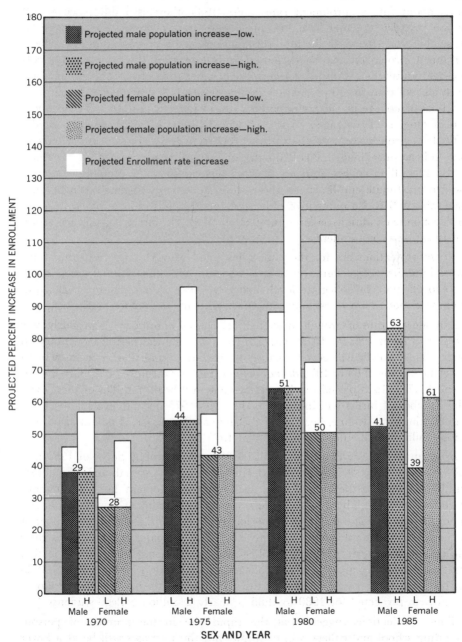

Note: The male population appears to be growing more rapidly than the female, but the different rate of growth is caused by the elimination of persons in military service and in institutions from the population base. Since a constant size was assumed for the Armed Forces, this makes the college eligible male expand more rapidly than the comparable group of females. For the total age group the male and female populations have about the same rate of growth.

Source: Tables I–7 and I–8.

Projections at the college level involve less uncertainty about population growth (since the college students of 1980 are already born), but much more uncertainty about future enrollment rates. For 1985, there is a difference of 1.2 million between the high and low projections of the population aged 18 to 21, so about one-fourth of the total difference between the high and low college enrollment projections can be attributed to differences in the projections of college-age population. Any of the enrollment rates projected seems reasonable; the high rate calls for 50 percent of the youth 18 to 21 years old to be enrolled in school or college in 1985, compared with 33 percent in 1963. The proportion of older students (aged 25 to 34) who will enroll in college is especially difficult to project accurately, and this proportion is a very substantial part of total college enrollment. Based on the high enrollment projection, 3 million of the 12 million college students of 1985 will be 25 to 34 years old, but this could overestimate enrollment of these older students by as much as a million. (See table I–8.) Enrollment of older students depends more heavily on social and economic conditions; a large proportion of the enrollment of this age group consists of part-time students.

These projections are for the population aged 5 to 34. In the future, substantial numbers of persons over 35 may be continuing their formal schooling at the subcollegiate or collegiate level, many of them on a part-time basis. No attempt is made here to estimate the enrollment of these older students.

A moderate rate of growth in elementary school enrollment is projected for the period from 1963 to 1975, and a higher rate for the period from 1975 to 1985. This growth will occur because of the large number of new families to be formed in the 1965 to 1975 decade, when the larger number of children born in the 1947 to 1955 period reach marriage age and begin families of their own. The number of births will increase in the 1965-1975 decade, even if the birth rate continues to decline, because of the increased number of potential parents whose children will enter school between 1975 and 1985.

By contrast, college enrollment will increase most rapidly between 1963 and 1970, and the rate of increase will decline thereafter, even though the actual numbers added to the college rolls each year will remain large throughout the entire period. The low projection of college enrollment implies a plateau in enrollment during the 1980-1985 period as a result of the declining number of births projected for the 1963-1967 period. The increases in enrollment rates will be balanced by declines in the college-age population. The high projection assumes continuing growth in the college-age population in the 1980 to 1985 period. When increased enrollment rates are applied to the larger age cohorts, the growth projected for 1980 to 1985 is nearly 2 million college students.

These projections suggest that the rapid rise in the number of persons attending school and college will continue, but the increases will be at a lower rate than during the 1950's and early 1960's. At the elementary and secondary levels the increases will be due primarily to population growth; at these levels

Table I–8.—HIGH AND LOW PROJECTION SERIES OF FALL SCHOOL ENROLLMENT, BY AGE AND SEX: 1963 TO 1985

[In thousands]

Projection, age, and sex	1963	1965	1970	1975	1980	1985
HIGH PROJECTION						
Total, 5 to 34 years old.....	50,356	52,997	58,757	65,449	73,517	84,007
Male.............................	26,243	27,845	31,109	34,869	39,326	45,077
Female...........................	24,113	25,152	27,648	30,580	34,191	38,930
5 and 6 years old.............	6,768	6,904	7,554	8,881	10,177	11,370
Male.............................	3,440	3,505	3,859	4,541	5,227	5,880
Female...........................	3,328	3,399	3,695	4,340	4,950	5,490
7 to 13 years old.............	26,203	27,264	28,749	30,861	35,079	39,805
Male.............................	13,280	13,837	14,603	15,685	17,852	20,280
Female...........................	12,923	13,427	14,146	15,176	17,227	19,525
14 and 15 years old...........	6,813	6,861	7,783	8,216	8,785	10,030
Male.............................	3,466	3,489	3,946	4,168	4,466	5,100
Female...........................	3,347	3,372	3,837	4,048	4,319	4,930
16 and 17 years old...........	5,704	6,046	6,836	7,451	7,629	8,827
Male.............................	2,936	3,098	3,503	3,810	3,922	4,543
Female...........................	2,768	2,948	3,333	3,641	3,707	4,284
18 to 21 years old............	3,330	3,936	5,100	6,364	7,300	8,737
Male.............................	1,957	2,366	3,081	3,831	4,382	5,280
Female...........................	1,373	1,570	2,019	2,533	2,918	3,457
22 to 24 years old............	745	872	1,235	1,506	1,823	2,024
Male.............................	588	693	967	1,169	1,401	1,544
Female...........................	157	179	268	337	422	480
25 to 34 years old............	793	1,114	1,500	2,170	2,724	3,214
Male.............................	576	857	1,150	1,665	2,076	2,450
Female...........................	217	257	350	505	648	764
LOW PROJECTION						
Total, 5 to 34 years old.....	50,356	52,356	56,572	57,954	60,511	66,019
Male.............................	26,243	27,473	29,896	30,822	32,280	35,048
Female...........................	24,113	24,883	26,676	27,132	28,231	30,971
5 and 6 years old.............	6,768	6,828	6,538	6,874	7,998	8,944
Male.............................	3,440	3,480	3,347	3,520	4,067	4,544
Female...........................	3,328	3,348	3,191	3,354	3,931	4,400
7 to 13 years old.............	26,203	27,266	28,751	27,456	28,676	32,682
Male.............................	13,280	13,839	14,605	13,982	14,608	16,621
Female...........................	12,923	13,427	14,146	13,474	14,068	16,061
14 and 15 years old,..........	6,813	6,835	7,744	8,183	7,560	8,125
Male.............................	3,466	3,477	3,932	4,153	3,840	4,128
Female...........................	3,347	3,358	3,812	4,030	3,720	3,997
16 and 17 years old...........	5,704	5,939	6,661	7,241	7,118	7,118
Male.....,.......................	2,936	3,065	3,439	3,724	3,670	3,666
Female...........................	2,768	2,874	3,222	3,517	3,448	3,452
18 to 21 years old............	3,330	3,725	4,581	5,479	6,053	5,886
Male.............................	1,957	2,239	2,784	3,332	3,684	3,568
Female...........................	1,373	1,486	1,797	2,147	2,369	2,318
22 to 24 years old	745	837	1,133	1,334	1,567	1,715
Male.............................	588	669	898	1,050	1,223	1,334
Female...........................	157	168	235	284	344	381
25 to 34 years old............	793	926	1,164	1,387	1,539	1,549
Male.............................	576	704	891	1,061	1,188	1,187
Female...........................	217	222	273	326	351	362

Source: Special computations described in appendix B.

there is not much possibility for increased enrollment rates, since nearly the entire age group is now enrolled. At the college level, both the increased size of the age group and the expected continued increase in demand for higher education will contribute to the rapid growth of enrollment.

Although the rise in demand for higher education in this country has been very rapid in the last decade, the spread of universal secondary education was even more rapid in the early 1900's. Figure I–3 provides a comparison of the growth in the ratio of secondary enrollment to the population aged 14 to 17 in the 40-year period from 1910 to 1950, with the growth in the comparable ratio of college enrollment to the population aged 18 to 21 in the period from 1940 to 1980.[19] Although the two trends were almost identical in the first decade of growth, the college ratio fell behind in the second decade; it will fall even further behind in the third and fourth decades, according to the low enrollment projection, but will match the earlier high school growth rate, according to the high projection.

Historical continuity favors the high enrollment projection, but there are factors which may result in the lower projection being the more realistic. The expansion of college enrollment is more complex and hence more costly for both students and society than was the earlier expansion of high school enrollment. The greater complexity and greater expense of increased college enrollment may tend to decelerate the trend reflected by the higher projection.

Regional variations in enrollment patterns

The preceding discussion focused on national trends in enrollment. Within this national pattern there have been some important variations in enrollment by different categories of the population and in different geographic regions.

Census statistics reveal some clear and marked regional differences in the development of education. Schools developed first in the New England and Middle Atlantic States, and by the time of the 1840 Census more than half the children aged 5 to 19 in these States were enrolled in school. During the 20 years between 1840 and 1860, education spread rapidly into the Midwest, and by the eve of the Civil War as many students were from the Midwest as from the Northeast.

Growth in the South and Southwest was much slower. In 1860, for example, over 60 percent of the children of school age in both the North Atlantic and North Central States were in school, while in the South Atlantic and South Central States the proportion was less than one-half as much. Only the free population was included in the census reports; if slaves had been included the picture for the South would have been even more unfavorable. (See tables I–2, I–3, and I–9.) By 1860, the South had already been outstripped by the West. In that sparsely settled area, despite the difficulties of providing schools, about 35 percent of the youth aged 5 to 19 were enrolled.

Figure I–3.—COMPARISON OF HIGH SCHOOL ENROLLMENT RATES WITH ACTUAL AND PROJECTED COLLEGE RATES 30 YEARS LATER: 1910 TO 1950, AND 1940 TO 1980

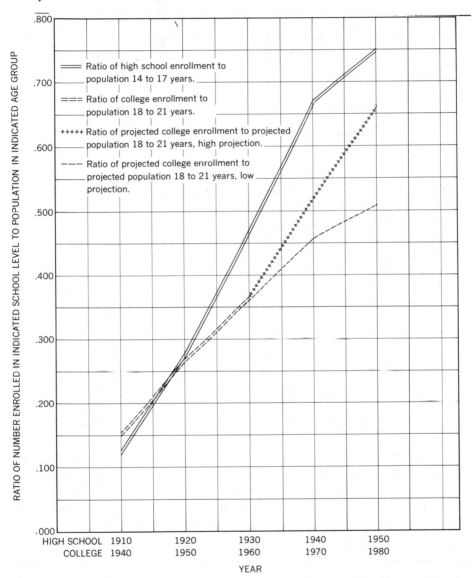

Source: Projections from table I–7 and enrollment ratios computed from U.S. Bureau of the Census, *Historical Statistics of the United States, Colonial Times to 1957; Continuation to 1962 and Revisions,* Series H-223 and 224.

Table I-9.—Percent Distribution of School Enrollment, by Geographic Division: 1840 to 1890

Geographic division	1890	1880	1870	1860	1850	1840
United States...............	100.0	100.0	100.0	100.0	100.0	100.0
North Atlantic....................	25.3	29.6	34.6	40.6	53.0	69.7
South Atlantic....................	13.6	12.4	6.9	7.2	8.9	7.0
North Central....................	39.1	41.1	47.3	41.2	29.3	18.1
South Central....................	17.9	13.8	9.1	10.2	8.7	5.1
Western.........................	4.1	3.0	2.2	0.8	(Z)	(NA)

NA Not available.
Z Less than 0.05 percent.

Source: Derived from table I-2.

It is impressive that schools spread so rapidly to the frontier. By 1850, enrollment rates in the North Central Region had exceeded the national average. By 1870, in the West, they had exceeded the national average. (See table I-10.) After the Civil War, the educational system of the Southeast and South Central States expanded, but by 1890 only 40 percent of the school-age youth were enrolled, a percentage which had been achieved nationally 50 years earlier. The Southeast and South Central States lagged behind the rest of the Nation in the development of universal education during the entire 19th century.

The slower development of education in the South may be explained in part by the following factors:

1. The aristocratic tradition, which favored private over public schools and was unconcerned about universal education.

2. The large Negro population, which received almost no education during the period of slavery, and very little in the second half of the 19th century.

3. The predominantly rural population.[20]

In 1860 the proportion of students attending private schools was definitely higher in the South than in other parts of the country. In most Southern States, 20 to 30 percent of the students were enrolled in private schools, compared with only 10 percent for the Nation as a whole.[21] However, even in 1860, public schools predominated in both North and South.

The large Negro population of the South accounts only in part for its low enrollment rates. In 1870, over 90 percent of all Negroes lived in the South Atlantic and South Central regions, and they were just as heavily concentrated in those regions in 1900. However, white enrollment rates in the South in 1870 were about one-half the rates for nonsouthern whites; by 1900, southern white enrollment rates were still only about three-fourths the rates for the non-South. (See figure I-4.)

Figure I–4.—Percent of the Population 5 to 19 Years Old Enrolled in School, by Race, for the South and the United States Excluding the South: 1870 and 1900

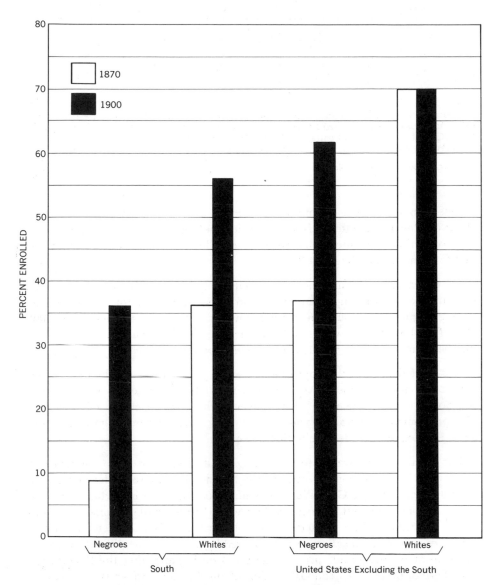

Source: Estimated from data in *Ninth Census of the United States: 1870, Population and Social Statistics,* table 9, and *Twelfth Census of the United States: 1900,* Vol. II, *Population,* Part 2, tables 35 and 40.

Table I-10.—Decennial Rate of Increase in School Enrollment, by Geo-graphic Division: 1840 to 1890

Geographic division	1880 to 1890	1870 to 1880[1]	1860 to 1870	1850 to 1860	1840 to 1850
United States...................	28.9	54.7	31.6	50.3	79.8
North Atlantic......................	9.9	32.5	12.2	15.1	36.7
South Atlantic......................	31.3	200.0	26.5	21.4	127.5
North Central......................	22.6	34.4	51.0	111.2	191.8
South Central......................	67.3	135.1	17.0	76.1	205.8
Western..........................	76.7	113.4	241.3	(2)	(NA)

NA Not available.

[1] Adjusted to include enrollment in schools not covered in the 1880 Census; estimates for 1880 (in thousands) are United States, 11,152; North Atlantic, 3,305; South Atlantic, 1,488; North Central, 4,584; South Central, 1,540; and Western, 335.

[2] 1850 base too small to yield meaningful percent increase.

Source: Derived from table I-2.

Less than 10 percent of southern Negroes were enrolled in school in 1870, about one-fourth the rate for Negroes outside the South. By 1900, slightly more than one-third of southern Negroes were enrolled, or about 60 percent of the rate for nonsouthern Negroes.

All the increase in enrollment rates nationally between 1870 and 1900 can be attributed to the improvement in enrollment among southern whites and among Negroes, both southern and nonsouthern. During this period enrollment rates for nonsouthern whites did not increase at all, even though the total number enrolled nearly doubled because of population increase.

A part of the lag in the South's educational progress was attributable to the concentration of Negroes. Another part might be attributed to the fact that the South was a more rural area; however, the North Central Division was also predominantly rural, as was the Far West, and enrollment rates in those areas equaled or exceeded the national average.

But even after allowance for the factors just mentioned there remained a substantial lag in enrollment rates in the South. Its failure to develop public education prior to the Civil War seems to be related in an important way to a social structure and set of social values which placed little emphasis on uni-versal education. The belated efforts following the Civil War to develop a system of universal education were hampered by the economic difficulties (not a problem of any magnitude prior to the War) during and after the Reconstruc-tion Period, by the tremendous backlog of uneducated former slaves, and by the persistence of values and attitudes which had slowed the development of southern public education in the first place. Considering these formidable obstacles, it is surprising that the South made substantial progress between 1870 and 1900 in providing more education for its citizens and that the Negroes made the most rapid progress. All this occurred at a time when the rest of the Nation was making little progress in expanding the proportion of youth served by education. The failure to expand the percent of youth enrolled in school in the non-South is explained in part by the large number of immigrants who entered the United States between 1870 and 1900.

The differential in enrollment rates between the South and the non-South has persisted during the 20th century, remaining about the same size between 1910 and 1960, while other differentials have been sharply reduced. (See figure I–5.) Enrollment rates in the South have lagged 5 to 7 percentage points behind the other regions at each census period since 1910, while differences in enrollment among the other regions have been small.

Although in the 19th century the size of the nonwhite population in the South and the rural character of the region were not considered sufficient reasons for the southern education lag, they now appear to be the main explanatory factor. Most of the continuing differentials in enrollment rates between the South and non-South can be explained by the higher proportion of nonwhites in the South and the lower proportion of urban residents. Among comparable color-residence groups, enrollment rates were generally lower in the South, but the differentials were small and in some groups favored the South.

Similar patterns were found by James Cowhig[22] in his thorough analysis of census data on dropout rates among urban and rural youth. Dropout rates, which are almost the inverse of enrollment rates, generally exhibited greater color and residence differentials than South-non-South differentials. The regional differential was typically small between southern and nonsouthern urban areas but much larger between southern and nonsouthern rural areas.

Enrollment rates by sex, color, and residence

In the last 50 years there has been a rapid but not always steady growth in the proportion of youth enrolled in schools for nearly every subgroup of the population. Enrollment rates for boys and girls have always been very similar. Up to age 15, the rates for females are slightly higher, but for the older ages, the rates are higher for males. At age 19, in 1960, enrollment rates for males were about 30 percent higher than for females.

The sex differential in enrollment rates at ages above 17 has been increasing since 1940. But it would not be correct to conclude from these figures that college enrollment rates have been going up more rapidly for men than for women. Actually, the percentage of men among college students in 1960 was about the same as in 1910 (66 percent), and the percent of male undergraduates has actually declined slightly.[23] The more rapid increase of enrollment rates for men at the older ages is explained by the decline in the proportion of students over age 17 enrolled in high school, where the sex distribution is approximately equal. It can be estimated that in 1910 about 72 percent of the enrollment of persons over 18 was below college level, while in 1950 com-

Figure I–5.—PERCENT OF THE POPULATION 5 TO 20 YEARS OLD ENROLLED IN
SCHOOL, BY REGION: 1890 TO 1960

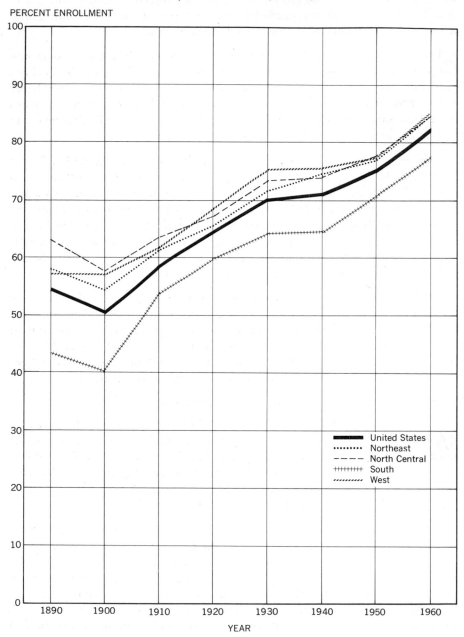

Source: Computed from enrollment statistics reported in the Decennial Censuses 1890 to 1960.

parable census figures for enrolled persons aged 18 to 24 indicate that only 36 percent of those over 18 were below the college level.

Census data do not reveal a uniform superiority of urban over rural youth in regard to enrollment rates. At the younger ages (5 to 15) urban enrollment rates have been higher than rural rates since 1920, when data were first available in comparable form, but the differentials between urban and rural rates have declined markedly since 1940. At the high school and early college ages (18 and 19) rural enrollment rates were actually higher in 1930, but urban rates were higher in 1940; the differential in favor of the urban areas widened until 1950, only to decrease in the last decade. Part of the change between 1940 and 1950 may have been a result of the change in the residence definition of college students. In 1940, college students were allocated to the residence classification of their parents, and students from farms were classified as rural by the Census. In 1950 and 1960, students living at college were counted at college, thus most of them were urban by definition, regardless of where their parents resided.

Another pattern revealed in the figures is the sharper separation between school and work in the urban environment. In the city, youths tend to stay in school full time until they take a full-time job and then they leave school. In rural areas, part-time work on the farm begins early and work and schooling continue simultaneously. This pattern undoubtedly increases retardation, which is greater in rural than in urban areas. Many rural youths stay in school to high school graduation, even though they are overage for the grade in which they are enrolled. However, not enough of the rural students remain in school to make their enrollment rates equal to those of their urban counterparts.

Census data show steady progress in reducing enrollment differentials between whites and nonwhites during the past half century. Reductions have been most pronounced at the younger ages. At ages 5 and 6, a differential that amounted to 14 percentage points in 1910 had been reduced to only 3 percentage points; at ages 7 to 13, a differential of over 20 percentage points had been reduced to only 2 percentage points. At age 16 and above, the differential had not been reduced very much.

Another way of expressing the gap is to indicate that, if the differential were entirely eliminated at ages 5 to 19 by raising nonwhite rates to the white level, nonwhite enrollment would be increased by about 200,000, which is only 4 percent of nonwhite enrollment and less than one-half of 1 percent of the Nation's total enrollment.

At the college level, nonwhite students have a pattern of enrollment quite different from that of white students. About 65 percent of the white students, but only about 53 percent of the nonwhite students, are male. (See table I–11.) The higher ratio of nonwhite female to male college students undoubtedly reflects the kinds of occupational opportunities open to nonwhites with advanced education.

Table I–11.—College Enrollment, by Year in Which Enrolled, Color, and Sex: 1960

[Numbers in thousands]

Year in which enrolled	White			Nonwhite		
	Total	Male	Female	Total	Male	Female
Number enrolled..............	2,743	1,777	966	192	101	91
1 to 4........................	2,376	1,469	907	169	85	84
5 or higher...................	367	308	59	23	16	7
Percent enrolled............	100.0	64.8	35.2	100.0	52.9	47.1
1 to 4........................	100.0	61.8	38.2	100.0	50.5	49.5
5 or higher...................	100.0	83.9	16.1	100.0	70.1	29.9

Source: Computed from *1960 Census of Population, Subject Reports, School Enrollment,* Series PC (2)–5A, table 1.

Elimination of enrollment rate differentials by sex, color, and residence would have had only a small effect on the total enrollment in the United States in 1960, adding less than 1 million students to a total of over 40 million in the 5 to 19 age range. The development of kindergartens as a universal feature of the American educational scene may add as many as 800,000 more children to the rolls. Enrollment rates can, of course, rise at the college level; the amount of increase in the college rates will depend on social norms regarding college attendance which have not yet been crystallized. With these exceptions, future enrollment will be determined almost entirely by changes in the size of the school age population.

Factors affecting enrollment rates

During the 120 years in which enrollment rates have been recorded, they have been influenced to some extent by several factors over a long period of time. These include urbanization, rising per capita income, and rising educational attainment of the adult population. Other factors, more specific and limited, include such forces as wars, depressions, and the effects of legislation, all of which may have altered the course of enrollments either temporarily or permanently. These specific forces will now be examined to see what effects, if any, they have had on the trend in enrollment.

Relation of school attendance laws to enrollment. Legislation designed to assure school attendance is often assumed to have had a positive effect in boosting enrollment. Between 1850 and 1920 all of the States enacted laws requiring children between certain ages to attend school, and most States also enacted laws prohibiting child labor. It has often been assumed that these laws had a substantial effect in raising enrollment rates. However, according to George Stigler, "The influence of legislation is difficult to isolate, but a brief investigation . . . suggests that on the whole compulsory school attendance laws have followed more than led the increase in enrollments of children over 14."[24]

An analysis of the effects of legislation on school enrollment is handicapped by the fact that 25 of the 48 States passed attendance laws prior to 1890, the first date when census enrollment data classified by age became available. These 25 States included all of the New England and Far Western States, and many of the Midwestern and Mountain States. They excluded all of the Southern States, which were last to pass school attendance laws. The census statistics limit the analysis to the Southern States plus six others scattered around the country.

The States exhibited two quite distinct enrollment patterns in 1890. (See table I–12.) In the industrial States of New England and elsewhere in the Northeast, children started school at about age 6 and attended until "time to quit and go to work" (at an early age). In the agricultural States, both South and Midwest, the children enrolled later, attended sporadically, but did not drop out at such young ages. The break between school and work was not so sharp. In both the industrial and the agricultural States an elementary education was probably the norm; it just took longer to achieve in the rural areas.

Table I–12.—Percent Enrolled in School, by Age, for Selected States: 1890

State	5 to 9 years old	10 to 14 years old	15 to 19 years old
Industrial States:			
Massachusetts........................	72.0	91.2	25.4
New York.......................	61.9	85.9	23.7
New Jersey.......................	59.4	84.7	21.2
Agricultural States:			
Indiana.......................	56.2	90.7	41.6
Wisconsin.......................	63.4	90.8	32.0
Kentucky.......................	40.3	75.5	36.4

Source: *Eleventh Census of the United States: 1890, Report on Education in the United States*, table 7.

In 1890 the median percent enrolled among the 10 to 14 age group was substantially higher in the States with attendance laws (89 percent) than in the States without such laws (71 percent). The laws at that time more often required attendance through age 14 than through age 16. The compulsory attendance age range was later raised in revisions of the laws in most States. Among the group aged 15 to 19, enrollment rates were nearly as high in the States without attendance laws (33 percent was the median) as in the States which had such laws (36 percent median).

While this comparison indicates a marked difference in enrollment rates between the States with attendance laws and those without, it does not indicate whether the change came before the law and was reinforced by the law, or whether the law itself actually raised the enrollment rates.

For the States which passed attendance laws after 1890, enrollment rates were compared with the national rate for the same decade. The resulting Index numbers (where the national rate of change equals 100) are shown in table I–13 for the States which enacted attendance laws between 1900 and 1919.

Table I–13.—INDEX OF CHANGE IN ENROLLMENT RATES AT THE TIME OF ENACTMENT OF COMPULSORY ATTENDANCE LAWS, FOR SELECTED STATES: 1900 TO 1919

[Minus sign (−) denotes decrease]

State	Compulsory school ages	Index of change in enrollment rates[1]				Change in the index	
		Decade prior to first compulsory attendance law		Decade following first compulsory attendance law		10 to 14 years old	15 to 20 years old
		10 to 14 years old	15 to 20 years old	10 to 14 years old	15 to 20 years old		
1900 TO 1909							
Arkansas	7 to 15	98.9	101.6	106.2	100.2	7.3	-1.4
Delaware	7 to 14	102.6	111.2	101.5	110.9	-1.1	-0.3
Iowa	7 to 14	97.1	91.2	93.5	90.4	-3.6	-0.8
Maryland	8 to 16	99.6	100.6	101.3	109.0	1.7	8.4
Missouri	8 to 16	97.4	95.2	99.4	92.5	2.0	-2.7
North Carolina	8 to 14	108.1	126.9	114.1	106.7	6.0	-20.2
Tennessee	8 to 16	96.4	100.2	108.1	105.6	11.7	5.4
Virginia	8 to 12	103.1	104.9	106.3	106.6	3.2	1.7
1910 TO 1919[2]							
Alabama	8 to 16	119.1	116.2	113.3	106.4	-5.8	-9.8
Florida	8 to 14	93.9	91.3	111.3	106.9	17.4	15.6
Georgia	8 to 14	112.3	118.2	106.2	103.8	-6.1	-14.4
Louisiana	7 to 14	112.0	129.7	119.8	118.7	7.8	-11.0
Mississippi	7 to 14	115.1	114.7	101.3	98.1	-13.8	-16.6
South Carolina	8 to 16	124.9	128.1	118.5	111.6	-6.4	-16.5
Texas	8 to 14	99.0	105.2	99.9	93.4	0.9	-11.8

[1] Percent of change in the State enrollment rate divided by percent of change in the national enrollment rate, for the same time period and age group (times 100).
[2] Period of enactment of first State Compulsory Attendance Law.

Source: See text for description of computations.

In the majority of States the enactment of an attendance law resulted in an acceleration of attendance rates greater than the national average acceleration for the same decade. However, 3 out of 22 States had lower rates than the United States for the 10 to 14 age group, and 4 out of 22 had lower rates for the 15 to 20 age group. Most of the States had rates of increase only slightly greater than those of the United States. Only 5 of the 22 States had enrollment rates for ages 10 to 14 that were 10 percent or more greater than the national rate in the decade in which they enacted attendance laws.

This suggests that the attendance laws had some influence in stimulating enrollment rates. However, this conclusion may not be warranted, because most of the States that enacted attendance laws after 1890 had lower enrollment rates and more room for improvement. The question is: How much of the higher enrollment growth was just normal "catching up" with the rest of the United States, and how much can be attributed to the attendance laws?

The rates of growth in the decades immediately before and immediately after the laws were enacted will give an indication of their influence.

Six of the 15 States had greater increases in enrollment rates relative to the national rates for ages 10 to 14 in the decade prior to the enactment of compulsory attendance laws than in the decade when the laws were passed. (See table I–13; comparisons are possible for only the 15 States enacting laws subsequent to 1900.) Most of the States (11 out of 15) had greater increases than the national average rate at ages 15 to 20 in the decade before the laws were passed. Enrollment rate increases were larger in most States when attendance laws were passed than in the next decade (data not shown). Out of 22 States, only 7 had larger increases in enrollment rates for the 10 to 14 group in the subsequent decade, and only 3 had larger increases for the 15 to 20 group. About one-third of the States showed much larger increases in enrollment rates in the decade of attendance law passage than in the next decade.

Compulsory attendance laws were enacted in most of the States (where comparisons can be made) during a period of rapid increase in enrollment relative to the national rates. These increases did not begin when the laws were passed. They had generally been underway for some time. In a majority of the States the attendance laws apparently had a small effect in boosting enrollment rates. While the rates generally continued to increase in the decade after the laws were passed, the increases were smaller. These data generally confirm the conclusions reached by Stigler.

Effect of the GI Bill on the education of the male population. The veterans rehabilitation and education program, popularly known as the GI Bill, was in effect the largest scholarship program in the Nation's history. It is therefore of considerable interest to assess the effect of this program on the educational level of the male population.[25] In 1952, young veterans of World War II (those aged 25 to 34) were definitely better educated than nonveterans of the same age. The former had a median of 12.3 years of school completed, while the latter had only 10.0 years of schooling.[26] A large part of this differential was the result of the initial selection procedures used by the Armed Forces. The mental tests used screened out those with the least education. It has been estimated that the average serviceman who was under 25 when he entered the Armed Forces had a median of 12.1 years of school completed, while for the population as a whole, men aged 18 to 24 in 1940 had an average of about 11 years of school completed.[27] Therefore, the veterans started out with a substantial educational advantage over their nonveteran counterparts.

It can be estimated that during World War II high school enrollment was lowered by 2 to 5 percent and college enrollment was reduced from about a million and a half to less than a million male students, as a result of young men entering the armed services. During the war years about half a million fewer high school diplomas and about 400,000 fewer college degrees were awarded than would have been expected from the prewar trends. The effects of World War II on enrollment were quite substantial.

A large number of veterans took advantage of their educational benefits. In the fall of 1947, about 110,000 veterans were enrolled in high school and 1.2 million (about 70 percent of all male college students) were enrolled in college. In 1956 nearly one-half million veterans of the Korean conflict (about 25 percent of all male college students) were enrolled in college. Even though large numbers attended formal school, only 16 percent of all veterans of World War II and the Korean conflict completed at least one year of formal training. These figures exclude those students who attended for less than one year, and also those who completed vocational, technical, and agricultural programs which were not a part of the formal school program.

Of special interest is the question of how many more of the veterans attended college because of the GI Bill benefits, and how many would have gone anyway. Two separate studies of veterans attending college reached the conclusion that between 20 and 25 percent probably would not have attended college without the benefits.[28] While this type of retrospective question about how a person might have acted under different circumstances is subject to substantial response error, the figures indicate that the GI Bill enabled many who could not otherwise have continued their education to do so, but a large majority would probably have gone on to college anyway. The GI Bill enabled some veterans to continue their education for a longer period than would otherwise have been possible, but there are no good estimates of the size of this effect. While 82 percent of those whose college attendance was interrupted by the war made use of their educational benefits, only one-half of all veterans did so, indicating that the program was more valuable to those students who had already identified college attendance as a goal.

The overall effects of veterans educational benefits were substantial. After World War II, 250,000 veterans graduated from high school. This represented a little less than 3 percent of the males who graduated from high school in the 1940 to 1955 period and about 1 percent of the total number of males in the population who had 12 years or more of schooling. At the college level the effects of the GI Bill were much greater. About 2,250,000 veterans completed at least one year of college after military service. These constitute about 55 percent of the men who completed at least one year of college between 1940 and 1955, and about 20 percent of all the men in the population with one or more years of college in 1955. Further, the approximately 1 million veterans who became college graduates after the war represented one-half of the men who graduated from college in the period from 1940 to 1955, and almost one-fourth of all male college graduates in the population in 1955.

Based on the limited evidence available about the percent of veterans who would not have been able to continue their education without the GI Bill, it appears that a substantial majority would have continued their education anyway, without any educational benefits. Although the number of college-trained men in the population increased substantially because of the postwar education of veterans, even if these benefits had not been available the educational attainments of the population would have continued to increase in the same way as in the past several decades. The GI Bill provided a 10 to 20 percent acceleration of that trend at the college level during the period in which it was operating. Looked at another way, the GI Bill not only helped to fill in the shortage of male college graduates created by the small graduating classes during the war, but also led to an increase of about 10 percent in the total number of male graduates produced in the 1940 to 1955 period over what might have been expected from the continuation of prewar trends. Since the "deficiency" in college degrees during World War II was about 400,000, its elimination is a substantial accomplishment.

Effects of economic conditions on enrollment rates. While school enrollment is compulsory for ages 7 to 16, both below and above this point attendance is voluntary and may be affected by a variety of economic conditions. Even at the compulsory ages, economic conditions may have an effect on enrollment rates in situations where attendance laws are not strictly enforced. The correlation between enrollment rates (for the population aged 5 to 19) and per capita personal income for 48 States (excluding Alaska and Hawaii) has been moderate for the past four decades. (See table I–14.) Both expenditures per pupil in public schools and the educational attainment of the adult population were more highly correlated with enrollment rates than enrollment rates were with per capita income, but the differences were not large. There does not appear to be any clear-cut trend toward an increasing or decreasing relationship between these variables and enrollment rates.

Table I–14.—CORRELATION COEFFICIENT OF THE LINEAR RELATIONSHIP OF STATE ENROLLMENT RATES FOR THE POPULATION 5 TO 19 YEARS OLD AND SELECTED ECONOMIC AND EDUCATIONAL VARIABLES: 1930 TO 1960

Year	Independent variables		
	Per capita personal income	Public school current expenditures per pupil	Educational attainment of adult population
1930...	.55	.78	(NA)
1940...	.53	.68	.70
1950...	.58	.61	.61
1960...	.56	.66	.62

NA Not available.

Source: Per capita personal income from U.S. Bureau of the Census, *Survey of Current Business* for August of the year following the census year; current expenditures per pupil in public schools from U.S. Office of Education, *Biennial Survey of Education,* 1929 and 1930, 1939 and 1940, 1949 and 1950, and 1959 and 1960; educational attainment of adult population from Censuses of 1940 to 1960.

One can also plot the trend in age-specific enrollment rates over several decades to see if there seems to be any correlation with economic conditions. Decennial census years are too far apart to be very effective in revealing any but major trends. Adverse economic conditions should reduce enrollment rates at the higher noncompulsory ages because some students will drop out of school to take a job. This might be counter-balanced by students remaining in school because they could not find a job.[29] Trends in enrollment rates showed no tendency to reflect the effects of the depression years of the 1930's at any ages except 5 and 6. The enrollment rates at these ages for the total population did not grow at all between 1930 and 1940; this suggests a halt in the expansion of kindergartens, and some delay in entering the first grade among children who did not have proper clothing to begin school at age 6. These hypotheses are not borne out by the trend in enrollment rates of nonwhites aged 5 and 6, whom we would expect to be more affected by the factors suggested. While enrollment rates for the group aged 5 and 6 among the total population were stationary during the decade of the depression, nonwhite enrollment rates increased at about the same rate as during the preceding and subsequent decades. For all other age groups, there is no evidence that enrollment rates were either boosted or retarded as a result of the depression.

NOTES

[1] Carroll Wright, *History and Growth of the United States Census.* Washington: U.S. Government Printing Office, 1900, p. 36.

[2] Wright, op. cit., p. 37.

[3] Herman Richey, "Reappraisal of the State School Systems of the Pre-Civil-War Period," *The Elementary School Journal,* Vol. XLI, Oct. 1940, pp. 118-129. Richey emphasizes the rapid growth of schools in the period just prior to the Civil War.

[4] The census institutional reports of enrollment growth are not consistent with the reports from individuals. The institutional reports indicate an increase in the percent enrolled between 1850 and 1890 from 42 to 64 percent, while the individual reports for the same time period indicate an increase from 47 to 51 percent (see tables I–2 and I–3). It would be expected that the institutional reports would contain a number of duplicate enrollments—and Wright, op. cit., as well as the census reports themselves, attest that this did occur. However, it appears that reporting of institutional data was very defective, especially in the South, because the individual data indicate larger total enrollment for both 1850 and 1860. The Eleventh Census, 1890, had a *Report on Education in the United States,* which gives the institutional statistics in great detail, including a summary for previous years. There is an extended discussion of problems of definition, collection, and reporting in this volume.

Although on a priori grounds it would seem that the collection of enrollment statistics from institutional sources would be easier and would be more likely to be complete, this apparently was not the case in the 1850 and 1860 Censuses.

[5] When the individual data from 1850 to 1900 are adjusted for some differences with the data collected since 1910, it seems likely that the actual increase in percent enrolled from 1850 to 1890 was more on the order of 8 to 14 percent than the 4 percent reported.

NOTES—Continued

At least two factors can be identified:

a. Enrollment reported in 1890 and 1900 asked for number of months enrolled. Where this was not known there was a tendency to report the student as not enrolled (see discussion Census of 1910, *Population,* Vol. I, pp. 1103, 1104). In the 1910 Census discussion, a large part of the 1900-1910 increase in percent enrollment was attributed to a more complete enumeration in 1910.

b. The percent enrolled in 1850, 1860, and 1870 was computed by dividing the *total* enrolled by the population 5 to 19. In 1890 and subsequently, the percent enrolled included only those within the age range 5 to 19 who were enrolled. While the 5 to 19 age group includes most of the persons enrolled, even in the mid-1800's there were some students (possibly 5 to 10 percent) who were outside this age range.

If the percent enrolled were lowered 2 to 5 percent in the earlier period and raised 2 to 5 percent in 1890 and 1900, we would obtain an estimate of the "true" increase in the percent enrolled of from 8 to 14 percent.

[6] This ignores the effect of the increases in the length of the school year which made school attendance a more significant fact during the later years. For the period 1870 to 1890, the average number of days attended increased about 10 percent. (Comprehensive data for earlier periods are not available.)

[7] Comparison of 1900 Census figures with those for 1890 and for 1910 indicates a substantial undercount of persons enrolled in school in 1900. For this reason, most of the discussion and statistics on school progress in the 20th century will use the 1910 Census as the base.

[8] Martin Trow, "The Second Transformation of American Secondary Education," *International Journal of Comparative Sociology,* Vol. II, No. 2, Sept. 1961, pp. 144-166.

[9] For a statement about universal higher education as a goal, see *Universal Opportunity for Education Beyond the High School,* Educational Policies Commission, National Education Association, 1964.

[10] U.S. Bureau of the Census, *Current Population Reports,* P-20, No. 126, Sept. 1963, table A.

[11] Beverly Duncan, "Drop-outs and the Unemployed," *Journal of Political Economy.* Vol. LXXIII, April 1965, pp. 121-134.

[12] George Strayer, *Age and Grade Census of Schools and Colleges.* Office of Education Bulletin, 1911, No. 5.

[13] Strayer, op. cit., p. 135.

[14] Frank Phillips, *An Age Grade Study in 900 City School Systems.* U.S. Office of Education. Statistical Circular No. 8, May 1927.

[15] There may be a practical upper limit on the amount of retardation somewhere between 50 and 75 percent. In any community or neighborhood group where retardation reaches these proportions, dropping out of school is probably sanctioned for the retarded student. The difficulties of operating schools with such a large proportion of retarded pupils suggests that school officials probably would see dropouts as a "reasonable" solution to their problems. If these speculations have validity, the American public school system between 1900 and 1930 was probably operating with a near maximum "load" of retarded pupils.

[16] The age-grade table in 1940 was prepared from the question, "What was the highest grade of school completed?" For persons enrolled in school, it was assumed that they would be in the next higher grade. However, internal evidence indicates that many people gave the grade in which the student was currently enrolled as the highest grade completed. There is no satisfactory way to adjust this data so that it is comparable with the 1950 and 1960 Census materials on the subject. On the basis of comparison with the Office of Education grade enrollment data, net over-reporting of grade enrolled in 1940 was about

NOTES—Continued

two-thirds of a grade; with improved question wording, the net over-reporting was reduced to about .2 of a grade in 1950.   See appendix A.

[17] Two years are defined as "normal" for each grade. Thus both 6- and 7-year-olds in the first grade at the time of the census are considered normal. Seven-and-eight-year-olds in the second grade are normal, and similarly for other grades.

[18] The method of making the enrollment projections is described in appendix B. They are based on the latest available Census Bureau population projections contained in *Current Population Reports,* P–25, No. 286, July 1964. Similar projections, utilizing somewhat higher population projections, and more conservative assumptions about enrollment rates can be found in Bureau of the Census *Current Population Reports,* "Illustrative Projections to 1980 of School and College Enrollment in the United States," P–25, No. 232, June 1961. A revision of these projections was released by the Bureau of the Census as this monograph was going to press.

[19] The major increases in the percent of youth attending high school occurred between 1910 and 1950. While the pattern of increase at the college level may not follow the earlier high school experience, some of the same forces seem to be operating. See Trow, op. cit., for an extended discussion.

[20] Herman Richey, "The Persistence of Educational Progress During the Decade of the Civil War," *The Elementary School Journal,* Vol. XLII, Jan. 1942, p. 359. He says: "These [regional] differences might be accounted for as easily in terms of conditions which characterized rural society, both North and South, as in terms of geographical location or social organization." (Quoted with the permission of the University of Chicago Press. Copyrighted 1942 by the University of Chicago.) The facts do not sustain this viewpoint very well. While the Northeast in 1850 was considerably more urban (26 percent) than the South (8 percent), the North Central Region (9 percent urban) and the West (6 percent urban) developed schools much more rapidly than the South, even though their proportion urban was similar to that in the South. The urban theory is a better explanation of the persistence of the South's lower enrollment rates in the last half of the 19th century; by 1900, the South was still only 18 percent urban compared with 66 percent in the Northeast, 39 percent in the North Central, and 41 percent in the West.

[21] Richey, "Reappraisal of the State School System of the Pre-Civil-War Period," op. cit., table 2.

[22] James Cowhig, "School Drop-out Rates" *Agricultural Economic Report,* No. 42, U.S. Department of Agriculture, table 6.

[23] U.S. Office of Education, *Biennial Survey of Education, 1956–58,* chapter 4, section 1, table 2; and the U S O E, *Total Enrollment,* 1959–60, OE–54205, table 1.

[24] George J. Stigler, *Employment and Compensation in Education.* New York: National Bureau of Economic Research, Occasional Paper No. 33, 1950, p. 8, and appendix B.

[25] For a more extended discussion, see Charles Nam "Impact of the 'G.I. Bills' on the Educational Level of the Male Population," *Social Forces,* 43, 1964, pp. 26-32.

[26] U.S. Bureau of the Census, *Current Population Reports,* Series P–20, No. 45, table 16.

[27] The President's Commission on Veterans Pensions, *A Report on Veterans Benefits in the United States,* Staff Report IX, Part A. Washington: U.S. Government Printing Office, 1956, p. 86, and U.S. Bureau of the Census, 1950, *Population,* Vol. II, U.S. Summary. Washington: U.S. Government Printing Office, 1953, table 115.

[28] Norman Fredrickson and W. B. Schraeder, *Adjustment to College: A Study of 10,000 Veteran and Non-Veteran Students in Sixteen American Colleges.* Princeton: Educational Testing Service, 1951, p. 34. A separate study by Strom is reported on p. 35.

[29] For a more complete analysis of the relation of employment conditions to school dropouts of teenagers, see B. Duncan, op. cit. She found a high correlation between unfavorable economic conditions and rising enrollment rates. This suggests that when it was relatively more difficult to obtain a job, male youth tended to stay in school.

CHAPTER II

SOCIAL FACTORS RELATED TO SCHOOL AND COLLEGE ENROLLMENT

Introduction

Chapter I traced the trend in school and college enrollment in the United States over a long part of the country's history, and examined some of the major social forces which affected that trend. The present chapter deals with those factors which influence school and college enrollment for different segments of American society, with emphasis on the factors operating at the family and individual levels.

School enrollment rates, school retention to higher grade levels and to graduation, scholastic attainment, and the proportions of students entering college and completing college, vary for different segments of the population because of numerous social and economic influences which hinder educational development for some groups and advance it for others. Wolfle divided the factors which determine who continues in school into two categories: "... those which are essentially related to school progress and those which are related, but not in any essential way."[1] In the essential category he placed four factors: ability of the type which can be measured by standardized aptitude tests; a record of satisfactory schoolwork; money; and the student's own desire for an education. Those he called related but not essential variables were sex, cultural background, geographic location, and ethnic and religious background.

Data from the decennial censuses and periodic sample surveys enable us to assess the effects of many of these factors.[2] Because compulsory school attendance laws require children to enter school by a certain minimum age and to remain in school until they have attained a specified higher age, the essential factors have only a limited effect on elementary and early high school enrollments. Neither the student nor his parents can choose to have him stay out of school. Moreover, publicly supported schools obviate the need for most large personal expenditures to keep children in school. Furthermore, although children who do not perform well may be kept from advancing, they are nevertheless generally kept in school. Among the essential factors, only ability—or the lack of it—significantly restricts enrollment at compulsory ages by excusing from school those children who are not mentally or physically capable of doing the work. At later high school and college ages, when attendance is voluntary rather than compulsory, the factors of educational choice, economic status, and satisfactory school achievement have a major effect on enrollment patterns. The related but not essential factors may have somewhat more effect than the essential factors at the lower educational levels, but their effects are more easily seen at the voluntary high school and college levels.

Discussion in the following pages centers on how these several factors are related to the early school years and scholastic progress, and how they may determine who stays in elementary and high school and who drops out, who enters college, and who stays in college and who drops out.

Early school years

Enrollment patterns at age 5. Enrollment rates for 5-year-olds tend to vary according to whether or not they live in densely populated areas where kindergarten is normally part of the education pattern. Table II–1 shows that in April 1960 the percentage of 5-year-olds enrolled in kindergarten or elementary school was highest in urban areas, with 57 percent enrolled in the central cities of urbanized areas and 55 percent in the urban fringe; about 42 percent in urban places of 10,000 or more population outside urbanized areas; 40 percent in urban places of 2,500 to 10,000 population; 35 percent in rural places of 1,000 to 2,500 population; and as low as 29 percent in other rural-nonfarm areas and 24 percent in farm areas.

Nationwide, more than four-fifths of the 5-year-olds in school in 1960 were in kindergarten. This proportion exceeded nine-tenths in urban fringe areas, but was only two-thirds in farm areas. As might be expected, the percentage of 5-year-olds enrolled in elementary school was higher in rural than in urban areas. In many rural areas, parents do not have the opportunity of sending their children to kindergarten before they are enrolled in elementary school. In urban-fringe areas, the effect of having the opportunity of sending children to kindergarten can be seen clearly: 5-year-olds in these areas who were enrolled were most likely to be attending kindergarten and least likely to be in elementary school.

Ethnic background is an important correlate of enrollment rates at age 5. In 1960, about 69 percent of Japanese and Chinese children and 66 percent of children of the Nation's less populous races (for example, Filipino, Hawaiian, Eskimo, Aleut, Korean, Asian Indian) were enrolled in school, compared with 56 percent of the white children of foreign or mixed parentage, 53 percent of foreign-born whites, 45 percent of the children of white natives, 42 percent of Negroes, and 32 percent of Indians. While these differentials were not as great in large urban areas as in other size-of-place categories, they did exist in all types of residence areas and indicate the importance of cultural factors in accounting for unequal school-beginning rates.

Table II–1.—Percent of 5- and 6-Year Olds Enrolled in School, by School Level, Residence, and Ethnic Status: 1960

Residence and ethnic status	5-year olds			6-year olds			
	Total	Kindergarten	Elementary school	Total	Kindergarten	First grade	Higher grade
United States................	44.8	38.1	6.8	83.4	16.7	60.6	6.1
RESIDENCE							
Urban........................	52.4	45.9	6.5	87.2	19.4	61.3	6.5
Urbanized areas....................	56.0	49.2	6.8	88.7	19.6	62.2	7.0
Central cities..................	56.9	48.4	8.5	87.7	17.2	62.0	8.5
Urban fringe....................	55.0	50.2	4.6	90.0	22.5	62.4	5.1
Other urban........................	40.8	35.2	5.6	82.2	19.0	58.4	4.8
Places of 10,000 or more.........	41.6	36.4	5.2	82.4	19.7	57.8	4.9
Places of 2,500 to 10,000.........	39.9	33.7	6.1	82.0	18.1	59.2	4.7
Rural........................	28.8	21.5	7.3	75.4	11.0	59.1	5.3
Places of 1,000 to 2,500............	35.3	29.4	5.9	80.2	15.4	60.2	4.6
Other rural........................	28.0	20.5	7.5	74.8	10.4	59.0	5.4
Nonfarm.........................	29.4	22.1	7.3	75.6	10.8	59.5	5.2
Farm............................	24.1	16.1	8.0	72.6	9.3	57.6	5.7
ETHNIC STATUS							
White........................	45.2	39.4	5.7	84.1	17.7	61.1	5.2
Native white........................	45.1	39.4	5.7	84.0	17.7	61.1	5.2
Native parentage.................	44.5	38.9	5.7	83.8	17.6	61.1	5.1
Foreign or mixed parentage.......	55.8	48.9	6.8	88.1	19.0	62.4	6.7
Foreign-born white.................	52.7	45.9	6.8	85.6	19.7	59.9	6.0
Nonwhite........................	42.7	29.7	13.0	79.1	10.4	57.3	11.4
Negro..........................	41.8	28.4	13.4	78.6	9.8	57.1	11.7
Indian.........................	32.3	21.0	11.3	72.3	14.6	49.3	8.4
Japanese and Chinese..............	68.9	61.3	7.6	84.4	17.8	69.6	7.6
Other races.....................	65.6	58.3	7.3	91.5	21.4	63.7	6.4

Source: *1960 Census of Population, Subject Reports, School Enrollment*, Series PC(2)–5A, tables 1 and 2.

Socioeconomic factors also help to explain differences in enrollment rates at age 5. Among boys at this age, the percentages enrolled varied with both the parents' educational level and the family income. For example, if the boy's father (or his mother, if his father was not present) had less than 8 years of schooling and the family had less than $3,000 annual income, the chances were 23 out of 100 that the boy was enrolled; if the parent was at least a high school graduate and the family income was at least $7,000, the boy's chances of being enrolled were 57 out of 100. Family income and parents' education each exerted an independent effect on enrollment; that is, when either factor was held constant, variations in the enrollment rate could still be observed by the other factor.

Census data do not provide an adequate basis for describing how socioeconomic factors operate to affect the enrollment rate at age 5, but one may speculate. Better educated parents presumably are more likely to place a high value on education and to want their children in school as early as possible. Parents from the higher economic strata are in a better position than those from the lower strata to enroll their children in school early. In some places only private kindergartens are available, and even where public kindergartens exist, parents must face certain costs, if nothing more than the cost of having their children reasonably well dressed and well groomed when they go to school. Where family income exceeded $7,000, 17 percent of the 5-year-olds enrolled were in private school, but of the comparable group from families with less than $3,000 income only 7 percent were in private school.

Some correlates of enrollment at ages 6 to 9. The vast majority of school children who were 6 years old in April 1960 were in the first grade, but a small percentage were in a higher grade, and a slightly larger percentage in kindergarten. The pattern of urban-rural differences noted for 5-year-olds held fairly well for 6-year-olds, primarily because residential differences in the availability of kindergartens were still an important factor (table II–1). Likewise, ethnic and socioeconomic factors remained operative. Though enrollment rates at age 6 were approaching the maximum rates held by slightly older children, some of the children were not yet covered by the compulsory attendance laws and there was room for variation in enrollment rates among population classes.

Nearly all children aged 7 to 9 were in school in April 1960. About 98 percent of the 8-year-olds were enrolled, and the same percent was recorded for every ethnic group except Negroes and American Indians, for whom the enrollment rates were 96 and 93 percent, respectively. Similarly, there was very little distinction in enrollment rates for socioeconomic groups. Among children aged 7 to 9, the percent in school ranged from 95 percent for those whose parents lacked an eighth grade education and whose family had less than $3,000 annual income, to 99 percent for those with a high school graduate parent and $7,000 or more family income.

Who stays in school and who drops out?

The person who fails to complete high school today is commonly regarded as unable to meet the job requirements of a technological society. Compared with the high school graduate, the high school dropout is at a disadvantage in that he has a harder time getting a job, may learn new skills more slowly, is not as well prepared to be a citizen, and makes less money.[3] Moreover, the disadvantage faced by the dropout is growing and the situation is likely to become worse.[4] A number of reasons have been offered to explain why students leave school: they are from low-income families and must contribute to family income, or they have been lured by their own needs for money; they are discouraged with their schoolwork because they are failing, or because they have been held back one or more grades; they are dissatisfied with the school or with teaching methods; they have a feeling of "not belonging"; or personal or family difficulties have left them physically or psychologically unfit to pursue their studies.[5]

Census data and population sample surveys provide no information about some of these topics, but they do reveal much about the traits that distinguish the dropouts from those who stay in school to graduation. While census data do not record a variety of important influences on the school progress of children and youth, and also fail to measure some of the effective causes of school attrition, they do serve to identify those groups within the population whose schooling is most deficient and to indicate where more intensive research into the causes of educational deficiency may be most productive.

Selectivity in school retention by age. Children who are physically and mentally capable are virtually certain to be in school by age 10, but from that age on the enrollment rate declines, and it declines more rapidly as the children reach the later teens. What are the patterns of social selectivity in school retention at these ages? Do the patterns change with age? The statistics we shall now examine are principally for three age groups—10 to 13, 14 and 15, and 16 and 17. Children in the first group are well within the compulsory age range, and 98 percent were in school in 1960. Scholastic attrition had begun to lessen the enrollment rate by ages 14 and 15. Of this group, 94 percent were in school in 1960. By ages 16 and 17, most youths are no longer subject to the compulsory attendance laws and dropping out of school is much more permissible than at earlier ages. In 1960, 81 percent of those aged 16 and 17 were in school.

Differentials in enrollment rates by urban-rural residence were slight at ages within the compulsory attendance range (table II–2). Even at ages 14 and 15, only 2 percentage points separated the residence group with the highest enrollment rate from the group with the lowest rate. At ages 16 and 17 the differentials were wider, although still not especially great. Rural-nonfarm residents and those living in large cities had the lowest enrollment rates. While these data probably reflect low educational status among urban minority groups, they may also indicate that in large cities and rural-nonfarm areas, more 17-year-olds had graduated from high school and gone to work by the time of the 1960 Census. The former explanation may be the more compelling, since, in the latter case, students graduating from high school at an early age might be expected to have gone on to college.

Little ethnic variation in enrollment rates can be observed at ages 10 to 13 (table II–2). Foreign-born white children were slightly less likely to be in school than other children at these ages; the percent enrolled for Negro children was 2 percentage points below, and that for Indian children, 4 percentage points below that for all children in the age group. At ages 14 and 15, ethnic differentials were slightly wider. The enrollment rate for Japanese and Chinese children was a few percentage points higher than the national average, while the rates for Negro and Indian children were several points lower. The percentages for native white children of native parentage and for children of

Aleut, Eskimo, and other minor nonwhite races were slightly higher than the average, and for foreign-born white children, slightly lower. Among youths 16 and 17 years old, differentials were greater. Japanese and Chinese youths had enrollment rates 13 percentage points above the average for the age group, and the rate for those of native parents was 8 points higher. White youths of foreign or mixed parentage had a slightly better-than-average chance of being enrolled, while the foreign-born whites had an enrollment rate 3 points below the national average, Negro youths 8 points below, and Indian youths 11 points below.

Table II–2.—Percent of the Population 10 to 17 Years Old Enrolled in School, by Age, Residence, and Ethnic Status: 1960

Residence and ethnic status	10 to 13 years old	14 and 15 years old	16 and 17 years old
United States......................	97.5	94.0	81.0
RESIDENCE			
Urban...............................	97.7	94.8	82.1
Urbanized areas...........................	97.7	94.9	82.0
Central cities.........................	97.2	93.8	79.6
Urban fringe..........................	98.3	96.3	85.6
Other urban............................	97.8	94.6	82.5
Places of 10,000 or more.............	97.8	94.6	81.9
Places of 2,500 to 10,000.............	97.9	94.6	83.1
Rural...............................	97.1	92.7	79.0
Places of 1,000 to 2,500.................	97.7	94.3	83.2
Other rural.............................	97.0	92.5	78.5
Nonfarm................................	96.9	92.3	76.7
Farm.................................	97.2	93.0	82.2
ETHNIC STATUS			
White...............................	97.7	94.6	88.6
Native white............................	97.8	94.6	88.5
Native parentage.......................	97.8	94.6	88.9
Foreign or mixed parentage.............	97.4	94.3	82.3
Foreign-born white.......................	96.5	93.3	77.5
Nonwhite.............................	95.9	90.2	73.8
Negro...................................	95.9	90.0	73.1
Indian.................................	93.4	88.7	69.9
Japanese and Chinese.....................	97.7	97.3	93.7
Other races.............................	97.2	95.2	81.4

Source: *1960 Census of Population, Subject Reports, School Enrollment*, Series PC(2)–5A, tables 1 and 2.

Between 1950 and 1960, enrollment rates increased for all ethnic groups, but particularly for those groups with the lowest rates in 1950. At ages 10 to 13, for example, the percent enrolled for Japanese increased from 96 to 98 percent, for Indian children from 81 to 93 percent, and for foreign-born white children from 92 to 97 percent. Thus, by 1960, enrollment differentials by ethnic status had narrowed considerably.

Family status is an important influence on a child's enrollment expectancy. The 1960 Census showed that enrollment rates, especially at ages 16 and 17, were somewhat lower for children from broken families (those disrupted by the loss of a parent through death or a broken marriage) than for those living with both parents. Furthermore, among children living with both parents, enrollment rates tended to be lower where the mother was the breadwinner or where neither parent was in the labor force than where the father was in the labor force. A child living with only one parent was slightly less likely to be enrolled if the parent was not in the labor force. The necessity of contributing to the family income apparently caused some dropouts, and since boys more often than girls help the family to earn a living, it is understandable that in homes where only the mother, or neither parent, was working, the enrollment rate for boys was lower than the rate for girls.

Among youths aged 16 and 17 not living with either parent, the enrollment rate was consistently lower than average, particularly for girls, many of whom had married or gone to work. This is borne out in table II–3, which shows 1960 Census data on the family status of high school dropouts (those who were not in school and who did not finish high school)[6] in the group aged 16 and 17. By these ages, girls were much more likely than boys to have established their own families, and about half of the married women who had dropped out of school had already had children of their own. Boys who had dropped out were more likely than girls to be living with nonrelatives or living alone. Of the dropouts of both sexes living with their parents or other

Table II–3.—FAMILY STATUS OF HIGH SCHOOL DROPOUTS 16 AND 17 YEARS OLD, BY COLOR AND SEX: 1960

[A "dropout" is defined here as a person who is not enrolled in school and did not finish high school]

Family status	Total		Nonwhite	
	Male	Female	Male	Female
Total..............................	538,587	545,245	88,051	90,227
Percent...........................	100.0	100.0	100.0	100.0
Family head or wife of head...............	3.2	35.6	2.5	28.3
Married, spouse present..................	3.0	32.7	2.1	22.4
With own children....................	1.1	16.1	1.2	14.3
Without own children.................	1.9	16.6	0.9	8.1
Other marital status....................	0.2	2.9	0.4	5.9
Family members other than head or wife.....	82.4	60.0	86.4	67.0
With family head—				
Single.................................	0.7	0.7	2.3	1.8
Married (except separated).............	66.6	48.1	58.1	44.6
Widowed, divorced, or separated........	15.1	11.3	26.0	20.6
Living alone or with nonrelatives..........	10.4	2.6	5.0	3.1
Institutional inmate......................	4.0	1.8	6.1	1.5

Source: *1960 Census of Population, Subject Reports, School Enrollment,* Series PC(2)–5A, table 14.

relatives, about one-fifth were in families in which the head was divorced or widowed.   About 1 in 20 male dropouts (all racial groups combined) and a smaller proportion of female dropouts were in institutions of one kind or another, many of them penal or correctional institutions.

The value of education for children is usually more appreciated by parents who are themselves well educated.   The higher the parents' educational attainment, the higher the enrollment rates of their children (table II–4).[7] Moreover, the education of each parent seems to be important in accounting for higher enrollment percentages.   For example, even for a fixed level of father's education, enrollment rates varied by the mother's educational level.

Among children aged 10 to 13 years, whether or not the parents had finished grade school or had attended college had only a modest effect on the uniformly higher percentages enrolled.   Where both parents lacked an eighth-grade education, 95 percent of the boys and girls aged 10 to 13 were in school.   By ages 14 and 15, as the overall dropout rate increased, the selective effect of parents' education became more noticeable.   Where both parents had failed to complete the eighth grade, about 88 percent of the children aged 14 and 15 were enrolled in school, but where both parents had attended college, about 99 percent were in school.

For each higher level of father's education, and for each higher level of mother's education, there was a small increment in the enrollment rate of the children.   Enrollment differentials by parents' education were considerably wider at ages 16 and 17.   Boys at these ages whose fathers had less than 8 years of schooling had 73 chances in 100 of being enrolled, while those whose fathers had gone to college had 96 chances in 100.   If the mother as well as the father had less than 8 years of school, the boy's chances were reduced to 66 in 100; if the mother as well as the father had some college, the chances were increased to 97 in 100.

This pattern of enrollment by parents' educational level for the different ages of children and youth was about the same whether the child was a boy or a girl, white or nonwhite, or from an urban or rural area.   There are a few minor variations in the pattern.   At ages 16 and 17, where the parents were not high school graduates, girls were somewhat more likely than boys to be enrolled, but the difference was small.   At the same ages, nonwhite boys and girls were less likely than their white counterparts to be enrolled, especially where the parents had completed high school, but the color differential even here was small compared with the differential by parents' educational attainment.   The enrollment rate for rural-farm boys 16 and 17 years old, both of whose parents lacked an eighth grade education (62 percent), was somewhat less than the rate for boys in urban-fringe areas whose parents had the same educational background (71 percent), but this differential by residence was considerably narrower where the parents were better educated.

Table II–4.—PERCENT ENROLLED IN SCHOOL FOR CHILDREN 10 TO 17 YEARS OLD
LIVING WITH BOTH PARENTS, BY AGE, SEX, AND EDUCATIONAL LEVEL OF MOTHER
AND FATHER: 1960

Educational attainment of mother and father	Male			Female		
	10 to 13 years old	14 and 15 years old	16 and 17 years old	10 to 13 years old	14 and 15 years old	16 and 17 years old
Total........................	97.6	95.1	85.3	97.9	95.3	87.2
Father less than 8 years............	96.3	90.8	72.7	96.5	90.9	77.7
Mother: Less than 8 years..........	95.1	87.9	66.1	95.5	88.0	71.9
8 years or more............	97.3	93.9	79.5	97.4	93.9	83.4
Father 8 to 11 years................	97.8	95.5	85.2	98.0	95.6	86.9
Mother: Less than 8 years..........	96.4	92.1	76.1	97.0	92.4	79.1
8 to 11 years.............	97.7	95.2	83.7	97.9	95.5	85.8
12 years or some college...	98.2	97.0	91.1	98.4	97.0	91.4
Father 12 years....................	98.4	97.1	92.1	98.3	97.3	91.9
Mother: Less than 12 years........	98.1	96.1	88.8	97.9	96.4	89.0
12 years..................	98.5	97.4	93.4	98.5	97.6	92.9
Some college..............	98.7	98.1	95.6	98.9	98.2	95.4
Father some college................	98.8	98.2	95.7	98.8	98.3	95.1
Mother: Less than college.........	98.6	97.8	94.4	98.7	97.8	93.8
Some college..............	99.1	98.5	97.2	98.9	98.9	96.7

Source: *1960 Census of Population, Subject Reports, School Enrollment,* Series PC(2)–5A, table 4.

What do we find when we introduce an index of economic status to the relationship between parent's education and school enrollment of young persons? From the data in table II–5 we can see that, for given levels of parent's education, the higher the family income the higher the enrollment rate of children and youth.[8] The effect of family income was most pronounced where the parent who was the household head had attained a low level of schooling. For example, among girls aged 14 and 15, the percent enrolled in school ranged from 88 percent in the lowest income category to 93 percent in the highest category where the parent lacked an eighth grade education, and from 96 percent in the lowest income category to 98 percent in the highest category where the parent was at least a high school graduate. Similarly, among boys aged 16 and 17, enrollment rates by family income varied from 66 to 77 percent for youths whose parent had not finished the eighth grade, and from 90 to 94 percent for those whose parent had completed high school. The enrollment rate differential between the lowest and highest parental education-income status groups for boys was 10 percentage points at ages 14 and 15, and 28 percentage points at ages 16 and 17. Although both parental educational level and family income affected a child's chances of being in school, particularly at ages 16 and 17, the effect of parental educational level was a little stronger (figure II–1).

The same general relationship between parental education, family income, and school enrollment was found in 1960 for each sex, color, and residence group, with little variation. Among the notable exceptions were the slightly

Figure II–1.—Percent of Boys 14 to 17 Years Old Not Enrolled in School, by Parent's Education, Family Income, and Age: 1960

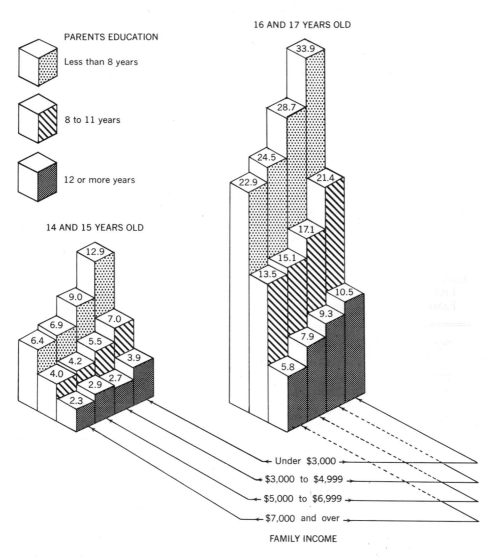

Source: Table II–5.

more favorable enrollment rate of girls aged 16 and 17 than of boys the same age whose parents were poorly educated; the somewhat lower enrollment rate of nonwhite than of white boys and girls in the same age group whose parents were moderately to well educated; and the slightly higher enrollment rates for farm than for urban boys and girls in the age group 16 and 17 years old whose families had low incomes. These exceptions, however, were minor when compared with the variation in enrollment generally associated with parents' education and income.

Whether an enrolled youth 16 or 17 years old was in a public or nonpublic (parochial or other private) school also varied according to his socioeconomic background. Only 2 percent of the boys in school at these ages whose parents had less than 8 years of school and less than $3,000 annual income were attending a nonpublic school, compared with 15 percent of those whose parents were high school graduates with a yearly income of $7,000 or more. Here, the income factor proved more important. Even among enrolled boys whose parents did not have as much as an eighth grade education, 10 percent whose families had at least $7,000 of income were attending nonpublic schools.

Table II–5.—Percent Enrolled in School for Children 10 to 17 Years Old Living With One or Both Parents, by Age, Sex, Education of Parent, and Family Income: 1960

Years of school completed by parent[1] and family income in 1959	Male			Female		
	10 to 13 years old	14 and 15 years old	16 and 17 years old	10 to 13 years old	14 and 15 years old	16 and 17 years old
Total.....................	97.7	94.8	94.2	97.8	94.9	86.1
Less than 8 years..................	96.1	90.3	71.5	96.4	90.5	76.1
Under $3,000....................	94.9	87.1	66.1	95.3	87.9	72.3
$3,000 to $4,999.................	96.6	91.0	71.3	96.8	91.4	77.2
$5,000 to $6,999.................	97.1	93.1	75.5	97.2	92.9	79.0
$7,000 and over..................	97.1	93.6	77.1	97.3	92.6	78.7
8 to 11 years.....................	97.6	95.1	84.0	97.8	95.2	85.8
Under $3,000....................	96.8	93.0	78.6	96.9	93.1	82.5
$3,000 to $4,999.................	97.5	94.5	82.9	97.8	94.8	84.9
$5,000 to $6,999.................	98.0	95.8	84.9	98.1	95.5	86.6
$7,000 and over..................	97.9	96.0	86.5	97.9	96.2	87.0
12 years or some college...........	98.5	97.4	93.1	98.5	97.6	92.8
Under $3,000....................	97.9	96.1	89.5	97.9	96.1	90.2
$3,000 to $4,999.................	98.1	97.3	90.7	98.0	96.8	91.2
$5,000 to $6,999.................	98.3	97.1	92.1	98.3	97.4	91.9
$7,000 and over..................	98.8	97.7	94.2	98.7	97.9	93.7

[1] Education of parent refers to father's education when child was living with both parents or father, and to mother's education when child's father was not living with the household.

Source: 1960 Census of Population, Subject Reports, School Enrollment, Series PC(2)–5A, table 5.

One other socioeconomic indicator for which census enrollment data by age are available is the occupation of the child's father. The figures in table II–6 are similar to those obtained when parents' education and family income by enrollment of children were analyzed.[9] Only small occupational differences, favoring children of white-collar workers, were found at ages 10 to 13. At the older school ages, the percent enrolled in school was much lower than average for children of farm laborers and also substantially less than average for children of blue-collar workers and farmers. Among boys 16 and 17 years old, 95 percent of those whose fathers were professionals were in school, compared with 90 percent of sons of clerical workers, 84 percent of sons of farmers, 82 percent of sons of operatives, 77 percent of sons of nonfarm laborers, and 64 percent of sons of farm laborers.

The pattern of enrollment by father's occupation differed for girls only in that, at ages 16 and 17, the daughters of men in farm occupations were more likely to have stayed in school than the sons. The pattern for nonwhites differed from that for whites primarily in lower nonwhite enrollment rates among boys and girls 16 and 17 years old whose fathers were sales workers or farmers, and among boys who were sons of professional workers. The pattern by residence varied only in that there was a slightly greater tendency in rural than in urban areas for children of farm laborers to be out of school.

In general, it can be said that socioeconomic factors are highly associated with enrollment differences, particularly at postcompulsory school ages. Their effect clearly overshadows such demographic factors as sex, color, and type of residence. A good part of the enrollment rate differentials between whites and nonwhites and between urban and rural populations can be ascribed to socioeconomic differences among these groups rather than to other factors associated with group membership.

Table II–6.—PERCENT ENROLLED IN SCHOOL FOR CHILDREN 10 TO 17 YEARS OLD LIVING WITH AN EMPLOYED FATHER, BY AGE, SEX, AND FATHER'S OCCUPATION: 1960

Major occupation group of employed father	Male			Female		
	10 to 13 years old	14 and 15 years old	16 and 17 years old	10 to 13 years old	14 and 15 years old	16 and 17 years old
Total[1]...................................	97.9	95.4	86.0	98.0	95.6	87.6
Professional, technical, and kindred workers......	98.7	98.0	95.4	98.8	98.2	95.1
Farmers and farm managers........................	97.6	94.0	83.7	97.9	94.8	89.0
Managers, officials, and proprietors, exc. farm...	98.7	97.5	92.9	98.6	97.6	92.9
Clerical and kindred workers.....................	98.1	96.4	90.2	97.9	96.8	89.8
Sales workers....................................	98.4	97.0	92.0	98.4	97.6	92.6
Craftsmen, foremen, and kindred workers...........	98.1	96.1	86.4	98.1	96.1	87.6
Operatives and kindred workers...................	97.6	94.6	81.7	97.7	94.3	83.6
Service workers..................................	97.7	95.2	84.8	97.6	94.4	84.9
Farm laborers and foremen........................	95.6	86.1	64.3	95.8	87.6	73.9
Laborers, exc. farm and mine.....................	96.7	91.7	76.7	97.1	92.4	79.6

[1] Includes persons whose father's occupation was not reported, not included in the distribution by occupation.

Source: 1960 Census of Population, Subject Reports, School Enrollment, Series PC(2)–5A, table 14.

Selectivity in school retention to high school graduation. Although a student's progress in school is closely related to his age, the correspondence of age and school grade, as indicated in the previous chapter, is far from perfect. The age at which children begin school varies and some children are not promoted regularly or are kept out of school temporarily for reasons of health or truancy. In terms of knowledge gained through formal schooling and of job opportunities in the world of work, the age to which a youngster continues in school is not nearly so important as how far he advances in the school system. With the great emphasis placed today on getting a high school diploma, it is of particular interest to know what differentiates the high school dropout from the high school graduate.

Table II–7 provides some measures of school retention by school level for various ethnic groupings. The data are for men and women 20 to 24 years old who ordinarily would have finished their secondary schooling during the late 1950's. There are some major differences in retention. Among those who had completed the fifth grade (in the immediate post-World War II period), less than two-thirds of the Puerto Ricans had continued as far as the ninth grade. The corresponding proportion was about two-thirds for Indians and persons of Mexican origin, roughly three-fourths for Negroes and foreign-born whites, and nine-tenths or more for native whites and persons of Oriental origin.[10]

Table II–7.—Selected Measures of School Retention for Persons 20 to 24 Years Old, by Ethnic Status and Sex: 1960

Ethnic status	Percent of persons--			
	Finishing 5th grade who completed some high school		Completing some high school who graduated	
	Male	Female	Male	Female
United States......................	86.5	89.8	73.6	73.9
Native white of native parentage...........	87.8	91.2	75.3	75.4
Native of foreign or mixed parentage.......	90.9	93.7	78.3	81.0
Foreign born................................	75.9	76.9	75.5	71.0
White persons of Spanish surname[1].........	68.3	69.2	55.8	58.4
Puerto Rican stock..........................	61.4	63.3	40.9	47.0
Negro.......................................	74.5	80.8	52.7	56.1
American Indian.............................	67.3	68.8	50.4	49.0
Japanese....................................	96.5	96.1	88.5	87.4
Chinese.....................................	92.7	92.9	85.2	84.9

[1] In 5 Southwestern States, largely persons of Mexican origin.

Source: *1960 Census of Population, Subject Reports, Persons of Spanish Surname,* Series PC(2)–1B, table 7; *Educational Attainment,* Series PC(2)–5B, table 1; *Nonwhite Population by Race,* Series PC(2)–1C, tables 19–22; *Puerto Ricans in the United States,* Series PC(2)–1D, table 6.

The ethnic factor in school retention became even more selective with advances in school level. Only 41 percent of young Puerto Rican males and 47 percent of the females who had completed the ninth grade went on to graduate from high school. For Indians in the same age group the figure was about 50 percent, and for Negroes and persons of Mexican origin, between 50 and 60 percent. The high dropout rate of Puerto Ricans, compared with that of Negroes, is all the more remarkable considering that the Puerto Ricans are concentrated in urban centers while many of the Negroes are rural residents. On the other hand, one-fourth of the Puerto Ricans were living in Puerto Rico five years before the census was taken and presumably passed through the school ages there rather than in the United States. The high school graduation rate for person 20 to 24 years old who had completed some high school was about 70 to 80 percent for native and foreign-born whites, and 80 to 90 percent for Japanese and Chinese.

To become a high school graduate, a student needs the mental ability to carry out his schoolwork successfully. However, until children are past the compulsory school ages, the tendency is to keep them in school regardless of their ability. Estimates from a sample survey conducted in 1959 and 1960 showed that children with below-average IQ's were more likely than those with above-average IQ's to be school dropouts, but a considerable proportion of the less intelligent children continued in school. About 2 percent of the potential number of high school seniors who were in the top half of the distribution of measured intelligence in 1959, and 39 percent of those in the bottom half of the distribution, failed to reach the senior year of high school; conversely, about 61 percent of those with below-average IQ's had continued in school to the senior year (table II–8).

Table **II–8.**—Selected Measures of School Attrition, by Intelligence Quotient: 1959 to 1960

Intelligence quotient (IQ)	Percentage of potential seniors who did not reach senior year of high school[1]	Percentage of high school seniors who did not graduate
Top quartile.......................	} 1.7	{ 5.3
Second quartile....................		6.5
Third quartile.....................	} 39.2	{ 12.0
Bottom quartile....................		20.1

[1] Derived by subtracting the estimated number of high school seniors in each category from the estimated number of 17-year-olds in each category. Not all of the high school seniors were 17 years old at the survey date; however, three-fifths were 17 years old, one-fifth were below that age, and one-fifth were above that age, so that little bias should be introduced by this procedure. It was assumed that half of the 17-year-olds were in the top half of the normal IQ distribution and that half of them were in the bottom half of the distribution.

Source: U.S. Department of Commerce, Bureau of the Census and U.S. Department of Agriculture, Economic Research Service, Census–ERS, Series P–27, No. 32, tables 1 and 4.

The percentage of high school seniors who did not graduate varied also by ability level. Only 5 percent of the seniors in the top quartile of the IQ distribution failed to graduate, but about 20 percent in the lowest quartile did not finish the senior year.[11]   When the seniors were classified according to their scholastic standing in the class, a similar pattern emerged: 3 percent in the top quarter scholastically did not graduate, compared with 20 percent in the lowest quarter.

Dropping out of school before high school graduation is more characteristic of youths from low-status families than of those from high-status families, although dropouts can be found at all levels of the social scale.   The 1959 sample survey showed that 41 percent of potential high school seniors from families with incomes of less than $3,000 did not reach the senior year, compared with 10 to 15 percent from families in higher income categories (table II–9).   The percentage of dropouts or failures in the senior year was about 16 to 19 percent for youths whose families had less than $6,000 of income, but 6 to 9 percent for those whose families had incomes of $6,000 and over.   Likewise, among seniors who failed to complete the last year of high school, a higher proportion came from households in which the head was either a manual or service worker, or unemployed, or not in the labor force, than from white-collar or farm households.

Table II–9.—SELECTED MEASURES OF SCHOOL ATTRITION, BY FAMILY INCOME IN 1959: 1960

Family income	Percentage of potential seniors who did not reach senior year of high school[1]	Family Income	Percentage of high school seniors who did not graduate
Under $3,000	41.4	Under $4,000	15.6
$3,000 to $4,999	9.9	$4,000 to $5,999	18.7
$5,000 and over	14.9	$6,000 to $9,999	6.4
		$10,000 and over	8.9

[1] Derived by subtracting the estimated number of high school seniors in each category from the estimated number of 17-year-olds in each category. Not all of the high school seniors were 17 years old at the survey date; however, three-fifths were 17 years old, one-fifth were below that age, and one-fifth were above that age, so that little bias should be introduced by this procedure. It was assumed that half of the 17-year-olds were in the top half of the normal IQ distribution and that half of them were in the bottom half of the distribution.

Source: U.S. Deparment of Commerce, Bureau of the Census and U.S. Department of Agriculture, Economic Research Service, Census–ERS, Series P–27, No. 32, tables 1 and 3.

These findings, based on national data, are quite consistent with those of other studies which were limited to specific areas of the country or to individual schools.[12]   Less consistent are the reports of underlying factors which make dropping out of school more likely for low-status youths.   Some studies have identified low job aspirations and low value placed on schooling, typical of lower class families, as important mechanisms leading to school attrition. Other studies point to the direct economic need of the family and the necessity for another full-time worker in the family to increase its earnings.[13] Still other studies suggest the explanatory significance of the low-status adolescent's disregard of and disdain for authority and education, the expectation of his status group that he will "grow up and get a job," and his inability to comprehend the middle-class values and goals which he finds increasingly imbedded in the educational process as he advances in the school system.[14] Finally, the studies do not determine to what extent lower levels of ability, the poorer educational background of parents, and other factors which tend to be correlated with low economic position, help to account for the inverse association between social status and dropping out of school.

Some economic consequences of dropping out of school. Is it really true that the school dropout is much worse off economically than his counterpart who has graduated from high school? Available data substantiate the popular notion that schooling "pays off."

The market position of high school dropouts in 1960 was clearly unfavorable in comparison with that of high school graduates of the same ages (table II–10). Among boys 16 and 17 years old, about the same proportion of dropouts and graduates were in the labor force (that is, either working or looking for work), but the unemployment rate was twice as high among dropouts. At ages 18 and 19, the number of boys in the labor force, both dropouts and graduates, had risen considerably, but the dropout was more likely not to be in the labor force at all. About 91 percent of the graduates and 82 percent of the dropouts in 1960 were either working or looking for work. Comparative unemployment rates hardly differed from rates at earlier ages; 17 out of 100 high school dropouts and 9 out of 100 high school graduates who were in the labor force were out of work. Moreover, the graduates were more likely to be in the Armed Forces, presumably because the dropouts were less able to pass the qualifying tests.

The employment status patterns for girls differed from those for boys at the same ages in that girls were less likely to be in the labor force, especially if they were not high school graduates. Those who had graduated from high school had slightly lower unemployment rates than boys. Consistent with the notion that girls, both married and unmarried, once out of school typically undertake domestic duties while boys out of school head for the job market, only half of the girl graduates at ages 16 and 17 and one-fourth of the dropouts at those ages were in the labor force, compared with about three-fifths of each group of boys at the same ages. Similarly, at ages 18 and 19, two-thirds of the girl graduates and one-third of the dropouts were in the labor force, compared with nine-tenths and eight-tenths, respectively, of the boys. Girls in the labor force were more than twice as likely to be unemployed if they had not finished high school. While the unemployment rate at ages 18 and 19 for girl graduates was 7 percent, it was 17 percent for girls the same ages who had dropped out (figure II–2).

Table II–10.—EMPLOYMENT STATUS OF CHILDREN 16 TO 19 YEARS OLD, BY ENROLLMENT STATUS, HIGH SCHOOL GRADUATION STATUS, AGE, COLOR, AND SEX: 1960

Employment status, color, and sex	16 and 17 years old			18 and 19 years old		
		Not enrolled in school			Not enrolled in school	
	Enrolled in school	High school graduate	Not a high school graduate	Enrolled in school	High school graduate	Not a high school graduate
MALE						
Total.....................	100.0	100.0	100.0	100.0	100.0	100.0
Labor force.....................	31.0	61.9	61.4	43.7	91.0	81.8
Armed Forces...................	0.2	6.8	7.9	1.7	23.7	14.4
Civilian labor force...........	30.8	55.1	53.5	41.9	67.3	67.4
Employed..................	28.0	49.9	42.6	38.4	61.0	56.1
White-collar worker........	8.0	16.5	5.0	12.8	18.9	6.0
Blue-collar worker.........	15.6	28.8	27.2	21.9	36.8	41.1
Farm worker................	4.4	4.6	10.4	3.7	5.3	9.0
Unemployed................	2.8	5.2	10.9	3.6	6.3	11.3
Unemployment rate.......	9.1	9.4	20.4	8.6	9.4	16.8
Not in labor force.............	69.0	38.1	38.6	56.3	9.0	18.2
Nonwhite...................	100.0	100.0	100.0	100.0	100.0	100.0
Labor force.....................	19.0	57.9	55.1	34.0	81.0	72.5
Armed Forces...................	0.1	4.8	2.1	1.1	17.4	4.7
Civilian labor force...........	18.9	53.1	53.0	32.9	63.6	67.8
Employed..................	16.4	42.4	42.2	28.8	53.9	55.5
White-collar worker........	2.4	9.8	1.5	4.1	9.0	3.1
Blue-collar worker.........	9.8	29.8	24.7	19.8	41.0	38.5
Farm worker................	4.2	2.8	16.0	4.9	3.9	13.9
Unemployed................	2.5	10.7	10.8	4.1	9.7	12.3
Unemployment rate.......	13.2	20.2	20.4	12.5	15.3	18.1
Not in labor force.............	81.0	42.1	44.9	66.0	19.0	27.5
FEMALE						
Total.....................	100.0	100.0	100.0	100.0	100.0	100.0
Labor force.....................	18.1	47.7	28.8	31.7	69.5	35.7
Employed..................	16.4	43.7	23.1	29.4	64.5	29.5
White-collar worker........	8.8	33.9	6.6	20.4	52.3	8.7
Blue-collar worker.........	7.1	9.5	15.3	8.7	11.9	19.8
Farm worker................	0.4	0.2	1.3	0.3	0.3	1.0
Unemployed................	1.7	3.9	5.7	2.2	4.5	6.1
Unemployment rate.......	9.4	8.2	19.8	6.9	6.5	17.1
Not in labor force.............	81.9	52.3	71.2	68.3	30.5	64.3
Nonwhite...................	100.0	100.0	100.0	100.0	100.0	100.0
Labor force.....................	9.3	31.3	25.5	20.8	53.8	36.0
Employed..................	7.7	26.3	18.6	17.9	43.5	28.2
White-collar worker........	1.6	7.8	0.8	5.5	15.7	1.6
Blue-collar worker.........	5.2	18.1	14.5	11.2	27.1	23.7
Farm worker................	0.9	0.5	3.3	1.1	0.7	2.8
Unemployed................	1.5	4.9	6.8	2.8	9.7	7.8
Unemployment rate.......	16.1	15.7	26.7	13.5	18.0	21.7
Not in labor force.............	90.7	68.7	74.5	79.2	46.2	64.0

Source: 1960 *Census of Population, Subject Reports, School Enrollment*, Series PC(2)–5A, table 14; *Employment Status and Work Experience*, Series PC(2)–6A, table 1; and *Occupational Characteristics*, Series PC(2)–7A, tables 6 and 7.

In view of their poorer educational preparation for jobs, and the increasing demand for better educated workers, it is understandable that dropouts face greater difficulties than those who remain in school when it comes to obtaining work. Their greater tendency to not look for work may be ascribed partly to futility stemming from the smaller number of jobs available to them, and partly to their lower motivation for work. According to a recent survey, 53 percent

Figure II–2.—WORK PATTERNS OF HIGH SCHOOL GRADUATES NOT ENROLLED IN COLLEGE AND OF HIGH SCHOOL DROPOUTS, 16 TO 19 YEARS OLD, BY AGE AND SEX: 1960

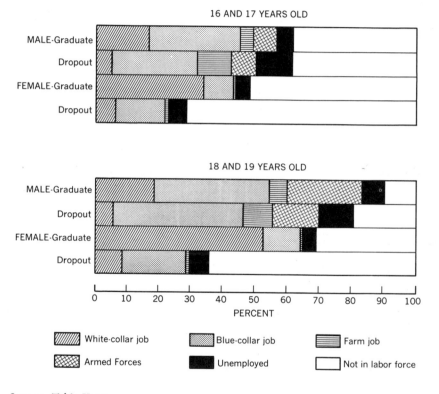

Source: Table II–10.

of the 1962 high school graduates who were not in the labor force were attending special schools for instruction and training in skills which would improve their job opportunities, whereas a mere 6 percent of the dropouts not in the labor force were taking such training.[15] If this kind of job preparation is regarded as a continuation of schooling, much greater disparity is found between the labor force participation rates of graduates and dropouts.

Although completion of high school greatly improved employment prospects for white youths, it had much less effect for nonwhite youths. In fact, among nonwhite boys 16 and 17 years old, graduates were as likely as dropouts to be out of the labor force or unemployed. By ages 18 and 19, a high school diploma was a decided advantage for nonwhite boys with regard to labor force participation, and a slight advantage with regard to employment, but the differential was not as great as for white boys at these ages. Work patterns for nonwhite girls were more like those for white girls, although nonwhite girls had higher unemployment rates.

Even among young employed people, completion of high school made a difference in the kinds of jobs they had. For boys 16 and 17 years old, there was a greater likelihood that the dropout with a job was engaged in farm work. Among those who entered nonfarm work, the proportion of graduates in white-collar jobs was twice as great as among dropouts. This finding may be explained not only by the graduates' better qualifications for white-collar jobs, but also by the preference of most employers for high school graduates even if the additional schooling is not necessary for the job. The occupational distribution by education for boys 18 and 19 years old was similar to that for the younger boys, except that the older boys who had high school diplomas were even more likely than those who did not to be in white-collar jobs. These occupational differences for graduates and dropouts were even larger among girls. Of the girls 18 and 19 years old who were not in school, 81 percent of the employed high school graduates and 29 percent of the workers who had not finished high school had white-collar jobs. The pattern for nonwhite youths was quite similar to that for all young men and women, although the percentage in white-collar work for both graduates and dropouts was somewhat less than for all youths.

The value attached to white-collar employment lies partly in the higher prestige and more desirable working conditions such employment affords, compared with blue-collar and farm jobs, and partly in the greater income it brings even for beginning workers. But, white-collar job or blue-collar job, the high school graduate earns more money than the high school dropout in the same type of employment. The graduate will more often be preferred by larger, better paying organizations; he is sometimes offered a higher starting salary than the dropout for the same type of work because of his greater promise to the company, and he stands a better chance of early promotion. Of course, many dropouts have higher earnings than graduates of the same age, partly because they have been working longer, but the average high school graduate is paid more than the average dropout. Among males 18 to 24 years old who held clerical jobs in 1960, 49 percent of those who had completed high school had earnings of $3,000 or more, as against 39 percent who had dropped out of high school. The comparison for retail salesmen and sales clerks was still sharper; 40 percent of the graduates and 26 percent of the dropouts had earnings of $3,000 or more. Even among nonfarm laborers, as in other occupations, the earnings of those in the same age group who had completed high school exceeded, on the average, the earnings of the high school dropouts. The education-occupation-earnings relationship was similiar for young women.

Factors related to scholastic retardation

As indicated in the previous chapter, not all pupils in school advance one grade each year. Some are required to repeat a grade, generally because their performance in that grade did not meet the minimum standard. Scholastic retardation[16] differs for different segments of the population in much the same way that enrollment rates differ.

Since scholastic retardation can begin with the first grade (in fact, the highest proportion of grade repeaters is found in the first grade), it should not be surprising that marked differentials in age-grade progress are already present by ages 10 to 13. The retardation rate at these ages in 1960 was highest in rural-nonfarm areas and lowest in urban-fringe areas (typically the suburbs), as shown in table II–11. The rate was slightly lower for farm than nonfarm rural areas, presumably because more farm than nonfarm rural children who are scholastically retarded drop out of school. Residence differentials were similiar at older ages although the level of the rates was higher.

Table II–11.—PERCENT SCHOLASTICALLY RETARDED FOR CHILDREN 10 TO 17 YEARS OLD, BY AGE, RESIDENCE, AND ETHNIC STATUS: 1960

[Scholastic retardation refers to enrollment in a grade below the modal grades for persons of a given single age]

Residence and ethnic status	10 to 13 years old	14 and 15 years old	16 and 17 years old
United States......................	9.8	14.6	15.1
RESIDENCE			
Urban..............................	8.2	12.1	13.2
Urbanized areas...........................	7.6	11.1	12.5
Central cities..........................	8.9	12.7	14.0
Urban fringe...........................	5.8	8.9	10.5
Other urban...............................	10.3	15.2	15.2
Rural..............................	13.0	19.3	18.8
Nonfarm.................................	13.2	19.9	19.3
Farm....................................	12.8	17.9	17.6
ETHNIC STATUS			
White..............................	8.2	12.5	12.9
Native white..........................	8.1	12.3	12.7
Native parentage......................	8.1	12.4	12.9
Foreign or mixed parentage.............	8.3	11.2	10.8
Foreign-born white........................	15.6	21.6	28.0
Nonwhite..............................	21.1	30.2	33.3
Negro..................................	21.6	31.1	34.4
Indian.................................	29.2	41.5	43.3
Japanese and Chinese......................	4.9	4.3	6.9
Other races...............................	11.2	15.2	17.5

Source: *1960 Census of Population, Subject Reports, School Enrollment*, Series PC(2)–5A, table 1.

Almost 30 percent of Indian children and more than 20 percent of Negro children 10 to 13 years old who were in school in 1960 were attending grades below those normally expected for their age (table II–11). The corresponding percentage was as low as 8 percent for native white children and 5 percent for Japanese and Chinese children.

Retardation differentials were significantly wider at ages 14 and 15. Forty-two percent of Indian children, 31 percent of Negro children, but only 4 percent of Japanese and Chinese children 14 and 15 years old who were enrolled in school were in grades below normal for their age. Retardation rates were only slightly higher for youths 16 and 17 years old than for those in immediately younger ages. The dropouts at these ages included many who had been scholastically retarded, thus the percentage of retardation went up only slightly despite a moderately large number of new retardates.

Figure II–3.—PERCENT SCHOLASTICALLY RETARDED AMONG PERSONS 10 TO 17 YEARS OLD ENROLLED IN SCHOOL, BY AGE AND ETHNIC GROUP: 1960

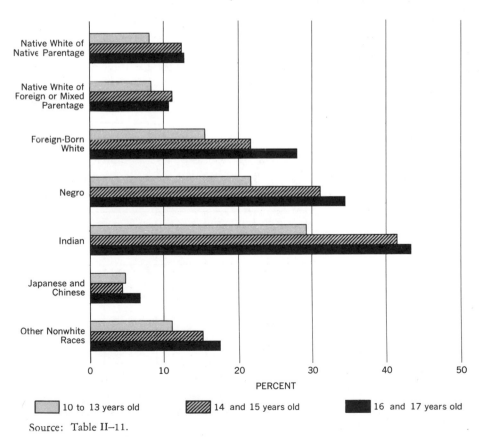

Source: Table II–11.

An overall reduction between 1950 and 1960 in the percent of enrolled pupils who were scholastically retarded was found for each of the ethnic groups shown in table II–11. Since, during this decade, the retardation rate was about halved for all ethnic groups in the 10 to 13 age group, for example, the differentials in scholastic progress had become considerably narrower (figure II–3).

How well a child keeps up with his age peers in school seems to be strongly associated with family status. The percent scholastically retarded was highest for children not in families, and considerably higher for children who were not living with both parents than for those who were living with both parents. This relationship existed for each age group and for girls as well as boys, with few exceptions.

As seen in table II–12, lack of grade progress was most frequent among children of poorly educated parents. About one-fourth of the boys 10 to 13 years old whose fathers did not have an eighth-grade education were scholastically retarded, compared with one-tenth of those whose fathers completed the eighth grade but did not finish high school, one-twentieth of those whose fathers were high school graduates, and nearly one-thirtieth of those whose fathers had some college education. If the boy's mother as well as the father had low educational attainment, his chances of being retarded were much greater. For instance, where both parents lacked an eighth-grade education, 35 percent of the boys were attending a grade below that expected for their age; where the mother had reached at least the eighth grade but the father had not, about 17 percent of the sons were retarded, half the rate found when both parents had the lower amount of education.

Table II–12.—PERCENT SCHOLASTICALLY RETARDED FOR CHILDREN 10 TO 17 YEARS OLD LIVING WITH BOTH PARENTS, BY AGE, SEX, AND EDUCATIONAL LEVEL OF MOTHER AND FATHER: 1960

Educational attainment of mother and father	Male			Female		
	10 to 13 years old	14 and 15 years old	16 and 17 years old	10 to 13 years old	14 and 15 years old	16 and 17 years old
Total........................	10.8	16.0	16.5	6.8	9.9	9.9
Father less than 8 years.............	25.6	34.3	33.3	17.4	22.8	21.5
Mother: Less than 8 years..........	34.8	44.8	43.6	25.1	31.8	30.9
8 years or more............	17.3	23.9	24.5	10.0	13.8	13.4
Father 8 to 11 years.................	10.3	14.5	16.2	5.8	8.5	9.2
Mother: Less than 8 years..........	21.4	28.1	29.9	13.0	18.3	18.9
8 to 11 years.............	11.1	15.5	17.3	6.2	8.8	9.7
12 years or some college...	6.3	8.6	10.4	3.1	4.6	5.6
Father 12 years.....................	5.3	7.8	9.4	2.9	4.6	5.3
Mother: Less than 12 years.........	7.9	11.9	13.4	4.9	6.9	7.6
12 years..................	4.4	6.1	7.8	2.2	3.7	4.3
Some college.............	3.3	5.5	6.3	1.8	2.6	3.5
Father some college..................	3.5	5.2	6.6	2.1	3.0	4.0
Mother: Less than college.........	4.3	6.4	8.0	2.6	3.3	4.7
Some college..............	2.6	4.0	5.2	1.7	2.6	3.2

Source: 1960 Census of Population, Subject Reports, School Enrollment, Series PC(2)–5A, table 4.

Where both parents were at least high school graduates, less than 5 percent of the sons 10 to 13 years old lagged in grade progress; where both parents had some college education, the rate was below 3 percent. With each increase in educational attainment of mother and father, the scholastic retardation rate of sons was reduced. The general relationship between parents' education and retardation observed for boys 10 to 13 years old was also found for girls, and for both sexes at older school ages. While the education of the mother and of the father were independently associated with relative school progress, and while the contribution of each was substantial, the mother's schooling seemed to be somewhat more closely related to the son's than the daughter's school progress, whereas the father's schooling was similarly related to the progress of both sons and daughters.

Is the child of a "normal" family (a family including both parents) more likely to be at the school grade expected for his age because the "normal" family provides a more satisfactory socioeconomic background for the child than does a family affected by death or marital dissolution? Broken families do tend to have lower socioeconomic status, and relatively more children from lower status families are scholastically retarded. However, a broken family exerts some effect on age-grade school progress that is independent of socioeconomic status (table II–13).

Table II–13.—Percent Scholastically Retarded for Males 14 and 15 Years Old, by Education of Parent, Presence of Parents, and Color: 1960

Presence of parents and color	Education of parent[1]			
	Total	Less than 8 years	8 to 11 years	12 years or more
Total:				
Living with both parents	16.0	34.3	14.5	6.7
Living with only one parent	24.3	43.1	22.5	10.4
White:				
Living with both parents	14.2	31.6	13.8	6.5
Living with only one parent	20.3	40.4	20.1	9.4
Nonwhite:				
Living with both parents	34.0	43.9	24.1	12.7
Living with only one parent	36.3	46.9	30.2	18.7

[1] For boys living with both parents, educational level of the father.

Source: 1960 Census of Population, Subject Reports, School Enrollment, Series PC(2)–5A, tables 4 and 5.

Family income also exerts an independent effect on scholastic retardation. For example, in 1960, among schoolgirls 10 to 13 years old whose parents had not completed the eighth grade, 26 percent were retarded where the family income was less than $3,000, but only 10 percent where the income exceeded

$7,000. Even among those whose parents were high school graduates, 5 percent were retarded where the family income was under $3,000, and 2 percent where it was $7,000 or higher. Here, too, the relationship held for both sexes and for all school-age groups. While the retardation rate was higher for nonwhites than for whites and higher in rural than urban areas, the pattern of socioeconomic differentials in retardation for all these population subgroups was quite similar, with one variation in the pattern. At the lowest end of the socioeconomic scale, the retardation rate in rural areas was particularly high (table II–14).

Table II–14.—Percent Scholastically Retarded for Children 10 to 17 Years Old, Living With One or Both Parents, by Age, Sex, Education of Parent, and Family Income: 1960

Education of parent [1] and family income in 1959	Male			Female		
	10 to 13 years old	14 and 15 years old	16 and 17 years old	10 to 13 years old	14 and 15 years old	16 and 17 years old
Total......................	11.5	17.0	17.4	7.2	10.7	10.7
Less than 8 years..................	28.9	35.6	34.9	18.3	24.1	23.0
Under $3,000......................	36.9	47.7	47.4	26.4	33.3	33.6
$3,000 to $4,999..................	24.5	33.6	35.7	16.2	22.7	22.3
$5,000 to $6,999..................	18.3	28.4	28.3	11.4	18.0	16.6
$7,000 and over..................	15.0	21.6	21.8	9.5	13.0	13.1
8 to 11 years.....................	11.0	15.6	17.3	7.1	9.1	10.0
Under $3,000......................	17.4	23.9	25.0	10.6	14.4	16.0
$3,000 to $4,999..................	12.9	18.3	20.9	7.6	11.0	12.2
$5,000 to $6,999..................	9.7	14.2	16.9	5.2	8.4	9.9
$7,000 and over..................	7.6	11.3	13.0	3.9	6.1	6.8
12 years or some college...........	4.8	7.1	8.5	2.7	4.1	4.9
Under $3,000......................	8.3	12.4	13.4	5.2	7.1	8.7
$3,000 to $4,999..................	7.0	10.6	12.4	3.9	6.0	7.2
$5,000 to $6,999..................	5.2	7.8	9.7	3.0	4.7	5.7
$7,000 and over..................	3.6	5.6	6.9	2.0	3.2	3.8

[1] Education of parent refers to father's education when child was living with both parents or father, and to mother's education when child's father was not living with the household.

Source: 1960 Census of Population, Subject Reports, School Enrollment, Series PC(2)–5A, table 5.

Differences in age-grade school progress in relation to the father's occupation reveal one more type of socioeconomic effect on scholastic retardation. In 1960, fully 37 out of 100 schoolboys 10 to 13 years of age whose fathers were farm laborers or farm foremen were one or more grades below the modal grades for boys of their age. The corresponding proportions were 21 out of 100 for sons of nonfarm laborers, 10 out of 100 for sons of craftsmen, and 3 out of 100 for sons of professional workers. In general, for both sexes and all ages, the higher the occupational status the lower the retardation rate (table II–15).

Table II–15.—Percent Scholastically Retarded for Children 10 to 17 Years Old Living With an Employed Father, by Age, Sex, and Father's Occupation: 1960

Major occupation group of employed father	Male			Female		
	10 to 13 years old	14 and 15 years old	16 and 17 years old	10 to 13 years old	14 and 15 years old	16 and 17 years old
Total.....................................	10.2	15.1	15.7	6.3	9.3	9.3
Professional, technical, and kindred workers......	3.3	5.3	6.8	2.1	2.8	4.1
Farmers and farm managers.........................	12.2	17.7	17.6	7.2	10.8	10.9
Managers, officials, and proprietors, exc. farm...	5.0	7.2	8.3	2.6	3.9	4.6
Clerical and kindred workers.....................	6.0	8.9	10.6	3.5	6.0	5.8
Sales workers....................................	4.8	7.9	9.2	2.6	4.2	4.8
Craftsmen, foremen, and kindred workers...........	9.5	14.8	15.8	5.3	8.5	8.9
Operatives and kindred workers....................	13.5	19.8	20.1	8.3	12.0	11.9
Service workers..................................	11.1	16.7	19.5	7.2	10.7	11.8
Farm laborers and foremen........................	37.2	45.5	41.7	27.7	34.8	29.6
Laborers, exc. farm and mine.....................	20.9	28.5	29.9	13.8	19.2	19.4

Source: *1960 Census of Population, Subject Reports, School Enrollment*, Series PC(2)–5A, table 7.

Who enters college?

While a high proportion of persons still do not attain higher education, it has increasingly become a goal for young people. The number and percent of jobs requiring some college education have risen. Moreover, some employers are now seeking the college-educated in occupations for which they formerly considered high school graduates suitable.

Another kind of attraction which higher education has for many young people is as an avenue to a style of life at relatively high status levels. In college one may acquire tastes and cultivate interests leading to personal and social benefits often unobtainable through other routes. College attendance not only provides access to high status levels, but also provides the basis for taking full advantage of the benefits which such status confers. A young man with high-status aspirations may profit from having a college-educated father, but unless the son also acquires some college education he is often likely to find himself handicapped in economic and social relationships.

Planning for college. A student, even if he is from a family in comfortable circumstances, will usually not attend college unless he has prepared for entrance well in advance. Preparation can take at least two forms: choice of a high school curriculum that is academically oriented, and nurture of motivation for college. Of course, some of those not so prepared do get to college, but they are quite unlikely to do so. Records of college attendance or nonattendance for high school graduates of the preceding summer were obtained in the fall of 1960 from high school principals in a national sample survey. About 7 out of 10 high school graduates who had been enrolled in a college preparatory curriculum, but only about 1 in 5 of those enrolled in some other curriculum, attended college in the fall of 1960.

Socioeconomic status modifies the association between type of high school curriculum and college enrollment. In the survey cited above, the proportion of graduates from white-collar households who had taken a college preparatory curriculum was twice as great as the proportion among other graduates; and of graduates who had gone through such a curriculum, those from high-status backgrounds were more likely to have enrolled in college. For example, among graduates with a college preparatory background in high school, 8 out of 10 of those from white-collar households and 6 out of 10 from other households were enrolled in college in the fall of 1960.

The kind of community one lives in is related to college attendance. It is probable that nearly all high schools in middle and upper class neighborhoods offer academic curricula, while many schools in lower class neighborhoods do not. However, once a college preparatory curriculum has been undertaken, socioeconomic differences in college attendance reflect economic ability to pay for college, as well as differences in plans and motivations.

For some students, the choice of an academic curriculum in the early high school years may be the most satisfactory even though college attendance is not initially a goal. Many of these students may decide subsequently on a college career. As the time for college draws near, however, college plans must become firm, since many colleges encourage application for entrance almost a year in advance. Data from a survey in the fall of 1959 showed that almost half of the high school seniors in the country had definitely planned to attend college in 1960, the following school year.[17]

Rural-farm high school seniors were much less likely than either urban or rural-nonfarm seniors to have definite college plans. At the same time, higher proportions of farm than of nonfarm students were undecided. These facts indicate significantly less planning for college on the part of farm youths.

College plans were almost as frequent among nonwhite as among white high school seniors. This finding would seem to run counter to other information about the educational attainments of whites and nonwhites, but it should be realized that school attrition occurs at earlier ages for the average nonwhite, and those who reach the senior year of high school are an educationally select group.

The decision of high school seniors to attend college also varies by socioeconomic circumstance. According to the survey, those from white-collar families more often had plans to attend college and less often were undecided. Likewise, there was a close association between college plans and the family's economic position. Over two-thirds of the high school seniors from families with incomes of $7,500 or more reported definite college plans, compared with somewhat less than one-fourth of the seniors in families with incomes of under $3,000. The proportion planning to attend college increased, and the proportion undecided about their plans decreased, as income increased.[18]

The relationship between family income and college plans may reflect both the association between economic status and college plans, and a realistic assessment of what the student may reasonably expect to do, given the financial resources available. Where family income is relatively low, the student may adjust his occupational and educational plans to economic realities. He may, for example, elect to take other than a college preparatory course in high school, and therefore may not be academically prepared for college.

Reasons given by high school seniors for not planning to attend college substantiate this assumption. About 39 percent of students in families with incomes of less than $5,000, but only about 14 percent of those in families with incomes of $5,000 or more, reported lack of money as a reason for not attending college. Seniors in higher income families who had foregone college reported reasons such as "marriage," "military service," and "taking a job" more frequently than did students in families with incomes of less than $5,000. Some of those reporting such reasons, it should be noted, may be candidates for college at a later date.

Realization of college plans. How accurate, we might ask, are college plans made nearly one year in advance, and what are some of the factors that affect the fulfillment of these plans? A Census Bureau followup study of the high school students whose educational plans were described above showed that, of those who graduated from high school, 42 percent actually enrolled in college in 1960 on either a full- or part-time basis, whereas 53 percent had planned in 1959 to attend college the following year. Of those who had definite plans in 1959 to attend college, 68 percent were enrolled in college in 1960; in addition, about 8 percent of those who did not plan to attend, and 20 percent of those who were undecided, were also enrolled in 1960 (table II–16).[19]

Table II–16.—PERCENT OF 1959 HIGH SCHOOL GRADUATES ATTENDING COLLEGE IN 1960, BY 1959 COLLEGE ATTENDANCE PLANS AND SEX

[Covers only persons reporting on both plans and attendance]

College plans in 1959 and sex	Total	Attended college, 1960	Did not attend college, 1960
Total............................	100.0	41.6	58.3
Planned to attend........................	100.0	68.4	31.6
Did not plan to attend...................	100.0	7.5	92.5
Undecided...............................	100.0	20.1	79.9
Male[1].................................	100.0	46.0	54.0
Planned to attend........................	100.0	71.7	28.3
Did not plan to attend...................	100.0	8.8	91.2
Female[1]...............................	100.0	37.5	62.5
Planned to attend........................	100.0	64.8	35.2
Did not plan to attend...................	100.0	6.5	93.5

[1] Includes persons who were undecided about college plans, not shown separately.

Source: U.S. Department of Commerce, Bureau of the Census and U.S. Department of Agriculture, Economic Research Service, Census–ERS, Series P–27, No. 32, table 6.

Boys were slightly more likely than girls to carry out their plans. Since we know that girls are equal to boys in ability needed for college, and that boys are subject to military service, and more often than girls must take jobs to provide economic aid to their families, the lesser fulfillment of college plans by girls must be ascribed partly to the fact that many girls marry after high school graduation and forego college and partly to their less realistic college plans. It may also mean that parents will sacrifice more to send a son than a daughter to college.

Relatively more whites than nonwhites successfully carried out their college plans. About 7 out of 10 white high school graduates, but 5 out of 10 nonwhite graduates, who had college plans at the beginning of their senior year went on to college. Hence, even though the goal of college attendance may be equally important to both white and nonwhite high school graduates, the chances of realizing the goal are less for nonwhites.

Both ability and social status differentiated the college planners who did attend college from those who did not. Among those who carried out their plans, the proportion of graduates in the highest IQ quartile and the highest quartile of scholastic standing was twice as high as the proportion in the lowest IQ quartile and the lowest quartile of scholastic standing, respectively. Similarly, among those who actually attended college in the year they graduated from high school, the proportion coming from white-collar families was about twice that from other families, and the percentage whose family income exceeded $10,000 was 3½ times as great as the percentage whose family income was less than $4,000. Thus, many students who apparently have the ability and motivation to go to college are thwarted in attaining their goal, and such youths are much more likely to be found among lower status groups.

Actual college attendance. The selective factors determining who plans for college and who is faithful to those plans continue to operate in terms of who, among all high school graduates, actually enrolls in college.

There is a close relationship between measures of ability and college attendance. About two-thirds of the graduates in the top IQ quartile and a similar proportion in the top scholastic standing quartile, enrolled in college in 1960. The proportion attending college was progressively lower in each of the other quartiles. Even in the lowest quartile, however, a substantial minority of high school graduates were enrolled in college (table II–17).

Ability and high school performance are not perfectly correlated. Persons who rank high on both measures stand the best chance of going to college. About two-thirds of the graduates in the top half of both distributions were enrolled in college in 1960; one-third of those in the upper half of IQ's but in the lower half of scholastic standings attended college; one-fourth of the graduates with a high scholastic rating but low IQ went to college; and only about

Table II–17.—Percent of High School Graduates Enrolled in College, by Intelligence Quotient and Scholastic Standing in High School: 1960

[Data refer to college enrollment in the fall for youths who graduated from high school earlier that year. Some additional graduates may have begun college at a later time]

Quartile	Intelligence quotient	Scholastic standing
Top	67.2	66.6
Second	38.2	43.6
Third	24.8	33.6
Bottom	15.5	19.2

Source: U.S. Department of Commerce, Bureau of the Census and U.S. Department of Agriculture, Economic Research Service, Census–ERS, Series P–27, No. 32, table 9.

a fifth of those ranking in the bottom half of each measure were enrolled in the fall of 1960.

A substantial proportion of the graduates with greater ability did not enroll in college and a significant minority of graduates of lesser ability did enroll. Furthermore, although a high ranking in terms of both IQ and scholastic standing was more closely related to college attendance than was a high ranking on only one measure, a high IQ seemed slightly more important than getting good grades in school.

Admittedly, the two measures are imprecise indicators of ability. Scholastic standing is a composite of teachers' judgments, the type of grading system used, the competition within a specific high school class, and the motivation of the student, as well as an objective measure of the youth's ability to absorb what he is taught. Although IQ tests are designed to be standard measures of intelligence for persons of a given age group in any social class, there is evidence that the tests deal with situations that are more generally experienced by children from middle class and upper class homes.[20] In spite of their weaknesses, the two measures are probably sufficiently correlated with ability to offer a useful indication of the ability dimension.

The importance of ability notwithstanding, it is sometimes said that a child's chances of going to college are largely determined at birth by the family's social position. There is some substance to this belief, even though the social status of families can change over an individual's early life span.

College enrollment rates for men in their early twenties were several times as large for men whose fathers were college graduates as for those whose fathers never finished high school (68 vs. 12 percent).[21] Sons were about twice as likely as daughters to be in college, but if the child's father had a college education, the probability of enrollment was much the same for daughters and sons. Similarly, although nonwhites in the age group studied were only half as likely to be in college as were white persons of the same age, their chances were relatively better when the father's educational level included college attainment.

Family income has an important effect on the relationship between the father's educational attainment and the college attendance of his child. Among young men and women whose fathers were not high school graduates, the proportion enrolled in college was 9 percent where family income was less than $5,000, but 44 percent where family income was $10,000 or more. The proportion of persons attending college whose fathers had also attended college was about 23 percent where the family income was less than $5,000, but rose to 70 percent where the family income was $10,000 or more. Of those attending college, the proportion whose fathers were well educated and whose family income was low, was roughly the same as the proportion with poorly educated fathers but high income. This indicates that the father's education and the family income are about equally associated with a person's chances of going to college.

The occupation of the household head was also closely related to college attendance. In another 1960 survey, it was found that twice as many 1960 high school graduates from white-collar households as from manual and service or farm households were enrolled in college in the fall of 1960. Even among families with $6,000 or more income, a significantly higher proportion of graduates from white-collar than from other households were enrolled (table II–18). This suggests that, while the several socioeconomic variables have similar relationships to college attendance, each has an independent influence on college-going.

Table II–18.—PERCENT OF HIGH SCHOOL GRADUATES ENROLLED IN COLLEGE, BY FAMILY INCOME AND OCCUPATION OF HOUSEHOLD HEAD: 1960

[Data refer to college enrollment in the fall for youths who graduated from high school earlier that year. Some additional graduates may have begun college at a later time]

Family income in 1959	Household head--	
	A white-collar worker	Not a white-collar worker
Under $6,000..........................	44.7	24.9
$6,000 and over........................	61.7	42.0

Source: U.S. Department of Commerce, Bureau of the Census and U.S. Department of Agriculture, Economic Research Service, Census–ERS, Series P–27, No. 32, table 13.

The cumulative effect of several variables on college attendance can be demonstrated through multiple regression analysis, in which the effect of each of a number of items can be measured. Such analysis, based on data for 13 independent variables (including demographic, socioeconomic, ability, and educational planning factors) showed a correlation coefficient of .68 between the combination of these items and college attendance. The items which correlated most highly with college attendance were college plans and type of high school curriculum. The correlation coefficient of these two items together and college-going was .64. Correlation coefficients of intelligence (IQ), scholastic standing, family income, and occupation of the household head, singly with enrollment in college were moderate, and the correlation coefficients for each of the remaining variables (number of siblings, urban-rural residence, region of residence, type of high school, size of high school class, color, and sex) and college attendance were positive but low.[22] Figure II–4 shows the percent of college attendance for several of the more important variables.

Since the "explained" variance was only 46 percent, it is evident that whether or not a high school graduate goes on to college depends on much more than his personal and family background, his ability, and his preparation for college. Motivations to become educated and to achieve high status, encouragement by family and friends, and educational traditions in their communities are among other factors which lead youths to acquire higher education.[23]

Two-year vs. four-year colleges. The growing enrollment in junior and community colleges, and the difference in the types of programs they offer compared with programs in the four-year colleges, makes the distinction between the two kinds of schools an important one. Are the high school graduates entering two-year colleges like or unlike those entering four-year colleges? Do factors affecting two-year college attendance differ from those affecting four-year college attendance? The 1959-1960 Census Bureau survey provides some answers to these questions.[24]

1. Youths who enter two-year colleges are less likely to have prepared for college than those entering four-year colleges. One-half of the two-year college students, compared with four-fifths of the four-year college students, had taken a college preparatory curriculum in high school; only three-fourths of the two-year college students, compared with nine-tenths of the four-year college students, had plans for college early in their high school senior year.

2. Presumably because of the typical city location of two-year colleges, and the lack of dormitories at many junior colleges, about 1 in 4 beginning college students in nonfarm areas, but only 1 in 10 from farms, were enrolled in a two-year college.

3. While college students as a group were generally drawn from the more able high school graduates, those going on to junior or community colleges were largely of lesser ability than those enrolled in four-year colleges. Over 40 percent of four-year college students were in the top quartile of their high school class on both IQ and scholastic standing, but less than 10 percent of two-year college students ranked that high; at the other end of the scale, only 7 percent of four-year college enrollees were in the bottom half of both indicators of ability, but about 28 percent of the two-year college students fell into that category.

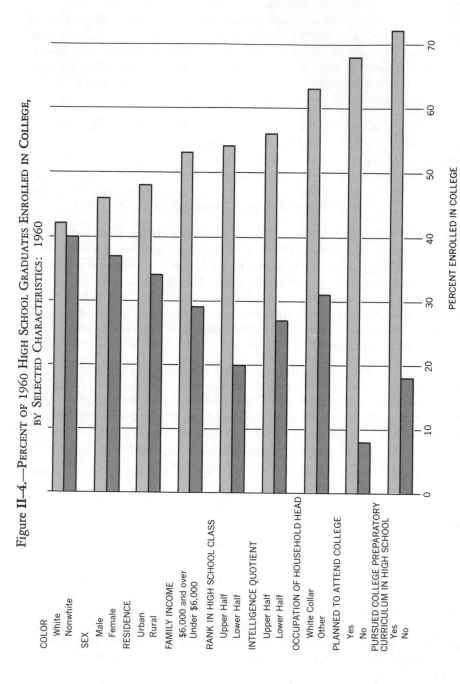

Figure II–4.—Percent of 1960 High School Graduates Enrolled in College, by Selected Characteristics: 1960

Source: U.S. Department of Commerce, Bureau of the Census and U.S. Department of Agriculture, Economic Research Service, Census–ERS, Series P–27, No. 32.

4. Two-year college students were recruited relatively more frequently than four-year college students from the "working" class. These differences in social origin were not great, and were larger for men than for women. Family income influenced the type of college attended less than did the occupational class of the household head.

5. Ability was the sharpest differentiator of whether a college-bound youth entered a two-year or four-year college. The extent of prior planning for college was less important than ability but more important than socioeconomic status.

Migration to college. An additional factor affecting college enrollment is the proximity of a college to a potential student's home. A person interested in college but not strongly motivated, or one of limited means, is probably more likely to attend if the college is within commuting distance. This condition is no doubt related to the growing number of junior and community colleges and their popularity.

Yet, as shown in several studies of college student migration, a large number of young people cross State lines to attend institutions of higher education.[25] In 1958, more than 1 out of 3 students in professional schools, and about 1 out of 4 in graduate schools, had been interstate migrants to school. Roughly 1 out of 6 at the undergraduate level attended college in a State other than the one they came from, and even 1 out of 10 junior or community college students crossed State lines to attend college. Not all college students who crossed State lines to go to college were migrants according to the Census definition. Many still lived with their parents and commuted to school in another State, particularly those who lived in large metropolitan areas located on State borders.

The effect of college student migration on enrollment in the various States was minimized by the largely compensating interchange of students among the States. The 1958 study showed that, while over a half million students crossed State lines to go to college, the net change in the number of college students, by State, was only about 50,000, or less than 10 percent.

Conceivably, such phenomena as the addition of new community colleges and the generally greater expansion of public than private colleges might result in a decline in the migration of future college enrollees. At present, however, the movement of college students from home to school may be classed as an important contemporary migration movement which has had a moderate effect on the geographical redistribution of college students.

Reasons for not entering college. Despite the increasing trend toward college enrollment, large numbers of high school graduates are not going on to college. What are their reasons for not attending college? A question on this subject, in the 1959 sample survey, was directed to persons 16 to 24 years old who had completed high school but had not gone to college. Presumably they met minimum college entrance requirements, yet less than 1 percent reported applying to a college but not being admitted (table II–19).

Table II–19.—Percent of High School Graduates 16 to 24 Years Old Not Enrolled in College, by Major Reason Reported for Not Enrolling and Sex: October 1959

Major reason reported for not enrolling in college	Male	Female
Total...	100.0	100.0
No desire to go......................................	32.1	31.8
Not admitted...	0.9	0.3
Lacked money...	24.9	15.2
Took a job...	18.5	22.9
Needed at home.......................................	1.4	0.3
Military service.....................................	12.5	0.2
Marriage...	5.0	22.1
Other reason...	2.7	6.3
Not reported...	2.0	0.9

Source: U.S. Department of Commerce, Bureau of the Census and U.S. Department of Agriculture, Economic Research Service, Census–ERS, Series P–27, No. 30, table 13.

Although we should not minimize the significance of economic considerations (which were important to one-fourth of the males, and about one-sixth of the females), other reasons given for not attending college are also important. Some respondents indicated no desire for a college education, others were entering military service, or getting married. This suggests that a substantial proportion of potential college students have other than economic reasons for not attending college.

Similar reasons for not going to college were reported by both urban and rural youths. Girls differed from boys mainly in that they mentioned marriage more often than economic considerations, and boys often cited military service as the factor preventing their college attendance. Economic constraints clearly differentiated color groups. Forty-five percent of the nonwhite high school graduates, but only 16 percent of the whites, reported lack of money as the reason for never attending college. Although the failure to control for some variables such as measured ability and the weaknesses of the question on reasons limit the interpretation of these data,[26] they suggest that many youths who graduate from high school forego college involuntarily, and that, for many of them, economic barriers stand in the way.

The college years

Many students who enter college drop out prior to graduation. The pattern of dropping out of college, like the pattern of leaving school below the college level, is selective of certain characteristics of the student body which are examined below, along with other characteristics which differentiate college students from the general population of college age.

Socioeconomic backgrounds of students. The selective processes which operate at points along the education continuum result in a group of college students whose socioeconomic backgrounds are quite different from those of the average person of college age. As shown in table II–20, college students in the fall of

1960 were less than half as likely as all persons of college age to come from families where family income was less than $5,000 and in which the father did not finish high school. On the other hand, they were 2½ times as likely to come from families where the income level was $7,500 or more and in which the father had attended college. Although both socioeconomic variables differentiated college students from the general population, the differences with regard to the father's education were greater than those with regard to family income.

Table II–20.—Income of Families With Persons 16 to 24 Years Old Who Were Not Household Heads or Wives, by Educational Level of Father and College Attendance: October 1960

Educational level of father and college enrollment status	Total	Family income			
		Under $5,000	$5,000 to $7,499	$7,500 to $9,999	$10,000 and over
PERSONS 16 TO 24 YEARS OLD					
Total.....................................	100.0	40.2	25.0	15.4	19.4
Father:					
Not a high school graduate...................	64.8	33.4	16.2	8.4	6.7
High school graduate, no college.............	17.8	4.5	6.0	2.6	4.6
Some college................................	17.4	2.2	2.8	4.3	8.1
COLLEGE STUDENTS 16 TO 24 YEARS OLD					
Total.....................................	100.0	20.7	25.5	21.9	32.0
Father:					
Not a high school graduate...................	38.4	13.2	12.3	6.7	6.2
High school graduate, no college.............	22.2	4.8	7.2	4.4	5.8
Some college................................	39.4	2.7	6.0	10.9	19.9
RATIO OF COLLEGE STUDENTS TO PERSONS 16 TO 24 YEARS OLD[1]					
Total.....................................	100	51	102	142	165
Father:					
Not a high school graduate...................	59	40	76	80	93
High school graduate, no college.............	125	107	120	169	126
Some college................................	226	123	214	253	246

[1] Computed by dividing the percent of college students 16 to 24 years old in each cell by the corresponding percent for all persons of the same age.

Source: Unpublished data from the U.S. Bureau of the Census, *Current Population Survey* for October 1960. Excludes persons for whom family income and father's education were not reported.

This social selection of college students appears to reflect mainly the selection in college entrance. As Wolfle found, after students get to college the influence of socioeconomic differences disappears almost entirely. The persistence in college was about the same for students whose fathers were in different occupations.[27] This finding is generally consistent with reasons given by students for leaving college, as reported in a Census Bureau survey.[28] About one-fourth of the males and roughly one-tenth of the females specifically cited financial reasons for dropping out; yet the majority of dropouts cited major reasons which were not necessarily related to socioeconomic status—loss of interest, poor grades, marriage, military service, and taking a job.[29]

No recent information is available on trends in the socioeconomic selection of college students. Have differentials been narrowing, widening, or staying the same? We may expect a leveling of the social and economic differentials in college attendance as junior and community colleges open up higher educational opportunities to persons with more limited economic means and of more culturally deprived backgrounds. The present strength of social factors affecting college enrollments suggests, however, that socioeconomic status will continue to play an important role in the selection of college students.

Marriage patterns. College attendance, involving as it usually does a serious commitment to learning and an interruption or postponement of some institutionalized social activities, has a marked effect on marriage patterns. Compared with the population of the same age not enrolled in school, college students are less likely to be married. For instance, at ages 20 and 21 in 1960, 9 percent of college men and 8 percent of college women were married, while 32 percent of men and 60 percent of women at these ages who were not enrolled in school were married.

Still, many young married persons pursue a college education and the proportion who are married increases with academic advancement. In 1960, among freshmen, only 12 percent of men and 8 percent of women were married. The corresponding percentages were 37 and 25 percent for senior men and women, and 54 and 37 percent, respectively, for those in graduate or professional schools (table II–21 and figure II–5).

One explanation offered for the increasing numbers of married students on campus is that the greater incidence of student marriages is part of a continuing national trend toward marriage at earlier ages. It has already been indicated that far fewer college students than persons not enrolled are married at a given age, for example, age 21. However, when the median age at first marriage of wives of college students is compared with the median age at first marriage of wives of all couples under 35 with similar educational attainment, there is very little difference between the two groups. Median age at marriage of women under 35 with 1 year of college is 20.3 years, identical with the median age of wives of undergraduate college students. From other data we can infer that the average college attainment level of wives of college students is probably 1 to 3 years. Census data support the idea that age-at-marriage patterns of college students are similar to those of all couples with similar educational attainment levels.

Not a great deal is known about trends in the proportion of college students who are married. Census Bureau data, available only since 1957, reveal no significant change in the college marriage pattern since that time. A sharp upward trend is indicated between the pre-World War II and postwar periods, but this is based on the findings of only a few studies of college classes and alumni from specific institutions of higher education.[30] How well these findings can be generalized to the United States as a whole and how much of the trend reflects changes in social values is unknown. Nonetheless, available statistics indicate that demographic and socioeconomic factors alone could account for most of the change. The average age of college students rose during the prewar to postwar period, primarily because many veterans were attending college, and apparently because an increasing proportion of students were coming from working-class homes. Both of these tendencies are associated in the general population with higher proportions of married students. Moreover, a working-class student may need the support of a working wife to carry him through school.

By providing more housing for married students, colleges and universities have no doubt made it more feasible for them to continue their education. Housing for married students was first provided on a large scale for veterans of World War II, and institutions of higher education have maintained or expanded such facilities for the later nonveteran generation of students. The GI's showed that married life and college-going were compatible.

Table II–21.—LIVING ARRANGEMENTS OF COLLEGE STUDENTS, BY MARITAL STATUS, COLLEGE CLASS, AND SEX: 1960

Marital status, living arrangements, and sex	All college students	Fresh-men	Sopho-mores	Juniors	Seniors	Graduates or professionals
Male..............................	100.0	100.0	100.0	100.0	100.0	100.0
Married, spouse present.................	27.4	11.5	19.7	24.9	37.3	54.2
Household head........................	26.4	10.9	18.8	24.0	35.9	53.3
In parents' household[1]..............	0.8	0.5	0.8	0.8	1.2	0.8
In other relative's household........	0.1	0.1	0.1	0.1	0.1	0.1
In nonrelative's household...........	0.0	0.0	0.0	0.1	0.1	0.1
Other marital status..................	72.6	88.5	80.3	75.1	62.7	45.8
Household head.......................	5.1	2.4	4.1	5.0	6.3	9.3
In parents' household[2]..............	29.0	40.5	35.9	26.8	21.3	12.0
In other relative's household........	2.0	2.6	2.4	2.0	1.6	1.1
In college dormitory[2]...............	24.4	32.5	26.3	27.5	20.3	10.5
In other living quarters.............	12.1	10.5	11.6	13.7	13.1	12.8
Female.............................	100.0	100.0	100.0	100.0	100.0	100.0
Married, spouse present.................	13.7	7.6	10.4	12.7	24.9	36.7
Wife of head........................	13.2	7.3	9.9	12.2	24.1	35.8
In parents' household[1]..............	0.4	0.3	0.4	0.4	0.7	0.8
In other relative's household........	0.1	0.1	0.1	0.0	0.0	0.1
In nonrelative's household...........	0.0	0.0	0.0	0.0	0.1	0.1
Other marital status..................	86.3	92.4	89.6	87.3	75.1	63.3
Household head.......................	3.8	1.9	2.4	3.5	5.9	16.4
In parents' household[1]..............	29.0	33.9	31.3	24.3	23.6	18.1
In other relative's household........	2.3	2.9	2.2	1.8	1.7	1.8
In college dormitory[2]...............	35.5	39.5	37.3	38.3	30.9	9.1
In other living quarters.............	15.7	14.2	16.3	19.4	12.9	17.8

[1] Includes parents-in-law.
[2] Includes sorority houses and fraternity houses.

Source: *1960 Census of Population, Subject Reports, School Enrollment*, Series PC(2)–5A, table 9.

Figure II–5.—LIVING ARRANGEMENTS OF COLLEGE STUDENTS, BY COLLEGE CLASS AND SEX: 1960

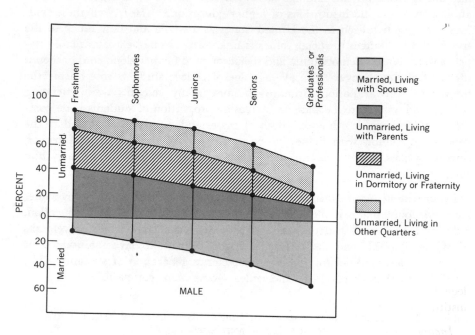

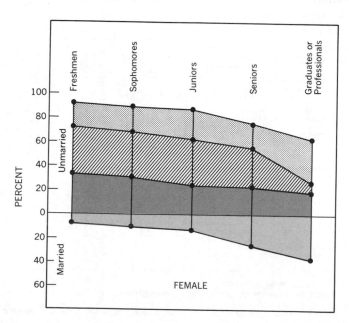

Source: Table II–21.

Living arrangements. Nearly all married students had their own households in 1960, some presumably in college-sponsored housing units and others in off-campus units. A very small percentage lived with their parents or other relatives.

Among the unmarried students, one-third of the undergraduate men and two-fifths of the undergraduate women were in college housing, with little distinction in these patterns by college class. The proportion of unmarried students at the graduate and professional level who lived in college housing units was considerably below that of the unmarried undergraduate students. Similar proportions of the unmarried students (two-fifths of the undergraduate men, one-third of the undergraduate women, and slightly smaller percentages of graduate students) were living with their parents.

A sizable proportion of the unmarried students had set up living quarters away from the campus and from their parents' home, mostly in rooming and boarding houses and apartments. Nearly one-fourth of all unmarried students had such living arrangements. The percentage tended to be small among freshmen but grew larger with each higher college class. Virtually half of the unmarried graduate and professional students fell into this category. These living patterns reflect, of course, the different percentages married at each college level, the college residence requirements laid down by the educational institutions, and the wishes and preferences of the students and their parents.

Income and work patterns. An important factor in a student's ability to continue through college is the cost involved. This varies widely, depending on the type of college, whether the student attends on a full- or part-time basis, and whether or not he lives at home. In any event the cost is significant.[31] In addition to paying direct college expenses, most students necessarily forego the income which they could have earned from full-time employment. Although this temporary loss of income may be more than counterbalanced in the long run, at the time of enrollment it may be an important consideration.[32]

College students generally have little opportunity to earn income to help defray college costs while they are in school, and what opportunity they do have usually produces only a small income. In 1960, about 88 percent of college men and 68 percent of college women reported some earnings during the previous year; however, a large group of these students had received all their earnings from summer work, presumably while on vacation from school. The percentages cited, therefore, refer to students who worked at some time during the year. Roughly 57 percent of the men and 40 percent of the women were working at the time they went to college (tables II–22 and II–23).

Of all male students with earnings during the year, slightly more than one-third had made less than $1,000, and some had received part of this income from sources other than earnings. About half of the college men with earnings during the year had incomes of $2,000 or more, but two-fifths of these men had incomes other than earnings to help bring them over the $2,000 mark. Of the female students with annual earnings, fully 70 percent made less than $1,000, and only one-sixth made $2,000 or more.

It is not surprising, therefore, that in 1959, 70 percent of college girls and 55 percent of college boys received some financial support from their parents, and 40 percent of the girls and 21 percent of the boys relied solely on their parents for the means to stay in college.[33] More than half of the students depended at least partly on their own work or savings to see them through college, and one-fifth supported themselves entirely. Some form of scholarship, excluding the GI Bill and grants from employers, was reported for 16 percent of all students.

Table II–22.—INCOME OF COLLEGE STUDENTS BY COLLEGE CLASS AND SEX: 1960

Income in 1959 by type and sex	All college students	Fresh-men	Sopho-mores	Juniors	Seniors	Graduates or profes-sionals
Male...........................	100.0	100.0	100.0	100.0	100.0	100.0
Earnings only.....................	63.8	69.8	67.1	63.1	58.7	55.7
Under $1,000.................	27.9	39.7	31.6	27.6	21.6	11.6
$1,000 to $1,999.............	14.7	14.7	16.3	16.9	14.6	10.4
$2,000 and over.............	21.2	15.4	19.2	18.7	22.6	33.7
Earnings and other income.............	23.8	15.1	20.3	25.4	29.9	34.4
Under $1,000.................	4.2	5.1	4.3	4.5	3.9	2.7
$1,000 to $1,999.............	5.2	3.4	4.9	6.4	7.0	5.1
$2,000 and over.............	14.5	6.5	11.2	14.4	19.0	26.6
Other income only.................	2.5	1.5	2.0	2.6	3.5	3.5
Under $1,000.................	1.3	1.0	1.1	1.3	1.7	1.5
$1,000 and over.............	1.2	0.5	0.9	1.3	1.8	1.9
Not an income recipient................	9.9	13.6	10.6	8.9	7.9	6.4
Female...........................	100.0	100.0	100.0	100.0	100.0	100.0
Earnings only.....................	59.2	57.5	58.9	60.2	60.3	64.3
Under $1,000.................	42.3	45.8	45.6	44.8	36.6	16.6
$1,000 to $1,999.............	7.0	6.1	6.6	7.4	8.2	10.1
$2,000 and over.............	9.3	5.7	6.6	7.9	15.4	37.6
Earnings and other income.............	9.1	8.0	8.4	9.0	9.9	17.1
Under $1,000.................	4.9	5.1	5.1	5.2	4.4	2.6
$1,000 to $1,999.............	1.7	1.3	1.6	2.1	2.2	2.6
$2,000 and over.............	2.5	1.5	1.7	1.7	3.3	11.9
Other income only.................	3.2	2.8	3.0	3.0	3.8	4.6
Under $1,000.................	2.1	2.1	2.1	2.0	2.4	1.9
$1,000 and over.............	1.0	0.7	0.9	1.0	1.4	2.7
Not an income recipient................	28.5	31.7	29.7	27.8	26.0	14.0

Source: *1960 Census of Population, Subject Reports, School Enrollment,* Series PC(2)–5A. table 10.

Working one's way through college, at least in part, becomes more common with advancement through the college system. Not quite half the freshman boys, but three-fifths of the seniors, were in the labor force while attending college. Moreover, the proportion whose income was $2,000 or more increased with each higher college class, being one-fifth for freshmen and two-fifths for seniors. It is probable, too, that students rely less and less on their parents for financial aid as they continue in college; although there are no data bearing on this assumption, it is known that a substantial proportion of advanced students attend college part time and work either part or full time.

One consequence of a higher marriage rate in each more advanced college class is that an extra burden is added to the already difficult task of procuring enough money for college. Married students in 1960 not only had spouses to support; 17 percent of the college men (two-thirds of those who were married) and 8 percent of the college women (over half of those who were married) had children as well. It should be noted, however, that marriage made college attendance possible for many persons. Most of the college women with children had husbands in the labor force. Presumably many of these women attended school part time and their husbands worked full time so that financial needs could be met without too much difficulty. Among married college men, 87 percent of those with children and 74 percent of those without children were in the labor force. For about 27 percent of those with children and 76 percent of those without children, the wife was in the labor force. Among married couples where the husband was in college, in one-tenth of the cases both husband and wife were in the labor force and many of the couples had children.

Table II–23.—Percent Distribution of College Students, by College Class, Family Status, Labor Force Status of Student and Spouse, and Sex: 1960

Family status, labor force status of student and spouse, and sex	All college students	Fresh-men	Sopho-mores	Juniors	Seniors	Graduates or profes-sionals
Male..........................	100.0	100.0	100.0	100.0	100.0	100.0
Married, wife present...................	27.4	11.5	19.7	24.9	37.3	54.2
Labor force..........................	22.5	10.3	17.1	19.8	29.2	44.1
Wife in labor force.................	9.2	4.2	6.7	8.7	12.2	17.6
With own children.................	3.7	1.8	2.9	3.5	4.7	7.0
Without own children.............	5.5	2.4	3.8	5.2	7.5	10.7
Wife not in labor force.............	13.3	6.1	10.5	11.1	17.0	26.5
With own children.................	11.4	5.1	8.9	9.5	14.5	23.2
Without own children.............	1.8	0.9	1.6	1.5	2.5	3.3
Not in labor force....................	4.9	1.2	2.5	5.2	8.0	10.1
Wife in labor force.................	3.0	0.8	1.6	3.4	5.0	5.9
With own children.................	1.0	0.3	0.5	1.1	1.7	1.8
Without own children.............	2.0	0.5	1.1	2.3	3.3	4.2
Wife not in labor force.............	1.9	0.5	1.0	1.8	3.1	4.2
With own children.................	1.3	0.3	0.6	1.1	2.1	3.1
Without own children.............	0.6	0.2	0.4	0.7	1.0	1.1
Other marital status....................	72.6	88.5	80.3	75.1	62.7	45.8
Labor force..........................	34.2	37.5	38.1	34.6	30.8	26.6
Not in labor force....................	38.5	50.9	42.2	40.4	31.9	19.2
Female..........................	100.0	100.0	100.0	100.0	100.0	100.0
Married, husband present.................	13.7	7.6	10.4	12.7	24.9	36.7
Labor force..........................	5.9	2.7	3.9	5.1	10.7	22.9
Husband in labor force.............	5.5	2.5	3.6	4.7	9.7	21.3
With own children.................	2.4	1.2	1.7	2.1	4.4	7.9
Without own children.............	3.1	1.3	1.9	2.6	5.3	13.4
Husband not in labor force.........	0.5	0.2	0.3	0.4	1.0	1.6
With own children.................	0.1	0.1	0.0	0.1	0.2	0.2
Without own children.............	0.4	0.1	0.2	0.3	0.8	1.3
Not in labor force....................	4.9	4.9	6.5	7.6	14.2	13.9
Husband in labor force.............	3.0	4.6	5.9	6.9	12.6	12.5
With own children.................	4.8	3.5	4.3	4.4	7.9	8.0
Without own children.............	2.2	1.0	1.6	2.5	4.7	4.5
Husband not in labor force.........	0.7	0.3	0.6	0.7	1.6	1.4
With own children.................	0.2	0.2	0.2	0.2	0.4	0.4
Without own children.............	0.5	0.1	0.5	0.5	1.2	1.0
Other marital status....................	86.3	92.4	89.6	87.3	75.1	63.3
Labor force..........................	34.5	31.0	36.0	37.7	33.2	43.0
Not in labor force....................	51.8	61.4	53.6	49.7	41.9	20.2

Source: 1960 Census of Population, Subject Reports, School Enrollment, Series PC(2)–5A, table 8.

NOTES

[1] Dael Wolfle, *America's Resources of Specialized Talent*. New York: Harper and Brothers, 1954, p. 140.

[2] The regular censuses and surveys of the Bureau of the Census are used to gather data on the school and college enrollment and educational attainment of the population, but on occasions special surveys have been taken to obtain data on ability and other factors related to high school graduation and college entrance.

[3] R. A. Tesseneer and L. M. Tesseneer, "Review of the Literature on School Dropouts," *Bulletin of the National Association of Secondary School Districts*, 42, May 1958.

[4] Jacob Shiffman, "Employment of High School Graduates and Dropouts in 1962," *Monthly Labor Review*, July 1963.

[5] See R. A. Tesseneer and L. M. Tesseneer, op. cit., for a general discussion of these points. Also S. M. Miller, Betty L. Saleem, and Herrington Bryce, *School Dropouts: A Commentary and Annotated Bibliography*. Syracuse University: Youth Development Center, 1964.

[6] This group includes youths who never went to school or who dropped out in the elementary grades, as well as those who dropped out in high school.

[7] Data are for children living with both parents in 1960. Census data are not available on the education of parents not residing with their children, or deceased.

[8] Data are for children living with one or both parents in 1960. See footnote 7 and footnote to table II–5.

[9] Data are for children having an employed father with whom they were living. Not included are children whose fathers were not residing with them, or living with them but not employed, or deceased.

[10] The ethnic groups with poorer educational experience had already had higher attrition rates before the fifth grade, so that ethnic differentials in attainment of some high school education were even greater than indicated by the statistics just cited. For further discussion of ethnic differences in educational attainment, see chapter V.

[11] Most studies in which intelligence or aptitude has been related to dropping out of school show dropouts to be more selective of the less able, but there is considerable variance in reports of the extent of the difference in ability between dropouts and graduates. See Tesseneer, op. cit.

[12] See Tesseneer, op. cit.

[13] Ibid.

[14] For a discussion of the lower class dropout and the middle class values of the American school system, see Edgar Z. Friedenberg, "An Ideology of School Withdrawal" in Daniel Schrieber, (ed.), *The School Dropout*. Washington: National Education Association, 1963.

[15] Jacob Schiffman, op. cit. A recent study by Beverly Duncan indicates that opportunities in the job market are an important determinant of whether or not some youths drop out of school. See "Dropouts and the Unemployed," *Journal of Political Economy*, Vol. LXXIII, April 1965, pp. 121–134.

[16] To some extent, scholastic retardation is also a function of age at time of beginning school; however, the method of measurement used (which identifies a person as retarded if he is enrolled below the two-grade mode) largely takes into consideration the variation in age at school entrance.

[17] James D. Cowhig and Charles B. Nam, "Educational Status, College Plans, and Occupational Status of Farm and Nonfarm Youths: October 1959." Census–ERS, Series P–27, No. 30, table 6.

[18] See ibid. for a more detailed discussion and data.

[19] Charles B. Nam and James D. Cowhig, "Factors Related to College Attendance of

NOTES—Continued

Farm and Nonfarm High School Graduates: 1960," Census–ERS,Series P–27, No. 32, table 6. These results are in close agreement with those of a 1955 study of public high school students. See *Background Factors Relating to College Plans and College Enrollment Among Public High School Students.* Princeton, New Jersey: Educational Testing Service, 1957.

[20] See Allison Davis, *Social Class Influence Upon Learning.* Cambridge, Mass.: Harvard University Press, 1950. Some persons have argued for dropping these tests as bases for placing and rating students; others have argued for their continued use but on a more discriminating basis and in conjunction with other information about the students. A distinction should be made between the use of tests for placing individual students and their use as a variable in research dealing with groups.

[21] U.S. Bureau of the Census, *Current Population Reports,* Series P–20, No. 110, "School Enrollment, and Education of Young Adults and Their Fathers, 1960."

[22] The low correlation between college attendance and color can be explained by the fact that a greater proportion of nonwhites than whites who drop out of school do so before reaching college age; nonwhites who graduate from high school tend to be much like whites with regard to measured ability and socioeconomic background.

[23] Since some of these factors are partly reflected in the variables included in the correlation analysis, it is difficult to believe that they can account for half the explained variance. The general failure to account for much of the explained variance in studies of social phenomena suggests possible methodological weaknesses in the approach. Part of the unexplained variance must be due to error and measurement variability. Perhaps more stress, therefore, should be put on the relative importance of the different variables measured than on the measured magnitude of each effect.

[24] The authors are grateful to A. J. Jaffe who sponsored this aspect of the 1959–1960 survey.

[25] Data cited from *Home State and Migration of American College Students, Fall 1958,* American Association of Collegiate Registrars and Admissions Officers, March 1959. This is one of a series of studies of college student migration, all the others having been conducted by the Office of Education. For a good historical review see H. T. Groat, "Internal Migration Patterns of a Population Subgroup, College Students 1887–1958," *American Journal of Sociology,* Vol. LXIX, January 1964, pp. 383–394.

[26] The survey question called for the major reason where there was more than one reason. The major reason reported by the respondent in some cases may not have been the primary or underlying reason.

[27] Wolfle, op. cit., p. 160.

[28] Cowhig and Nam, op. cit.

[29] The survey data showed that "taking a job" did not necessarily represent an economic constraint, since this reason for not attending college was given by a larger proportion of students in families with incomes of $5,000 or more than in families with lower incomes.

[30] For a report on marriage trends of college students as revealed by several localized studies, see Nahum Medalia, "Explaining the Increase in College Student Marriage," paper presented at the annual meeting of the Eastern Sociological Society, April 1964.

[31] It has been found that costs are higher for full-time than part-time students, for those living at college rather than at home, for those attending private rather than public colleges, and for those attending a university rather than a junior college or liberal arts college. See John B. Lansing, Thomas Lorimer, and Chikashi Moriguchi, *How People Pay for College,* Survey Research Center, The University of Michigan, 1960, p. 18.

[32] See chapter VI for a discussion of the economic benefits of a college education.

[33] Cowhig and Nam, op. cit., pp. 4-5.

CHAPTER III

TEACHERS IN AMERICAN SOCIETY

Introduction

This chapter traces the growth and change of the teaching profession and provides a demographic description of its members. Since census materials on teachers were limited prior to 1900, the present analysis deals primarily with the years between 1900 and 1960—a period of major changes in teachers' characteristics. More details on this subject are reported in the 1960 Census than in any of the earlier censuses.

Census statistics on teachers, like those on any other occupational group, are subject to errors of coverage, reporting, and classification. (A detailed discussion of these errors and comparisons with statistics from the U.S. Office of Education will be found in appendix A.) The major problems of comparability between the Census data and OE statistics arise in the consideration of college teachers. Many part-time college teachers who are reported in the census according to their primary occupation (doctor, chemist, and so on), are also included in the OE reports on college faculty members. Figures from the Office of Education on the number of college teachers are about 25 percent higher than the census figures for 1960. Most of this difference probably is caused by differences in definition. At the elementary and secondary levels the two series are in closer agreement, but the comparisons indicate that the OE statistics probably failed to include many private school teachers, especially in the years before 1960.

The characteristics of teachers prior to 1900 cannot be accurately documented statistically. Data on the number of teachers, but not on their characteristics, were first available in 1870 from the Office of Education. Although these early figures, like the enrollment statistics for the same period, are probably subject to substantial errors, they indicate the general trends in the number of teachers.

In 1870 there were about 200,000 public school teachers and about 5,000 to 6,000 college teachers. (Good estimates of the number of private school teachers below the college level are not available.) The average public school teacher was reported to receive an annual salary of about $200 for teaching 35 to 40 pupils. About 40 percent of the public school teachers, and about 90 percent of the college teachers, were men.

By 1900 the number of teachers in public schools had more than doubled to 423,000 (Office of Education figures), and the number in colleges had increased to 24,000. The number of private elementary and secondary teachers was estimated to be about 35,000. The average teacher received about $300 a year salary, and at the elementary level taught an average of about 37 pupils. The proportion of male teachers had declined to about 30 percent despite the rise in salary (or perhaps because the salary was still so low). At the college level the proportion of men teachers had probably also declined to about 80 percent.[1]

It is important to remember that in 1900 elementary teachers outnumbered secondary teachers by about 20 to 1. By 1920 this ratio had declined to 6 to 1, by 1930, to 3 to 1, and since 1950 the ratio has been less than 2 to 1. The characteristics of teachers vary in a number of ways at different levels of teaching, and these variations affect a number of other comparisons. For example, at every period secondary teaching attracted more men than elementary teaching, paid higher salaries, and was characterized by smaller numbers of pupils per teacher.

Beginning with the 20th century, there has been more comprehensive statistical data on the characteristics of teachers. Information in the 1940, 1950, and 1960 Censuses and in a special report by Kaplan and Casey[2] enable us to develop an estimate of the total number of teachers from census occupational statistics. This estimate includes not only college teachers, public school teachers, and private school teachers, but also a part of other occupational categories, such as artists and art teachers, musicians and music teachers, and librarians. The method of developing this estimate, described in appendix A, provides a useful overall measure of the number of people whose major job is teaching.

Throughout the 20th century, teachers have been the largest occupational group among professional workers. In 1900 they comprised 40 percent of all professional workers, but in 1950, despite a threefold increase, they made up only 28 percent of all professionals. Between 1950 and 1960, due to the tremendous growth of enrollment, the number of teachers grew at about the same rate as the number of other professionals, and in 1960 they comprised 28.5 percent of all professionals (see figure III–1). In 1900 teaching was almost the only profession open to women, and 85 percent of all professional women were teachers. This percentage declined steadily to 1950, when women teachers were just half of all women professionals. Since 1950 the number of women in teaching has been increasing at the same rate as the number of all women professionals.

Among male professionals, for the past 60 years, the number who were teachers (at any level) has been close to 15 percent. The number increased fivefold during this 60-year period, but there was also a fivefold increase in the number of male professionals. The decline in the percentage of all professionals who are teachers is a result of larger percentages of women entering the nonteaching professions. Teaching remains by far the largest professional occupation for women, but it has more competition today than 60 years ago from other professions that attract women.

Figure III–1.—PERCENT OF TEACHERS AMONG PROFESSIONAL WORKERS, BY SEX:
1900 TO 1960

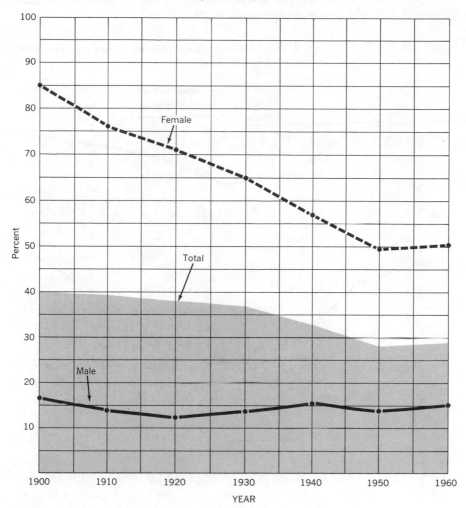

Source: See appendix A for derivation of figures; Kaplan and Casey, *Occupational Trends in the United States, 1900 to 1950*, U.S. Bureau of the Census, Working Paper No. 5, 1958; and *1960 Census of Population, Subject Reports, Occupation by Industry*, PC(2)–7C.

Elementary school teaching has been largely a woman's occupation. Secondary teaching has also attracted more women than men, although at least 30 percent of secondary teachers have always been men. College teaching has always been more open to men than women. Over the past 60 years the proportion of men in teaching has fluctuated, declining at all levels between 1900 and 1920, and rising since 1930 at secondary and college levels (see figure III–2). These trends suggest that elementary teaching is likely to remain predominantly a woman's profession, and that college teaching is likely to continue to be predominantly a profession for men, with secondary education attracting varying proportions of men, depending on economic conditions, available labor supply, and the relative attractiveness of secondary teaching compared with alternative occupational opportunities.

Figure III–2.—Percent of Males Among Teachers, by Level of Teaching: 1900 to 1960

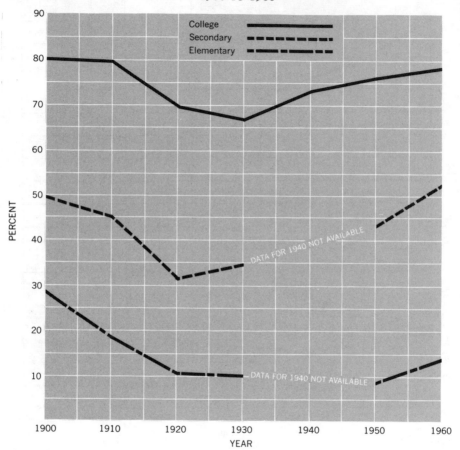

Source: U.S. Bureau of the Census, *Historical Statistics of the United States, Colonial Times to 1957, Continuation to 1962 and Revisions.*

Changes in marriage patterns of teachers

One of the most striking changes in the last 60 years has been the rise in the percent of women teachers who are married. As recently as 1920, 90 percent of women teachers were single. School boards often had rules against hiring married women, and the figures suggest that they seldom made exceptions to the rule. A rapid and steady decline in the percent of unmarried women teachers began in the 1920's, and by 1960 only 29 percent of the women teaching in elementary and secondary schools were single. There has also been a substantial change in marriage patterns for men. In 1900, 53 percent of all men teachers were single; by 1940, 27 percent were single; in 1950 and in 1960, only about 16 percent of those teaching in elementary and secondary schools were single.

Among women teachers, the proportion who are widowed and divorced has increased gradually from about 3 to 12 percent in the last 60 years (see figure III–3); but among men teachers the proportion has been very low (not more

Figure III–3.—FEMALE ELEMENTARY AND SECONDARY TEACHERS, BY MARITAL STATUS: 1900 TO 1960

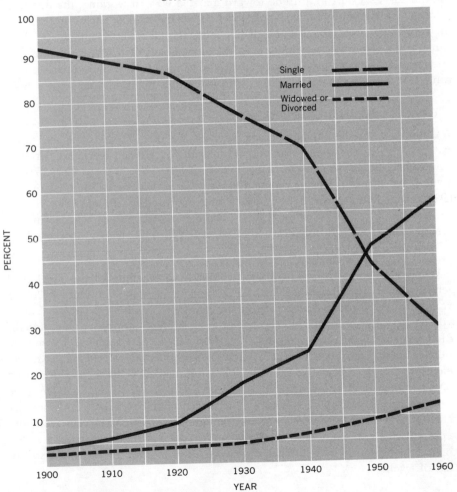

Source: U.S. Census of Population Reports—
1900: *Occupations*, table LXXXII.
1910: Vol. IV, *Occupations*, table 9, p. 698.   (Distribution of widowed and divorced esti-
       mated.)
1920: Ibid.
1930: Vol. V, *General Report on Occupation*, table 9, p. 278.
1940: Vol. III, *The Labor Force*, Part 1, table 68.
1950: Vol. II, *Characteristics of the Population*, Part 1.
1960: Vol. I, *Characteristics of the Population*, Part 1.

than 2.5 percent) during the entire period. It is possible that this low proportion of unmarried men was a result of a working association with a large
number of eligible women; however, the percent of male teachers who were
widowed and divorced was at about the same level as that of all professional
men.

The rise in the proportion of married women teachers and the consequent
decline in the proportion who are single is probably the result of several
factors, including the general decline in age at marriage, and an increase in
the proportion of the population who are married. But the trend also reflects
such factors as a shift in attitude toward married women working, the difficulty
of obtaining enough qualified single teachers for the rapidly expanding schools,
the increasing professionalization of teaching, the increased length of teaching
careers, and the associated increase in the average age of teachers. If pay and
other working conditions are more adequate, women will be more likely to continue teaching after marriage, or to return to it after their children begin school.

Changes in the age of teachers

Changes in teachers' characteristics during the past 60 years are also illustrated by the changing age distribution, especially of women teachers. In 1900
almost half of all women teaching below college level were under 25; the
median age was 26. During the next 20 years there was very little change. In
1920 the median age was 27, by 1930 it had increased to 29, and since then it
has risen rapidly to 44 years in 1960. The age distribution of teachers in the
first decade of the 20th century suggests that the median length of teaching
careers was 5 years or less.

We do not know the average age at entry into teaching in the 1900-1920
period, but it was probably 20 to 22 years. With a median age of 26 for
women teachers, the average teaching career was only about 5 years. Young
women typically entered teaching when they finished normal school, taught
a few years until they married, and then dropped out of teaching. Those who
did not marry continued to teach. A 1909 sample study of secondary school
teachers by E. L. Thorndike indicated that the median years of teaching were
5.5 for women and about 8 for men.[3] In a 1931 survey, E. S. Evenden gave
the median years of service (men and women combined) as 8 for elementary
teachers and 6 for secondary.[4] Even though these sample surveys were not
representative nationally of all teachers, and had substantial nonresponse rates,
they are consistent with estimates developed from a study of the age distribution of teachers.

Two sample surveys taken in 1956 and 1960 by the National Education
Association provide additional data on average length of service. In 1956 the
median was 8 years of service for men, 15.4 for women, and 13.5 for both
sexes combined. In 1960 the median number of years of service was 7.1 for

men and 14.2 for women.[5] These changes in career patterns are clearly reflected in the changing age structure of teachers (see figure III–4). In 1930
one-third of all teachers were under 25, and there was no evidence in the age
distribution of women teachers of their return to teaching at the end of the
childbearing period. In both the 1950 and 1960 age distribution the dropout
and return to teaching among women is quite evident. Reentry to teaching
usually occurs at ages 35 to 44 when their own children are in school or college.

Figure III–4.—PERCENT DISTRIBUTION OF FEMALE ELEMENTARY AND SECONDARY
TEACHERS, BY AGE: 1930 TO 1960

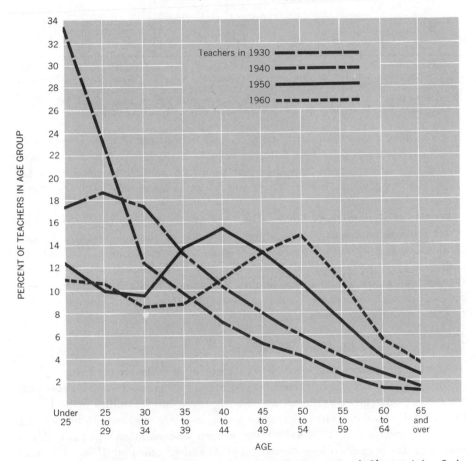

Source: *1960 Census of Population, Subject Reports, Occupational Characteristics,* Series
PC(2)–7A, tables 6 and 7; *1950 Census of Population,* Vol. IV, *Special Reports, Economic
Characteristics,* Part IB, *Occupational Characteristics,* tables 6 and 7; *1940 Census of Population, The Labor Force,* Part 2, chapter 2, *Occupational Characteristics,* tables 1 and 2; and
1930 Census of Population, Vol. V, *General Report on Occupation,* chapter 4, tables 6 and 9.

For nonwhite women and for women in college teaching, the age distributions are different. Nonwhite elementary and secondary teachers do not

Table III–1.—MEDIAN AGE OF TEACHERS, BY LEVEL OF TEACHING, COLOR, AND SEX: 1930 TO 1960

Color and census year	Male		Female	
	Elementary and secondary	College	Elementary and secondary	College
TOTAL				
1960	35.3	39.1	44.5	43.3
1950	37.9	38.6	41.2	40.5
1940	33.7	39.8	33.9	41.1
1930	32.1	38.7	28.8	35.9
NONWHITE				
1960	35.8	38.3	37.8	39.8
1950	36.9	37.7	36.2	33.9
1940	34.2	36.7	32.0	30.5
1930	37.7	34.5	28.2	29.0

Source: *1960 Census of Population, Subject Reports, Occupational Characteristics*, Series PC(2)–7A, tables 6 and 7; *1950 Census of Population*, Vol. IV, *Special Reports, Economic Characteristics*, Part IB, *Occupational Characteristics*, tables 6 and 7; *1940 Census of Population, The Labor Force*, Part 2, chapter 2, *Occupational Characteristics*, tables 1 and 2; and *1930 Census of Population*, Vol. V, *General Report on Occupation*, chapter 4, tables 6 and 9.

drop out during the childrearing ages. It may be that nonwhite women cannot afford to stop teaching. This different pattern of work is reflected in a lower median age among nonwhite than among white women teachers: 2 years lower in 1940, 5 years lower in 1950, and 6.7 years lower in 1960. (See table III–1.)

Women college teachers have a later age at entry (because of the greater educational requirements) and a higher percent of them are single than of elementary and secondary teachers. Slightly more than one-half of women college teachers were single in 1960, while only 29 percent of women elementary and secondary teachers were single. The age distribution of women college teachers is more like that of men college teachers than that of women elementary and secondary teachers.

Changes in the education of teachers

Another important changing characteristic of teachers is their rising level of formal education. Census data on educational attainment are available only since 1940, but earlier estimates are possible from sample studies made by the Office of Education. The Thorndike study in 1908[6] estimated that among *secondary* teachers about one-half the women and about 55 percent of the men had less than a college degree. The Evenden[7] study in 1930-1931 indicated that 88 percent of elementary teachers had less than 4 years of college, while among secondary teachers only 13 percent had less than 4 years of college. This suggests a very substantial increase in the educational level of secondary teachers between 1908 and 1930; it also illustrates the sharp difference that existed then between the educational levels of elementary and secondary teachers.

The level of teachers' education rose substantially between 1930 and 1940; it is not possible, however, to make precise comparisons, as the sample data referred to above for 1930 are tabulated by level of teaching and not by sex, while the 1940 Census tabulated the data by sex but not by level of teaching. The 1940 Census showed that about one-fourth of male teachers and almost one-half of female teachers had less than 4 years college education. (See table III–2.) Substantial gains in educational attainment were reported for all groups between 1940 and 1960, especially among nonwhites and rural male teachers, who had relatively more room for improvement. By 1960, a higher percentage of college graduates was found among nonwhite than white teachers, regardless of their sex. Possibly this reflects greater competition for nonwhite teaching jobs, as well as a greater tendency for nonwhite females, once qualified, to remain in teaching, thus reducing the number of temporary or replacement teachers required each year.

The largest improvement in the educational attainment of teachers has occurred at the elementary level. The 1930-1931 survey by Evenden indicated that 2 percent of elementary teachers had 1 or more years of graduate education, while the 1960 Census indicated 24 percent of the same group had had this much schooling. Evenden's survey also indicated that 88 percent of elementary teachers had *less* than 4 years of college; by 1960 this proportion had contracted to 29 percent.

Table III–2.—PERCENT OF ELEMENTARY AND SECONDARY TEACHERS WITH LESS THAN 4 YEARS OF COLLEGE, BY URBAN AND RURAL RESIDENCE AND SEX: 1960 AND 1940

Urban and rural residence and sex	1960	1940	Percent decrease, 1940 to 1960
UNITED STATES			
Total			
Male	13.3	26.3	49.4
Female	28.8	48.3	40.4
Nonwhite			
Male	12.3	32.3	61.9
Female	17.6	59.9	70.6
URBAN			
Male	13.0	20.1	35.3
Female	25.5	41.3	38.3
RURAL			
Male	13.9	32.8	57.6
Female	37.8	58.7	35.6

Source: *1960 Census of Population, Subject Reports, Characteristics of Teachers*, Series PC(2)–7D, table 4; and *1940 Census of Population, The Labor Force*, Part 2, chapter 2, *Occupational Characteristics*, table 3.

In 1930, only 13 percent of secondary (excluding junior high school) teachers had less than 4 years of college; by 1960 this figure had decreased to 9 percent. In 1930, 29 percent of secondary teachers had 5 or more years of college; by 1960 this figure had risen to 53 percent.

Teachers with 4 or more years of college education comprise a substantial fraction of all college graduates. Male teachers (elementary, secondary, and college) with college degrees comprised about 11 percent of all college men in 1940, 9 percent in 1950, and 11 percent in 1960. For women, the comparable figures were 26 percent in 1940, 21 percent in 1950, and 28 percent in 1960. The rapid expansion of enrollments at all levels in the 1950's brought a larger proportion of all college graduates into teaching. In 1960, it would have required only about 1½ percent of the total supply of men with college degrees to replace all the men in the teaching profession who had less than 4 years of college. To replace the women who had less than 4 years of college with women who had graduated would have required about 11 percent of all women in the population with college degrees.

Teachers of both sexes 35 to 44 years old are better educated than either younger or older teachers. (See figure III–5.) Younger teachers include a much smaller proportion with master's degrees, while teachers over 45 are survivors of a group who entered teaching at an earlier date when educational attainment was generally lower. There is very little decline in educational attainment at the older ages; this reflects both selective retention of teachers who meet educational standards, and selective reentry of better educated teachers who left teaching to raise a family.

Changes in income of teachers below college level

Changes in the levels of compensation for teachers have accompanied the rise in educational level and the increased length of service. (College teachers' earnings are analyzed in the next section.) Office of Education figures on salaries go back to 1870; the figures are for average salaries paid by the public schools to regular teachers. The Census has provided information on teachers salaries since 1940. Census income statistics include information on all persons who worked as teachers either full or part time. In 1940 and 1950, members of religious orders who were teaching but not receiving a salary were included in the census compilations of median salaries. If teachers who worked less than 27 weeks and teachers with no income are excluded, the median earnings of teachers for the calendar year 1959, reported in the 1960 Census, were only about 5 percent less than the estimated average salary reported to the Office of Education.[8] The average dollar salary of teachers was more than 10 times as great in 1960 as in 1910 (see table III–3), but in dollars or constant purchasing power, teachers' incomes had increased a little less than 3½ times since 1910.

Figure III–5.—EDUCATIONAL ATTAINMENT OF ELEMENTARY AND SECONDARY
TEACHERS, BY AGE, COLOR, AND SEX: 1960

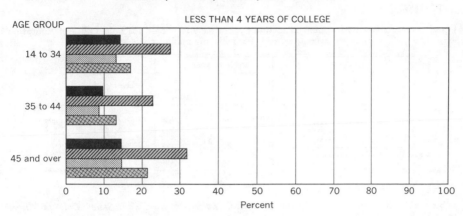

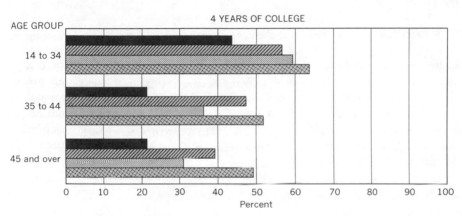

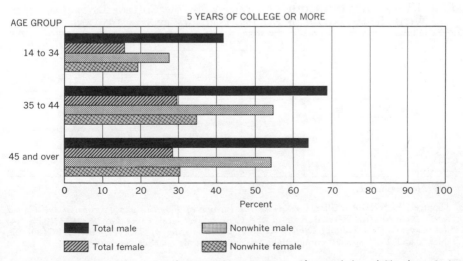

Source: *1960 Census of Population, Subject Reports, Characteristics of Teachers,* Series
PC(2)–7D, table 4.

Table III–3.—INCOME OF TEACHERS BELOW COLLEGE LEVEL AS SHOWN IN STATISTICS FROM THE U.S. OFFICE OF EDUCATION AND THE BUREAU OF THE CENSUS: 1910 TO 1960

[Census reports *median* income and includes part-time and unpaid teachers, Office of Education figures are *average* salaries for full-time public school teachers]

Year	Office of Education		Census	
	Current dollars	Constant (1947–49) dollars	Current dollars	Constant (1947–49) dollars
1960	5,174	4,056	4,449	3,487
1950	3,010	2,928	2,687	2,614
1940	1,441	2,406	1,105	1,845
1930	1,420	1,989	(NA)	(NA)
1920	871	1,016	(NA)	(NA)
1910	485	1,194	(NA)	(NA)

NA Not available.

Source: U.S. Bureau of the Census, *Historical Statistics of the United States, Colonial Times to 1957*, Series H–235.

Salaries of teachers have risen about twice as much as the per capita income of the population as a whole since 1920, but relative gains in income have been quite uneven in different decades. Teachers' earnings made large gains relative to earnings of all employed persons between 1920 and 1930, about held their own from 1930 to 1940, lost ground between 1940 and 1950, and gained again between 1950 and 1960. A more pertinent comparison is between earnings of teachers and of all professionals. The growth rate of teachers' salaries was similar to the rate for all professionals in the 1950-1960 period, but female teachers increased their earnings a little more rapidly than all professional women, and male teachers increased their earnings a little more slowly than all male professionals. (See table III–4.)

Table III–4.—MEDIAN INCOME OF TEACHERS BELOW COLLEGE LEVEL, COMPARED WITH MEDIAN INCOME OF ALL PROFESSIONALS, BY SEX: 1959 AND 1949

Year and sex	Median income in 1959 dollars				Teachers' income as percent of professionals' income
	Professionals	Teachers	Percent increase since 1949		
			Professionals	Teachers	
Male:					
1949	4,902	4,304	(X)	(X)	87.8
1959	6,710	5,571	36.9	29.4	83.0
Female:					
1949	2,785	2,956	(X)	(X)	106.1
1959	3,606	4,043	29.5	36.8	112.1

X Not applicable.

Source: Herman P. Miller, *Trends in the Income of Families and Persons in the United States, 1947 to 1960*, U.S. Bureau of the Census, Technical Paper No. 8, 1963, table 14; *1960 Census of Population, Subject Reports, Characteristics of Teachers*, Series PC(2)–7D, table 7; and 1950 special unpublished tabulations of data about teachers.

Compared with other professional women, female teachers have slightly higher earnings. Their earnings in 1959 were about 12 percent higher than for all women professionals. As teachers below the college level constitute about 43 percent of all professional women, their average earnings are probably about 20 percent above the earnings of nonteaching professional women.

Male teachers, by contrast, earn about 17 percent less than the average for all professional men. Men teaching below the college level earn an average of 38 percent more than women and in spite of this differential, they still lag behind the earnings levels of other professional men. Since teaching as a profession provides salaries that place it above the average for all professional women and below the average for all professional men, we might expect that the proportion of men in teaching should be declining. However, the opposite is true; the proportion of men rose at both the elementary and secondary levels between 1950 and 1960.

There are substantial State and regional differences in teachers' pay. In general, the Northeast and Far West have paid salaries above the national average, and the South has paid salaries below the national average. (See table III–5.) These differences in teacher compensation parallel regional differences in per capita income, but the regional differences in teachers' salaries are generally less than the differences in per capita income. Regional differentials in teachers' salaries narrowed somewhat between 1940 and 1960. In 1940, median salaries in the South (the lowest region) were about 55 percent of those in the Northeast (the highest region), but by 1960 median salaries in the South were about 76 percent of the median salaries in the West (the highest region).

Table III–5.—MEDIAN INCOME OF TEACHERS BELOW COLLEGE LEVEL, BY REGION AND SEX: 1960, 1950, AND 1940

[In current dollars]

Area and sex	1960	1950	1940	Percent increase	
				1940 to 1960	1940 to 1950
MALE					
United States.................	5,571	3,516	1,475	278	138
Northeast.........................	5,874	3,843	1,946	202	97
North Central....................	5,668	3,625	1,459	288	148
South.............................	4,732	2,940	1,071	342	174
West.............................	6,144	3,837	1,727	256	122
FEMALE					
United States.................	4,043	2,415	984	311	145
Northeast.........................	4,617	2,792	1,446	219	93
North Central....................	4,025	2,398	926	335	159
South.............................	3,558	2,089	812	338	157
West.............................	4,693	3,040	1,353	247	125

Source: *1960 Census of Population, Subject Reports, Characteristics of Teachers*, Series PC(2)–7D, table 7; 1950 special unpublished tabulations of data about teachers; and *1940 Census of Population, The Labor Force*, Part 1, U.S. Summary, table 73.

Earnings of nonwhite teachers are lower than those of white teachers. This gap was partially closed between 1950 and 1960, especially for women teachers (see table III–6), but it is still substantial. It might be assumed that the color differential was largely regional, since about three-fourths of the non-white teachers are concentrated in the South, and since salaries in the South have already been shown to be lower than in other regions. Data from the 1950 Census indicate that the color differential had almost disappeared for nonsouthern women teachers, but that it still existed for southern male and female teachers and nonsouthern male teachers. The presence of a color differential among nonsouthern males may reflect the small numbers involved and the instability of the figures, or possibly the greater difficulty of nonwhite male teachers in achieving administrative positions and other higher paying teaching jobs. If census figures were available on teachers' earnings in 1960, by region and by color, we might find that all of the color differential is related to regional differentials in earnings, since the regional differential in 1960 was larger (for females) than the color differential.

Table III–6.—Ratio of Median Earnings of Nonwhite Teachers to Those of White Teachers, for the United States and Selected Major Regions, by Sex: 1959 and 1949

| Year and sex | United States | | South, total | All other regions, total |
	Total	With 4 years of college		
1959				
Male.....................................	.78	.82	(NA)	(NA)
Female...................................	.91	.91	(NA)	(NA)
1949				
Male.....................................	.68	(NA)	.76	.76
Female...................................	.76	(NA)	.82	.96

NA Not available.

Source: *1960 Census of Population, Subject Reports, Characteristics of Teachers*, Series PC(2)–7D, tables 7, 9, and 10, and 1950 unpublished tabulations of median earnings.

Characteristics of college teachers

Although the earnings of college teachers increased in the 1940-1960 period, the increase in earnings of constant purchasing power has been only a little more than a third of that for public school teachers. As table III–7 shows, college teachers actually lost real income in the 1940-1950 period, when the cost of living increased more rapidly than their salaries. In the 1950-1960 period, gains in real income for college teachers and for other teachers were quite comparable in magnitude. Male college teachers registered greater increases than other male teachers, while female college teachers registered slightly smaller gains than other female teachers.

Table III–7.—Percent Increase in Median Earnings of Constant Purchasing Power for College Teachers and Elementary and Secondary School Teachers, by Sex: 1940 to 1960

[Percent based on data deflated to constant dollars by Consumer Price Index. Minus sign (—) denotes decrease]

Level of teaching and sex	1940 to 1950	1950 to 1960	1940 to 1960
MALE			
College level......................	-9	40	27
Below college level...............	39	28	78
FEMALE			
College level......................	5	32	36
Below college level...............	43	37	93

Source: Salaries of noncollege teachers, see table III–5; College salaries, *1960 Census of Population, Subject Reports, Characteristics of Teachers*, Series PC(2)–7D, table 7; *1950 Census of Population*, Vol. IV, *Special Reports, Occupational Characteristics*, table 22; *1940 Census of Population, The Labor Force*, Vol. 3, Part 1, table 72.

Most college teachers being males, changes in their marital status, age, and other characteristics have been much less dramatic during the past 50 years than for teachers below the college level. The number of college teachers reported by the census has increased twenty-four times since the turn of the century, compared with a fourfold increase in teachers below the college level, but in spite of this much more rapid growth, during the last 60 years the demographic characteristics of college teachers have changed less than the characteristics of other teachers.

Summary of changes in the characteristics of teachers

During the past 50 years the teaching profession underwent much growth and change. Most of the changes can be described under two major headings: growth in the number of teachers, and an increasing professionalization of teaching.

The number of teachers has increased fourfold since 1900, and although teaching is still the largest profession, the proportion of all professionals who are teachers has declined from 40 to 28 percent. Male teachers have comprised between 12 and 16 percent of all male professionals in the last 60 years; female teachers were 85 percent of all women professionals in 1900 but the figure has declined steadily to 50 percent in 1960.

Teaching as an occupation has become more professionalized in the last 60 years and especially in the last 30 years. Since 1930 the average length of teaching careers has about doubled; it is now about 14 years. The educational level of teachers has risen, and a college degree has become the standard for entry into teaching at the elementary as well as the secondary level. Between

1940 and 1960 the percent of male teachers without college degrees was cut in half, and the percent of female teachers lacking the baccalaureate was reduced by 40 percent. There is still room for improvement; in 1960, about one-fourth of teachers still did not have 4 years of college education. Improved compensation has contributed to the professionalization of teaching. In dollars of constant purchasing power the salaries of teachers (below college) have increased more than threefold since 1910, and have almost doubled since 1940. Professionalization and higher pay have meant that more women teachers stay in teaching, or return to it after marriage. These factors have brought about a rise since 1930 in the number of men teaching at the secondary level.

Characteristics of teachers in 1960

The first part of this chapter described the growth and change of teaching groups since the turn of the century. The next part will deal with more detailed information about the characteristics of teachers provided by the 1960 Census.

Teachers are distributed by residence and region in the same way as the total population and the pupils they serve. As would be expected, there are a few exceptions to this rule. For example, college teachers are more concentrated in urban than in rural areas. (See table III–8.) The biggest concentration of teachers, relative to the total population, occurs in small cities, not in large urbanized areas. This is true for elementary and secondary teachers (21 percent in small urban areas compared with 16 percent of the total population), and to an even greater extent for college teachers (29 percent in small urban areas compared with 16 percent of the population). The "typical" college town was traditionally a small town, and despite the establishment and growth of colleges in metropolitan areas, the vestiges of the earlier pattern are still evident. Nonwhite teachers, like the nonwhite population as a whole, are concentrated in the central cities of large urbanized areas; 29 percent of all teachers below college level, but 47 percent of nonwhite teachers, are located in the central cities of urbanized areas. However, as shown in table III–8, nonwhite teachers include a slightly lower proportion of central city residents than does the total nonwhite population.

The regional distribution of teachers is also closely related to the distribution of population and pupils. The ratio of pupils to teachers ranges from 23 in the Northeast to 25 in the South. At the college level the range is from 16 in the North Central and South to 18 in the West.

Regional differences in the ratio of teachers to total population are small at the elementary and secondary levels and larger at the college level. There is a college teacher for every 905 persons in the West, and one for every 1,169 persons in the South. These differences reflect the lower proportion of college-age youth in the South who attend college.

Table III–8.—RESIDENCE PATTERNS OF TEACHERS, BY LEVEL OF TEACHING, AND OF
THE TOTAL POPULATION, BY COLOR: 1960

Area of residence and color	Percent distribution			Teachers per 100,000 population	
	Total population	College teachers	Teachers below college level	College teachers	Teachers below college level
Total............................	100.0	100.0	100.0	99	938
Urbanized areas......................	53.4	58.3	50.4	108	884
Central city.........................	32.3	36.0	28.8	110	834
Urban fringe........................	21.1	22.3	21.6	105	960
Other urban......,.................	16.4	28.9	21.4	174	1,226
Rural nonfarm.......................	22.7	12.0	22.4	52	926
Rural farm..........................	7.5	0.8	5.8	11	731
Nonwhite......................	100.0	100.0	100.0	42	703
Urbanized areas......................	58.9	65.2	54.5	47	650
Central city.........................	50.5	50.1	47.4	42	660
Urban fringe........................	8.4	15.1	7.1	76	590
Other urban.........................	13.5	22.4	24.0	70	1,250
Rural nonfarm.......................	19.8	12.2	17.1	26	609
Rural farm..........................	7.8	0.2	4.4	1	394

Source: *1960 Census of Population, Subject Reports, Characteristics of Teachers,* Series
PC(2)–7D, table 1.

Although the situation is changing, nonwhite teaching opportunities have
been heavily concentrated in the South. In 1940, about 89 percent of nonwhite teachers were located in the South; in 1950, about 86 percent; and in
1960, about 71 percent. The proportion of all nonwhite population living in
the South was 74 percent in 1940, 66 percent in 1950, and 56 percent in 1960.

Teaching opportunities for nonwhites vary markedly by region. (See table
III–9.) When the number of nonwhite teachers in each region is compared
with the number of nonwhite pupils, it may be seen that teaching opportunities
for nonwhites have been greatest in the South, where a largely segregated system still existed in 1960. The figures in table III–9 should *not* be interpreted
to mean that nonwhite pupils outside the South are in more overcrowded
schools than are other pupils. This may or may not be true, but the ratios also
reflect the greater tendency in the North and West for nonwhite pupils to have
white teachers.

At the college level, opportunities for nonwhite teachers are also more
heavily concentrated in the South, where there is a nonwhite teacher for every
18 nonwhite college students. (See table III–10.) In the rest of the country
the ratio is 28 nonwhite college students for every nonwhite teacher. Nearly
all the nonwhite college teachers in the South are Negro (94 percent), but
elsewhere this proportion is only 31 percent. The opportunities for Negro
college teachers are as heavily concentrated in the South (which has 81 percent of all Negro college teachers) as are the opportunities for elementary
and secondary teachers (79 percent of all Negro elementary and secondary
teachers are concentrated in the South).

There is very little difference in the proportion of female teachers in communities of different size. Although there is some tendency for the percent of female teachers to be highest among teachers living on farms, and lowest among those living in rural-nonfarm areas, the differences are not large. Teachers living on farms are older than other teachers. Age differences in cities of different size and in rural nonfarm areas are generally very small. There is no evidence in the census statistics that the fast-growing suburbs have larger proportions of young teachers than do other areas.

Table III–9.—RATIO OF PUPILS TO ELEMENTARY AND SECONDARY SCHOOL TEACHERS, BY REGION AND COLOR: 1960

[Numbers in thousands]

Region and color	Teachers	Pupils	Ratio[1]
Northeast:			
Total......................................	412	9,519	23.1
Nonwhite.................................	12	700	58.3
North Central:			
Total......................................	485	11,868	24.5
Nonwhite.................................	17	894	52.6
South:			
Total......................................	509	12,818	25.2
Nonwhite.................................	102	3,083	30.2
West:			
Total......................................	276	6,629	24.0
Nonwhite.................................	13	575	44.2

[1] Many of the nonwhite pupils outside the South are taught by white teachers. These ratios do not indicate the extent of crowding or the lack of it in schools serving nonwhites, see text.

Source: *1960 Census of Population, Subject Reports, Characteristics of Teachers*, Series PC(2)–7D, table 4, and *1960 Census of Population*, Vol. I, *Characteristics of the Population*, Part 1, U.S. Summary, table 102.

Age differences among teachers in different regions are also small; no one part of the country appears to be attracting a disproportionate number of young or old teachers. No regional median age of teachers differed from the national median for the same sex and level of teaching by as much as two years.

Table III–10.—NONWHITE COLLEGE TEACHERS AND COLLEGE STUDENTS, BY RACE, FOR THE UNITED STATES, THE SOUTH, AND ALL OTHER REGIONS: 1960

Subject	Total	Negro	Other
United States:			
Teachers................................	8,704	5,910	2,794
Students[1].............................	189,649	145,496	44,153
Ratio....................................	21.8	24.6	15.8
South:			
Teachers................................	5,132	4,803	329
Percent.................................	100.0	93.6	6.4
All other regions:			
Teachers................................	3,572	1,107	2,465
Percent.................................	100.0	31.0	69.0

[1] Enrollment data for college students limited to 17-to-34-year-old population.

Source: *1960 Census of Population, Subject Reports, Characteristics of Teachers*. Series PC(2)–7D. table 1. and *School Enrollment*. Series PC(2)–5A. table 1.

Mobility of teachers

There is a sharp contrast between the mobility of college teachers and those in elementary and secondary schools. Comparisons for 1960 are limited to the State of birth and State of residence in 1960. Elementary and secondary teachers are slightly less mobile than the total population in the labor force or than all professional workers. About two-thirds of all elementary and secondary teachers are still living in the State where they were born; for the total population the comparable figure is 60 percent. By contrast, college teachers more often come from other areas. Only about one-third were living in their native State in 1960, and nearly an equal number were born in a region other than the one in which they were then teaching. (See table III-11.)

Table III–11.—Distribution by Birthplace and Residence of Teachers, persons in the Civilian Labor Force, and Professional Workers, by Color and Sex: 1960

Occupation group and color	Total	Same region		Different region	Foreign born	Other and unknown
		Same State	Different State			
MALE CIVILIAN LABOR FORCE						
Total.............................	100.0	60.5	13.1	16.6	6.6	3.2
Professional workers....................	100.0	52.1	18.0	22.9	6.3	0.7
College teachers......................	100.0	30.6	24.7	33.5	10.0	1.2
Elementary teachers....................	100.0	64.0	15.4	18.0	2.1	0.5
Secondary teachers....................	100.0	64.2	16.7	16.4	2.1	0.6
Nonwhite..........................	100.0	52.5	12.2	25.9	3.9	5.5
Professional workers....................	100.0	48.3	15.1	23.2	12.5	0.9
College teachers......................	100.0	23.7	24.6	18.0	32.6	1.1
Elementary teachers....................	100.0	68.2	12.7	17.6	0.9	0.6
Secondary teachers....................	100.0	69.8	16.1	12.5	1.4	0.2
FEMALE CIVILIAN LABOR FORCE						
Total.............................	100.0	59.9	13.6	16.9	6.1	3.5
Professional workers....................	100.0	58.3	17.0	19.2	4.6	0.9
College teachers......................	100.0	38.7	23.8	27.9	8.1	1.5
Elementary teachers....................	100.0	66.6	15.1	15.7	2.0	0.6
Secondary teachers....................	100.0	63.6	17.9	15.5	2.4	0.6
Nonwhite..........................	100.0	53.3	12.9	26.2	2.4	5.2
Professional workers....................	100.0	58.6	13.5	22.6	4.2	1.1
College teachers......................	100.0	35.7	29.7	22.5	10.6	1.5
Elementary teachers....................	100.0	73.2	11.7	13.7	0.7	0.7
Secondary teachers....................	100.0	69.8	16.4	12.2	0.9	0.7

Source: *1960 Census of Population, Subject Reports, Occupational Characteristics*, Series PC(2)-7A, table 8.

These lifetime percentages of migrants have not been adjusted for differences in age between teachers and all professionals, or between teachers and all workers. If the percentages had been adjusted, the teachers would have appeared to be somewhat less mobile, since their average age is greater than that of the total labor force.

Nonwhite elementary and secondary teachers include a slightly higher percentage of persons working in their own State of birth than do all elementary and secondary teachers. At the college level, a high percent of nonwhite teachers are foreign born—33 percent for men, 11 percent for women. Since about two-thirds of nonwhite college teachers are Negro, and most Negroes are native, these figures indicate that most of the nonwhites who are not Negroes are foreign born.

Although elementary and secondary teachers are no more likely to have moved away from their State of birth than are other workers, unpublished data from the 1950 Census for elementary and secondary teachers indicate that they are more likely than the population as a whole to be migrants. In 1950, 12.4 percent of male teachers, 7.0 percent of female teachers, and only 5.6 percent of the total population was comprised of migrants.[9] The 1960 Census indicates that professional workers are much more migratory than all workers, male professionals are almost twice as migratory, and female professionals about 58 percent more migratory. This indicates that teachers move across county lines more often than the general population, but elementary and secondary teachers do not tend to move away from the State and region of their birth.

Family status of teachers

In the earlier part of this chapter we described the rise in the percent of married women teachers. Most of the women in the teaching profession are members of families, and a majority of the families include children under 18. However, the types of families of women who are college teachers and of nonwhite women who are teachers differ from the general pattern.

Compared with other women teachers, women in college teaching are much more likely to be single. If they are married and living with their husbands they are about as likely as other women teachers to have children under 18, but more likely to have children under 6. The college teachers are less likely than other women teachers to drop out of teaching while their children are under 6. (See table III–12.)

There is a sharp contrast between women public school and college teachers both in their careers and family patterns. Public school teachers do not defer marriage for a career. Between 51 and 62 percent of the married elementary and secondary teachers who are living with their husbands have children under 18. Teachers below the college level tend to drop out of teaching when their children are young, and to reenter when all their children are in school. The proportion of married teachers with children aged 6 to 17 (35.7 percent) actually exceeds the national percentage (26.1) although the percent of teachers with children under 6 is only about half the national average. (See table III–13.) These differences are partly due to the older average age of married teachers compared with the average age of all married women.

Table III–12.—FAMILY STATUS OF FEMALE TEACHERS, BY LEVEL OF TEACHING AND COLOR: 1960

Level of teaching and color	Total	Single	Children under 18 years old				No children under 18 years old	
			Married, spouse present		Other		Married, spouse present	Other
			Children under 6	Children 6 to 18	Children under 6	Children 6 to 18		
TOTAL								
College......................	100.0	50.3	9.5	8.8	0.9	2.2	17.0	11.3
Elementary school:								
Public......................	100.0	22.0	10.6	22.5	0.8	3.2	30.9	10.0
Private.....................	100.0	54.8	7.2	15.9	0.5	2.0	14.4	5.2
Secondary school:								
Public......................	100.0	30.3	10.4	20.0	0.8	2.7	27.2	8.7
Private.....................	100.0	65.7	5.3	8.6	0.4	1.3	13.4	5.3
NONWHITE								
College......................	100.0	24.6	12.1	14.4	0.7	5.1	19.5	23.6
Elementary school:								
Public......................	100.0	18.3	17.4	15.8	2.8	4.0	26.7	15.0
Private.....................	100.0	22.1	14.0	15.6	4.0	6.0	22.7	15.6
Secondary school:								
Public......................	100.0	24.0	16.5	14.4	2.7	3.9	24.9	13.6
Private.....................	100.0	36.3	9.6	7.7	4.5	3.0	24.9	14.0

Source: *1960 Census of Population, Subject Reports, Characteristics of Teachers,* Series PC(2)–7D, table 5.

The proportion of private school teachers who are single is more than double that of public school teachers, probably because many private school teachers are members of religious orders.

Women college teachers differ from other women teachers primarily in deferring marriage for careers. If they do marry and have children, they are less likely to drop out of teaching and reenter later. Reentry into college teaching where great stress is placed on keeping knowledge current, is probably more difficult than reentry into elementary teaching, where patterns of reeducation and retraining are well established.

Table III–13.—PERCENT OF EVER-MARRIED WOMEN IN HUSBAND-WIFE FAMILIES, AND DISTRIBUTION OF HUSBAND-WIFE FAMILIES BY NUMBER OF OWN CHILDREN, FOR ALL WOMEN AND WOMEN ELEMENTARY AND SECONDARY SCHOOL TEACHERS, BY COLOR: 1960

Marital status and number of own children	Total		Nonwhite	
	All women	Women elementary and secondary school teachers	All women	Women elementary and secondary school teachers
Women ever married............................	100.0	100.0	100.0	100.0
In husband-wife families........................	76.6	82.0	62.3	72.9
Husband-wife families...........................	100.0	100.0	100.0	100.0
With own children under 18 years old.............	59.3	53.2	57.8	55.4
One or more own children under 6 years old....	33.2	17.5	37.5	29.1
All own children 6 to 17 years old.............	26.1	35.7	20.3	26.3
With no own children under 18 years old.........	40.7	46.8	42.2	44.6

Source: *1960 Census of Population,* Vol. I, *Characteristics of the Population,* Part 1, U.S. Summary, table 176; *Subject Reports, Families,* Series PC(2)–4A, table 51; and *Characteristics of Teachers,* Series PC(2)–7D, table 5.

The family patterns of nonwhite women teachers differ from those of other women teachers in that the former are less likely to drop out when their children are young. This is probably due more to economic necessity than to the need to maintain professional competence, as is the case with women college teachers. Nonwhite college teachers exhibit other variations in the family pattern: a much higher percent are married than among white women college teachers, but they rank highest in the proportion (nearly 30 percent) who are separated, divorced, or widowed.

To summarize, the basic family pattern for women teachers below college is marriage, temporary retirement from teaching when the children are of preschool age, and reentry to teaching when the children are older. For college teachers and nonwhites there are a number of variations on this family pattern which seem to relate to both professional requirements and family economic conditions.

Occupations of spouses of teachers

Nearly all male teachers and a majority of female teachers live in families with their wives or husbands. The occupation of the spouse has a bearing on the teacher's economic position, family status, and relation to his job.

As we might expect, the husbands of most women teachers are employed. The figure is over 90 percent for most categories of women teachers, and the proportion of working husbands is about the same for elementary, secondary, and college teachers. We might also expect that male teachers with higher salaries would be less likely than those with lower salaries to have working wives. Although available data do not permit a direct test of this assumption, we can compare the percent of working wives of male teachers by teaching level and color, which are indirect measures of income. Table III–14 shows that there is a relationship of the sort expected; only 34 percent of the wives of college teachers work, 44 percent of the wives of secondary teachers work, and 47 percent of the wives of elementary teachers work. A much higher percent of the wives of nonwhite teachers work, which may indicate differing family patterns and traditions as well as economic differences. This is illustrated by the fact that nonwhite male college teachers earn about the same as all male teachers below college, but have a substantially higher percent of working wives.

There are large regional variations in the percent of wives of male teachers who work. The highest percent of working wives is found in the South where salaries are lowest, and the second highest percent in the West, where salaries are highest. Perhaps the higher percent of working wives of teachers in the West reflects greater prosperity and thus greater job availability, or perhaps it merely reflects less commitment in the West to the traditional idea that women should keep house rather than work. Since male teachers in each region have about the same median age, the higher percent of working wives in the West is not a reflection of age differences.

Table III–14.—Percent of Married Teachers With Spouse Present Having Spouse in the Labor Force, by Level of Teaching, Type of School System, and Color: 1960

Level of teaching and color	Total	Male	Female
ALL CLASSES			
College teachers..........................	40.7	34.3	91.9
Elementary teachers.......................	83.9	47.0	91.8
Public.................................	83.6	47.2	91.6
Private................................	86.7	44.2	93.3
Secondary teachers........................	62.1	44.4	92.4
Public.................................	62.5	45.1	92.5
Private................................	56.3	36.5	91.9
NONWHITE			
College teachers..........................	68.3	59.3	95.3
Elementary teachers.......................	88.0	67.1	92.4
Public.................................	88.2	67.8	92.7
Private................................	84.7	50.4	89.2
Secondary teachers........................	81.6	70.9	93.7
Public.................................	81.9	71.4	94.1
Private................................	72.4	62.7	85.1

Source: *1960 Census of Population, Subject Reports, Characteristics of Teachers,* Series PC(2)–7D, table 6.

If a male teacher has a working wife, she also is likely to be a teacher. About one-third of college teachers' wives who work do so as teachers, while slightly over one-half of male elementary and secondary teachers' wives who have jobs are teachers. The percent of husbands of women teachers who are also teachers is unlikely to be as high as the figures given above, since there is an excess of women over men among teachers. If all of the men in teaching below the college level were married to women teachers, the percent of married women teachers with teacher husbands could be a maximum of 66 percent. Actually about 19 percent of women secondary teachers have husbands who are also teachers, while 13 percent of women elementary teachers have teacher husbands. (See table III–15.) There is a noticeable tendency for husbands and wives who are both teachers to work at the same level of school.

The husband-wife teacher combination is even more prevalent among non-whites than among all teachers. This undoubtedly reflects the concentration of professional opportunities for nonwhites in teaching. About 70 percent of the wives of nonwhite male teachers who have jobs are also teachers. About one-half of all wives of nonwhite male elementary and secondary teachers are also teachers; of the remainder, 20 percent work at other jobs and 30 percent are not working. For all male teachers, only about one-fourth have wives who also teach, another 20 percent have wives who work at other jobs, and about 55 percent have nonworking wives. There is probably no other large occupational group in which so high a proportion of both husbands and wives work in the same profession.

Table III–15.—Occupational Distribution of Teachers' Spouses in the Labor
Force, by Teachers' Sex, Color, and Level of Teaching: 1960

Level of teaching, color, and sex	Total in labor force	Occupation of spouse					
		College teacher	Secondary teacher	Other teacher	Other professional	Other white collar	Other occupation[1]
TOTAL							
Male							
College........................	100.0	9.4	8.5	18.8	27.5	29.4	6.4
Elementary....................	100.0	0.3	6.3	45.9	11.9	26.2	9.4
Secondary.....................	100.0	0.7	15.7	34.6	14.1	27.7	7.2
Female							
College........................	100.0	28.0	5.3	2.6	31.2	20.8	12.1
Elementary....................	100.0	1.2	6.8	5.5	17.4	30.7	39.4
Secondary.....................	100.0	2.6	12.9	3.2	21.1	32.2	28.0
NONWHITE							
Male							
College........................	100.0	18.7	11.4	24.6	22.8	16.0	6.5
Elementary....................	100.0	0.3	8.8	61.0	8.5	10.8	10.6
Secondary.....................	100.0	1.1	21.2	46.8	12.8	8.8	9.3
Female							
College........................	100.0	34.6	8.2	3.3	21.3	8.1	24.5
Elementary....................	100.0	1.1	9.0	10.1	13.3	17.1	49.4
Secondary.....................	100.0	2.6	18.9	7.0	13.8	18.4	39.3

[1] Includes occupations not reported.

Source: *1960 Census of Population, Subject Reports, Characteristics of Teachers,* Series
PC(2)–7D, table 6.

The need to supplement the income of the household is one reason why large
proportions of teachers are in families where both husband and wife are working. Some teachers supplement their income by moonlighting, or working at
more than one job. Studies of multiple-job holders by the Bureau of Labor
Statistics in December 1959 and December 1960[10] found that 23.5 percent of
the male teachers in 1960, and 22.1 percent in 1959, had more than one job. On
the other hand, only 2.5 percent of the women teachers at that time had more
than one paid job. In December moonlighting is undoubtedly high because of
the Christmas season. It should be noted that an earlier survey, taken in July
1958, indicated that only about 9 percent of the men teachers had more than
one job. Very few teachers would have been working as teachers in July, so the
figures are not comparable with the later surveys taken in December.

Income of teachers by age

In general, the rise in teachers' earnings with increasing age is relatively
modest. The differential in earnings at ages 18 to 24, when most teachers earn
starting salaries, and earnings at 45 years and over is about 50 percent for
women elementary teachers, about 70 percent for women secondary teachers,

F. Lee Bushong.

about 75 percent for men elementary teachers, and 80 to 110 percent for men secondary teachers. (See figures III–6 and III–7.)   These are differences in income that existed in 1960 for teachers of different ages.   Actual income changes in the next 25 years of the cohort of teachers 20 to 24 years old may be quite different from these cross-sectional statistics.   The earnings differential by sex is greater than the differential in earnings between elementary and secondary teachers.   The earnings differential between men and women teachers at the beginning ages is small (about $100 a year difference in median earnings), but by ages 30 to 34 the differential in favor of the men is about $1,000, and remains about the same for ages above 35.

Figure III–6.—MEDIAN EARNINGS OF ELEMENTARY AND SECONDARY TEACHERS WITH 4 YEARS OF COLLEGE EDUCATION, BY SEX, AGE, AND LEVEL OF TEACHING: 1960

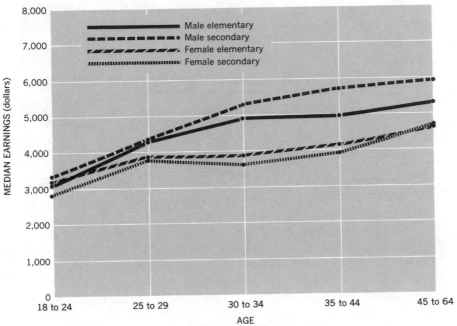

Source: *1960 Census of Population, Subject Reports, Characteristics of Teachers*, PC(2)–7D, table 10.

Since most school systems have a salary schedule which pays men and women equally for equal work, how can this large sex differential in income be explained?   Several factors seem to be involved.   First, as indicated earlier, women are likely to drop out of teaching while their children are young; thus the women teachers aged 30 to 34 may have less experience on the average than their male counterparts.   Second, over 20 percent of the men supplement their teaching income with earnings from other jobs, while only about 2 percent of the women hold other jobs. Third, most part-time teachers are women. About 16 percent of women elementary, secondary, and college teachers worked less than 27 weeks in 1959, while the comparable percentages for men were 5 to 7 percent. Fourth, men are more likely than women to move into administrative positions which will add to their income.

Figure III–7.—MEDIAN EARNINGS OF TEACHERS, BY AGE, LEVEL OF TEACHING, AND TYPE OF SCHOOLING: 1960

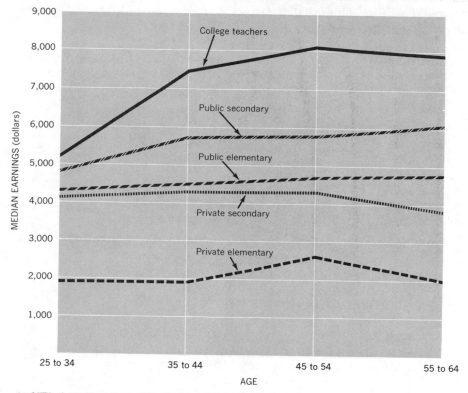

Source: *1960 Census of Population, Subject Reports, Characteristics of Teachers,* PC(2)–7D, table 7.

The percent of men teachers with master's degrees is more than twice the comparable figure for women at every age (figure III–5), and the percent of men with less than a college degree is about half the comparable percent for women. Since most school systems pay more to teachers with additional education, a good part of the sex difference in pay reflects differences in educational attainment.

The differential in earnings between persons with 4 years of college and those with 5 or more is also substantial. At ages 18 to 24 the differential is $300 to $700 a year; by ages 30 to 34, it is $900 to $1,300 a year; and it remains at that level for older ages. This differential reflects not only the salary increments paid by school systems for additional education, but also the tendency of persons with advanced degrees to stay in teaching and to have more years of experience even at the same age level; hence the teacher between 30 and 34 who holds a master's degree has probably had several years more experience than the teacher with only a bachelor's degree who may have dropped out of the profession for several years.

The earnings differential by color was much greater for men than for women. Nonwhite male teachers had earnings $1,000 to $1,400 a year lower than all male teachers, while for women the comparable differential was $400 to $500. This suggests that part of the differential was the result of fewer chances for a second job for nonwhite men, and part was a reflection of regional factors—high proportions of nonwhites live in the South, where all teaching salaries are lower.

Total family income of teachers

The male teacher is usually the major breadwinner in his family, in the sense of earning more than half of the family income. Female teachers in the highest earnings category (above $7,000 a year) also make the major contribution to the family income, but those with lower levels of earnings usually have husbands who make as much as or more than they do. (See table III–16.)

While it is not possible to identify these relationships precisely, it appears that no matter what the level of the wife's earnings as a teacher, the average contribution of husbands to family income is about the same. That is, the husband's income (for those in the labor force) is about $5,500 a year when the wife earns $3,000 to $5,000 a year at teaching, and about $6,000 a year when the wife earns $5,000 or more. Another way of saying the same thing is that income of women teachers is not correlated with their husband's income.

Since a high proportion of women teachers have husbands who are professionals, or who hold other white-collar jobs, it appears that the median income of their husbands is below average for their occupation. The husband's income relative to the average for his occupation is undoubtedly an important determinant of whether the wife continues in teaching. If the husband's income is below the average for his occupation the wife will be under considerable economic pressure to remain in teaching, or, if she has dropped out to raise children, to return as soon as possible.

Wives of men teachers in the lowest income bracket ($3,000 to $5,000) contribute about one-third of the family income—an average of about $2,000 a year; for men teachers in the middle income group ($5,000 to $7,000), the wives' contribution to family income declines sharply to less than $1,000 a year, but in the highest teacher-income bracket ($7,000), the wives' contribution rises again—to $2,000 a year. This suggests that men teachers in the $5,000 to

$7,000 income range may have families with small children, and hence a lower proportion of working wives; by the time the man's income has risen above $7,000 his children may be old enough to allow his wife to reenter the labor force.

Table III–16.—MEDIAN INCOME OF FAMILIES WITH TEACHERS AND ESTIMATED PERCENT OF TOTAL INCOME CONTRIBUTED BY TEACHERS, BY LEVEL OF TEACHING, COLOR, SEX, AND INCOME OF TEACHERS: 1960

Level of teaching, color, and sex	Median income of families with teachers earning—			Estimated percent of family income contributed by teachers earning—		
	$3,000 to $4,999	$5,000 to $6,999	$7,000 and over	$3,000 to $4,999	$5,000 to $6,999	$7,000 and over[1]
TOTAL						
Male						
College..........................	5,092	6,783	11,723	79	88	68
Elementary......................	5,977	6,909	9,794	67	87	82
Secondary.......................	5,846	6,884	10,197	68	87	78
Female						
College..........................	9,682	11,467	13,317	41	52	60
Elementary......................	8,721	11,444	13,592	46	52	59
Secondary.......................	8,979	11,376	13,802	45	53	58
NONWHITE						
Male						
College..........................	(B)	8,080	11,871	(B)	74	67
Elementary......................	6,402	8,841	11,508	62	68	70
Secondary.......................	6,390	8,907	12,010	63	67	67
Female						
College..........................	(B)	(B)	(B)	(B)	(B)	(B)
Elementary......................	7,186	10,840	12,967	56	55	62
Secondary.......................	7,809	10,290	(B)	51	58	(B)

B   Base less than 1,000.

Source: *1960 Census of Population, Subject Reports, Characteristics of Teachers,* Series PC(2)–7D, table 11.

Teachers in the labor reserve

In 1960, for the first time, the census provided information about the characteristics of former teachers. (See table III–17.) Persons who had taught at any time in the 10 years preceding the 1960 Census were defined as members of the "labor reserve." While some were quite likely to return to teaching, others probably were not; hence the total number in the labor reserve is not a good estimate of those who could readily return to teaching if they were offered a job.[11] It is possible to identify some of the characteristics of teachers in the labor reserve, and to make some estimates of the number who might return to teaching under present conditons. If salaries and working conditions for teachers changed substantially, for better or for worse, then the proportion of the labor reserve that might be drawn back into teaching would vary accordingly.

Nearly all teachers in the labor reserve are women. If men leave teaching they go to another job; up to age 55, the number of male teachers in the labor reserve is less than 2 percent of the number in the labor force.

Table III–17.—COMPARISON OF LABOR RESERVE WITH LABOR FORCE, BY LEVEL OF TEACHING, AGE, AND SEX: 1960

Level of teaching and age	Male			Female		
	Persons in labor force	Persons in labor reserve	Labor reserve as percent of labor force	Persons in labor force	Persons in labor reserve	Labor reserve as percent of labor force
25 TO 34 YEARS OLD						
College teachers...................	41,288	2,135	5.2	8,219	4,350	52.9
Public elementary.................	60,785	1,170	1.9	169,061	142,641	84.4
Public secondary..................	104,426	2,239	2.1	47,906	35,812	74.8
35 TO 44 YEARS OLD						
College teachers..................	40,631	541	1.3	8,824	3,267	37.0
Public elementary.................	33,988	528	1.6	171,463	52,449	30.6
Public secondary..................	68,645	832	1.2	51,247	15,253	29.8
45 TO 54 YEARS OLD						
College teachers..................	25,962	271	1.0	8,842	1,314	14.9
Public elementary.................	20,810	369	1.8	249,310	33,230	13.3
Public secondary..................	50,035	593	1.2	67,563	7,859	11.6
55 TO 64 YEARS OLD						
College teachers..................	15,794	584	3.7	6,626	1,211	18.3
Public elementary.................	10,427	730	7.0	144,298	27,575	21.2
Public secondary..................	27,383	1,378	5.0	42,168	7,951	21.0

Source: *1960 Census of Population, Subject Reports, Characteristics of Teachers*, Series PC(2)–7D, tables 3 and 12.

In contrast, the number of women teachers in the labor reserve at ages 25 to 34 is almost 80 percent of the number of women at the same ages who are actually teaching. This figure drops to 30 percent for women aged 35 to 44 and to 12 percent for women aged 45 to 54. These figures suggest that there is a tremendous potential for rapid expansion of the teaching force, if need be. However, these figures may be deceptive, since many of the women who have left teaching have no intention of returning, while others who might like to return may be too old, or may lack enough education to be readily employable. There is no way to determine people's intentions from census data, but some members of the labor reserve have characteristics which suggest that they are not likely to reenter teaching. For example, about 106,000 women teachers in the labor reserve (22 percent) are over age 55, and about 123,000 of those under 55 have less than 4 years of college. People with these characteristics are probably less likely than others to return to teaching. About 140,000 teachers in the labor reserve aged 20 to 34 have children under 6 years old. These women constitute about 70 percent of the married teachers in their age group in the labor reserve. Some of them will probably return to teaching when their children are older. The characteristics of the teachers in the labor reserve suggest that probably no more than one-fourth to one-half could be expected to return to teaching unless there is a sharp change in incentives for teachers.[12] Barring a war or other major crisis, the number of college graduates prepared for teaching will be about 75 percent greater in the next decade, and teachers in the labor reserve may have more competition from college graduates when they try to reenter teaching.

It is important to realize that the number of teachers entering the profession each year is quite large. According to estimates from the U.S. Office of Education, there were between 175,000 and 200,000 new teachers each year for the period from 1960 to 1963.[13] Thus, even if 40 percent of the teacher labor reserve were to reenter teaching, they would match in numbers only one year's supply of entering teachers.

Future teacher supply and demand

Since the growth of enrollment at the elementary and secondary levels will be only about one-half as great between 1965 and 1974 as it was between 1955 and 1964, the total need for new teachers will not be as great in the next 10 years as in the past 10. Specific areas characterized by heavy immigration, low salaries, or unfavorable working conditions, may continue to experience shortages even though the national picture improves. The slowdown in enrollment growth will have less effect on national needs than might be imagined, however, since even in the period of rapid enrollment growth from 1955 to 1964, about two-thirds of all entering teachers were replacements for existing teachers.[14] In the period of enrollment growth at a lower rate during the next decade, "replacement" teachers will constitute 75 to 80 percent of all teachers added.[15] Estimation of the replacement need, or the number of teachers who will leave teaching each year, is the principal problem in determining how many new teachers there must be. The Office of Education has used an annual replacement rate of 8 percent,[16] which implies an average teaching career of 12.5 years in an occupational group of stable size. Since teaching has been expanding rapidly in the last decade, an 8 percent replacement rate would be consistent with an average teaching career of about 10 years. This is inconsistent both with NEA survey data which indicate an average teaching career of about 13.4 years, and with a median age of about 44 years for women teachers in 1960. The continued rise in the real income of teachers, the acceptance of the pattern of working wives, and the importance of teachers' income in the total family income, all indicate that the length of teaching careers may continue to increase; certainly there is no reason to assume that they will decrease.

An annual replacement rate of 6.7 percent would be consistent with a 15-year teaching career, a 5-percent rate with a 20-year career. These lower rates of attrition would produce substantial decreases in the number of teachers needed in the next decade. (See table III–18.) It has been estimated that in 1960 about 175,000 new teachers entered the profession. The projections indicate a slight decline in the annual needs for new teachers between 1965 and 1970, and a rise in 1975 and 1980 to levels slightly above those of 1960. Although these projections are lower than those of the Office of Education and the Bureau of Labor Statistics (because of the lower replacement rate used), all show a relatively constant level of demand for new teachers, fluctuating between 160,000 and 180,000 a year in the Office of Education projections, between 186,000 and 206,000 in the Bureau of Labor Statistics projections, and between 140,000 and 170,000 in our own projections.[17]

Table III–18.—PROJECTED ANNUAL NEEDS FOR NEW ELEMENTARY AND SECONDARY
TEACHERS: 1960 TO 1980

[Numbers in thousands]

Year	Total number of teachers	Number needed for enrollment growth[1]	Number needed for replacement[2]		Annual total of teachers needed
			High rate	Low rate	
1960	1,682	53	112	112	175
1965	1,917	33	128	115	148–161
1970	2,079	31	138	111	142–169
1975	2,249	46	150	120	166–196
1980	2,479	46	165	132	178–211

[1] From U.S. Office of Education estimate.

[2] Assumes high enrollment projection. High replacement rate is 6.67 percent annually; low replacement rate declines from 6.67 percent to 5.33 percent between 1960 and 1970 and is constant thereafter. Projections assume no change in teacher-pupil ratios at either elementary or secondary levels.

Source: Derived from enrollment projections in table I–7.

Between 1960 and 1970 there will be an increase of about 80 percent in the annual number of bachelor's degrees awarded in education, and an increase of about 67 percent in master's degrees. Increases in degrees granted in other major fields from which teachers are drawn will be comparable. It is clear that with a greatly increased supply of potential teachers, and a relatively stable demand, teacher recruitment may change substantially.

Additional demands for people trained as teachers may also be generated by the newly developing antipoverty programs and other social service programs. No quantitative assessment of their magnitude has been made, but their impact on the future teacher recruitment situation could be substantial. Further sharp declines in the number and percent of teachers with less than a college degree seem likely. Teachers who drop out of teaching for family or other reasons may find it more difficult to reenter teaching in competition with recent graduates. A more adequate total supply of teachers will not solve all problems of teacher shortage, because there are many problems of distribution; shortages may continue in low-paying isolated rural schools and in slum schools, while middle class suburban schools may have several applicants for each vacancy.

Whether the greater availability of candidates will lead to improved selectivity is not clear. The schools will have an opportunity to obtain better teachers from the larger supply that will be available if educational administrators are willing and able to select them on merit and to retain those who prove effective.

NOTES

[1] Census figures for 1900 indicated that about 90 percent of the college teachers were male, while the Office of Education indicated only 80 percent were male; the Office of Education figures are more consistent with data from later decades.

[2] David Kaplan and Claire Casey, *Occupational Trends in the U.S. 1900 to 1950*, Bureau of the Census, Working Paper No. 5, 1958.

[3] U.S. Bureau of Education, *The Teaching Staff of Secondary Schools in the U.S.*, Bulletin 1909, No. 4. Based on questionnaire sent to 5,000 secondary schools.

[4] U.S. Office of Education, *National Survey of the Education of Teachers*, Bulletin 1933, No. 10, Vol. 6, by E. S. Evenden and others.

[5] N E A Research Bulletin, "The Status of the American Public School Teacher," Vol. 35, No. 1, February 1957, and *The American Public School Teacher 1960-61*. National Education Association Research, Monograph 1963-M2.

[6] E. L. Thorndike, op. cit. Table (unnumbered) Years of Education Beyond the Elementary Course.

[7] Evenden, op. cit., Vol. 6, table 2, p. 42.

[8] Median teacher (below college) income in 1959 reported in the census was $4,744 for teachers who worked 27 weeks or more. Office of Education average salary reported was $4,939 in 1958-1959, and $5,135 in 1959-1960; approximately $5,017 for *calendar* year 1959; salary averages are for full-time regular teachers in public schools.

[9] Figures for 1950 refer to a county of residence in 1950 other than that in 1949, figures for 1960 refer to a county of residence in 1960 other than that in 1955; specific figures on the migration of teachers between 1955 and 1960 are not available in the 1960 Census.

[10] U.S. Bureau of Labor Statistics, *Special Labor Force Report, No. 18,* "Multiple Job Holders in December 1960"; and No. 9, "Multiple Job Holders in December 1959."

[11] None of the members of the labor reserve are seeking work; if they were, they would be defined as members of the labor force.

NOTES—Continued

[12] Two recent Office of Education surveys on turnover of public school teachers in 1957-1958 and 1959-1960 indicate that almost one-fourth of new elementary teachers hired were reentries. See U.S. Office of Education, *Teacher Turnover in the Public Schools 1957-58* (1959), p. 4; and *Teacher Turnover in Public Elementary and Secondary Schools 1959-60* (1963), p. 9. These figures appear consistent with a return of one-fourth to one-third of the teaching reserve. One-fourth of entering teachers would represent a group of 45,000 to 50,000 returning to teaching each year from the labor reserve.

[13] *Projections of Educational Statistics to 1973-74* (1964 Edition). Washington: U.S. Government Printing Office, OE 10030, tables 14 and 15.

[14] Ibid., tables 14 and 15.

[15] Maxine Stewart, "A New Look at Manpower Needs in Teaching," *Occupational Outlook Quarterly,* Vol. 8, May 1964, estimates that more than 4 times as many teachers will be needed for replacement as for growth in the next 10 years (1965-1975).

[16] Ibid. Gives an annual separation rate of 8.4 for elementary women teachers, 9.9 for secondary women teachers, 6.0 for elementary men, and 6.5 for secondary men. These separation rates for women include a second separation for a substantial fraction of the women, perhaps as much as 25 percent. Reduction of the separation rates to allow for multiple separations by about a fourth of the women would make the separation rates consistent with a 15-year average teaching career, and would also explain the apparent paradox that men have lower separation rates but shorter teaching careers.

[17] *Projections of Educational Statistics to 1973-74* (1964 Edition). Washington: U.S. Government Printing Office, OE 10030, tables 14 and 15, and Maxine Stewart, op. cit.

CHAPTER IV

TRENDS AND PATTERNS
OF ILLITERACY

Introduction

Literacy, or the ability to read and write in some language, was the first measure of educational attainment reported in a census of the United States. The 1840 Census, the first to ask a question on school attendance, was also the first to include a question on literacy, and the question was asked in each census thereafter through 1930. Since then the literacy question has not been used. By the time of the 1940 Census most people in the United States could read and write, and thus literacy rates were no longer an adequate measure of educational attainment among different population groups. However, literacy questions have been asked periodically in national sample surveys of the Census Bureau, most recently in 1959.

It is not surprising that the earlier censuses used literacy as a measure of educational attainment. During the middle decades of the 19th century, before school systems had fully developed and when relatively small numbers of Americans reached secondary school, illiteracy was widespread and was much more common among some groups than among others. Furthermore, the rapid growth of industry and technology generated an increasing need for people who could read and write, and those who possessed these skills stood a better chance of acquiring preferred jobs and advancing within their fields.

Literacy and illiteracy have been variously defined in the several censuses. In this country, literacy is usually defined as the ability to read and write in either English or some other language. In the censuses of 1870 through 1920, separate questions were asked on ability to read and ability to write, and literacy was operationally defined as the ability to write regardless of ability to read. Since the data showed that nearly all persons who were able to write could also read, the different definitions did not greatly affect the statistics. Moreover, many people who were reported as able to write but not able to read could probably write no more than their names. Even though census enumerators were usually instructed not to accept signatures as evidence of writing ability, but rather to identify as literate only those who could write at least a simple message, it is likely that this distinction was sometimes lost, since there was no writing test.[1]

Apart from problems of definition, the measurement of literacy has been affected by variations in data-collecting techniques and in the population covered by the literacy questions. In 1840, the head of the family was asked for the total number of illiterates in the family, a method which undoubtedly led to some understatement of illiteracy; in subsequent censuses, the question was asked about each individual separately. The literacy statistics for 1840, 1850, and 1860 were collected for persons 20 years old and over; from 1870 through 1930, for those 10 years old and over; and in later surveys for persons 14 years old and over.

Historical trends in illiteracy

Colonial to pre-Civil War Period. Prior to 1840, there were no national statistics on literacy and local statistics were scant. Where such data did exist, they had been obtained by the conventional technique of noting what proportion of persons "made their mark" on public documents. Obviously, this method was quite inadequate as a means of measuring illiteracy, and served to understate illiteracy levels as they would be estimated by present-day techniques, since many who signed their names (that is, who could make more than a mark) probably could not write more than their names, and literate men were more likely than illiterate men to be engaged in signing public documents.

It is interesting to note, however, the reports of illiteracy for the Colonial Period. Kilpatrick found the American Dutch to be somewhat more literate than the people of other colonies. Of a small sample of men at Albany in the mid-1600's, 21 percent made their marks; in Flatbush, at the same time, 19 percent of a sample of similar size made their marks. Of a larger sample of 17th century male Virginians who signed jury lists, 46 percent made their marks, as did 40 percent of a still larger sample who signed deeds and depositions. Of German male immigrants 16 years old and over who came to Pennsylvania in the early part of the 18th century, 26 percent made their marks. In all of these colonies, we are told, the illiteracy figures for women were considerably higher than those for men.[2] Obviously, these data can only be used to illustrate the magnitude of illiteracy at the time, since the extent to which these groups were representative of the national, or even other local, populations cannot be determined. It would probably not be far wrong, however, to say that in the Colonial Period one-third to one-half of the adults could not read or write.

It was not until the 1840 Census was published that the public had at least a fair knowledge of the status of illiteracy in the country as a whole. This Census showed that 1 out of 5 persons was illiterate. But the statistics were woefully weak and needed revision. Furthermore, the 1840 Census gave an illiteracy report for whites only; to determine a total illiteracy rate, one must make assumptions about the rate for nonwhites. It is often assumed that all slaves were illiterate[3] and that the rate for the "free colored" population was the same in 1840 as in 1850.[4] By adjusting the reported data accordingly, it may be calculated that about 22.0 percent of the total population 20 years old and over in 1840 was illiterate.

A comparison of the 1840 statistics with those of succeeding censuses and with other information led some observers to regard the published illiteracy level for 1840 as much too low. Leigh reported that Horace Mann judged himself within bounds when he added to the figures of the census on this point "only 30 percent for its undoubted underestimate," and he raised the number of illiterates for 1840 from 550,000 to 700,000. Leigh gives the basis for Mann's revision of the figure, as follows:

> In corroboration of this he quotes from the message of Governor Campbell, of Virginia, in 1839, statements derived from the most reliable sources, the court records of five city and borough courts and ninety-three county courts (out of one hundred and twenty-five counties in the State), to the effect that ". . . almost one-quarter part of the men applying for marriage licenses were unable to write their names." The census report for 1840 gave 58,787 illiterate white adults in Virginia; Governor Campbell's proportion would raise the number to 82,489, or 40 per cent more. From such facts as this, and from careful comparisons of the census reports for the several States, and for the several years 1840, 1850, and 1860, there can be no doubt that the figures of the census may be relied on as much below the painful truth.[5]

Although the basis for revision used by Mann was quite unsubstantial, the method of asking for the total number of illiterates in each household in the 1840 Census, and comparisons of the 1840 figures with other sources, suggest that the reported figures were too low; for the country as a whole, the true illiteracy rate in 1840 for the population 20 years old and over was probably in the range of 25 to 30 percent.

By 1850, when enumeration of illiterates on an individual basis was first introduced, about 22.6 percent of the total population 20 years old and over were reported as illiterate; by 1860, just prior to the Civil War, the reported illiteracy rate was 19.7 percent. Between 1850 and 1860, the illiteracy rate for the white population showed a decline from 10.7 to 8.9 percent. Although statistics for this period were still likely to be unreliable, they were accurate enough to document the downward trend. The development of the public school systems, particularly in the Northern States, had begun to have its effect by this time and the trend toward almost universal literacy in the Nation was well on its way.

Civil War to post-World War I period. The census reports for 1870 showed that 20.0 percent of the population 10 years old and over was illiterate (table IV–1 and figure IV–I). This rate was slightly higher than that recorded for 1860, despite the fact that the 1870 figures included data for the more literate group 10 to 19 years old. Probably the major reason for the apparent increase was the fact that the 1870 Census provided for separate answers to questions about reading and writing, a procedure which no doubt contributed to more ac-

Table IV–1.—PERCENT ILLITERATE AMONG PERSONS 10 YEARS OLD AND OVER, BY RACE AND NATIVITY: 1870 TO 1959

Year[1]	Total	White			Nonwhite		
		Total	Native	Foreign born	Total	Negro	Other races
1959[1]	2.2	1.6	(NA)	(NA)	7.5	(NA)	(NA)
1952[1]	2.5	1.8	(NA)	(NA)	10.2	(NA)	(NA)
1947[1]	2.7	1.8	(NA)	(NA)	11.0	(NA)	(NA)
1940	[2]2.9	[2]2.0	[2]1.1	[2]9.0	[2]11.5	(NA)	(NA)
1930	4.3	[3]3.0	[3]1.6	[3]10.8	[3]16.4	16.3	[3]19.4
1920	6.0	4.0	2.0	13.1	23.0	22.9	25.6
1910	7.7	5.0	3.0	12.7	30.5	30.4	31.6
1900	10.7	6.2	4.6	12.9	44.5	44.5	44.5
1890	13.3	7.7	6.2	13.1	56.8	57.1	45.2
1880	17.0	9.4	8.7	12.0	70.0	(NA)	(NA)
1870	20.0	11.5	(NA)	(NA)	79.9	81.4	20.1

NA Not available.

[1] Percents for these years apply to the population 14 years old and over, and are undoubtedly slightly higher than for the population 10 years old and over. Data on illiteracy were not collected for persons 10 to 13 years old at those dates. For a discussion of other factors affecting the comparability of figures for different years, see source.

[2] Estimated.

[3] Figures revised to include Mexicans as white who were classified with "Other races" in 1930.

Source: U.S. Bureau of the Census, *Current Population Reports—Population Characteristics*, Series P–20, No. 99, table A, and Census records.

curate statistics and hence to less understatement of illiteracy. On the other hand, the new definition of literacy as the ability to write may have led to some reporting of literacy that would not have been so recorded in earlier censuses, when both reading and writing ability were required to classify a person as literate.

The 1870 figures also showed the wide differential in literacy rates between whites and Negroes. Compared with 11.5 percent of whites who were illiterate, 81.4 percent of Negroes could not write even a short message. By 1880, the general illiteracy rate had declined to 17.0 percent; for whites it stood at 9.4 percent, and for nonwhites at 70.0 percent. Only about 12.0 percent of the foreign-born whites were reported to be illiterate, despite the low educational levels of many of the newly arrived immigrants.

Data for 1890 and 1900 showed that there had been a continued decline in the illiteracy of the total population, as well as in that of the native white and Negro populations. In fact, for these groups the illiteracy rate in 1900 was roughly half of what it had been in 1870. In 1900, only 5 out of 100 native whites and 45 out of 100 Negroes 10 years old and over could not write.

There was an increase in illiteracy among foreign-born whites from 1880 to 1890, which was partially offset by a decrease from 1890 to 1900. This decrease appeared only in the youngest and oldest age groups. In the group 15 to 34 years old, which included most of the immigrants of the period, the proportion of illiterates was higher in 1900 than in 1890. This pattern seemed to be related to the changing nationality composition of our immigration. The percentage of immigrants from Southern and Eastern Europe, whose literacy levels were relatively low, had been increasing, while the percentage from Northern and Western Europe, where literacy rates were higher, had been decreasing. Thus, whereas one-eighth of all foreign-born persons 10 years old and over in the Nation were reported as illiterate at the turn of the century, about one-fourth of the immigrants admitted to the country at that time could neither read nor write.[6] This undoubtedly contributed to a slowing down of the national improvement in literacy.

Figure IV–1.—Percent Illiterate Among Persons 10 Years Old and Over, by Race and Nativity: 1870 to 1959

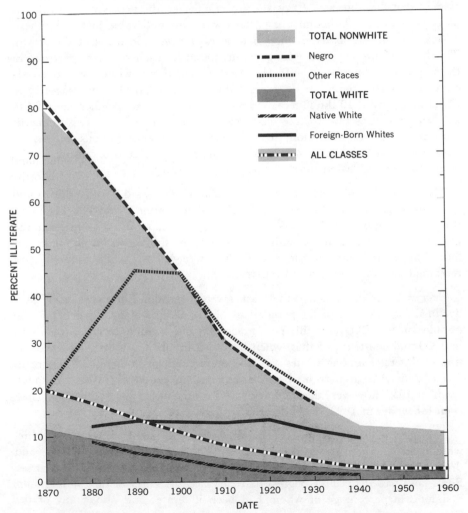

NOTE: Data for 1947, 1952, and 1959 refer to the population 14 years old and over.

Source: Table IV–1.

Analysis of the 1900 Census data on illiteracy by age reveals some very interesting facts about the effect of historical factors on illiteracy. First, the marked changes in opportunities for Negroes to receive formal schooling were reflected in the strikingly different illiteracy rates between the older and younger groups. Four-fifths of the Negroes 55 to 64 years old, who had spent their years of school age under the slavery system, were unable to read and write, compared with less than one-third of the Negroes who were in their teens. Second, among the native white population of native parentage the illiteracy rate for the group 45 to 54 years old was higher than for the next older as well as for the next younger age groups. Since those persons who were between 45 and 54 years old in 1900 had been between 5 and 14 when the Civil War broke out, it is evident that the illiteracy of this age group reflected the poor school conditions of the war years. Although this pattern was most noticeable in the Southern States, it could be observed, though to a lesser extent, in areas of the North. Third, lower illiteracy rates were generally found for each younger age group in the population down to age 10. However, among native whites of native parentage, the illiteracy rate in 1900 was higher at ages 10 to 14 than at ages 15 to 24, although by 1910 the illiteracy rate of the younger group (then aged 20 to 24) was as low as that for the older group (aged 25 to 34). This apparent pattern of "belated education," or the tendency for some persons to learn to read and write after they had become adults, was most pronounced in the South but also appeared in other areas of the country.[7]

The proportion of illiterates in the population decreased further during the first two decades of the 20th century. By 1920, shortly after World War I, 6 0 percent of the population 10 years old and over was illiterate. The rate for the native white population was only 2.0 percent, for the nonwhite population it had dropped to 23.0 percent, and for the foreign-born white group it had remained generally level at 13.1 percent.

Recent decades. During the past several decades, illiteracy rates have declined for all classes of the population. In 1959, only about 2 percent of the population was illiterate; this percentage was one-third of what it had been in 1930 and one-tenth of that which prevailed in 1870. In 1959, the proportion of illiterates among whites was 1.6 percent and for nonwhites, 7.5 percent —a considerable drop from the rates reported in pre-World War I decades. Even in 1959, however, the illiteracy rate for nonwhites was as high as it had been for whites in 1890, seven decades earlier.

The percentage of foreign-born persons who were unable to read and write, which had remained steady from 1880 to 1920, began to decline in 1930 and dropped even further by 1940. Two factors could account for this change: First, laws passed by the Congress had curtailed the entry of new immigrants, a significant percentage of whom had been illiterate; and also, many of the foreign born already in this country who had been illiterate had died, or had acquired the ability to read and write. Second, after the quota system was initiated in 1920, the majority of immigrants came from Northern and Western European countries, and few immigrants from these countries were illiterate.

Although the *percentage* of the population which was illiterate dwindled to a relatively low level, the *number* of illiterates remained substantial. In 1959, about 2.6 million persons not in institutions were reported to be illiterate; 1.7 million of these were white and nearly 1 million were nonwhite. Additionally, an estimated quarter of a million inmates of institutions (persons in mental hospitals, homes for the aged, prisons, and the like) could not read and write. The problem of illiteracy can thus be regarded as still important for American society. Furthermore, since nearly 1 million of the illiterates in 1959 were in the labor force and about 11 percent of these were unemployed, it is obvious that illiteracy presents substantial economic problems.

No matter by what standards we view the prevalence of literacy in the rates were 1.0, 1.3, and 1.5 percent, respectively, there was a relatively lower United States today, we have made noteworthy progress over the past century In the North Central States, the West, and the Northeast, where illiteracy in reducing illiteracy. The United States ranks among the few countries in the world with illiteracy rates under 5 percent. According to a UNESCO report[8] only 32 of 198 countries for which estimates of illiteracy could be made for the period around 1950 had illiteracy rates under 5 percent, 12 had rates between 5 and 10 percent, 12 had rates between 10 and 20 percent, 45 had rates between 20 and 50 percent, and 97 had rates of 50 percent or over. Sixty of the last mentioned, mostly African and Asian nations, had rates exceeding 80 percent. It is interesting to note that the illiteracy rate for nonwhites in the United States around 1950 was lower than the total rates for almost four-fifths of the countries.

States and residence areas. Illiteracy within the United States has varied from area to area. In 1959, the rural-farm population 14 years old and over had a higher illiteracy rate (4.3 percent) than the rural-nonfarm population (2.2 percent) or the urban population (1.7 percent). In 1930 the corresponding rates (for the population 10 years old and over) were 6.9, 4.8, and 3.2 percent, so that gains in literacy were effected in all residence areas during that period of time.

In 1959, inability to read and write was more prevalent in the South, where 4.3 percent of the population was illiterate, than in any of the other regions. proportion of nonwhites than in the South. In 1930, the corresponding rates (for the population 10 years old and over) were 8.3 percent for the South and and 1.9, 2.7, and 3.5 percent, respectively, for the North Central States, the West, and the Northeast. Thus, gains in literacy were also common to all major regions of the country.

An examination of the data for States shows further variations within regions. According to table IV–2, illiteracy rates in 1900 for persons 15 years old and over by States (as presently constituted) ranged from a low of 2.6 percent (in Nebraska) to a high of 40.6 percent (in Alaska). By 1960, the range of estimated illiteracy rates was from 0.7 percent (in Iowa) to 6.3 percent (in Louisiana). In 1900, 12 States had illiteracy rates under 5 percent, whereas in 1960, 47 States and the District of Columbia had rates so low; in 1900, 17 States and the District of Columbia had rates between 5 and 10 percent and 21 States had rates of 10 percent or higher, whereas in 1960, only 3 States had rates over 5 percent. Figure IV–2 portrays the State variations in illiteracy rates for 1960, and figure IV–3 shows the convergence of illiteracy rates for geographic divisions between 1900 and 1960.

Table IV–2.—Percent Illiterate Among Persons 15 Years Old and Over, by State: 1960, 1930, 1900

Region, division, and State	Number illiterate, 1960	Percent illiterate			Region, division, and State	Number illiterate, 1960	Percent illiterate		
		1960[1]	1930	1900			1960[1]	1930	1900
United States...	3,055,000	2.4	4.8	11.3	SOUTH--Con.				
					South Atlantic--Con.				
NORTHEAST					Dist. of Columbia.	11,000	1.9	1.7	9.4
					Virginia.........	94,000	3.4	9.7	24.3
New England:					West Virginia.....	35,000	2.7	5.5	12.6
Maine............	9,000	1.3	3.0	5.5	North Carolina....	125,000	4.0	11.5	30.1
New Hampshire.....	6,000	1.4	3.0	6.7	South Carolina....	87,000	5.5	16.7	37.4
Vermont..........	3,000	1.1	2.4	6.4	Georgia...........	120,000	4.5	10.4	32.1
Massachusetts.....	83,000	2.2	4.0	6.5	Florida...........	92,000	2.6	7.7	23.4
Rhode Island.....	15,000	2.4	5.5	9.2	East South Central:				
Connecticut.......	41,000	2.2	5.1	6.5	Kentucky..........	70,000	3.3	7.3	18.1
Middle Atlantic:					Tennessee.........	88,000	3.5	8.0	21.9
New York.........	355,000	2.9	4.1	6.1	Alabama...........	93,000	4.2	14.0	35.1
New Jersey........	99,000	2.2	4.3	6.5	Mississippi.......	71,000	4.9	14.8	34.1
Pennsylvania.....	166,000	2.0	3.5	6.9	West South Central:				
					Arkansas..........	45,000	3.6	7.6	21.3
NORTH CENTRAL					Louisiana.........	137,000	6.3	15.1	39.6
					Oklahoma..........	32,000	1.9	3.1	11.7
East North Central:					Texas.............	272,000	4.1	7.3	15.6
Ohio.............	99,000	1.5	2.5	4.5					
Indiana..........	40,000	1.2	1.8	5.2					
Illinois.........	128,000	1.8	2.7	4.8	WEST				
Michigan..........	84,000	1.6	2.2	4.8					
Wisconsin........	35,000	1.2	2.1	5.4	Mountain:				
West North Central:					Montana...........	5,000	1.0	1.9	6.6
Minnesota........	23,000	1.0	1.4	4.6	Idaho.............	4,000	0.8	1.2	5.1
Iowa.............	14,000	0.7	0.9	2.7	Wyoming...........	2,000	0.9	1.8	4.4
Missouri.........	52,000	1.7	2.5	7.0	Colorado..........	15,000	1.3	3.1	4.5
North Dakota.....	6,000	1.4	1.7	6.1	New Mexico........	24,000	4.0	14.9	35.7
South Dakota.....	4,000	0.9	1.4	5.8	Arizona...........	33,000	3.8	11.0	30.0
Nebraska.........	9,000	0.9	1.3	2.6	Utah.............	5,000	0.9	1.4	3.6
Kansas...........	14,000	0.9	1.4	3.3	Nevada............	2,000	1.1	4.8	13.8
					Pacific:				
SOUTH					Washington........	18,000	0.9	1.1	3.4
					Oregon............	10,000	0.8	1.1	3.7
South Atlantic:					California........	203,000	1.8	2.8	5.3
Delaware.........	6,000	1.9	4.4	13.2	Alaska............	5,000	3.0	20.5	40.6
Maryland.........	41,000	1.9	4.2	12.1	Hawaii............	21,000	5.0	17.5	35.2

[1] Estimated. Based on population 14 years old and over.

Source: U.S. Bureau of the Census, *Current Population Reports—Technical Studies,* Series P–23, No. 8, for 1930 and 1900. For estimating technique for 1960, see text.

Illiteracy by age. The results of extending educational opportunities from decade to decade are brought out clearly by the statistics on illiteracy for the various age groups, shown in table IV–3. At all dates and for both sexes, the percentage of illiteracy was highest among the oldest segment of the population and progressively lower with each younger age group. In 1959, for example, 6.5 percent of the population 65 years old and over was illiterate, compared with 2.2 percent of the population aged 45 to 54 and only 0.6 percent of persons aged 14 to 24.

Figure IV–2.—Estimated Percent Illiterate Among Persons 14 Years Old and Over, by State: 1960

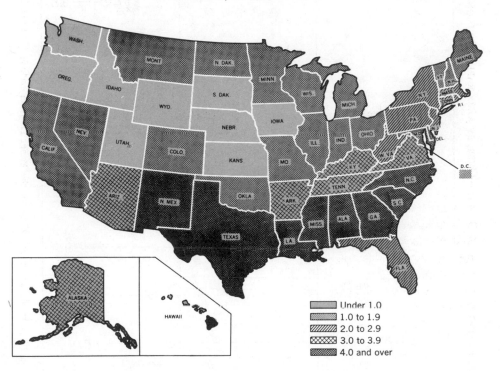

Under 1.0
1.0 to 1.9
2.0 to 2.9
3.0 to 3.9
4.0 and over

Source: Table IV–2.

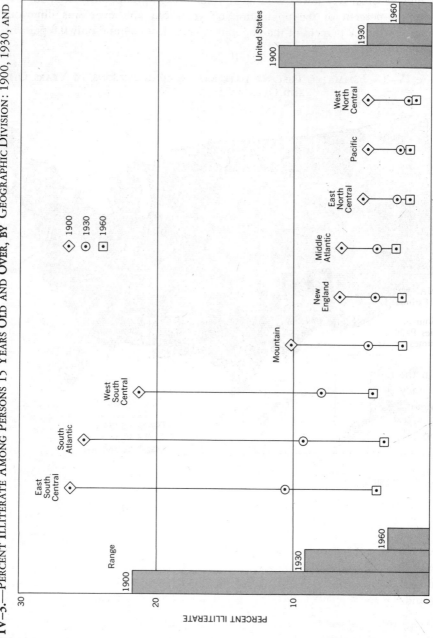

Figure IV-3.—Percent Illiterate Among Persons 15 Years Old and Over, by Geographic Division: 1900, 1930, and 1960

NOTE: Data for 1960 are for the population 14 years old and over. Data for the Pacific Division exclude Alaska and Hawaii.

Source: Computed from data in table IV-2.

Table IV–3.—Percent Illiterate Among Persons 14 Years Old and Over,by Age and Sex: 1910 to 1959

Age and sex	1959	1950[1]	1940[1]	1930	1920	1910
BOTH SEXES						
14 to 24 years....................	0.6	1.9	2.1	2.2	[1]3.4	[1]5.6
25 to 34 years....................	1.1	1.8	2.4	3.3	5.6	7.3
35 to 44 years....................	1.4	2.3	4.0	5.2	7.0	8.1
45 to 54 years....................	2.2	3.4	5.8	6.6	8.2	9.9
55 to 64 years....................	3.2	5.7	7.0	7.2	9.1	12.0
65 years and over.................	6.5	7.6	8.8	9.7	12.0	14.5
MALE						
14 to 24 years....................	0.8	2.2	(NA)	[1]1.7	[1]3.9	[1]6.3
25 to 34 years....................	1.3	2.1	(NA)	3.4	5.6	7.6
35 to 44 years....................	1.9	2.7	(NA)	4.9	6.9	7.6
45 to 54 years....................	2.9	3.5	(NA)	6.5	8.0	8.7
55 to 64 years....................	3.7	6.1	(NA)	7.0	8.4	10.6
65 years and over.................	6.9	8.2	(NA)	8.9	11.0	12.5
FEMALE						
14 to 24 years....................	0.3	1.5	(NA)	[1]2.7	[1]3.1	[1]5.0
25 to 34 years....................	0.9	1.5	(NA)	3.1	5.6	7.0
35 to 44 years....................	0.9	1.9	(NA)	5.4	7.1	8.6
45 to 54 years....................	1.5	3.2	(NA)	6.8	8.3	11.3
55 to 64 years....................	2.8	5.3	(NA)	7.5	9.8	13.6
65 years and over.................	6.2	7.0	(NA)	10.5	13.0	16.5

NA Not available.
[1] Estimated.

Source: U.S. Bureau of the Census, *Current Population Reports—Population Characteristics,* Series P–20, No. 99, for 1959; and Nos. 20 and 45 for 1940 and 1950; and Decennial Census volumes for 1910, 1920, and 1930.

In the half century between 1910 and 1959, there were sharp reductions in illiteracy in all age groups. While the overall rate dropped from 7.7 to 2.2 percent, the rates in specific groups declined accordingly. For males, the reduction in percentage points of illiteracy was similar for all 10-year age groups, so that the difference in number of percentage points of illiteracy among age groups was actually the same at the end of the period as at the beginning. For females, the reduction in percentage points of illiteracy was greater at the older than younger ages; hence, there was some narrowing of the absolute differentials. For both males and females, although the absolute differentials did not change much, the relative differentials widened. In 1910, the illiteracy rate for males was about twice as large, and for females about 3 times as large, at ages 65 and over as at ages 14 to 24. By 1959, the rate for males was about 8 times as large, and for females, 20 times as large, at the oldest as at the youngest age groups. These findings reflect the great improvements in schooling and the consequent sharp gains in literacy among the young population.

Analysis of age cohorts (groups of persons born in the same time period) as they age through successive census periods suggests that very little of the reduction in illiteracy has been a result of formal or informal adult education. Most of the gains made in literacy have been attained through the more adequate schooling of young persons who, as they grew up, replaced the older cohorts of persons who had less formal training. Furthermore, some of the apparent reduction in illiteracy in some cohorts may represent nothing more than unintentional errors of reporting or classification, or misreporting by persons embarrassed by the stigma of not being able to read, a stigma that has probably grown sharper over the last fifty years. The trend in illiteracy rates for several of the cohorts, showing a decline in the rate up to the peak ages of employment, when the advantages of claiming literacy are most obvious, and a return to the level of earlier rates by the older ages provides some support for believing that a certain amount of intentional misreporting occurred. This effect could reflect some gain and a subsequent "relapse" from literacy for a small group of persons, but this is quite unlikely.[9] In any event, it is clear that the overall reduction in illiteracy has resulted from declines in all age groups, and that we may expect continued declines, particularly at the older ages, which should further reduce the total illiteracy rate.

Correlates of illiteracy. Data presented earlier showed that the ability to read and write differed among States, regions, urban and rural areas, and among age and color groups. Illiteracy tended to be greater in the South, in rural areas, among older persons, and among Negroes. Furthermore, there were indications that the size of the differentials among these groups was diminishing as the older illiterates died and the persons entering the older age groups were members of a generation which had received a better education. As the American school system expanded, it increasingly reached educationally disadvantaged groups—particularly farm residents and Negroes.

Other data have shown that birth rates and infant death rates are directly correlated with illiteracy. Winston found that, in 1920, there was a significant relationship between illiteracy and birth rates, even when the extent of urbanization and economic status were statistically controlled. He also found that the gross relationship between illiteracy and infant mortality was a significant one, and that when the percentage of urbanization and per capita current income were controlled the relationship turned out to be even more significant.[10] These findings suggest that the illiterate's inability to read and write may have limited his access to and understanding of knowledge of modern methods of disease control and means of family limitation.

The simple correlation between illiteracy and migration across State lines was low but significant. When the extent of urbanization and the percent of male wage earners engaged in manufacturing (an index of industrialization) was held constant, the relation between illiteracy and interstate migration increased. No relationship was discovered between ability to read and write and the suicide rate, even when controls were used for urbanization, marital status, and ethnic status; however, illiteracy may be related to other measures of personal and social disorganization.[11]

A Census Bureau study in 1959 found that illiteracy was greater among those not in the labor force than among those in the labor force; and within the labor force, the unemployed were more likely than the employed to lack the ability to read and write. Among workers, illiteracy was most common among manual workers, particularly male farm and nonfarm laborers. Furthermore, persons with low levels of income were far more likely to be illiterate than those with higher incomes. It should be noted, however, that these differences in illiteracy rates for certain economic groups can be explained, in part, by differences in age composition and by the distribution of other characteristics. Moreover, the rates for even the most illiterate groups were not extremely high. The highest rate, that for male farm laborers and foremen, was 15 percent. The lowest income group in the census classification (men with under $1,000 income) had an illiteracy rate of 7 percent, and unemployed men had a rate of less than 5 percent.

Occupation groups are not only economic groups, they are social groups as well, and the occupation of the family breadwinner is generally a key to the style of life the family leads. For this reason, occupational categories are sometimes referred to as socioeconomic categories. Table IV–4 shows illiteracy rates for males by broad socioeconomic groupings for 1890 and 1959. An analysis of this table brings out the following highlights: (1) At both points in time, illiteracy rates were inversely related to the level of socioeconomic status; that is, illiteracy rates were higher for farm and manual and service workers than for white-collar workers; (2) Whereas the size of the male population was nearly twice as great in 1959 as in 1890, the number of illiterates was only about one-fourth the number in 1959 as in 1890; hence, the overall illiteracy

Table IV–4.—MALE ILLITERATES, BY SOCIOECONOMIC GROUP: 1959 AND 1890

Year and socioeconomic group	Population	Illiterate	
		Number	Percent of population
1959			
Total	[1]31,063,000	687,000	2.2
White collar	11,659,000	32,000	0.3
Manual and service	16,259,000	391,000	2.4
Farm	3,145,000	264,000	8.4
1890			
Total	[2]18,790,000	2,589,000	13.8
White collar	2,942,000	37,000	1.3
Manual and service	7,178,000	742,000	10.3
Farm	8,670,000	1,810,000	20.9

[1] Civilian noninstitutional males 14 years old and over employed and reporting an occupation.
[2] All males 10 years old and over engaged in gainful occupations.

Source: Data for 1959 derived from U.S. Bureau of the Census, *Current Population Reports —Population Characteristics*, Series P–20, No. 99, table B; data for 1890 based on 1890 Census, shown in Eli Ginzberg and Douglas W. Bray, *The Uneducated*. New York: Columbia University Press, 1953, chapter 3.

rate declined from 14 to 2 percent; (3) about one-fourth of the reduction in the overall illiteracy rate between the two dates could be accounted for by an upgrading of the occupational structure (that is, the increase in percentages of skilled manual and white-collar jobs for which literacy was required). However, three-fourths of the reduction was due to declines in the percent of illiterates within each socioeconomic group. In terms of causation, it was probably a two-way relationship, for to some extent the upgrading of the occupational structure was made possible by the improved literacy of the population.

Illiteracy and formal schooling

A major implication of the historical patterns of illiteracy is that the extension of, and advances in, formal schooling for the general populace contributed greatly to the decline in illiteracy. This relationship can be demonstrated more directly in the following ways:

First, as school enrollment rates of young persons increased during a given time period, literacy rates of the adult population increased after an appropriate time lag. For example, among girls 10 years old (a peak age for enrollment), 90 percent were enrolled in school in 1910; of the same group 10 years later (when they were 20 years old), 96 percent were literate. Among 10-year-old girls in 1920, 93 percent were enrolled, and 98 percent of the same cohort in 1930 were literate. Similarly, the enrollment rate of nonwhite 10-year-olds went from 70 to 80 percent between 1910 and 1920, whereas the literacy rate of nonwhite 20-year-olds rose from 83 to 87 percent between 1920 and 1930. The small differences between the enrollment rates and later literacy rates can be accounted for by persons who learned to read even though they had dropped out of school before age 10.

Second, there is also a high, but less than perfect, relationship between illiteracy and the number of years of school completed by the general population. In 1959, as shown in table IV–5, 74 percent of the population with no school years completed were unable to read and write in any language, and the corresponding percentages were 59 percent of those with only 1 year of school, 33 percent of those with 2 years of school, and 17 percent of those with 3 years. The rate dropped off sharply to 5 percent among those with 4 years of school and 2 percent among those with 5 years. It was assumed in the survey that all persons with 6 or more years of formal education were literate.

The inverse relationship between the illiteracy rate and years of school completed was generally found in all age, color, sex, and residence groups. Likewise, there was little variation in these rates between 1947 and 1959. Hence, a minimum number of years of formal education appears to be the main requisite for literacy. Whether a person is white or nonwhite, old or young, male or female, or from the city or the farm, seems to be of much less importance. It is clear that future reductions in illiteracy will come mainly from further reductions in the proportion of the population with no or with few years of schooling.

Table IV–5.—PERCENT ILLITERATE AMONG PERSONS 14 YEARS OLD AND OVER, BY AGE, COLOR, AND SEX, AND YEARS OF SCHOOL COMPLETED: 1959

Age, color, and sex	Years of school completed					
	None	1	2	3	4	5
Total, 14 years and over.....	73.5	59.3	32.5	16.5	5.0	2.0
AGE						
14 to 24 years.....................	[1]91.8	[1]27.3	[1]45.0	[1]27.7	[1]14.2	2.2
25 to 34 years.....................	[1]83.8	[1]64.3	[1]51.9	22.4	8.7	5.1
35 to 44 years.....................	78.8	[1]70.4	[1]35.9	22.0	5.1	2.2
45 to 54 years.....................	74.3	[1]72.6	[1]40.7	18.9	3.9	1.4
55 to 64 years.....................	72.4	[1]57.3	25.4	15.9	4.0	1.2
65 years and over.................	70.3	50.8	24.1	10.3	3.6	1.7
COLOR AND SEX						
Male.............................	71.8	64.7	38.6	17.6	6.6	2.4
Female...........................	75.3	51.5	24.4	15.1	3.1	1.6
White..........................	70.2	49.0	29.3	14.4	4.6	2.0
Male.............................	67.7	54.4	34.9	15.7	6.0	2.3
Female...........................	72.7	[1]41.9	22.4	12.9	2.8	1.7
Nonwhite......................	82.6	74.4	38.6	21.6	6.3	1.9
Male.............................	81.6	[1]78.2	44.7	22.3	8.3	2.7
Female...........................	83.9	[1]67.8	[1]28.6	20.8	3.8	1.2

[1] Base less than 150,000.

Source: U.S. Bureau of the Census, *Current Population Reports—Population Characteristics,* Series P–20, No. 99, tables 7 and 8.

The small differences in illiteracy rates by years of schooling that do exist for color and residence groups (a few percentage points) may indicate differences in the quality of educational facilities and teaching and differences in the socioeconomic and cultural backgrounds of children in urban and rural areas and in white and nonwhite neighborhoods. Also, total illiteracy rates reflect, in great part, the illiteracy rates for the aged and the school conditions of previous decades, which tended to be poorer for rural and nonwhite neighborhoods. When rates for young adults are compared by subgroup, they are found to be more alike than the rates for all adults.

Several conclusions can be derived from these data: First, that the statement reported in several earlier censuses that, "In general, the illiterate population as shown by the census may be assumed to comprise only those persons who have had no education whatever."[12] is faulty. The available statistics show that not all persons reported as illiterate lacked formal schooling. Some with a few years of school had never acquired reading and writing skills, and others, through disuse, had lost the skills they had once acquired. This situation may reflect the poor quality of educational training in some parts of the country. It may also indicate that some persons lack, or fail to take advantage of, the opportunity to make use of reading and writing skills on their jobs, and that some have little opportunity or inclination to use them at home.[13]

Second, the data show that not all people without schooling are illiterate. Some persons who never attended a regular school are self-taught or have had informal educational training. Stories of immigrants to the United States include many accounts of the night courses they attended in order to learn English. Many had received some formal schooling in their native countries or elsewhere, and could read and write their native language or another language; others, lacking formal education, were eager to acquire the skills that would enable them to enter business or take on more responsible jobs.[14] In recent years, organized groups in the United States have made large-scale attacks on illiteracy (particularly in the South and in rural areas where the problem is most prevalent), by means of television programs, home instruction, and adult education classes. These efforts have undoubtedly helped many people who lacked the advantages of formal schooling to become literate.

A third conclusion to be drawn from the foregoing analysis is that illiteracy, or inability to read and write, must be clearly distinguished from "functional illiteracy." This term was first used in the literacy training programs of the Civilian Conservation Corps in the 1930's (when it was applied to persons having fewer than 3 years of school) and by the Army in the early years of World War II (when it referred to persons with fewer than 4 years of school) to describe men who could not function effectively in basic civilian or military jobs.[15] Because estimates of functional illiteracy for different areas and population groups could only be made conveniently from census data, and since the census classified persons according to whether or not they had completed fewer than 5 years of school but not according to whether or not they had completed fewer than 4 years of school, the definition in terms of less than 5 years of school became standard.[16] The number of functional illiterates greatly exceeds the number of illiterates. In 1959, there were over 8 million persons 14 years old and over in the United States with fewer than 5 years of schooling, compared with roughly 3 million illiterates of the same age.

Illiteracy in the future

The discussion in this chapter suggests a number of questions concerning the course of illiteracy in the United States: What is the likely trend of illiteracy in the years ahead? Will illiteracy differentials widen or narrow? Of what importance is illiteracy, as customarily defined, for the individual's way of living and for the functioning of the economic and social systems of the country.

Projections of illiteracy. It is almost certain that the percentage of persons in the Nation who are illiterate will continue to decline.[17] However, the rate of decline is uncertain and will depend on a number of factors. Among these are the percentage of persons who are not mentally capable of becoming literate, the time it will take for all young persons with the mental capacity to attain a minimum of schooling, the effectiveness of future adult education programs, the level of the mortality rates for older illiterate persons, and the trend of the birth rate, which affects the proportion of younger, and hence more literate, persons in the population.

In 1959, only 0.3 percent of the females and 0.8 percent of the males 14 to 24 years old were illiterate. Clearly, the low illiteracy rate for this age group was related to its level of educational attainment. For instance, only a small fraction of 1 percent of the females had no schooling whatever and less than 2 percent had fewer than 5 years of schooling. Although these percentages are already quite low, the percentages for future generations could be slightly lower. It stands to reason, however, that there will always be a small group of persons who are uneducable; to these, reading and writing skills cannot be taught because they are mentally or physically handicapped.

On the basis of a projection of the present age-sex pattern of literacy and on the assumption that adult education programs will have only a moderate effect on the literacy rate, it would take at least half a century for the general population 14 years old and over to achieve a literacy rate of 99.7 percent, a level reached by females 14 to 24 years old in 1959. In the next 50 years, however, one might expect a gradual rise in the rate from the present level of about 98 percent. Since the largest proportion of illiterates is at the older ages, an effective program to reduce adult illiteracy could hasten the rate of improvement. With the size of the national population increasing, however, the *number* of illiterates probably will remain substantial for some time even while the illiteracy *rate* declines.

A narrowing of illiteracy differentials among racial, regional, urban-rural, and socioeconomic groups, both absolutely and relatively, can be expected in the future. The rates for the more literate subgroups are already low and are approaching a minimum, while those for the less literate subgroups should, as in the past, decline progressively.

The meaning of illiteracy. Of what significance is it that only a small proportion of the population in the United States is not able to read and write a simple message in some language? This question can be answered in only a general way but there are some pertinent data on which to base the answer.

That the relatively low illiteracy rates of 1920 did not portray the true picture of illiteracy in the United States was the point of a post-World War I magazine editorial.[18] Citing information collected through Army literacy tests during World War I, in which the definition of literacy was "ability to read and understand newspapers and write letters home" rather than the less stringent "ability to read and write a simple message," the editorial points out that in 13 out of 28 Army camps where the tests were administered, at least 25 percent of the soldiers failed to pass the test. In none of the remaining camps was the percentage lower than 13 percent. Furthermore, in many of these camps the high illiteracy rate could not be accounted for by the percentage of Negroes taking the tests. A major aim of the editorial was to warn against a complacent attitude toward educational reforms and programs to reduce illiteracy further, a warning which has been repeated in succeeding decades.

The experience of the Armed Forces in World War II similarly indicated that the standard definition of literacy did not serve to discern the limited ability of many servicemen to communicate with their fellow men. Ginsberg and Bray estimated that approximately 435,000 illiterates were accepted into the armed services during the war.[19] However, not only these illiterates but also some literate men with a few years of schooling were found to be incapable of performing basic military functions. Studies of these men showed that, in general, a fourth grade education served to differentiate the "functional illiterate" from the "functional literate." Training programs designed to give the equivalent of fourth-grade schooling succeeded in making the men "functionally literate" to the extent that they "...were able to read and understand military communications, were capable of writing letters home, and had improved in their adjustments to military living."[20]

According to the standard definition, the ability to read and write in some language classified a person as literate. However, in terms of the individual American's ability to participate effectively in the economy, to exercise many of his rights and duties as a citizen, and to enjoy many of the pleasures of daily living, literacy in English is required.

Some immigrants and members of their families, and even some native Americans, are literate but not in English. The 1930 Census, the last to include a question on literacy, also included a question on ability to speak English. The census showed that, of the foreign-born white population 10 years old and over counted as *literate,* about 3 percent (over one-third of a million in 1930) could not speak English.[21] Presumably, these persons could read and write in their native language but had no command of the language of the country in which they lived. Of the *illiterates* in the same population group, 37 percent could not speak English; for these persons, communication problems must have been particularly severe. Inability to speak the English language may be a deterrent to assimilation for many Puerto Ricans, Cubans, Mexicans, Eastern Europeans, and others who have entered the United States in large numbers in recent years. Inability to read and write English, or to speak English, may put a strain on the effectiveness of community institutions which, to function well, must be in communication with all of the people they serve.

The foregoing discussion suggests that illiteracy, as usually defined, measures only the lower limit of what might be called the inability to communicate the written or printed word, and it describes only the barest minimum level of educational attainment of the population.[22] For this reason, much greater attention in the United States is now paid to the amount of formal schooling a person has completed. A discussion of years of school completed as an index of educational attainment begins in the next chapter.

NOTES

[1] Previous studies in Yugoslavia and Iran show that census reports of literacy are generally accurate when evaluated in terms of later tests of reading and writing ability. The same studies conclude, however, that literacy is a continuous variable and definitions must be specific and clearly understood to get consistent results. See S. S. Zarhovic, "Sampling Control of Literacy Data," *Journal of the American Statistical Association,* Vol. 49, Sept. 1954, pp. 510-519; and Charles Windle, "The Accuracy of Census Literacy Statistics in Iran," ibid., Vol. 54, Sept. 1959, pp. 578-581.

[2] William Heard Kilpatrick, "The Dutch Schools of New Netherland and Colonial New York," United States Bureau of Education, Bulletin, 1912, No. 12. Washington: U.S. Government Printing Office, 1912, pp. 228-229.

[3] In defense of these assumptions, Brinkley pointed out that, while it is known that the laws against teaching slaves to read were not rigorously enforced and that some slaves received private instruction, it seems unlikely that any appreciable proportion of the slaves learned to write. See Sterling G. Brinkley, "Growth of School Attendance and Literacy in the United States Since 1840," *The Journal of Experimental Education,* Vol. 26, Sept. 1957, p. 54. Franklin cited estimates to the effect that 1 slave in 50 in the Southwest was literate, and possibly 1 in 80 in Georgia. See John Hope Franklin, *From Slavery to Freedom.* New York: Alfred A. Knopf, 1947, p. 201.

[4] Since the illiteracy rate for "free colored" persons changed very little between 1850 and 1860, using the 1850 rates for 1840 would not seem to introduce much error.

[5] Edwin Leigh, "Illiteracy in the United States," *Report of the Commissioner of Education.* Washington: U.S. Government Printing Office, 1870, pp. 468-469.

[6] Bureau of the Census, *Illiteracy in the United States,* Bulletin 26. Washington: U.S. Government Printing Office, 1905, p. 11.

[7] For further details, see Bureau of the Census, *Twelfth Census of the United States: 1900.* Supplementary Analysis and Derivative Tables. Washington: Government Printing Office, 1906, pp. 328, 333, and 341. A number of deficiencies in the 1900 Census suggest that the latter finding may be the result of reporting errors.

[8] United Nations Educational, Scientific, and Cultural Organization. *World Illiteracy at Mid-Century.* Paris: UNESCO, 1957, pp. 38-44.

[9] Moreover, the unreliability of the estimates for 1940 and the possible effect of educational selectivity in mortality at the older ages make interpretation of cohort analysis of illiteracy trends difficult.

[10] Sanford Winston, *Illiteracy in the United States.* Chapel Hill: The University of North Carolina Press, 1930, pp. 92-98.

[11] Ibid., pp. 107-124.

[12] Bureau of the Census, *Fifteenth Census of the United States, Population: 1930,* Volume II. Washington: Government Printing Office, 1933, p. 1219.

[13] Also reflected here is the variable meaning of a "year of schooling." See chapter V for further discussion of this point.

[14] For description and analysis of the schooling of immigrants during the peak decades of immigration, see Frank V. Thompson, *The Schooling of the Immigrant.* New York: Harper and Brothers, 1920.

[15] Nicholas A. Fattu, Edmund Mech, and Lloyd S. Standlee, *A Review of Literacy Training Programs in the Armed Services During World War II.* Bureau of Navy Personnel Technical Bulletin 53-4, Institute of Educational Research, Indiana University, 17 December 1953, p. 6.

NOTES—Continued

[16] More recently, bills proposed in Congress to support adult education programs have used the cutoff of less than six years of school to define "functional illiteracy." The usefulness of less than five years of schooling as an index of "functional illiteracy" has been questioned in a recent study of the abilities of public welfare recipients, which reported that most of the persons studied (mostly Negro women) had five or more years of school but a large number of them scored below the estimated fifth grade level on an achievement test. See Cook County Department of Public Aid, *A Study to Determine the Literacy Level of Able-Bodied Persons Receiving Public Assistance*, prepared under the direction of Deton J. Brooks, Jr.

[17] It may actually increase in some places, as was estimated for the District of Columbia between 1950 and 1960, because of compositional changes in the population. See source of table IV-2.

[18] "The Attack on Illiteracy," *The Independent*, March 22, 1919, pp. 391-392.

[19] Eli Ginsberg and Douglas W. Bray, *The Uneducated*. New York: Columbia University Press, 1953, p. 73.

[20] Fattu, et. al., op. cit.

[21] Bureau of the Census, op. cit., p. 1348.

[22] For a comprehensive treatment of international approaches to measuring illiteracy, and of the definitions and meanings of the term, see United Nations Educational, Scientific, and Cultural Organization, op. cit., pp. 18-34.

CHAPTER V

TRENDS IN EDUCATIONAL ATTAINMENT

Introduction

The virtual elimination of illiteracy in the United States took place during a time when the population was growing and the educational system was expanding and also evolving facilities and programs which offered increasing opportunities for access to secondary and higher education. It was clear by the late 1930's, when the 1940 Census was being planned, that illiteracy was approaching very low levels and that the need for a census inquiry on ability to read and write was overshadowed by the need for data on how well educated the people had become. A question on years of schooling completed was added to the census, and for the first time an inventory of the educational attainment of the population became available.

The information on educational attainment obtained in the 1940 Census and the two subsequent decennial censuses covers a span of only 20 years, but these were years of great educational expansion, and are very important years for an analysis of trends in attainment of education. Furthermore, while census data on years of schooling were not collected before 1940, it is possible through analytical methods to estimate fairly accurately the educational attainment of the population at earlier periods.[1]

Trends for the total adult population

Before 1910. Not even sound analytical methods will provide reliable estimates of educational attainment for specific dates before 1910. However, some notion of the level of schooling of the population for earlier dates can be obtained by examining the data for aged persons in the 1960 Census. Persons who were 75 years old and over in 1960, most of whom would have been born in the 1870's and 1880's and would have attended school in the closing decades of the 19th century, reported an average of 8 years of formal schooling. About 17½ percent were high school graduates and about 3 percent were college graduates. Of the persons aged 70 to 74 in 1960 (those who would normally have obtained their education in the early 1900's), slightly more than one-fifth reported no more than a fourth grade education, nearly 19 percent were high school graduates, and 4 percent were college graduates. These reports of education received in a much earlier period are probably subject to substantial reporting errors.

1910 to 1960. In the 50 years prior to the 1960 Census, the educational status of the American people progressed steadily, advancing most rapidly during the 1940's and 1950's. Table V–1 and figure V–1 show the trend for the population 25 years old and over in terms of selected indicators of educational attainment. The decline in the percentage of the population with less than 5 years of schooling was greatest in the 1920's and 1930's, whereas the increase in the percentage of the population with a high school or college education was generally greatest in the later decades.

Table V–1.—SELECTED MEASURES OF EDUCATIONAL ATTAINMENT, FOR THE POPULATION 25 YEARS OLD AND OVER: 1910 TO 1980

Year[1]	Median school years completed	Percent with--		
		Less than 5 years of school	High school, 4 years or more	College, 4 years or more
Estimate:				
1910..........................	8.1	23.8	13.5	2.7
1920..........................	8.2	22.0	16.4	3.3
1930..........................	8.4	17.5	19.1	3.9
Census:				
1940..........................	8.6	13.7	24.5	4.6
1950..........................	9.3	11.1	34.3	6.2
1960..........................	10.5	8.3	41.1	7.7
Projection:				
1970..........................	11.9	5.7	49.3	10.2
1980..........................	12.3	3.4	58.9	13.3

[1] Figures for 1910 to 1930 are estimates based on retrojection of 1940 Census data on education by age. Figures for 1970 to 1980 are projections. All other figures are from Census reports. Figures for 1950 to 1980 include Alaska and Hawaii; those for earlier years do not.
[2] Based on retrojection of reported 1940 Census data on education by age.

Source: Series A (high) projections are shown for 1970 and 1980; *1960 Census of Population,* Vol. I, *Characteristics of the Population,* Part 1, U.S. Summary, table 173; and *Current Population Reports—Population Estimates,* Series P–25, No. 305, table 1; *1950 Census of Population,* Vol. II, *Characteristics of the Population,* Part 1, U. S. Summary, table 115.

The Nation had largely achieved the goal of a minimum level of schooling for nearly everyone at a time when large numbers of persons were not continuing their education through high school and into college. The latter goal was to be reached later. The educational level of the adult population increased greatly between 1910 and 1960. The proportion of adults with no more than 4 years of schooling decreased from 24 out of 100 in 1910 to 8 out of 100 in 1960, and the proportion completing high school increased from 14 out of 100 in 1910 to 41 out of 100 in 1960. About 3 percent of the adults in 1910 were college graduates, compared with 8 percent in 1960. The average adult in 1910 had completed elementary school, while his counterpart in 1960 **had attained** a partial high school education.

Educational expansion in the United States is also reflected in the growing *numbers* of high school and college graduates in the population. In 1940, the number of high school graduates was estimated to be 26 million, and the number of college graduates nearly 4 million. By 1960 these numbers had surpassed 50 million and 8 million, respectively.   Similarly, the *proportion* of persons aged 15 and over who were high school graduates rose from 26 to 41 percent, while the proportion of persons aged 20 and over who were college graduates went up from 4½ to 7½ percent.   (See table V–2.)

Figure V–1.—Percent of the Population 25 Years Old and Over With Indicated Number of Years of School Completed or More: 1910 to 1960

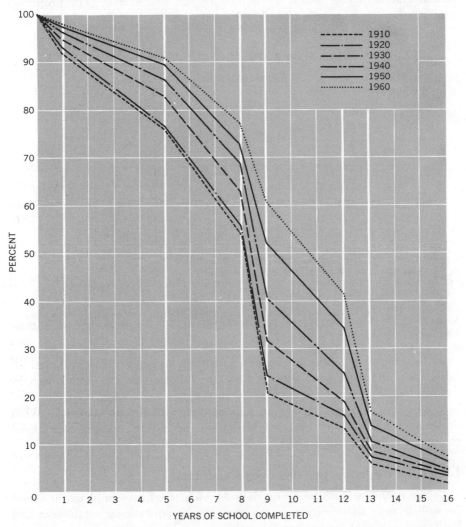

Source: Computed from data in sources used to compile table V–1.

Projections to 1980. If past trends continue, it is possible that by 1980 more than half the adults in the United States will be high school graduates. Carried to 1980, this projection indicates that only 3 percent of the population aged 25 and over will have fewer than 5 years of schooling, which is only one-seventh of the percentage recorded in 1910 and less than one-half the percentage recorded in 1960. About 59 percent will be high school graduates, or more than four times the proportion found in 1910, and nearly half again greater than the proportion for 1960. Over 13 percent will be college graduates, or five times the percentage in 1910 and nearly double the percentage in 1960. By 1980, the population is expected to include about 95½ million high school graduates and almost 17 million college graduates. (For projection methods, see source note in table V–2.)

Table V–2.—High School and College Graduates: 1940 to 1980

[Numbers in thousands]

Year	High school graduates[1]		College graduates[2]	
	Number	Percent of population 15 years old and over	Number	Percent of population 20 years old and over
Census:				
1940..........................	25,670	26.0	3,852	4.5
1950..........................	38,293	35.0	5,951	6.0
1960..........................	50,389	40.8	8,236	7.5
Projection:				
1970[3]......................	69,959	48.0	11,227	8.9
1980[3]......................	95,526	56.3	16,770	11.3

[1] Persons who completed 4 years of high school or more.
[2] Persons who completed 4 years of college or more.
[3] Estimates based on continuation of 1950–60 trend in percent of persons under 25 years old completing high school and college.

Source: U.S. Bureau of the Census, *Current Population Reports—Population Estimates,* Series P–25, No. 305, table 1. *1960 Census of Population,* Vol. I, *Characteristics of the Population,* Part 1, U.S. Summary, table 173.

The foregoing describes the general long-term trend in the educational attainment of the adult population as a whole. But how do these trends vary by age, and what generational changes do they reveal? What has been the trend in educational differentials among various classes of the population? What do we know about the geographic distribution and redistribution of educational resources in the United States over time?

Limitations in educational concepts and data

Before further describing census data on years of school completed, it would be well to note shortcomings in the measures of educational attainment and limitations inherent in the data themselves.

First, the census data on years of school completed refer to schooling obtained in either the regular public and private schools and colleges of the United States or in equivalent schools of other countries. The data do not include schooling in other types of schools or training programs. The measure of educational attainment includes only schooling which may lead to an elementary school certificate, high school diploma, or college degree. Educational training which may contribute to improvement in the skills and knowledge of individuals (such as commercial courses, on-the-job training, industrial classes, and informal educational programs) is not included in the years of schooling reported in the census.

Second, there have been variations both over time and in different parts of the United States in the content and quality of a "year of school." The consistency of historical data on years of schooling, and the comparability of such data for population groups in different parts of the country, is thus somewhat impaired.

Third, even within the limits set by the definitions employed and the nature of schooling obtained, there is a tendency for many persons to misreport the true number of years of schooling completed. There is, however, a tendency for both underreporting and overreporting, hence the net amount of misreporting on census statistics is considerably less than the gross amount.

On balance, although these shortcomings can have a disturbing effect on the analysis of census data on education, as indicated by the more elaborate discussion in appendix A, they are not so great as to invalidate the analysis of the attainment information, especially when the effects of the variations themselves are considered in making interpretations.

Cohort and generational factors in attainment trends

Educational attainment data will be examined in two ways: first, by analyzing differences in attainment by cohorts of different ages at a single census date. Since the older cohorts were educated at an earlier period, years of school completed for successive age groups can be used to identify historical trends in attainment. This type of analysis also permits identification of the effects of changing age composition on the attainment levels of the total population. The second type of analysis will utilize data for successive generations of the same family. This analysis not only reveals trends in attainment over time, but also indicates the influence of family background on educational attainment.

Cohort effects. The data in table V–3 show selected indicators of educational attainment by age for 1920, 1940, and 1960, and projections to 1980. First, for each date there is an inverse relationship between age and years of schooling; that is, each younger cohort in the population shows higher educational attainment. The data for 1960 provide a recent picture of education by age. The median number of school years completed was 8.3 for persons 65 years and over (born before 1896) compared with 8.7 for those 55 to 64 years (born 1896-1905), 10.2 for those 45 to 54 (born 1906-1915), 12.1 for persons 35 to 44 (born 1916-1925), and 12.2 for the group 25 to 34 years old (born 1926-1935). Correspondingly, the percent with less than 5 years of school completed ranged from 20.5 percent for the oldest of these age groups to 3.1 percent for the youngest; the percent who were high school graduates ranged from 19.1 to 58.1 percent; and the percent who were college graduates, from 3.7 percent for the oldest group to 11.0 percent for the youngest group.

Table V–3.—SELECTED MEASURES OF EDUCATIONAL ATTAINMENT, FOR THE POPULA-
TION 25 YEARS OLD AND OVER, BY AGE: 1920 TO 1980

Age and year	Median school years completed	Percent with--		
		Less than 5 years of school	High school, 4 years or more	College, 4 years or more
25 TO 34 YEARS OLD				
Estimate: 1920.....................	8.4	16.8	19.6	4.0
Census: 1940.....................	10.0	6.5	35.7	6.1
1960.....................	12.2	3.1	58.1	11.0
Projection: 1980...................	12.6	1.0	68.0	18.3
35 TO 44 YEARS OLD				
Estimate: 1920.....................	8.3	19.7	16.7	3.4
Census: 1940.....................	8.7	10.9	25.4	5.1
1960.....?.....´..........	12.1	4.3	51.7	8.8
Projection: 1980...................	12.4	1.7	66.4	17.1
45 TO 54 YEARS OLD				
Estimate: 1920.....................	8.1	23.5	13.6	2.8
Census: 1940.....................	8.4	16.8	19.6	4.0
1960.....................	10.2	6.7	37.9	7.3
Projection: 1980...................	12.2	3.1	58.2	11.8
55 TO 64 YEARS OLD				
Estimate: 1920.....................	8.0	26.0	11.7	2.4
Census: 1940.....................	8.3	19.7	16.8	3.4
1960.....................	8.7	11.7	26.7	5.6
Projection: 1980...................	12.1	4.1	51.9	8.7
65 YEARS OLD AND OVER				
Estimate: 1920.....................	7.9	28.6	9.9	1.8
Census: 1940.....................	8.1	24.2	13.1	2.6
1960.....................	8.3	20.5	19.1	3.7
Projection: 1980...................	9.5	8.4	34.1	6.6

Source: *1960 Census of Population*, Vol. I, *Characteristics of the Population*, Part 1, U.S. Summary, table 173; and *Current Population Reports—Population Estimates*, Series P–25, No. 305, table 1; *1950 Census of Population*, Vol. II, *Characteristics of the Population*, Part 1, U.S. Summary, table 115; and estimates.

Since each younger age group was educated at a more recent date, the rise in educational attainment for the younger groups is a further indication of the increased output of the school systems, discussed in chapter I. These data also show that, while some improvement in the educational level of adults may have contributed to the increasing educational attainment of the total adult population, the main factor in the increase has been the death of older persons, who as a class had lower than average education, and entrance into adulthood of younger persons with higher than average amounts of schooling.

How long should it take the adult population as a whole to attain the current educational level of the youngest adult age group? The 1960 Census showed that, among persons 25 to 29 years old, 3 percent had fewer than 5 years of school, 61 percent were high school graduates, and 11 percent were college graduates. Projections in table V–1 show that the first two percentages will almost be reached by the total adult group by 1980, and the college graduation percentage is likely to be reached by 1975. Thus it is clear that in educational attainment, the younger generations in the United States have made vast gains over the older generations. The United States, with 6 out of 10 young persons completing high school, had established a record which had not yet been reached by any other country, and which few, if any, other countries are likely to achieve in the near future.

The age profile of educational attainment is important also because the age composition of the population has been changing over time as a result of fluctuations in the trend of births and increases in life expectancy. In 1920, almost one-third of the population 25 years old and over was in the age group 25 to 34 years old. As of 1940, the proportion had declined to 29 percent. By 1960, the proportion was less than one-fourth, but by 1980 it is expected to rise again to the 1940 level. Simultaneously, the percentage of persons 65 years old and over has risen steadily, from 9 percent in 1920 to 16 percent in 1960, and projections indicate that this percentage will continue to increase to about 18 percent by 1980.

What is the significance of this shifting age composition for educational levels of the adult population? Because older persons tend to be less well educated than younger persons, the general aging of the population has depressed the educational level.   To illustrate the magnitude of the effect, if the relatively younger age distribution of the population in 1920 had remained the same until 1960, the percent of all adults in 1960 with less than 5 years of schooling would have been 6.8 instead of the recorded 8.3 percent; the percent who had completed high school would have been 45.0 instead of 41.1 percent; and the percent who were college graduates would have been 8.4 instead of 7.7 percent. Thus, while the effect of age changes on educational attainment during the 40-year period was not substantial, it was noticeably unfavorable and slowed down the rate of educational improvement of the total adult population.

Generational effects. The importance of the age structure for the educational level of the population lies in its relation to improvements over time in educational opportunities and the contribution of different cohorts to the educational stock of the population. Generational patterns add to the analysis of attainment because parents are a primary source of a youth's educational and occupational aspirations and achievements, and they provide the educational and cultural backgrounds which strongly influence the educational attainments of their children. In the present context, we are most interested in knowing the rate of educational change between generations and its effect on the educational level of the adult population. This interest can be posed in several questions which available data on the education of men and their fathers can answer: (1) How well educated is the sons' generation as a group compared with their fathers'? (2) What are the rates of upward educational movement between generations for men whose fathers had differing educational attainments? (3) How much of the total amount of measured educational mobility can be attributed to the upgrading of the national educational structure, and how much to individual and family effects on the mobility of sons?

Table V–4 and figure V–2 show how the schooling of the fathers' and sons' generations compare on an overall basis.[2] Fifty-two percent of the fathers, but 84 percent of the sons, had at least an eighth grade education; 19 percent of the fathers, but 50 percent of the sons, were high school graduates; and 8 percent of the fathers, but 23 percent of the sons, had one or more years of college. In these terms, intergenerational educational change has been quite great. From the data by age an even sharper picture is discerned of the gains in education made by the sons as compared with their fathers. For each of the indices described, the educational advantage of sons over fathers was greater for each younger age group of men, thus indicating increases over time in net upward educational mobility.

Similar findings are revealed when the percentages of sons who had higher, the same, or lower educational attainments than their fathers are examined. Of the men 55 to 64 years old, 42 percent had the same amount of education as their fathers; for men 25 to 34 years old, the corresponding figure was 30 percent. About 47 percent of the older men, but 64 percent of the younger men, exceeded their fathers' educational level. The percentage of men with lower attainments than their fathers was 11 for the older group and 7 for the younger group.

Not only was the percentage of upwardly mobile sons greater for each younger age group as a whole, but it was greater for younger men within each category of father's education. For example, 60 percent of the men 55 to 64 years old whose fathers lacked an eighth grade education had 8 or more years of schooling themselves, whereas the figure was 83 percent for men aged 25 to 34. Similarly, 31 percent of the older men whose fathers were high school graduates themselves had one or more years of college, while the comparable figure among the younger men was 44 percent. This pattern of generational differences can be generalized for all age groups and all categories of father's education; that is, the percentage of sons with the same educational level as their fathers was lower, and the percentage whose level exceeded that of their fathers was higher, in each younger age group, both for the age group as a whole and for each category of fathers' education.

Table V–4.—Selected Measures of Educational Attainment, for Sons 25 to 64 Years Old, by Age, and for Their Fathers: March 1962

Educational attainment of sons and their fathers	Age of son				
	Total, 25 to 64 years old	25 to 34 years old	35 to 44 years old	45 to 54 years old	55 to 64 years old
PERCENT WITH LESS THAN 8 YEARS OF SCHOOL					
Sons	16.3	8.8	13.0	19.0	28.0
Fathers[1]	48.1	37.4	48.2	52.4	56.9
PERCENT WITH 4 YEARS OF HIGH SCHOOL OR MORE					
Sons	50.3	64.7	54.3	44.2	30.3
Fathers[1]	19.1	24.8	19.0	16.7	14.2
PERCENT WITH 1 YEAR OF COLLEGE OR MORE					
Sons	22.9	30.3	24.8	19.2	14.5
Fathers[1]	7.9	10.5	8.0	7.0	5.5

[1] Includes fathers whose education was not reported. Allocation was based on fact that such fathers were distributed, with regard to other characteristics, much like those fathers who had less than 8 years of school. Of the 48.1 percent in the total column, 12.0 percent were not reported. The percent not reported varied from 7.1 for the youngest age group to 17.4 for the oldest.

Source: Unpublished tabulations from the U.S. Bureau of the Census, *Current Population Survey.*

One problem in interpreting these findings is that the educational structure of the United States has undergone considerable change over the past decades. There has been a proliferation of educational institutions and broadened facilities, educational opportunities have been made more readily available to all people and all areas of the country, and public attitudes toward education have improved considerably. As a result, the national educational structure has been upgraded. Even apart from these changes, there has been some educational mobility between generations. In effect, the net educational movement between the fathers' and sons' generations can be ascribed to two major factors: first, changes in the relative size of the educational strata over time resulting from increased educational opportunities and an increasing demand for educated persons; and second, the educational mobility of sons as a result of personal and family factors. Using a technique employed by Goldhamer and Rogoff for measuring occupational mobility,[3] we have measured the rates of educational mobility for the different age groups of men, separating the first of the factors mentioned above. This technique compares the reported educational attainment of sons with the educational attainment that would be expected if

Figure V–2.—Selected Measures of Educational Attainment for Sons 25 to 64 Years Old, by Age, and for Their Fathers: 1962

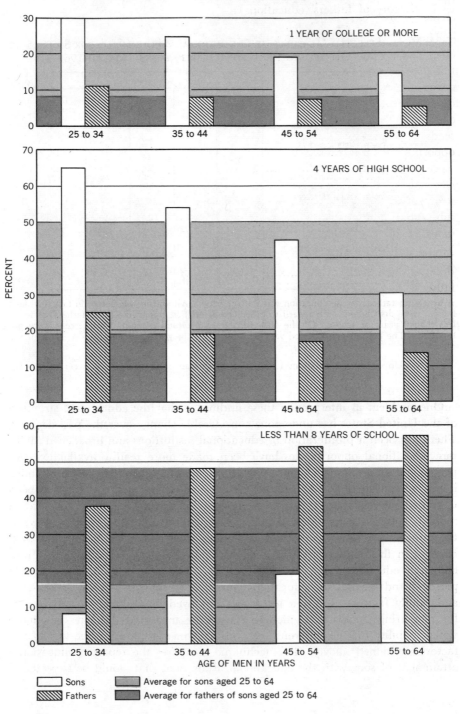

Source: Table V–4.

there were no association between the education of a son and that of his father; that is, if within the existing educational structure every son had the same chance of attaining a particular educational level.

This analysis yields two important findings. First, it shows that if a son's chance of attaining a particular educational level is uninfluenced by the educational attainment of his father, but was the same for all members of an age group, the expected number of sons whose educational level is the same as that of their fathers proves to be far lower than the actual number at the same educational level. The inference is clear that there is a generational link which tends to terminate a son's education at the father's level, despite the fact that opportunities for education grow more widespread and that the stimulus to seek more education grows stronger and more pervasive in our culture. This educational "inheritance," as it may be called, understandably was found to be strongest in the lowest and the highest educational attainment levels, but was substantial at intermediate levels as well. It was greatest for father-son pairs in which the father had completed some college education.

The second finding relates to those sons whose educational attainment level differed from that of their fathers. In these cases, the drift away from the father's educational attainment level appears to be mainly attributable to the upgrading of the educational structure, with little discernable effect attributable to the father's level of education.

Thus, it may be said that personal and family influences, crudely measured by the father's educational level, tend to inhibit generational educational mobility by a form of inertia, as it were. When the inertia is overcome, and the son falls free of what might be called the "gravitational" influence of the father, and takes greater advantage of the opportunities society provides for his education, his progress is virtually independent of his father's. Still unanswered, however, is the question of what factors determine whether inertia or free mobility prevails.

These actual-to-expected ratios, by age, when examined indicate the extent to which educational opportunities are "opening" or "closing," over and above those provided by a change in the total educational structure. In other words, it can be seen whether a man's chances of reaching an educational level different from that of his father are improving or lessening as a result of individual mobility.

Analysis of these ratios indicates that opportunities for sons to attain a different educational level from that of their fathers, apart from the effect of the changing educational structure, have not changed much over the past few decades. For the four age groups of men (55 to 64, 45 to 54, 35 to 44, and 25 to 34), the average *total* mobility rates were .89, .73, .76, and .74, respectively. The corresponding average *upward* mobility rates were 1.12, 1.03, 1.10, and 1.07. In other words, at all points in time it has been an expansion of educational opportunity that has led to increases in the educational level of the population.

Educational opportunities are determined by several important factors: (1) Economic factors, because continuation of one's education depends in part on the ability to pay, and because much of American education is keyed to meeting the educational requirements of the occupational structure; (2) educational institutional factors, because the amount of schooling a person receives, particularly at the college level, is a function of the quantity and availability of educational facilities; and (3) individual attitudes toward education, because public demand for education will influence the improvement of educational opportunity. These three factors have combined to open up channels of educational mobility and to greatly increase the educational level of the population. Their importance will be discussed in the next chapter.

Trends in educational differentials

Despite the rapidly rising educational level, large differences remain in the average attainments of many classes of the population and of people living in various areas of the country. This pattern of differentials raises two important questions: (1) Have all groups in the population benefited from the increasing educational level? (2) Have the differentials been narrowing over time? In the following pages we will examine these questions for both sexes, for racial and ethnic groups, religious denominations, urban and rural residence categories, regions of the country, and States. For most of the comparisons, census data are analyzed separately for the population 25 years old and over, and for persons 25 to 29 years old. The statistics for the younger adults indicate fairly recent educational differentials, while those for persons 25 years old and over describe differentials in the adult population as a whole. A high proportion of the adults received their schooling in the more distant past. Because of data restrictions, many of the comparisons relate to different time periods, but the data should reveal the trends in differentials.

Men and women. A significant feature of the American educational system is that, unlike many foreign systems, it provides almost equal opportunities for both sexes. Moreover, equality of educational attainment of the sexes goes back many years in the country's history.[4] This has been less true of college education than of elementary and secondary schooling. Traditionally, college has been the training ground for professional men. Although many women have continued their schooling through teachers colleges, fewer women than men have enrolled in liberal arts colleges and universities and in professional programs in business, engineering, law, and some other professional fields. Below the college level, the opportunity for a high school education has been extended equally to men and women, and the statistics indicate that proportionately more women than men have attained a complete high school education.

In terms of the median or average level of educational attainment, adult women have been slightly better educated than adult men at least since 1910, and the differential appears to be widening (see table V–5). But differences in averages often are not good indications of differences in distributions, as is clearly the case with the schooling of men and women. As table V–5 shows, while in 1960 smaller percentages of adult women than adult men lacked a fifth grade education, and larger percentages of women completed high school, men were far more likely to have graduated from college. More detailed statistics show that in 1960 adult women exceeded their male counterparts in completing each level of schooling through the last year of high shcool, but larger percentages of men were found at each level beginning with the first year of college.

Among the youngest adult age group (ages 25 to 29), the educational distributions of men and women in 1960 differed in the same way as among the total adult group, with two exceptions: First, the median number of school years completed was the same for males and females even though their educational distributions varied in the way described above. Second, the differential in

Table V–5.—SELECTED MEASURES OF EDUCATIONAL ATTAINMENT, FOR PERSONS 25 YEARS OLD AND OVER, AND 25 TO 29 YEARS OLD, BY SEX: 1910 TO 1960

	Male				Female			
		Percent with--				Percent with--		
Age and year[1]	Median school years completed	Less than 5 years of school	High school, 4 years or more	College, 4 years or more	Median school years completed	Less than 5 years of school	High school, 4 years or more	College, 4 years or more
25 YEARS OLD AND OVER								
Estimate:[2]								
1910	8.1	25.9	12.4	3.4	8.2	21.6	14.6	1.9
1920	8.2	23.0	14.5	3.9	8.3	19.1	17.1	2.4
1930	8.3	19.1	17.5	4.6	8.5	15.9	20.7	3.1
Census:								
1940	8.6	15.1	22.7	5.5	8.7	12.4	26.3	3.8
1950	9.0	12.2	32.6	7.3	9.6	10.0	36.0	5.2
1960	10.3	9.4	39.5	9.7	10.7	7.4	42.5	5.8
25 TO 29 YEARS OLD								
Estimate:[2]								
1910	8.2	21.2	15.7	4.1	8.4	17.3	18.5	2.6
1920	8.4	16.7	19.2	4.9	8.5	14.6	22.1	3.4
1930	8.7	10.6	24.6	6.5	8.9	8.9	29.1	4.5
Census:								
1940	10.1	6.9	36.0	6.9	10.5	5.0	40.1	4.9
1950	12.0	5.4	50.6	9.6	12.1	4.0	55.0	5.9
1960	12.3	3.4	59.7	14.4	12.3	2.2	61.7	7.8

[1] Data for 1950 and 1960 include Alaska and Hawaii, those for earlier years do not.
[2] Based on retrojection of reported 1940 Census data on education by age.

Source: *1960 Census of Population*, Vol. I, *Characteristics of the Population*, Part 1, U.S. Summary, table 173; *1950 Census of Population*, Vol. II, *Characteristics of the Population*, Part 1, U.S. Summary, table 115.

college attainment by sex favoring the males was greater than that for the total adult group.

For both the 25 years and over and the 25 to 29 years age groups, the reduction between 1910 and 1960 in the percentage of persons with less than 5 years of schooling was sharper for men than for women, resulting in some narrowing of the differential at that educational level. The differential favoring women at the high school graduation level, for both the total and youngest groups of adults, widened somewhat during the first few decades after 1910 and then narrowed again, so that by 1960 the differential was only slightly greater than in 1910 for all adults, and slightly smaller than in 1910 for young adults. At the college graduation level, the differential by sex has widened since 1940, especially for young adults. While there has been a substantial increase over the years in the relative numbers of women completing college, the increase has been still greater for men.

Some insight into the dynamic factors producing educational differentials between men and women can be gained from the data for 1960 on the schooling of men and women in the 20 to 24 years age group according to the educational attainment of their fathers.[5] About 68 percent of the men and 70 percent of the women were high school graduates, but 35 percent of the men and 25 percent of the women had attended college at some time. Among those whose fathers had not completed high school, 57 percent of the men and 62 percent of the women were high school graduates, and 23 percent of the men but 14 percent of the women had attended college. This is a relationship similar to the total pattern.

Among those whose fathers had graduated from high school, 92 percent of the men and 91 percent of the women were high school graduates, but 65 percent of the men and 52 percent of the women had some college education. Where the fathers had attended college, 95 percent of both the men and the women were high school graduates, and 80 percent of the men and 73 percent of the women had themselves attended college. Thus it seems that women are more likely than men to complete high school if their fathers were poorly educated, but not if their fathers had graduated from high school or gone on to college. The statistics also suggest that, while sons are more likely than daughters to attend college, a daughter's chances of attending college tend to be relatively more like a son's if their fathers were well-schooled. These findings support a widely held assumption that, among lower status families, college attendance is most often vocationally oriented and based on economic motives, whereas among higher status families going to college, particularly for girls, is a status-enhancing practice and is often based on social motives. It also suggests that in the future the differential favoring women at the lower educational levels will be further reduced, and that the differential favoring men at the college level may also be reduced.

Whites and nonwhites. The strong efforts made in recent years to equalize educational opportunity and educational achievement among the races in this country have come after many decades of substantial improvement in the educational status of the population, white and nonwhite. Attempts to equalize the educational attainment of racial groups pose important questions: What have been the relative educational gains of the white and nonwhite populations? Has the color gap in educational attainment been closing?

Table V–6.—SELECTED MEASURES OF EDUCATIONAL ATTAINMENT, FOR PERSONS 25 YEARS OLD AND OVER, BY COLOR: SELECTED DATES, 1920 TO 1960

[Data for 1960 include Alaska and Hawaii, not included in data for earlier years]

Age, color, and year	Median school years completed	Percent with--		
		Less than 5 years of school	High school, 4 years or more	College, 4 years or more
25 YEARS OLD AND OVER				
White				
1940.................................	8.7	10.9	26.1	4.9
1960.................................	10.8	6.7	43.2	8.1
Nonwhite				
1940.................................	5.8	41.8	7.7	1.3
1960.................................	8.2	23.5	21.8	3.5
25 TO 29 YEARS OLD				
White				
1920[1].................................	8.5	12.9	22.0	4.5
1940.................................	10.7	3.4	41.2	6.4
1960.................................	12.3	2.2	63.7	11.8
Nonwhite				
1920[1].................................	5.4	44.6	6.3	1.2
1940.................................	7.0	27.0	12.3	1.6
1960.................................	10.8	7.2	38.6	5.4

[1] Based on reports for persons 45 to 49 years old in 1940, who generally would have been 25 to 29 years old in 1920.

Source: *1940 Census of Population*, Vol. IV, U.S. Summary, table 18; *1960 Census of Population*, Vol. I, *Characteristics of the Population*, Part 1, U.S. Summary, table 173.

Data in table V–6 show that there was a slight narrowing of the color differential in the median years of school completed between 1940 and 1960 for the total adult population. During the same time, however, there was an extremely sharp reduction of the differential in the percent with less than 5 years of schooling and a widening of the differentials favoring whites at the high school and college graduation levels. (See figure V–3.) The reduced differential in the median can thus be accounted for largely by substantially greater school attainment for nonwhites at the lower levels of education, with the result that proportionally more nonwhites than whites passed the median level established earlier by their group. In 1940, the median for nonwhites was 5.8 compared with a median of 8.7 for whites, so that the median for nonwhites could have been raised by net movement into the upper elementary grades while that for whites had to be raised by gains in high school attainment. By 1960, the median for the nonwhite adult group still stood at only 8.2, whereas the median for white adults had risen to 10.8. With few exceptions, the pattern of change in color differentials observed for both sexes in the country as a whole held for males and females in each major region.

The results of recent educational efforts can better be studied by looking at data for persons 25 to 29 years old. These data, for 1920, 1940, and 1960, are also shown in table V–6. The 40-year reduction in the percent of nonwhites in this age group with less than 5 years of schooling was appreciable, dropping from 45 percent in 1920 to 7 percent in 1960. During the same period, the corresponding percentage for whites declined from 13 to 2 percent. This reduction in the differential (from 32 percentage points in 1920 to 5 points in 1960) was continuous over the period for which data are shown. At the high school graduation level, on the other hand, the color differential among young adults widened considerably between 1920 and 1940 and narrowed again only slightly between 1940 and 1960. By the latter date, 64 percent of the whites and 39 percent of the nonwhites were high school graduates. Although the college graduation rate for both white and nonwhite young adults increased, the percentage-point difference favoring the whites continued to grow larger between 1920 and 1960. Comparisons of the color groups over time show the nature of the lag in nonwhite education. Among those 25 to 29 years old, the percentage without a fifth-grade education among the nonwhites in 1960 had already been reached by whites about 1930. The percentage of the nonwhite group in 1960 that had finished high school, and the percentage holding college degrees, had each been attained by the white group prior to 1940. It probably will not take another 20 years for young nonwhite adults to reach the educational level attained by white adults in 1960.

Father-son education data for whites and nonwhites, as shown in table V–7, are instructive. Among the group of men 25 to 64 years old in 1962, 45 percent of the white fathers and 14 percent of the white sons lacked an eighth grade education, while the corresponding figures for nonwhite fathers and nonwhite sons were 72 and 40 percent, respectively—a generational difference of a little over 30 percentage points for each color group. About 20 percent of the white fathers and 53 percent of the white sons were high school graduates, compared with 9 percent of the nonwhite fathers and 26 percent of the nonwhite sons, a generational difference of 33 percentage points for whites, but only 17 percentage points for nonwhites. Eight percent of the white fathers and 24 percent of the white sons had completed one or more years of college, compared with 4 percent of the nonwhite fathers and 10 percent of the nonwhite sons, a difference of 16 percentage points between the generations for whites, and 6 percentage points for nonwhites.

Thus it appears that the nonwhite population has not only been less well educated than the white population, but its net movement into higher levels

Figure V–3.—PERCENT OF THE POPULATION 25 YEARS OLD AND OVER WITH INDICATED NUMBER OF YEARS OF SCHOOL COMPLETED OR MORE, BY COLOR: 1940 TO 1960

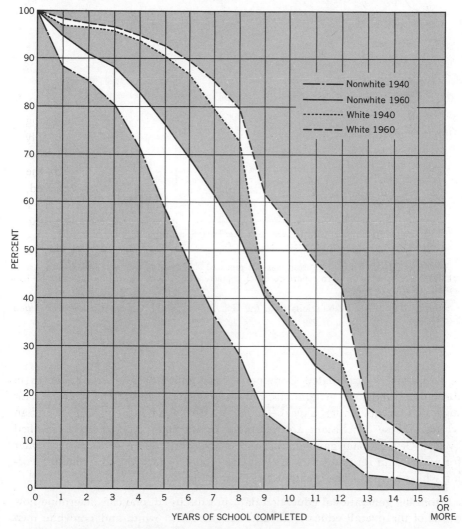

Source: 1940 Census of Population, Vol. IV, U.S. Summary, table 18; *1960 Census of Population,* Vol. I, *Characteristics of the Population.* Part 1, U.S. Summary, table 173.

Table V–7.—Selected Measures of Educational Attainment for Sons, 25 to 64 Years Old, and Their Fathers, by Age and Color: March 1962

Educational attainment of sons and their fathers by color	Total, 25 to 64 years old	Age of son			
		25 to 34 years old	35 to 44 years old	45 to 54 years old	55 to 64 years old
PERCENT WITH LESS THAN 8 YEARS OF SCHOOL					
White					
Sons........................	14	7	10	16	24
Fathers[1]...................	45	35	46	50	54
Nonwhite					
Sons........................	40	21	36	51	65
Fathers[1]...................	72	60	72	78	85
PERCENT WITH 4 YEARS OF HIGH SCHOOL OR MORE					
White					
Sons........................	53	68	58	47	33
Fathers[1]...................	20	26	20	18	15
Nonwhite					
Sons........................	26	38	31	20	7
Fathers[1]...................	9	12	7	8	7
PERCENT WITH 1 YEAR OF COLLEGE OR MORE					
White					
Sons........................	24	32	26	20	16
Fathers[1]...................	8	11	9	7	6
Nonwhite					
Sons........................	10	14	12	8	2
Fathers[1]...................	4	5	3	2	3

[1] Includes fathers whose education was not reported. Allocation was based on fact that such fathers were distributed, with regard to other characteristics, much like those fathers who had less than 8 years of school.

Source: Unpublished tabulations from the U.S. Bureau of the Census, *Current Population Survey.*

of education, as calculated from percentage-point educational differences in the fathers' and sons' generations, has lagged behind that of the whites. This suggests that nonwhites have been less upwardly mobile educationally than whites. These conclusions are reinforced by the same types of data classified by age. Generational gains at the high school and college levels were greater for whites than for nonwhites in every age group; in fact, the differential favoring whites seemed to be greater at younger rather than older ages.

From the generational education data just discussed, one can determine how much of the overall educational difference between white and nonwhite men can be explained statistically by the poorer educational attainment of the fathers of the nonwhite men and associated socioeconomic factors, and how much by the poorer educational experience of the nonwhite men themselves. Both "educational inheritance" and the men's own experiences appear to have important influences. Because of the high correlation between a father's education and that of his son, the educational distribution of the fathers is a potent factor in accounting for the educational distribution of the sons.

Among men 25 to 64 years old, the percentage of fathers who had not completed the eighth grade was three-fifths higher for nonwhites than for whites, the percentage who had finished high school was more than twice as high for whites, and the percentage with college degrees was exactly twice as high for whites as for nonwhites. On the other hand, within each category of father's education, and for every age group, white men had more schooling than nonwhite men. The difference was most pronounced at the higher educational levels. In fact, among men at all ages whose fathers were college graduates, 57 percent of the whites but only 13 percent of the nonwhites had themselves completed college. This large difference was observed among young men as well as old. (See table V–8.)

Table V–8.—Educational Attainment of Sons 25 to 64 Years Old, by Color, and Educational Attainment of their Fathers: March 1962

[In thousands]

Educational attainment of father	White				Nonwhite			
	Total	Less than 8 years	12 years or more	16 years or more	Total	Less than 8 years	12 years or more	16 years or more
Total....................	100	14	53	14	100	40	26	4
Less than 8 years..............	100	23	37	7	100	48	19	2
12 years or more..............	100	3	78	23	100	21	57	14
16 years or more..............	100	1	92	57	100	13	79	13

Source: Unpublished tabulations from the U.S. Bureau of the Census, *Current Population Survey.*

It is clear that much of the difference between the educational attainment of white men and nonwhite men is related to their color, for even when the fathers of both groups of men have had the same level of educational attainment, the white sons outstrip the nonwhite sons in educational level. In other words, being nonwhite seems to have been a greater handicap in getting more schooling than having a father whose education was limited. We can illustrate this point by showing the effect of one factor on educational attainment when the differential impact of the other factor is removed. For example, among men 25 to 64 years old, 14 percent of the whites and 40 percent of the non-whites lacked an eighth-grade education. If we assume that there had been no difference in the attainment distributions of white and nonwhite fathers, about 33 percent of the nonwhite men would have been expected to have less than 8 years of school. If we assume that the educational distributions of the fathers still differed, but that within each category of father's education white and nonwhite sons had the same educational distribution, then about 18 percent of the nonwhite men would have been expected to have failed to complete 8 years of school.

If the measure of education is high school graduation, a similar pattern emerges: 53 percent of the white men had completed high school, compared with 26 percent of the nonwhite men; under the first set of assumed conditions the percentage for nonwhites would have been expected to be 34 percent, and under the second set, 45 percent. In both examples, differences in the fathers' distributions could explain about one-fourth of the color differential in educational attainment of men. About three-fourths of the difference remained to be explained by other factors which could account for the poorer average educational attainment of nonwhite men even when their fathers were as well educated as the fathers of white men. The factor of educational differences among white and nonwhite fathers accounted for only a minor fraction of the total educational differential of white and nonwhite men in each age group; this factor, however, explained somewhat more variation at the younger than older ages, particularly at the lower end of the educational continuum. This was due to the fact that reductions in the color differential, especially in terms of percentages of men with little schooling, have been more noticeable among the sons' generation than among the fathers' generation, a concomitant of the more rapid rise in school enrollment rates in recent years.

Ethnic groupings. The findings afforded by comparison of the white and nonwhite populations may lead one to speculate about the relative educational status of specific white and nonwhite ethnic groups. How well educated, for example, are certain European foreign-stock groupings compared with various racial groups or other foreign-stock groupings? Table V–9 shows selected measures of educational attainment for nine such ethnic groups, and compares them with the attainment levels of native-white Americans of native parentage. The data are shown separately for two age groups: persons 45 to 64 years old, and those 25 to 34 years old. Differences in schooling between the two age groups provide a general indication of educational change over time.

Among the older ethnic groups, the Northern or Western European and Central or Eastern European foreign-stock groupings and the Japanese compared favorably with native-white Americans of native parentage in educational attainment. The Negro, Puerto Rican, Latin American, and American Indian groups ranked in the lower part of the educational scale. The Chinese and the Southern European stock had attainment levels intermediate to the other two combinations of ethnic groups. For the younger adult age group, however, there were some reversals in the ordering of ethnic groups by amount of schooling. The Japanese were the best educated among the groups, with the Northern and Western European, Central and Eastern European, and Chinese groups ranking higher than the native-white Americans of native parentage and the Southern European stock ranking just below the native Americans. In this age group, the Chinese had the highest percentage of any group with one or more years of college completed.

The Puerto Ricans in the United States—many of them recent migrants to the mainland and schooled in Puerto Rico—were at the bottom of the educational ladder in the 25 to 34 years age group, and the American Indians, Latin Americans, and Negroes were next in order above them. A comparison of the older and younger age groups shows that the Negroes were apparently more educationally mobile upward than the Latin American, Indian, or Puerto Rican groups.

Table V–9.—SELECTED MEASURES OF EDUCATIONAL ATTAINMENT FOR PERSONS IN SPECIFIED ETHNIC GROUPS 25 TO 34 YEARS OLD, AND 45 TO 64 YEARS OLD, BY SEX: 1960

Ethnic group and sex	25 to 34 years old			45 to 64 years old		
	Percent with--			Percent with--		
	Less than 5 years of school	High school, 4 years or more	College, 1 year or more	Less than 5 years of school	High school, 4 years or more	College, 1 year or more
MALE						
Native white of native parentage..................	3	59	27	7	34	16
Northern or Western European foreign stock.........	1	67	35	3	33	16
Central or Eastern European foreign stock.........	1	68	21	8	32	18
Southern European foreign stock...................	2	54	23	15	18	8
Mexican, Central or South American foreign stock..	10	31	15	43	16	7
Puerto Rican stock................................	19	20	6	33	11	5
Negro...	12	30	11	36	11	5
American Indian...................................	18	24	8	31	14	5
Japanese..	1	82	40	9	38	15
Chinese...	6	71	51	37	25	13
FEMALE						
Native white of native parentage..................	2	63	19	5	40	17
Northern or Western European foreign stock.........	1	70	22	2	37	14
Central or Eastern European foreign stock.........	1	70	22	11	28	10
Southern European foreign stock...................	2	57	11	18	14	4
Mexican, Central or South American foreign stock..	18	32	10	43	15	5
Puerto Rican stock................................	21	21	6	42	9	3
Negro...	6	36	11	25	14	6
American Indian...................................	17	25	6	29	15	5
Japanese..	1	77	22	15	29	7
Chinese...	12	64	34	40	28	14

Source: *1960 Census of Population, Subject Reports, Nonwhite Population by Race,* Series PC(2)–1C, tables 19–22; *Puerto Ricans in the United States,* Series PC(2)–1D, table 6; and *Educational Attainment,* Series PC(2)–5B, table 1.

Religious denominations. Nationality is one cultural factor that produces differences in educational attainment; religion is another. According to survey data collected by the National Opinion Research Center in the mid-1950's[6] Jews and Episcopalians were the best educated among household heads in the United States, and Presbyterians ranked third but significantly higher than other religious groups. Of the major denominations, Baptists, Roman Catholics, and Lutherans were among the least well educated. The religious factor is of course interwoven with nationality, and the joint effect reflects the different values and attitudes toward education held by various ethnic groups.

Geographic regions, States, and counties. Among the four major regions of the country, educational attainment, like enrollment rates, has been lowest in the South and highest in the West. With few exceptions, this relation is found to be the same for 1960 as it was for 1940 among the old and the young, among men and women, and among whites and nonwhites. (See table V–10.)

Table V–10.—SELECTED MEASURES OF EDUCATIONAL ATTAINMENT, FOR PERSONS 25 YEARS OLD AND OVER, AND 25 TO 29 YEARS OLD, BY REGION, COLOR, AND SEX: 1960 AND 1940

Age, color, sex, and years of school completed	1960				1940			
	North-east	North Central	South	West	North-east	North Central	South	West
25 YEARS OLD AND OVER								
Less Than 5 Years of School								
Male:								
White..........................	6.6	5.4	11.8	5.5	12.0	9.0	17.9	8.8
Nonwhite.......................	15.1	16.7	38.0	17.9	25.5	26.0	55.0	30.2
Female:								
White..........................	6.6	4.3	8.4	4.2	11.0	7.1	13.5	6.5
Nonwhite.......................	11.1	11.4	26.3	13.8	20.1	20.5	44.1	28.6
4 Years of High School or More								
Male:								
White..........................	40.9	40.7	38.1	50.0	23.5	23.2	22.4	32.2
Nonwhite.......................	25.7	23.8	13.2	35.6	11.2	11.6	4.4	17.7
Female:								
White..........................	42.9	44.7	41.3	53.7	25.4	27.7	26.8	38.8
Nonwhite.......................	29.2	28.2	16.6	38.9	12.1	13.6	6.3	19.5
25 TO 29 YEARS OLD								
Less Than 5 Years of School								
Male:								
White..........................	1.8	1.5	4.5	2.4	1.7	1.4	10.0	2.2
Nonwhite.......................	4.4	4.4	14.9	5.1	10.9	9.0	41.3	15.3
Female:								
White..........................	1.7	1.0	3.2	1.4	1.7	1.1	6.8	2.0
Nonwhite.......................	2.5	2.2	6.5	4.9	7.5	5.8	26.5	13.4
4 Years of High School or More								
Male:								
White..........................	63.8	64.7	56.7	67.4	38.2	41.6	31.2	51.1
Nonwhite.......................	40.9	39.9	27.0	58.4	17.7	21.6	6.6	30.8
Female:								
White..........................	67.9	68.0	57.0	67.7	40.0	47.0	37.4	56.9
Nonwhite.......................	46.6	44.9	32.3	59.0	19.7	23.8	10.4	35.4

Source: *1960 Census of Population*, Vol. I, *Characteristics of the Population*, Part 1, U.S. Summary, table 241; *1940 Census of Population*, Vol. IV, U.S. Summary, table 39.

Between 1940 and 1960, the educational level of all subgroups of the population increased in all four regions, but the rates of increase were somewhat uneven and, as a result, some regional differentials in education narrowed and others widened. The main tendency was toward a narrowing at the lower end of the educational continuum and a widening at the upper end. This pattern of change held true for men as well as women and for whites as well as non-whites. At the youngest adult ages, 25 to 29 years, widening of the regional differentials at the higher educational levels was not very pronounced; in fact, for white males the differential narrowed somewhat at the level of high school graduation. As levels of schooling rise and as high school completion and college attendance become more widespread, we may expect a narrowing of regional differentials at the higher educational levels.

Table V–11 and figures V–4 and V–5 indicate that the regions are not entirely homogeneous with regard to educational status. Data for States show substantial variation in educational attainment within regions. Furthermore, rates of change for the States were sufficiently different to cause a change in rank of 5 or more places in 20 States between 1940 and 1960 in terms of years of schooling completed by the 25 to 29 age group.

Using high school completion among all adults in 1960 as the measure of education, we find that the New England States, and particularly Massachusetts, have ranked above the other States in the Northeast Region. Among young adults in 1960, however, the percent finishing high school was higher in New Jersey, Pennsylvania, and New York than in any of the New England States except Massachusetts and Connecticut. Four of the North Central States—Nebraska, Kansas, Iowa, and Minnesota, all in the western part of the regional grouping—exceeded other States in the region in the percent of high school graduates among all adults. Nebraska ranked first in the percent of persons 25 to 29 years old who had completed high school, and Minnesota, Iowa, Kansas, and Wisconsin ranked among the first 10 States in the country.

States in the South largely held their low positions between 1940 and 1960 in the hierarchical ordering of States by percentages of persons completing high school. The District of Columbia, where the racial composition had changed drastically during the 20-year period (from 28 percent nonwhite in 1940 to 55 percent in 1960), dropped considerably down the list. The West Region of the United States includes one State (Utah) with a consistently high educational record, a number of other States which rank in the top 10 in terms of the percentage of the population completing high school, and 2 States (New Mexico and Arizona) where the educational attainment levels fall much below those of the other States in the West. The figures in table V–11 for persons 25 to 29 years old in 1960 suggest that in several of the Western States educational attainment is not increasing at the rate observed for many States in the country, and consequently the rankings of these Western

Table V–11.—PERCENT OF THE POPULATION 25 YEARS OLD AND OVER, AND 25 TO 29 YEARS OLD, WHO WERE HIGH SCHOOL GRADUATES, BY STATE: 1960 AND 1940

Division and State	Percentage				Rank[1]			
	25 years old and over		25 to 29 years old		25 years old and over		25 to 29 years old	
	1960	1940	1960	1940	1960	1940	1960	1940
NEW ENGLAND:								
Maine	43.2	28.8	58.2	44.2	20	15	32	18
New Hampshire	42.9	26.8	62.8	41.6	21	18	24	22
Vermont	42.9	27.9	60.4	42.8	22	17	31	20
Massachusetts	47.0	31.0	68.5	48.5	13	9	11	12
Rhode Island	35.0	21.1	56.0	32.4	39	38	37	36
Connecticut	43.8	25.1	66.0	38.1	18	22	17	28
MIDDLE ATLANTIC:								
New York	40.9	23.4	63.3	38.3	28	31	22	27
New Jersey	40.7	23.0	63.9	34.9	30	32	18	33
Pennsylvania	38.1	21.2	63.5	35.0	36	37	19	32
EAST NORTH CENTRAL:								
Ohio	41.9	25.7	61.2	45.2	25	20	28	16
Indiana	41.8	24.8	60.7	46.2	26	24	30	15
Illinois	40.4	24.3	63.5	40.9	32	28	20	24
Michigan	40.9	24.7	62.1	41.0	29	25	26	23
Wisconsin	41.5	22.4	69.3	41.7	27	34	8	21
WEST NORTH CENTRAL								
Minnesota	43.9	25.1	72.3	44.2	17	22	3	19
Iowa	46.3	28.9	72.1	52.1	14	13	4	7
Missouri	36.6	22.2	61.4	36.8	38	35	27	30
North Dakota	38.8	22.5	63.2	38.4	35	33	23	26
South Dakota	42.2	25.1	66.3	44.7	24	22	16	17
Nebraska	47.7	28.9	73.2	51.6	12	14	2	10
Kansas	48.2	28.5	71.1	51.7	9	16	5	9
SOUTH ATLANTIC:								
Delaware	43.4	23.9	62.4	36.5	19	29	25	31
Maryland	40.0	21.1	56.4	32.2	33	39	34	37
District of Columbia	47.8	41.2	61.1	53.2	11	1	29	6
Virginia	37.9	21.6	52.7	28.7	37	36	39	40
West Virginia	30.6	17.8	51.1	28.9	43	43	40	39
North Carolina	32.3	19.0	48.3	25.2	41	40	43	43
South Carolina	30.4	18.4	43.2	22.5	45	41	49	45
Georgia	32.0	17.4	47.6	21.9	42	45	46	47
Florida	42.6	26.6	56.1	30.5	23	19	36	38
EAST SOUTH CENTRAL:								
Kentucky	27.6	15.7	44.2	25.2	49	48	48	44
Tennessee	30.4	18.1	47.7	25.4	45	42	45	42
Alabama	30.3	15.9	48.5	21.3	46	47	42	49
Mississippi	29.8	16.2	44.2	21.6	47	46	47	48
WEST SOUTH CENTRAL:								
Arkansas	28.9	15.1	48.3	22.1	48	49	44	46
Louisiana	32.3	17.7	49.8	25.6	40	44	41	41
Oklahoma	40.5	24.5	63.4	39.4	31	27	21	25
Texas	39.6	24.7	56.1	34.3	34	26	35	34
MOUNTAIN:								
Montana	47.8	29.4	67.3	48.2	10	12	12	14
Idaho	48.5	30.5	66.3	49.7	7	10	15	11
Wyoming	52.0	32.9	69.2	51.9	3	7	9	8
Colorado	52.0	32.1	69.4	48.3	4	8	7	13
New Mexico	45.5	23.8	57.1	34.0	16	30	33	35
Arizona	45.7	29.4	55.5	37.9	15	11	38	29
Utah	55.8	37.0	73.2	58.6	1	3	1	1
Nevada	53.3	35.6	66.4	55.0	2	4	14	4
PACIFIC:								
Washington	51.5	33.6	70.5	56.3	5	5	6	2
Oregon	48.4	33.1	69.1	54.3	8	6	10	5
California	51.5	37.3	66.6	55.6	6	2	13	3
Alaska	54.7	26.6	61.8	(NA)	(NA)	(NA)	(NA)	(NA)
Hawaii	46.1	20.5	71.6	(NA)	(NA)	(NA)	(NA)	(NA)

NA Not available.

[1] Ranks do not include Alaska and Hawaii since some data for these States are lacking.

Source: *1960 Census of Population,* Vol. I, *Characteristics of the Population,* Part 1, table 103 for each State; *1940 Census of Population,* Vol. IV, U.S. Summary, table 12 for each State.

Figure V–4.—Percent of the Population 25 Years Old and Over Who Are High School Graduates, for the States of the Conterminous United States: 1940 and 1960

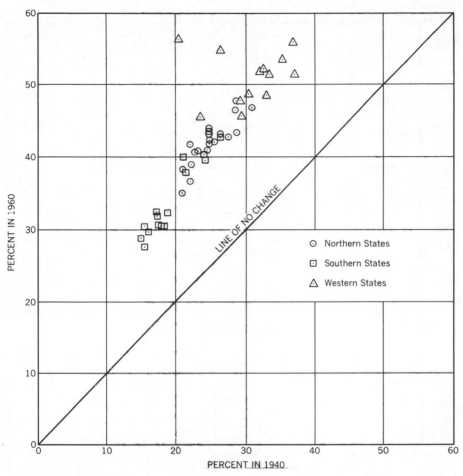

Source: Table V–10.

States have been lowered. It should be noted that all of the changes described are due not only to different rates of improvement in the output of the school systems, but also to educational selectivity in migration between States.

Urban and rural areas. To a great extent, regional and State variations in educational attainment can be attributed to differences in the urban-rural composition of the areas. Styles of living associated with urban, rural-nonfarm, and rural-farm areas are quite distinctive, and are related to differences in the adequacy of the school systems and in attitudes toward education. In 1960, for example, 7 percent of urban adults, 11 percent of rural-nonfarm adults,

Figure V–5.—Percent of the Population 25 to 29 Years Old Who Are High School Graduates, for the States of the Conterminous United States: 1940 and 1960

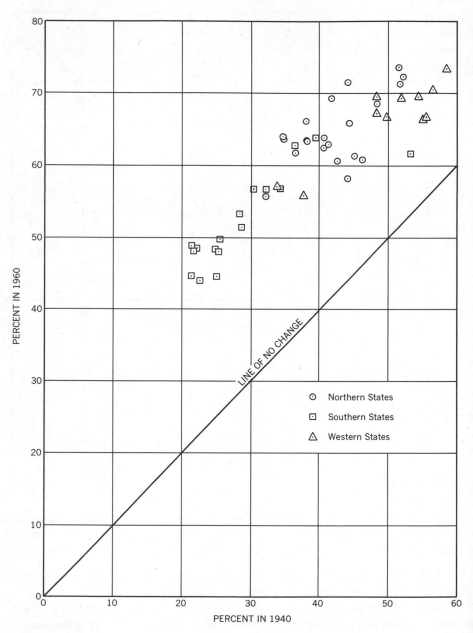

Source: Table V–10.

and 12 percent of rural-farm adults had less than 5 years of schooling (table V–12). Among the youngest adults these percentages were 2, 4, and 7 percent for urban, rural-nonfarm, and rural-farm persons, respectively. For both age groupings, these differentials tended to narrow between 1940 and 1960, although there was a slight widening between the rural-nonfarm and farm rates for all adults. In terms of high school graduation, percentages in 1960 for the three residence groups stood at 44, 35, and 29 percent for adults as a whole, and 64, 55, and 51 percent for young adults. Here again one could find a diminution of the differentials, except between the nonfarm and farm parts of rural areas.[7]

Table V–12.—Selected Measures of Educational Attainment for Persons 25 Years Old and Over, and 25 to 29 Years Old, by Urban and Rural Residence: 1960 and 1940

Years of school completed and residence	25 years old and over		25 to 29 years old	
	1960[1]	1940	1960[1]	1940
LESS THAN 5 YEARS OF SCHOOL				
Urban..........................	7.3	11.4	2.1	3.3
Rural nonfarm..................	10.9	13.9	4.1	6.9
Rural farm.....................	11.5	20.6	6.7	13.5
4 YEARS OF HIGH SCHOOL OR MORE				
Urban..........................	44.2	28.8	63.8	43.8
Rural nonfarm..................	34.5	23.3	54.6	35.7
Rural farm.....................	29.4	12.4	51.4	22.3

[1] Data for 1960 include Alaska and Hawaii, not included in data for 1940.

Source: *1960 Census of Population*, Vol. I, *Characteristics of the Population*, Part 1, U.S. Summary, table 173; *1940 Census of Population*, Vol. IV, U.S. Summary, table 18.

Educational distribution by counties. Table V–13 shows the number of counties within each State in the conterminous United States according to the percent of high school graduates among the county's adult population in 1960, and the changes in these distributions between 1940 and 1960. With one exception, out of 3,083 counties classified, the 73 counties with less than 15 percent of adults having completed high school by 1960 were all in the South Region, 50 of them in Kentucky and Tennessee. In 1960, seven States (Tennessee, Georgia, Alabama, Kentucky, Arkansas, Louisiana, and Mississippi) had less than 25 percent of adults who had finished high school in more than half of their counties, and in four other States (South Carolina, West Virginia, North Carolina, and Virginia) more than a third of the counties were in this category. The map in figure V–6 reveals that the poorest educated

Table V–13.—Number of Counties in Conterminous United States, by Specified Percent of High School Graduates in the Population 25 Years Old and Over, and Change in Distribution Since 1940, by State: 1960

Division and State	Total counties	Counties with specified percent of high school graduates in 1960					Change, 1940 to 1960				
		Under 15 percent	15 to 24 percent	25 to 34 percent	35 to 44 percent	45 percent and over	Under 15 percent	15 to 24 percent	25 to 34 percent	35 to 44 percent	45 percent and over
NEW ENGLAND:											
Maine.................	16	-	-	1	10	5	-	-3	-11	+9	+5
New Hampshire.........	10	-	-	-	6	4	-	-2	-8	+6	+4
Vermont...............	14	-	-	4	7	3	-	-5	-5	+7	+3
Massachusetts.........	14	-	-	1	5	8	-	-1	-8	+1	+8
Rhode Island..........	5	-	-	1	4	-	-	-5	+1	+4	-
Connecticut...........	8	-	-	1	6	1	-	-5	-2	+6	+1
MIDDLE ATLANTIC:											
New York..............	62	-	-	10	45	7	-	-44	-6	+43	+7
New Jersey............	21	-	-	5	11	5	-	-15	-1	+11	+5
Pennsylvania..........	67	-	-	27	33	7	-2	-54	+17	+32	+7
EAST NORTH CENTRAL:											
Ohio..................	88	-	1	17	55	15	-3	-51	-15	+54	+15
Indiana...............	92	-	1	24	44	23	-6	-51	-10	+44	+23
Illinois..............	102	-	14	27	50	11	-21	-41	+3	+48	+11
Michigan..............	83	-	2	21	53	7	-10	-56	+7	+52	+7
Wisconsin.............	71	-	-	27	36	8	-9	-54	+20	+35	+8
WEST NORTH CENTRAL:											
Minnesota.............	87	-	2	35	40	10	-14	-64	+29	+39	+10
Iowa..................	99	-	-	3	55	41	-	-34	-57	+50	+41
Missouri..............	115	1	30	44	31	9	-43	-24	+28	+30	+9
North Dakota..........	53	-	8	19	22	4	-8	-29	+13	+20	+4
South Dakota[1].......	67	-	3	17	36	11	-4	-40	-	+33	+11
Nebraska..............	93	-	-	7	47	39	-	-50	-34	+45	+39
Kansas................	105	-	-	4	45	56	-	-36	-57	+37	+56
SOUTH ATLANTIC:											
Delaware..............	3	-	-	1	1	1	-	-2	-	+1	+1
Maryland..............	24	-	-	14	8	2	-7	-15	+13	+8	+1
District of Columbia..	1	-	-	-	-	1	-	-	-	-1	+1
Virginia[2]...........	113	2	38	47	19	7	-44	-9	+33	+14	+6
West Virginia.........	55	2	21	24	8	-	-32	+2	+22	+8	-
North Carolina.......	100	-	40	44	12	4	-50	-3	+37	+12	+4
South Carolina.......	46	-	20	20	6	-	-16	-9	+19	+6	-
Georgia..............	159	7	107	32	11	2	-119	+78	+29	+10	+2
Florida..............	67	-	17	21	19	10	-26	-8	+8	+16	+10
EAST SOUTH CENTRAL:											
Kentucky.............	120	32	50	30	6	2	-52	+17	+27	+6	+2
Tennessee............	95	18	52	18	6	-	-54	+32	+15	+6	+1
Alabama..............	67	-	46	15	6	-	-55	+35	+14	+6	-
Mississippi..........	82	3	41	30	6	2	-45	+10	+27	+6	+2
WEST SOUTH CENTRAL:											
Arkansas.............	75	3	46	22	3	1	-57	+32	+22	+2	+1
Louisiana............	64	2	33	19	8	2	-44	+17	+17	+8	+2
Oklahoma.............	77	-	16	33	15	13	-19	-27	+20	+13	+13
Texas................	254	3	42	114	67	28	-54	-88	+63	+52	+27
MOUNTAIN:											
Montana[3]...........	56	-	-	1	29	26	-1	-17	-33	+26	+25
Idaho[3].............	44	-	-	1	17	26	-	-12	-28	+14	+26
Wyoming[3]...........	23	-	-	-	2	21	-	-1	-17	-3	+21
Colorado.............	63	-	2	7	22	32	-2	-13	-34	+17	+32
New Mexico[4]........	31	-	5	6	15	5	-7	-9	-2	+13	+5
Arizona..............	14	-	1	4	7	2	+5	-7	+3	+7	+2
Utah.................	29	-	-	-	4	25	-	-4	-18	-3	+25
Nevada...............	17	-	-	1	5	11	-	-2	-10	+2	+10
PACIFIC:											
Washington...........	39	-	-	-	13	26	-	-6	-29	+9	+26
Oregon...............	36	-	-	-	16	20	-	-1	-32	+13	+20
California...........	58	-	-	6	21	31	-	-11	-31	+11	+31

— Represents zero.

[1] Armstrong County annexed to Dewey County; Washington County annexed by Shannon County between 1940 and 1960.

[2] Excludes 8 independent cities created between 1940 and 1960 and the counties in which they were originally located.

[3] Excludes part of Yellowstone National Park.

[4] Los Alamos County not included.

Source: *1960 Census of Population*, Vol. I, *Characteristics of the Population*, chapter C, for each State; *1940 Census of Population*, Vol. IV, for each State.

counties (in terms of high school graduates) are concentrated in the Appalachian Mountain Region, and the counties where less than one-fourth of the adults had completed high school are primarily in the rural parts of the South.

Turning to the counties with better educated adults (those with 45 percent or more of high school graduates), we find that nine States (Wyoming, Utah, Washington, Nevada, Idaho, Oregon, California, Colorado, and Kansas) had more than half of their counties in this category. The District of Columbia also fell in this grouping.

The data in table V–13 in conjunction with figures V–5 and V–6 lead to two generalizations about changes in the geographical pattern of educational attainment in the United States between 1940 and 1960: First, the increase in educational attainment for the Nation as a whole during this 20-year period was widespread. A considerable proportion of the counties raised their percentage of high school graduates enough to place them in a higher category in 1960 than in 1940. Data not shown indicate that every county in the United States had accomplished at least some increase in the percentage of high school graduates. Second, improvement in the adult level of education of counties was so uniform throughout the country that the pattern of geographical differentials seen for 1940 was largely the pattern observed for 1960.

Distributional inequalities in education and other socioeconomic resources. One way of summarizing the pattern of educational differentials among subgroups of the population is to compute the percentage of the aggregate years of schooling held by given percentages of the best educated or the poorest educated.[8] These figures are shown for men in table V–14.

For the country as a whole, more equal distributions of educational attainment occurred at the younger ages. Among men 75 years old and over, the most poorly educated third of the population had 13 percent of the aggregate years of schooling; at ages 45 to 49, the figure was 20 percent; and at ages 25 to 29, as high as 22 percent—still a considerable distance from the 33 percent that would indicate distributional equality. Variations for the different subgroups are found within the different age groups. Among the oldest non-white men in the rural-farm parts of the South, the most poorly educated third had only 3 percent of the aggregate educational attainment. Considering the men 25 to 29 years old, the percentage of aggregate education possessed by the best educated third of the population was 49 percent among nonwhites in the South as a whole, 50 percent among North Carolina nonwhites, and 53 percent among Mississippi nonwhites. Overall, educational inequalities seem to be declining, but even among our recently educated population inequalities are still substantial. The distribution in 1960 in the South for rural-farm male nonwhites between 25 and 29 years old was the same as that for men 75 and over in the country at large.

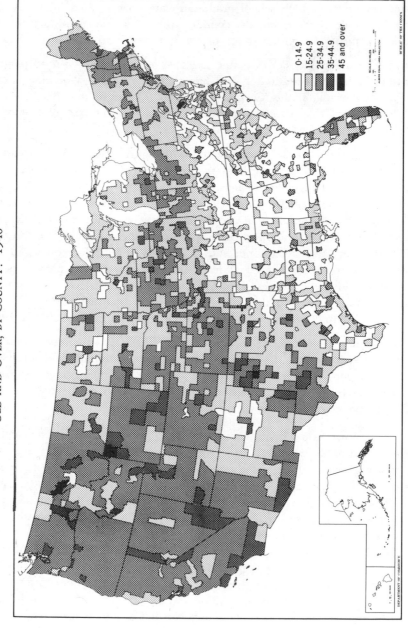

Figure V–6.—Percent of High School Graduates in the Population 25 Years Old and Over, by County: 1940

Source: 1940 Census of Population, Vol. II, table 21.

Figure V-7.—PERCENT OF HIGH SCHOOL GRADUATES IN THE POPULATION 25 YEARS OLD AND OVER, BY COUNTY: 1960

0 - 14.9
15 - 24.9
25 - 34.9
35 - 44.9
45 and over

1960 *Census of Population,* Vol. I, *Characteristics of the Population,* table 83.

Table V–14.—Distributional Inequalities in Years of Schooling and in Other Socioeconomic Resources: Circa 1960

Item	Percent of aggregate amount of indicated resource possessed by—			
	Lowest 5 percent of the distribution	Lowest 33 percent of the distribution	Highest 33 percent of the distribution	Highest 5 percent of the distribution
YEARS OF SCHOOLING				
Men 25 to 29 Years Old				
United States	1	22	43	8
Rural	2	23	43	7
Rural nonfarm	1	21	43	8
Rural farm	1	20	44	8
Northeast	2	23	43	7
North Central	2	24	42	8
South:				
Total	1	20	45	8
Nonwhite	1	17	49	9
Rural farm nonwhite	(Z)	14	54	10
North Carolina:				
Total	1	19	46	8
Nonwhite	1	16	50	10
Mississippi:				
Total	1	18	47	8
Nonwhite	(Z)	15	53	11
Iowa	2	25	41	7
Men 45 to 49 Years Old				
United States	1	20	46	9
South—rural farm nonwhite	(Z)	11	57	13
Men 75 Years Old and Over				
United States	(Z)	13	53	12
South—rural farm nonwhite	(Z)	3	69	18
Mississippi—rural farm nonwhite	(Z)	3	69	17
OTHER SOCIOECONOMIC CHARACTERISTICS				
Occupational status[1]	(Z)	12	54	10
Family income[2]	(Z)	12	58	13
Net worth[3]	(Z)	1	81	27
Health expenditures[4]	(Z)	5	75	27
Value of owned home[5]	1	14	56	14
Gross rent of rented home[6]	1	19	50	11

Z Less than 0.5 percent.

[1] Data for men in the experienced civilian labor force in 1950. Occupational weights are those cited in *Methodology and Scores of Socioeconomic Status*, U.S. Bureau of the Census, Working Paper No. 15.

[2] Data on income in 1959 for family units in 1960.

[3] Data for spending units in 1953.

[4] Data for family units in 1957–58.

[5] Data for owner-occupied housing units in 1960.

[6] Data for renter-occupied housing units in 1960 where cash rent is paid.

Source: *1960 Census of Population*, Vol. I, *Characteristics of the Population*, Part 1, U.S. Summary and selected State reports; *1953 Survey of Consumer Finances, Federal Reserve Bulletin*, 1953, supplementary table 5, p. 11; Odin W. Anderson, Patricia Collette, and Jacob J. Feldman, *Family Expenditure Patterns for Personal Health Services, 1953 and 1958; Nationwide Surveys, Health Information Foundation Research*, Series 14, p. 21; *1960 Census of Housing*, Vol. I, *States and Small Areas*, U.S. Summary, table 8; and records.

Of all socioeconomic resources, education seems to be the most equally distributed. Table V–14 shows six specific socioeconomic "resources" (occupational status, family income, net worth, health expenditures, value of owned homes, and gross rent of rented homes) which are distributed by aggregate amounts of the resource in various population sectors. Although the units for which these resources are reported vary, they generally refer to families or households. No family or household measure of educational attainment has been used, but a close approximation is obtained by referring to the attainment distribution for men 45 to 49 years old. Only the distribution of rental values of homes comes near the equality of years of schooling. If rental and owned home values were combined to get a universal measure of housing status, the distribution would be less equal than that for education. Occupational status and family income, two socioeconomic items most closely associated with education, are found to be distributed in the population far more unequally, and health expenditures and net worth have a distinctly uneven aggregate distribution when compared with years of schooling.

NOTES

[1] Data on educational attainment for 1910, 1920, and 1930 were estimated by retrojecting the 1940 data by age and sex (that is, tracing age cohorts in 1940 back in time). For example, males 45 to 49 years old in 1930 were assumed to have had the same relative educational distribution as that for males 55 to 59 years old in 1940. No allowance was made for possible bias in the estimates for earlier years due to differential mortality, or for misreporting of educational attainment in 1940, especially by older persons. (See section on "Limitations in Educational Concepts and Data Used" for further discussion of the latter limitation.) For a more refined estimate of the educational attainment of the adult population from 1910 to 1960, see Susan O. Bearrentine, "An Estimate of the 'True' Educational Distribution of the United States Adult Population: 1910 to 1960" (unpublished thesis, Florida State University, 1966).

[2] Since the data were based on a representative national sample of men in 1962, references to the father's generation do not cover a representative sample of men living during the father's lifetime, nor even to a sample of fathers, since some members of the father's male generation were unmarried, and some who were married had no sons.

[3] Natalie Rogoff, *Recent Trends in Occupational Mobility*. Glencoe, Illinois: The Free Press, 1953, pp. 29-33, 46. Similar methodological techniques were used in a study of occupational mobility in Great Britain. See David V. Glass (ed.), *Social Mobility in Britain*. Glencoe, Illinois: The Free Press, 1954, appendix I.

[4] There have been exceptional periods of time, such as the post-World War II period, when preference in college entrance was often given male war veterans.

[5] These data, some of which are unpublished, were obtained in connection with the October 1960 Current Population Survey.

[6] These data were cited in Donald J. Bogue, *The Population of the United States*. Glencoe, Illinois: The Free Press, 1949, pp. 700-702. See also Andrew M. Greeley, *Religion and Career*. New York: Sheed and Ward, 1963.

NOTES—Continued

[7] Census definitions of types of residence were changed somewhat between 1940 and 1960; hence, historical comparability may be affected. The extent of the net effect is not known, but the maintenance of rural nonfarm-farm differentials may be a function of definitional changes which based the farm definition on more rigorous criteria than before.

[8] This technique of measuring distributional inequalities in education was developed by C. Arnold Anderson and illustrated with 1950 Census data in his article, "Inequalities in Schooling in the South," *The American Journal of Sociology*, 60:6, May 1955, pp. 557-560.

CHAPTER VI

EDUCATIONAL ATTAINMENT, OCCUPATION, MIGRATION, AND FAMILY PATTERNS

Introduction

This chapter analyzes education as it relates to such key elements of the social structure as occupation, migration, family composition, and marriage patterns. The relationship between education and income will be treated only briefly since this subject is discussed comprehensively in the 1960 Census Monograph, *Income Distribution in the United States,* by Herman P. Miller.[1] The trends in educational attainment reported in chapter V provide a background for the more detailed information of this chapter, which is drawn primarily from the 1940, 1950, and 1960 Censuses.

Limitations of the data on educational attainment, discussed in chapter V and appendix A, will be referred to here only when they materially affect the conclusions.

Trends in educational attainment of occupational groups

There are at least two major approaches to the analysis of the education-occupation relationship. The first may be called the economic or labor market approach, which focuses on the direct relation of education to jobs. It is well represented in the works of Harris,[2] Blank and Stigler,[3] and to a lesser extent in the work of Havighurst.[4] In these studies, the *economic demand* for educated persons is assumed to be the major determinant of the supply of persons with given levels of education. While there may be temporary imbalances, if supply exceeds demand economic forces will be set in motion to slow down the expansion of the supply; if demand exceeds supply the same forces will operate in the opposite direction to increase the supply. The market perspective on the education-occupation relationship leads the researcher to concentrate on past and future changes in the occupational structure, since these changes are assumed to be the causative factors in the operation of the relationship.[5]

In 1949, Seymour Harris, using a supply-demand analysis, predicted a surplus of college graduates. In his words: ". . . college students within the next twenty years are doomed to disappointment after graduation, as the number of coveted openings will be substantially less than the numbers seeking them."[6]

Manpower studies conducted during the 1950's focused mostly on narrow segments of the occupational distribution and generally projected shortages in these areas. A few years ago, Havighurst analyzed the relation of educational output to occupation from a broader perspective, but one which was heavily influenced by economic factors, and came to a similar but qualified conclusion:

> If our estimates of future trends in supply and demand are close to reality, we shall soon enter a period in which supply equals demand for college men, followed by a period in which the supply may exceed the demand, unless ideological factors enter to supplement the economic factors we have considered.[7]

The conclusions of supply-demand analysis seem to be clear: that we have had a period of educational shortage, that we are entering a period when there may be some shortage areas, but that there will generally be a surplus of educated persons.

A second approach to the study of the education-occupation relationship is based on the consumer-demand or educational opportunity concept. As Trow, noting the rise in college enrollments, expresses it:

> These figures are related to a subtle change in the educational standard of living of the population, which is making of college not a special privilege for especially bright or well-to-do children, but for increasing parts of the population, simply the normal, expectable thing for one's children, just as a high school education became part of the normal expectations for nearly the whole population during the first half of this century. This basic shift in educational norms and values, rooted in but now developing independently of the changes in occupational structure means, in my opinion, that college enrollments are not merely rising, but will do so indefinitely, until there is near universal experience of some sort and duration in institutions of higher education. This entails a shift in perspectives that many observers have not yet made: there is still talk of the demand for college places "leveling off," and still efforts to link future enrollments to the demands of the occupational structure. I believe these perspectives are rooted in older conceptions of a higher education as something very special, and for the minority (even a large minority of students) who because of special talents can profit from it and are needed in the professional and technical occupations. These older conceptions of higher education are less and less appropriate to the character of the mass higher education that is developing all around us; we can see that more clearly in California than anywhere else in the world at this moment.[8]

Although Trow may be overly optimistic about rising trends in college education, he is suggesting that the growth of educational attainment in America is not so much the result of the demands of the economy as it is the belief that education is good in itself, and that educational opportunity is part of everyone's expectations. This is a different conception of the education-occupation relationship, and it suggests that in the future there may be less relationship between the growth of formal education and changes in occupational opportunities. Havighurst expressed a similar thought.

> Ideology will play a more important part in determining developments in higher education in the 1960's than it played during the 1950's. . . . Consequently we shall be more explicitly concerned with the *social* goals of higher education than we were

during the 1950's. The social goal of training people for certain occupations will lose some of its priority, and . . . [other] social goals will become more important in the decisions that are made.[9]

There is also the possibility that economic supply-demand factors are still dominant, but that analysts have given inadequate attention to educational upgrading within occupations, in contrast to shifts between occupations. As Denison comments:

> It would be interesting to know the extent to which the advance of education in the labor force has meant an increase in educational levels occupation-by-occupation, and the extent to which it has been absorbed by the disproportionate rise in the better educated occupations.[10]

An examination of the trends in occupation, in formal education, and in their relationship may provide the answer to the question Denison raises.

The long-term rise in educational attainment, deriving from continued expansion of the school systems and the extension of schooling to all groups and areas of the country, is well documented and needs only brief mention. Among men 25 to 64 years old, a group which closely approximates the males of labor force age, we find that in 1910, 25 percent had less than 5 years of schooling; by 1960, only about 7 percent had so little schooling. In 1910, 13 percent of the men between 25 and 64 were high school graduates and less than 4

Table VI-1.—EDUCATIONAL ATTAINMENT OF THE MALE POPULATION 25 TO 64 YEARS OLD: 1910 TO 1980

[Numbers in millions]

Years of school completed	Estimated		Reported		Projected	
	1910	1920	1940	1960	1970	1980
Total......................	21.2	25.1	33.1	40.6	43.9	51.3
No school years completed.........	1.8	1.7	1.1	0.6	0.4	0.3
Elementary: 1 to 4 years.........	3.6	3.9	3.4	2.2	1.6	1.2
5 to 7 years..........	4.7	5.4	6.1	5.3	4.2	3.2
8 years..............	7.0	8.1	9.4	6.6	5.1	3.9
High school: 1 to 3 years..........	1.4	2.2	5.2	8.2	9.4	10.7
4 years..............	1.3	1.9	4.3	9.6	12.1	15.8
College: 1 to 3 years..........	0.6	0.9	1.7	3.8	4.6	6.3
4 years or more.......	0.7	1.0	1.9	4.3	6.5	9.9
PERCENT DISTRIBUTION						
Total......................	100.0	100.0	100.0	100.0	100.0	100.0
No school years completed.........	8.2	6.8	3.4	1.5	0.9	0.6
Elementary: 1 to 4 years.........	17.0	15.5	10.2	5.4	3.6	2.3
5 to 7 years..........	22.3	21.6	18.5	13.1	9.6	6.2
8 years..............	32.8	32.3	28.3	16.3	11.6	7.6
High school: 1 to 3 years..........	6.8	8.7	15.6	20.2	21.4	20.9
4 years..............	6.3	7.5	13.1	23.6	27.6	30.8
College: 1 to 3 years..........	3.0	3.5	5.2	9.3	10.5	12.3
4 years or more.......	3.5	4.0	5.8	10.6	14.8	19.3

Source: Data for 1910 and 1920 are estimates based on retrojection of 1940 age cohorts by education. Data for 1940 are from *1950 Census of Population*, Vol. I, *Characteristics of the Population*, Part 1, U.S. Summary; for 1960, from *1960 Census of Population*, Vol. I, *Characteristics of the Population*, Part 1, U.S. Summary. Projections for 1970 and 1980 are from U.S. Bureau of the Census, *Current Population Reports—Population Estimates*, Series P-25, No. 305, and are based on Series B assumption at younger ages.

percent were college graduates; by 1960, the corresponding percentages were 44 and 11 percent. (See table VI–1.)

This "educational revolution" had its strongest surge during and after World War II, although improvements in educational attainment have been noted for each decade at least back to 1910 (the earliest date for which estimates are available). Census Bureau projections to 1980 indicate that we can still expect substantial increases in the educational level of the working population. The proportion of "functional illiterates" among men 25 to 64 years old may well be cut in half by 1980, the percentage who are high school graduates may rise to 62 percent of the group at that time, and the proportion who are college graduates may reach 19 percent.[11]

The trend in the occupational composition of the male population since the turn of the century has been one of numerical increases among white-collar workers and among skilled, semiskilled, and service workers. (See table VI–2.) There was some increase early in the century, and a decrease in later

Table VI–2.—Employment of Men, by Major Occupation Group: 1900 to 1975

[Numbers in millions. Data for 1900 and 1920 refer to civilian gainful workers 10 years old and over; for 1940, to persons 14 years old and over in the experienced civilian labor force; for 1960 and projections to 1975, to employed persons 14 years old and over]

Major occupation group	Estimated			Reported	Projected
	1900	1920	1940	1960	1975
Total....................................	23.7	33.6	39.2	43.5	56.5
Professional, technical, and kindred workers.......	0.8	1.3	2.3	4.7	7.9
Managers, officials, and proprietors, exc. farm....	1.6	2.6	3.4	4.9	7.9
Clerical and kindred workers......................	0.7	1.8	2.3	3.2	4.6
Sales workers.....................................	1.1	1.5	2.5	3.1	3.6
Craftsmen, foremen, and kindred workers...........	3.0	5.4	6.1	8.9	10.9
Operatives and kindred workers....................	2.5	4.8	7.1	9.1	10.3
Service workers...................................	0.7	1.2	2.4	2.8	4.5
Laborers, exc. farm and mine......................	3.5	4.7	4.7	3.1	3.6
Farmers and farm managers.........................	5.5	6.2	5.2	2.5	1.8
Farm laborers and foremen.........................	4.4	4.1	3.3	1.3	1.3
PERCENT DISTRIBUTION					
Total....................................	100.0	100.0	100.0	100.0	100.0
Professional, technical, and kindred workers.......	3.4	3.8	5.8	10.8	14.0
Managers, officials, and proprietors, exc. farm....	6.8	7.8	8.6	11.3	14.0
Clerical and kindred workers......................	2.8	5.3	5.8	7.4	8.1
Sales workers.....................................	4.6	4.5	6.4	7.1	6.4
Craftsmen, foremen, and kindred workers...........	12.6	16.0	15.5	20.5	19.3
Operatives and kindred workers....................	10.4	14.4	18.0	20.9	18.2
Service workers...................................	3.1	3.7	6.1	6.4	8.0
Laborers, exc. farm and mine......................	14.7	14.0	12.1	7.1	6.4
Farmers and farm managers.........................	23.0	18.4	13.3	5.7	3.2
Farm laborers and foremen.........................	18.7	12.1	8.4	3.0	2.3

Source: Data for 1900, 1920, and 1940 are from David L. Kaplan and M. Claire Casey, *Occupational Trends in the United States, 1900 to 1950*, Bureau of the Census, Working Paper No. 5, 1958. Data for 1960 are from *1960 Census of Population*, Vol. I, *Characteristics of the Population*, Part 1, U.S. Summary. Projections for 1975 are based on unpublished data provided by the U.S. Bureau of Labor Statistics, and are consistent with projections of occupations for both sexes published in the March 1963 issue of the *Monthly Labor Review*.

decades, in the number of nonfarm unskilled laborers, and a general decline in the number of persons in farm occupations. The relative occupational composition has also changed significantly. White-collar workers constituted 17.5 percent of the male work force in 1900 and more than double that percentage in 1960, with the professional and technical fields expanding most rapidly during the 1940 to 1960 period. The proportions of workers in craft, operative, and service jobs rose gradually over the decades, although they leveled off somewhat during the last decade or so. The proportion in non-farm laboring occupations, which was steady during the early decades of the century, dropped rapidly in later decades, while the proportion in farm occupations has in recent years continued the sharp drop that had already been observed at the turn of the century.[12]

Projections to 1975, based on reports of the Bureau of Labor Statistics, indicate a general continuation of the occupational trends noted in the past. The most rapid increases may be expected in the professional and managerial fields. The proportion of white-collar jobs among men will be approaching one-half of the male labor force. Skilled and semiskilled manual jobs, while increasing in number, will comprise a decreasing percentage of jobs in all occupations. Nonfarm labor may possibly increase slightly, whereas the farm segment of the male labor force can be expected to continue to decline, both relatively and absolutely.[13]

Association of education and occupation

Since higher levels of education are usually required for better jobs, it is not surprising that there is a direct association between levels of education and occupation. The 1960 Census, like those of 1940 and 1950, shows that the average level of educational attainment is highest for the professional and technical occupations, not quite so high for other white-collar jobs, still lower for skilled and semiskilled jobs, and lowest for farm occupations and unskilled nonfarm laborers. (See table VI–3.)

Granted that there is an association between education and occupation, how strong is the association? And is it becoming stronger or weaker? Because of data limitations, we have analyzed the relationship only for white males 35 to 54 years old in nonfarm occupations in 1940, 1950, and 1960. (The data for 1940 are limited to the native-born, which probably has some effect on the results.) Using as an index the measure, gamma, described by Goodman and Kruskal, we find: .52 in 1940, .50 in 1950, and .39 in 1960.[14] The index for 1940 probably would have been higher if we had been able to include foreign-born persons.[15] At any rate, the results clearly show in summary fashion that the association of education and occupation has been moderate but is declining.[16] Whatever the cause for this decline, it holds important implications for the analysis of educational supply and demand.

Table VI–3.—Percent of White Males 35 to 54 Years Old in the Experienced Civilian Labor Force Who Have Completed Specified Levels of School, by Major Occupation Group: 1960 and 1940

Major occupation group	Less than 5 years of school		High school graduates		College, 1 year or more	
	1960	1940[1]	1960	1940[1]	1960	1940[1]
Professional, technical, and kindred workers.........	0.2	0.4	91.3	84.7	74.5	72.7
Farmers and farm managers...........................	6.1	13.4	32.5	9.5	7.5	4.1
Managers, officials, and proprietors, exc. farm......	1.0	2.2	68.0	46.7	35.4	23.5
Clerical, sales, and kindred workers................	0.8	1.2	65.6	47.1	28.0	20.4
Craftsmen, foremen, and kindred workers.............	3.0	4.9	36.4	15.8	8.0	4.4
Operatives and kindred workers......................	5.7	8.1	24.9	10.9	4.0	2.9
Service workers.....................................	5.2	5.4	34.0	15.2	8.1	4.4
Farm laborers and foremen...........................	29.2	21.2	12.1	6.3	2.7	1.9
Laborers, exc. farm and mine.......................	12.3	13.5	17.2	7.3	2.8	2.0

[1] Data for 1940 are for employed native white males only.

Source: Data for 1960 are from 1960 Census of Population, Subject Reports, Educational Attainment, Series PC(2)–5B; for 1940 from 1940 Census of Population, Special Report, Educational Attainment by Economic Characteristics and Marital Status.

What can be said about the factors which affect the education-occupation relationship, and which may help to explain the declining association? Katz followed one approach to analyze changes in educational attainment levels within occupational groups for the 1952 to 1959 period, using data from the Census Bureau's Current Population Survey.[17] Computing an "expected" occupational distribution for 1959 that would have been obtained if the "demand for workers at each attainment level had remained the same in the various occupational groups as in 1952" and comparing it to the actual 1959 occupational distribution, he concluded that "The differences between the 'expected' and the actual 1959 occupation structure mainly depict an increasing demand for better educated workers." The data and analysis presented by Katz do not, however, really answer the question: Did the "demand" rise because the supply increased, or did the "demand" really stimulate the growth of the supply?

Some insight into this question, and the relative strength of demand factors, can be obtained by analyzing the extent to which the rise in the educational level of workers can be accounted for by shifts in the occupational distribution. How much of the rise in the educational level of the labor force is due to shifts from jobs requiring little education to those requiring more education, and how much of it can be attributed to rises in educational attainment within occupations? This is the question posed by Denison. The analysis again is confined to employed white males 35 to 54 years old, an age group for which shifts in and out of the labor force, as well as occupational and educational changes, should be minimal. The changes considered took place between 1940 and 1960.

During this period, the population in the age group increased from 10.6 million to 18.5 million, and its median level of educational attainment increased from 8.5 to 11.5 years of school completed. The group grew in size about twice as fast from 1940 to 1950 as from 1950 to 1960, but its educational attainment rose more rapidly in the second decade. The rise in educational attainment was subdivided into a component due to changes in occupational composition and a component due to increases in educational attainment within occupational groups.[18] (See table VI–4.)

Most of the educational change that occurred in the 1940 to 1960 period for the age group considered could be attributed to a rise in the level of educational attainment within occupational groups. Overall, about 85 percent of the rise in educational attainment may be attributed to increased educational

Table VI–4.—Components of Change in Educational Attainment of Employed White Males, 35 to 54 Years Old: 1940 to 1960

[Numbers in thousands]

Period and years of school completed	Total change in educational attainment	Educational change due to--		
		Change within occupation	Shifts in employment between occupations	Standardization difference (absolute)
	(1)	(2)	(3)	(4)
1940 TO 1960				
No school years completed........	-71	-35	-36	10
Elementary: 1 to 4 years........	-452	-291	-161	85
5 to 8 years........	-4,013	-3,549	-464	3
High school: 1 to 3 years........	794	694	100	63
4 years...........	2,414	2,363	51	126
College: 1 to 3 years........	595	505	90	9
4 years or more.....	734	314	420	25
1940 TO 1950				
No school years completed........	3	17	-14	3
Elementary: 1 to 4 years........	-27	54	-81	18
5 to 8 years........	-1,557	-1,417	-140	40
High school: 1 to 3 years........	299	255	44	29
4 years...........	861	828	33	5
College: 1 to 3 years........	193	171	22	13
4 years or more.....	228	91	137	27
1950 TO 1960				
No school years completed........	-71	-57	-14	1
Elementary: 1 to 4 years........	-415	-344	-71	16
5 to 8 years........	-2,109	-1,823	-286	35
High school: 1 to 3 years........	424	404	20	13
4 years...........	1,360	1,321	39	53
College: 1 to 3 years........	354	288	66	1
4 years or more.....	457	212	245	11

Note: Computation—Col. (1) represents the amount of change in educational level that would have occurred if the number of males 35 to 54 years old had remained constant during the period. Decreases equal increases. Cols. (2) and (3) distribute the changes into a component due to shifts in percent employed in different occupations (col. 3) and a component due to the increase in educational level within each occupational category during the period specified (col. 2). Since there is a difference in standardizing the occupational distribution on education and the educational distribution of occupation, an average of the two was used. Col. (4) gives the absolute size of the difference in the two computations.

Source: Data for 1960 from *1960 Census of Population, Subject Reports, Educational Attainment*, Series PC(2)–5B; for 1950, from *1950 Census of Population, Special Reports, Education*, table 11; for 1940, from *1940 Census of Population, Special Reports, Educational Attainment by Economic Characteristics and Marital Status*.

levels within occupations, and only 15 percent to shifts in the occupational structure from occupations requiring less education to occupations requiring more. This was true to about the same extent in the 1940 to 1950 period as in the 1950 to 1960 period, even though the labor force was expanding at a more rapid rate, relative to increases in educational attainment, during the earlier period than in the later period.

Only at the extremes of the attainment distribution (that is, for college graduates and for persons with no education) was as much as one-half the change in educational attainment attributable to shifts between occupations. At the college end of the distribution the change seems to reflect the continuing "demand" for college-trained personnel; at the other end of the distribution, where the changes were negative, they reflect the rapid shrinkage of jobs for persons without formal education. (See table VI-5.)

Table VI-5.—Percent Change in Educational Attainment Attributable to Changes in Occupational Structure, for Employed White Males 35 to 54 Years Old: 1940 to 1960

Years of school completed	1940 to 1960	1940 to 1950	1950 to 1960
No school years completed....................	51	45	20
Elementary: 1 to 4 years....................	36	60	17
5 to 8 years....................	12	9	14
High school: 1 to 3 years....................	13	15	5
4 years.......................	2	4	3
College: 1 to 3 years....................	15	11	19
4 years or more................	57	60	54

Note: Computation—Col. (3) of table VI-4 divided by the sum of Cols. (2) and (3) without regard to sign.

Source: Table VI-4.

It should be noted that this analysis deals with very broad occupational categories. As a result it may obscure shifts within these categories from occupations requiring less education to those requiring more. For example, within the occupational group classified as "managers, officials, and proprietors," which has increased its educational attainment level more rapidly than other white-collar groups, there was a rapid increase in the number of salaried officials of large businesses, for whom substantial education is required, while the number of self-employed proprietors of retail establishments, for whom formal education is less important, was actually declining.

Changes in median educational level between 1950 and 1960 for a number of detailed occupations are shown in table VI-6. The occupations requiring a higher skill level, generally found in the top half of the table, are also the occupations where the skill level is most likely to have risen between 1950 and 1960. These occupations seem to be a little less likely than those in the bottom half of the table to have large within-occupation rises in educational attainment. Occupations which are stable or shrinking in size, and where the educational level of workers in 1950 was less than 12 years, are those in which the educational attainment level rose most rapidly between 1950 and 1960. The rapid rise in attainment of the workers in these occupations (for example, locomotive firemen) seems to be due to the replacement of older, poorly educated workers with a smaller number of younger, better educated ones, rather than to any change in the skill level required by the job.

Table VI–6.—MEDIAN YEARS OF SCHOOL COMPLETED BY MALES IN THE EXPERIENCED CIVILIAN LABOR FORCE, BY SELECTED OCCUPATIONS: 1960 AND 1950

[Numbers in thousands]

Detailed occupation group	1960	1950	Median years of school completed	
			1960	1950
Accountants and auditors	396	327	15.3	14.7
Clergymen	196	158	17.1	16.2
Designers	55	29	13.8	12.7
Draftsmen	206	113	12.9	12.8
Engineers, technical	862	521	16.2	16.1
Medical and dental technicians	53	34	12.8	12.5
Managers (salaried):				
Manufacturing	611	383	13.1	12.7
Wholesale trade	190	145	12.7	12.5
Retail trade	522	426	12.4	12.3
Officials, public administration	160	127	12.9	12.7
Managers (self-employed):				
Manufacturing	160	218	12.3	12.2
Wholesale trade	128	170	12.3	12.1
Retail trade	830	1,133	11.7	11.2
Bank tellers	40	34	12.7	12.6
Mail carriers	198	164	12.3	12.2
Truck and tractor drivers	1,655	1,377	9.1	8.9
Barbers	176	199	9.2	8.9
Railroad conductors	45	55	10.5	9.4
Locomotive firemen	40	55	11.7	10.5
Railroad brakemen	67	79	10.8	9.9
Laborers, exc. farm	3,393	3,581	8.7	8.0

Source: *1960 Census of Population, Subject Reports, Occupational Characteristics,* Series PC(2)–7A.

It is also clear from table VI–6 that a number of occupations experienced very small rises in within-occupation attainment levels between 1950 and 1960. A substantial part of the within-occupation rise in educational level reported above can be attributed to the breadth of the occupational categories used; if data were available to permit this analysis with detailed occupations a different picture would emerge.[19]

The data in table VI–6 undoubtedly overstate the amount of flexibility in educational requirements because the occupational categories are so broad, but nonetheless indicate that the educational levels of workers in various occupations do change and reflect the "supply" of persons as well as the occupational demand. How much of the change reflects increased skill requirements for specific occupations, and how much is due to the availability of better educated persons for the same jobs, cannot be finally determined from these data.

Projections of educational attainment and the occupational structure

The projection of the occupational composition of the labor force (table VI–2) for 1975 can be compared with the projections of the educational attainment levels of the civilian labor force for the same date, to provide estimates of the adequacy of the future supply of persons at various educational levels.[20]

It is necessary to make some estimate of the educational levels required for the occupations of 1975; the first and easiest assumption is that the educational attainment distribution within each occupation will remain the same as it was in 1960. If this assumption turns out to be correct, there will be more high school and college graduates available in 1975 than will be required (table VI–7). In fact, there will be about 3.1 million more high school graduates, 850,000 more persons with some college education, and 3.3 million more college graduates than will be required to maintain the 1960 educational status quo within each occupation.

Table VI–7.—Projection of the Educational Attainment Level of the Male Civilian Labor Force Under Two Different Assumptions: 1975

[Numbers in millions]

Years of school completed	Required attainment distribution[1]	Projected attainment distribution[2]	Difference of required distribution from projected distribution	
			Amount	Percent
Elementary: Less than 5 years	3.46	1.86	-1.60	-86.0
5 to 8 years	15.72	9.59	-6.13	-63.9
High school: 1 to 3 years	11.01	11.51	+.50	+4.3
4 years	13.23	16.33	+3.10	+19.0
College: 1 to 3 years	5.66	6.51	+.85	+13.1
4 years or more	7.32	10.60	+3.28	+30.9
Total	56.40	56.40	0.00	(X)

X Not applicable.
[1] To maintain 1960 educational attainment levels within each major occupation group.
[2] From school graduation figures "available distribution."

Source: Available distribution computed by adjusting figures in U.S. Department of Labor, *Manpower Report of the President, 1965*. Table E5 adjusted to the attainment projections for males contained in U.S. Bureau of the Census, *Current Population Reports—Population Estimates*, Series P–25, No. 305; the distribution required to maintain 1960 educational attainment distribution within each occupational group was computed by applying the 1960 percent distribution of educational attainment within each occupation to the projected 1975 occupational totals.

The assumption of no change in the educational level within occupations has already been shown to be unrealistic. A more pertinent question is whether or not the future supply of persons at the higher educational levels will accelerate the future rate of educational upgrading above the rates of improvement observed between 1950 and 1960. If continued educational upgrading of occupations can be anticipated, which occupations will be affected most?

Between 1950 and 1960 most of the increase of college graduates in the labor force went into professional jobs, where 933,000 of the approximately 1,450,000 increase was concentrated. (See table VI–8.) But the professional occupations did not register much increase in the *proportion* of college graduates between 1950 and 1960. Only 12 percent, or a little over 100,000 of the added workers, contributed to upgrading the level of educational attainment in the professional category.[21] Between 1950 and 1960 about one-half million more males with four or more years of college were added to the labor force than were required to maintain the 1950 educational attainment levels; about 225,000 of these went into managerial occupations, 100,000 into the professions (as indicated above), almost 100,000 into sales occupations, and the remainder were scattered through the other occupations. In contrast, most of the additional persons with high school attainment were concentrated in the craftsmen and operatives occupations. The categories in table VI–8 which have both a large numerical increase and a high percentage of that increase attributable to higher educational attainment levels are the points in the occupational structure which absorbed the better educated workers between 1950 and 1960.

Table VI–8.—Increase in the Number of Males 25 Years Old and Over in Selected Levels of Major Occupation Groups, and Percent of the Increase Attributable to Improved Educational Levels Within the Occupation: 1950 to 1960

[Numbers in thousands. Negative percent indicates failure to achieve 1950 attainment level for the given category]

Major occupation group	High school				College			
	1 to 3 years		4 years		1 to 3 years		4 years or more	
	Amount of increase	Percent of increase due to attainment levels	Amount of increase	Percent of increase due to attainment levels	Amount of increase	Percent of increase due to attainment levels	Amount of increase	Percent of increase due to attainment levels
Professional, techn'l, & kindred wkrs...	77	–4	216	–11	279	13	933	12
Mgrs., off'ls, & propr's, exc. farm.....	95	14	227	26	218	70	281	80
Clerical and kindred workers............	118	31	179	3	119	51	53	36
Sales workers..........................	83	1	116	–17	123	48	130	68
Craftsmen, foremen, & kindred workers...	577	38	726	53	185	65	50	44
Operatives and kindred workers.........	536	47	484	62	93	68	–	–
Service wkrs., excl. private household..	135	58	138	64	50	82	–	–
Laborers..............................	114	100	82	99	–	–	–	–
Farm laborers.........................	–	–	–	–	–	–	–	–
Farmers..............................	–158	26	–	–	–	–	–	–

—Figures not shown where change is less than 20,000.

Source: Computed from *1960 Census of Population, Subject Reports, Educational Attainment*, PC(2)–5B, table 8; and *1950 Census of Population, Special Reports, Education*, PE–5B, table 11.

There is no assurance that the trends occurring between 1950 and 1960 will continue to 1975, but if they do, the majority of the additional male high school graduates will be absorbed into the blue-collar occupations, while a majority of the additional college-educated men will be absorbed by managerial, sales, clerical, and some craftsmen occupations. (Professional occupations, where educational levels are already high, have experienced relatively little educational upgrading.) If the amount of educational upgrading in the period 1950 to 1960 is expressed as a ratio to the total in each educational attainment category in 1960, and compared with the the anticipated ratio for the 1960-1975 time period (adjusted for the difference in length of the period), it can be seen that relatively more college graduates must be absorbed in the next decade than were added in the period 1950-1960, and relatively fewer men with one to three years of college or one to three years of high school. For convenience, this relationship will be called the "absorption ratio."

	High school		College	
	1-3 years	4 years	1-3 years	4 years
Ratio 1950-1960	.11	.13	.17	.12
Ratio 1960-1975	.03	.13	.09	.21

The absorption ratios for the period 1960-1975 are fairly similar to the ratios for the 1950-1960 period, even though the actual numbers of additional high school and college graduates to be absorbed are much larger. This is partly because the projections postulate a much higher total growth in the male labor force over age 25 between 1960 and 1975 (17.4 million) than occurred from 1950 to 1960 (5.0 million). Lower growth rates would probably create serious problems in absorbing the additional educated men, besides creating even more serious problems of unemployment among the poorly educated.

These data are not sufficiently detailed to permit easy identification of specific occupations where additional educated persons can be absorbed, or those occupations where no further educational upgrading is likely. At most, we can identify those occupations where nearly everyone now has a graduate degree; any further educational upgrading in these occupations (if it occurs) will be of a sort that the census does not measure. If a million additional college graduates are available to be absorbed by the managerial occupations in the period 1960 to 1975 (and this seems reasonable, based on the 1950-1960 experience), which specific occupations will be educationally upgraded? How much of the increase will be absorbed by structural changes within this broad occupational category, such as an increase in better educated salaried managers of manufacturing plants, while the number of self-employed proprietors of retail establishments with less education continues to decline? How much of the increase will occur because of rising educational standards within specific occupations? How much of the increase will be absorbed by the development of new jobs unknown in 1960? More detailed cross tabulations could add a good deal to our knowledge of this complex and important subject.

Education and income

The relation of education to income has been a topic of considerable interest during the past decade. Some of the studies have examined the "effects" of education on the level of economic activity in the country. Typically they have tried to answer the question: How much of the growth of the national economy is attributable to the educational attainment of the population?[22] Other studies of the relation of education to income have examined the effect of an individual's education on his income.[23] This approach seeks to identify the effects of educational attainment on annual and on lifetime earnings. Most of the analyses have used census data, and most of them have limited their analysis to men 25 to 64 years old, since nearly all of this group have completed their education and are working. The effects of education on individual earnings can be examined in detail with census materials. Since Miller devotes an entire chapter to this topic in his census monograph on income, the subject will be treated in a summary fashion here.[24]

The increase in annual and in lifetime income with increasing education is substantial, and has persisted for the three Censuses (1940, 1950, and 1960) for which data are available. High school graduates earn 70 to 80 percent more than elementary school graduates of comparable ages, while college graduates earn 50 to 75 percent more than high school graduates of comparable ages. Not only do better educated persons earn more initially, but their peak earnings are higher in relation to their initial earnings. The differential in earnings associated with education remained fairly stable between 1939 and 1959,[25] in spite of the rise in educational level of the population and the increase in the size of the labor force.

Much of the relation between education and income is a reflection of the occupations persons enter. Occupations that generally require a higher level of education for entry also tend to command higher incomes. Using an indirect method of measurement, Duncan concluded:

> . . . about 57 percent of the gross educational difference in income is accounted for by major occupation groups, and about 73 percent by detailed occupation. Certainly these data suggest that an educational advantage is translated into an income advantage primarily, though not exclusively, by pursuing an occupation in which the prevailing income level is comparatively high.[26]

While the process described by Duncan obviously occurs, the ratio of the income of college graduates to that of high school and eighth grade graduates remains substantial within broad occupations and even within specific occupations. Between 1939 and 1959 the ratio of earnings of white males 35 to 44 years old with a college education to the comparable group with only an eighth grade education was 2.25 for all workers; 2.02 for sales workers; 1.95 for proprietors, managers, and officials; and 1.86 for professionals. For these broad occupation groups, the educational differential within occupations was

80 to 90 percent as great as the differential for all workers. Even among operatives, laborers, and clerks, the occupation groups with the smallest differentials, the differentials were 60 to 70 percent as large as for all workers. Since few persons enter the professional occupations without a college education, and few persons with a college education enter any of the blue-collar occupations, the major part of the variance in the income-education relationship is "explained" by the occupational choices people make. But even within specific occupational groups such as engineers or electricians, the earnings differential between elementary and college graduates may be 25 to 50 percent. The educational differential in earnings disappears in only a few occupations, apparently those where there is neither a difference in the technical requirements of jobs within the occupation, nor an entrepreneurial opportunity in specific jobs in the occupational category. In occupations with entrepreneurial opportunities—for example, proprietors or sales workers—the educational differential in earnings is large, and educational attainment may be a proxy variable for initiative, motivation, and intelligence.

Migration and education

The migration of talent from one part of the country to another and from rural to urban areas has been a subject of interest to researchers for a long time. The educational selectivity of migration streams could have a substantial effect on both the sending and receiving areas if it continued long enough, if migration rates were high, and if selectivity was of sufficient magnitude. For obvious reasons, interest has been greatest in educational selectivity of migration for some of the larger and long-continuing migration streams— for example, the movement from farms to cities, from east to west, and from south to north. In this section we shall first review the extent of educational selectivity in migration, and follow that with an examination of the effects of such selectivity on the educational levels of the population in both places of origin and destination.

In general, the better educated are more migratory than the less well educated, although there are exceptions to that generalization. Table VI–9 shows the general pattern for long-distance migrants between census divisions in 1955 and 1960. College-educated persons were about twice as heavily represented among migrants as among the general population, while persons with an eighth grade education or less were underrepresented among migrants. Higher rates of migration among the college educated occur in a wide variety of migration streams. Bogue and Hagood[27] found this to be true for a majority of streams of short-distance migrants in the Cotton and Corn Belts between 1935 and 1940. Shryock and Nam[28] also found that migrants between regions of the United States had a much higher proportion of college-educated persons than did nonmigrants and migrants within regions. The patterns of migration are more variable for the poorly educated. In some streams they are under-represented (table VI–9), while in others they are overrepresented. For example, Hamilton[29] reports that among older net migrants from the South between 1940 and 1950, the poorly educated were more amply represented than the better educated.

Table **VI–9.**—EDUCATIONAL ATTAINMENT BY MIGRATION STATUS, FOR INTERDIVISIONAL MIGRANTS 25 YEARS OLD AND OVER: 1960

Educational attainment	Total population	Migrants between census divisions 1955 to 1960
Number....................thousands..	99,438	7,588
Percent............................	100.0	100.0
Elementary: Less than 5 years...........	8.4	4.4
5 to 7 years...............	13.9	8.3
8 years...................	17.5	10.9
High school: 1 to 3 years...............	19.2	18.1
4 years...................	24.6	28.9
College: 1 to 3 years...............	8.8	13.4
4 years or more............	7.7	16.0

Source: For total population—*1960 Census of Population,* Vol. I, *Characteristics of the Population,* Part 1, U.S. Summary, table 76. For interdivisional migrants—*1960 Census of Population, Subject Reports, Lifetime and Recent Migration,* Series PC(2)–2D, table 7.

The poorly educated are about as likely as the well educated to make a short-distance move. (Persons who moved from one house to another without crossing a county line are defined as "movers" by the census.) The well educated are much more likely to make a long-distance move, and the greater the distance, the greater the differential between the well educated and the poorly educated. This is true for both white and nonwhite men, and for older as well as younger men. (See table VI–10.)

Even if persons with more education are more likely to move, the effects of this movement may not be very great if the numbers involved are small, or if each migration stream has a return stream which cancels its effects.

Migration in the United States tends to be ineffective in cumulative impact, as a high gross migration produces a low net migration for many streams. (Effectiveness is measured by the ratio of net migration to gross migration.) This is especially true for short-distance movements, but is also true for many of the long-distance streams shown in table VI–11. For the 1949-1950 streams the migration of the better educated was more effective than the migration of the poorly educated, while for the longer 1955-1960 period the reverse appeared to be true. One might expect the better educated to be better informed about opportunities, and that their migration would thus be more effective. The data presented do not support this contention, although it is important to realize that the migration may be quite beneficial for the individual concerned,

Table VI–10.—Percent of Males 25 to 29 Years Old, and 45 to 64 Years Old, by Selected Level of Educational Attainment, Mobility Status Since 1955, and Color: 1960

Age and mobility status	White			Nonwhite		
	Persons with less than 5 years of school	High school graduates with no college completed	College graduates	Persons with less than 5 years of school	High school graduates with no college completed	College graduates
25 TO 29 YEARS OLD						
Total......................	100.0	100.0	100.0	100.0	100.0	100.0
Movers[1]......................	59.1	73.9	81.7	64.5	67.5	62.7
To different county..............	17.8	30.3	57.9	16.4	22.0	35.2
Different State...............	7.9	17.7	36.9	8.0	16.8	24.4
Noncontiguous State..........	4.4	12.8	26.0	5.4	13.6	20.3
45 TO 64 YEARS OLD						
Total......................	100.0	100.0	100.0	100.0	100.0	100.0
Movers[1]......................	37.1	34.4	36.3	39.5	38.1	35.6
To different county..............	8.9	11.4	16.4	6.0	7.1	11.3
Different State...............	3.4	5.7	9.4	2.5	4.2	7.0
Noncontiguous State..........	1.8	3.6	6.4	1.3	2.7	4.8

[1] Persons who moved to a different house during the time period.

Source: *1960 Census of Population, Subject Reports, Mobility for States and State Economic Areas,* Series PC(2)–2B, table 6.

even if his movement is counterbalanced by the movement of a similarly educated person in the opposite direction.

The volume of net migration shown in table VI–11 could still produce considerable redistribution of the educational resources of the Nation if net movements that were educationally selective were concentrated in a few streams. The following examination of selected streams will provide information on the overall effects of migration in redistributing the Nation's educational resources.

Educational selectivity in rural-urban migration

Movement from farm to city has been going on for a long time in the United States, and there has been an interest in the possibility that the best educated people are leaving the farm. In reviewing the research on rural-urban migration in the prewar period, Dorothy Thomas reported ". . . most of these investigations suggest that the better educated are selected in cityward migration. . . ."[30] The 1940 Census provided the first direct information on migration and on educational attainment; the migration data relate to the period from 1935 to 1940. The 1950 Census obtained information on migration in the 1-year period 1949-1950, while the 1960 Census provided information on the 5-year period 1955-1960. Although the census also obtains information on the State of birth and the State of current residence, it is impossible to tell from these statistics whether the person moved before, during, or after his formal education, nor do the statistics identify urban or rural locations within the State of birth. Therefore, the analysis of rural to urban migration must be limited to the census data for the periods 1935-1940, 1949-1950, and 1955-1960.[31]

Table VI–11.—EFFECTIVENESS OF INTERREGIONAL MIGRATION FOR PERSONS 25 YEARS OLD AND OVER, BY AGE, COLOR, AND YEARS OF SCHOOL COMPLETED: 1949 TO 1950, AND 1955 TO 1960

[Effectiveness ratio not shown where base is less than 500 in 1949-50, or 400 in 1955-60]

Years of school completed and color	Ratio of net migration to gross migration				
	25 to 29 years old	30 to 34 years old	35 to 44 years old	45 to 64 years old	65 years old and over
1949 TO 1950					
White					
Elementary: Less than 5 years	3.5	7.0	8.1	12.7	22.0
5 to 8 years	9.3	4.9	6.4	15.2	20.2
High school	9.9	11.3	12.6	21.5	30.2
College	13.1	14.9	13.5	21.0	30.8
Education not reported	40.6	43.1	28.2	38.3	38.9
Nonwhite					
Elementary: Less than 5 years	22.1	16.6	11.3	9.3	31.5
5 to 8 years	10.4	11.6	8.6	5.5	26.5
High school	13.1	12.0	11.9	21.3	(Z)
College	13.8	12.7	17.8	30.7	(Z)
Education not reported	(Z)	(Z)	(Z)	(Z)	(Z)
1955 TO 1960					
White					
Elementary: Less than 5 years	32.7	25.9	29.0	32.4	(Z)
5 to 8 years	21.6	17.1	28.1	41.0	(Z)
High school	15.4	28.6	34.0	46.0	(Z)
College	17.9	18.9	22.9	34.3	(Z)
Nonwhite					
Elementary: Less than 5 years	57.7	55.7	49.5	42.9	(Z)
5 to 8 years	60.5	50.7	50.2	45.7	(Z)
High school	47.6	38.4	35.7	39.4	(Z)
College	43.9	35.2	32.5	34.2	(Z)

Source: *1960 Census of Population*, Vol. II, *Subject Reports, Lifetime and Recent Migration*, PC(2)–2D, table 8; Henry S. Shryock, Jr., "The Efficiency of Internal Migration in the United States," in *Proceedings of the International Population Conference*, Vienna, 1959, pp. 685-694.

There is a substantial response bias in the answers to the census question on rural-urban residence before migration. People who lived in rural-farm or rural-nonfarm locations before migration tended to give the name of the nearest town as their residence, or if they lived in the unincorporated suburbs, to indicate that they lived in the city. This leads to underreporting of previous rural residence and overreporting of previous urban residence. This response bias was present in the Censuses of 1940, 1950, and 1960; as the census migration tabulations omit information on residence classification in 1955 for specific streams of migrants, the only kind of rural-urban migration that can be examined in relation to educational attainment as shown in the 1960 Census is the metropolitan-nonmetropolitan migration.

Bogue and Hagood[32] reported that farm to city within-State migration, among those 25 to 34 years old in the period 1935-1940, was heavily over-selective of the better educated compared with the educational attainment in the area of origin of the migrants. When compared with the educational attainment in the area of destination (the cities) the migrants—especially those in the Cotton Belt—were less well educated than the population in the area to which they migrated. This is an example of migration that lowers the educational attainment level in the communities of both origin and destination.

The information on this topic in the 1960 Census is limited to movement in and out of metropolitan areas. Between 1955 and 1960, there was a net in-migration of whites with four years of college to large metropolitan areas with populations of over a million. (See tables VI–12 and VI–13.) In-migrants had about twice as high a percent of college graduates as the resident population in the big cities, but about the same percentages as out-migrants to other metropolitan areas. Among white out-migrants from large metropolitan areas to nonmetropolitan areas, the percentages of college graduates were about half-way between those of in-migrants and the resident population. The total impact of migration on the educational level of the large metropolitan areas in the country is very small. The net in-migration of 40,000 college graduates to these big cities (table VI–13) represents only 1.2 percent of the college graduates living there in 1960.

Even in the rapidly growing metropolitan areas, the influence of migration appears to be small. While the rate of net in-migration of college graduates to the rapidly growing standard metropolitan statistical areas (those that grew 20 percent or more by migration between 1955 and 1960) was 10.7 between 1955 and 1960, compared with 1.2 for the large metropolitan areas, the educational attainment level of the rapidly growing cities did not rise much. This is because the attainment levels in the metropolitan areas that attract migrants were already high, and because the dominance of the better educated in these streams is not great. Two examples may make this point clearer. Fort Lauderdale had the highest rate of net in-migration of college graduates (44 percent) of any standard metropolitan statistical area (SMSA) in the period 1955-1960. This net in-migration had the same median attainment level as the resident population, so the median attainment level of the 1960 population (12.1 years) was unchanged by the heavy in-migration.

Table VI–12.—Percent of College Graduates Among Nonmigrants and in
Selected Streams of Metropolitan-Nonmetropolitan White Migrants:
1955 to 1960

Group	Percent with 4 years of college or more
Total resident 1960 population	10.0
In central cities	8.5
In the ring	11.3
Total in-migrants to central city	20.8
From another metropolitan area	22.7
From nonmetropolitan area	16.9
Total to the ring	22.1
From another metropolitan area	24.1
From nonmetropolitan area	18.4
Out-migrants:	
To metropolitan area	21.1
To nonmetropolitan area	14.4

Note: Data are for metropolitan areas of 1 million inhabitants or more in 1960, and for
the population 25 years old and over, except that origins for in-migrants from another metropolitan area include all metropolitan areas and destinations for out-migrants to another
metropolitan area include all metropolitan areas.

Source: *1960 Census of Population, Subject Reports, Mobility for Metropolitan Areas,*
Series PC(2)–2C, tables 4 and 5.

Table VI–13.—Migration Between Metropolitan and Nonmetropolitan
Areas, for All White Migrants and Those With 4 Years or More of
College: 1955 to 1960

[Numbers in thousands. Minus sign (−) denotes decrease]

Migration status	Total	Metropolitan areas	Nonmetro-politan areas
TOTAL WHITE MIGRANTS			
In-migrants	2,869	1,905	964
Out-migrants	3,076	2,079	997
Net migrants	−207	−174	−33
WHITE MIGRANTS WITH 4 YEARS OF COLLEGE OR MORE			
In-migrants	623	450	173
Out-migrants	583	439	144
Net migrants	40	11	29

Source: *1960 Census of Population, Subject Reports, Mobility for States and State Economic
Areas,* Series PC(2)–2B, table 6.

By contrast, Washington, D.C. had very high educational selectivity in its
net in-migration (the median educational level of white net in-migrants was
16 years), but the net number of well-educated migrants added was small,
raising the median attainment level of the metropolitan area by less than a
tenth of a year.

It is clear that census data are not very useful in the study of the educational selectivity of rural-urban migration, because of the response bias in reporting previous residence. The 1935 to 1940 migration statistics indicate a selection of the better educated in rural to urban migration, but the magnitude of the effects cannot be accurately assessed. The 1955 to 1960 metropolitan-non-metropolitan migration was also selective of the better educated in the movement to the cities; and these streams should not be affected much by the response bias in reporting place of residence in 1955. However, the effect of migration in changing the educational level of either large metropolitan areas or rapidly growing ones was small. Migration to and from metropolitan areas does appear to be maintaining the differentials that already exist in educational attainment between rural and urban areas, and between the central cities and their suburbs. In this sense, migration may exert a considerable influence on the long-run distribution of educational attainment.

Effects of interregional migration on educational attainment

The effect of migration on the educational level of different regions of the United States can be examined for the periods 1935-1940, 1949-1950, and 1955-1960. Shryock and Nam have analyzed educational differentials in inter-regional migration, and the effect of lifetime migration from birth to 1950 on the educational level in different regions. They conclude:

> The observed medians by region for persons 25 years old and over in 1950 are sur-prisingly similar to those that would have occurred had there been no lifetime inter-regional migration and if migration did not affect the education received. Moreover, it is the South that appears to have profited slightly from the interregional migration.[33]

They then present a table indicating a difference of about two-tenths of a year for males and about one-tenth of a year for females in median attainment be-tween those born in the South, and the total population living in the region in 1950. As they comment:

> The effect [of interregional migration] is somewhat more evident in the proportion of college graduates in the adult population, although even here the gain by the South is less than a percentage point (5.9 to 6.8 percent for males, 5.0 to 5.5 for females).[34]

Price analyzed the effect of nonwhite out-migration between 1955 and 1960 on the educational level of the East South Central Census Division.[35] He reported that out-migration of nonwhite males aged 25 to 29 reduced the median level of education about .3 of a year between 1955 and 1960, and that in-migration during the same period raised the median about .1 of a year for a net decrease of about .2 of a year. The out-migration of nonwhite females aged 25 to 29 had a similar effect on the attainment level of the remaining population, and for both sexes the effects at ages 30 to 34 on attainment level were smaller because there was less migration.[36]

The effects on educational attainment levels of out-migration of nonwhites from the South, described by Price, are larger than any found for migration streams of the total population. (See table VI–14.) In this analysis special attention was focused on the effects of the two major interregional movements: north-south migration, and westward migration. Between 1955 and 1960, the South Atlantic Division had a net in-migration of about 600,000 persons over 25 years of age. This is a heterogeneous area which includes the rapidly growing Washington and Baltimore metropolitan areas and Florida, as well as States with much smaller growth rates. The East South Central Division had a very small net out-migration of 30,000, while the West South Central area had a net in-migration of 125,000. Both the Mountain and Pacific Divisions grew rapidly by migration; the former by 250,000 and the latter by 1,000,000 net in-migrants in the period 1955-1960. Of these migration streams, only the movement to the South Atlantic Division had any effect on the educational attainment of the people in the Division; and it was small—adding only one-tenth of a year to the educational level. There was a large net in-migration to the Pacific Coast and Mountain States in this period, but since the migrants had almost the same attainment distribution as the adult resident population, the migration did not change the educational level of the region appreciably.

Table VI–14.—Net Migration as a Percent of the Resident Population 25 Years Old and Over, by Educational Attainment, for Selected Census Divisions: 1955 to 1960

[Minus sign (—) denotes decrease]

Attainment level	South			West	
	South Atlantic	East South Central	West South Central	Mountain	Pacific
Total..........................	5.8	-0.6	1.8	9.9	11.9
Elementary: Less than 5 years........	2.6	-0.6	1.6	8.5	18.7
5 to 7 years.............	2.8	-1.1	1.4	5.6	11.8
8 years.................	6.1	-0.9	1.9	7.3	10.2
High school: 1 to 3 years............	5.9	-0.4	1.7	9.2	11.2
4 years.................	8.0	0.5	2.5	11.0	10.5
College: 1 to 3 years............	9.0	(Z)	2.6	13.1	12.2
4 years or more..........	9.0	-3.1	0.5	13.0	16.9
Median..........................	12.1	(¹)	11.2	12.3	12.2
Median for 1960 nonmigratory resident population........................	10.0	9.1	10.4	12.1	12.2

[1] The median attainment level of net migration streams is ambiguous in meaning when some streams are positive and others negative. Net migration in the case above is so close to zero that it does not produce any change in the attainment level of the Census division.

Source: Computed from data in the *1960 Census of Population, Subject Reports, Lifetime and Recent Migration,* Series PC(2)–2D, table 7.

This analysis reinforces the conclusion of Shryock and Nam that the effects of interregional migration on the educational attainment of the resident population are small. Their conclusion was based partly on lifetime migration data where the education could have been obtained after migration; these data minimize that possibility since they refer to persons who were 25 years old and over in 1960, and consider only the migration of the past five years. Most of these persons would have completed their education before migration. Price's data show that, even when the total group is not affected, migration can affect the educational level of a subgroup of the population. It is quite possible that in the South, out-migration could lower the attainment level of nonwhites at the same time that in-migration was raising the level of attainment of the white population. For all groups, however, these changes are small when measured against the rise that occurred between 1950 and 1960 in the educational attainment levels of the population in all areas of the country.

Educational attainment and marriage

Marriage often follows shortly after school is completed, and in many cases contributes to the termination or interruption of formal education. Therefore, a close relationship between educational attainment and age at marriage might be expected. There has been interest in the increased number of couples who continue high school and college education after marriage. Are the married students on campus a temporary phenomenon, or are they merely a manifestation of a general trend toward more marriages and younger marriages in which nonstudent couples also participate?

The amount of education a person obtains affects age at marriage much more than it affects the chances of eventually marrying. The lowest percentages of married persons are found at the extremes of the educational distribution—those with only an eighth grade education, or less, and those with a college education. (See table VI–15.) The college educated are more likely to defer marriage; at ages 20 to 24 the proportion of women with 4 years of college education who are married may be as much as 20 percentage points below the proportion of women high school graduates who are married. By ages 30 to 34 this differential is only about 8 percentage points for women and 2 percentage points for men. The general patterns were the same in 1950 and 1960, with slightly higher percentages of married persons among all educational groups at the latter date. The lower percent of married people among the poorly educated reflects the values of groups in our society who may be less able to afford the costs of marriage, and who sometimes may not place the same value on marriage as middle-class Americans do.

For many women, there is only a short time between the end of formal education and marriage. The relation is not so close for men. The normal age for completing a specified level of education (18 years for high school, 22 years for college) also turns out to be the modal age at marriage for all women at that attainment level, for every attainment level from the third year of high school to the fourth year of college. (See table VI–16.) At each educational level shown in table VI–16, between a fourth and a fifth of the women were married at the age corresponding to the normal age for completing that level of education. From other data on the amount of school retardation, it seems reasonable to estimate that 15 to 25 percent of these women were overage for their grade level. We also know that there is some overstatement of educational attainment (see appendix A) and some acceleration in school. These two effects would work in opposite directions. If the figures on the percent of persons who married before the normal age for completing their school level can be accepted as reasonable estimates of the total percent who attended school at any time after marriage, this indicates that about 15 percent of the girls without a college education, and about 30 percent of those who attended college, went to school for some time after marriage. Since we know that in 1960 about 7.5 percent of the girls enrolled below the college level and about 14 percent of those enrolled in college were married, it appears that the duration of school attendance for girls after marriage is brief.

Some substantial changes have occurred since the 1920's in the effects of educational attainment on age at marriage. Figure VI–1 shows the proportions of those who married before age 22 and after age 28 for three groups: those who married between 1920 and 1929; those, between 1930 and 1939; and those married between 1955 and 1960.

Table VI–15.—PERCENT MARRIED, WITH SPOUSE PRESENT, BY EDUCATIONAL ATTAINMENT, AGE, AND SEX: 1960 AND 1950

Year, age, and sex	Less than 8 years	High school		College	
		1 to 3 years	4 years	1 to 3 years	4 years or more
1960					
Male					
20 and 21 years old...................	35.7	37.4	30.7	19.1	27.0
22 to 24 years old....................	57.2	62.1	57.5	47.5	45.9
25 to 29 years old....................	74.1	77.9	78.4	73.5	71.7
30 to 34 years old....................	80.9	84.8	85.3	84.7	83.8
Female					
20 and 21 years old...................	58.4	68.0	58.4	25.8	36.3
22 to 24 years old....................	69.5	79.1	77.1	64.0	53.0
25 to 29 years old....................	76.8	83.3	85.7	81.2	74.7
30 to 34 years old....................	80.2	86.1	87.9	85.8	80.4
1950					
Male					
20 and 21 years old...................	26.8	27.8	19.3	8.1	11.8
22 to 24 years old....................	50.5	56.1	49.1	32.9	34.7
25 to 29 years old....................	68.6	74.9	73.9	66.8	64.6
30 to 34 years old....................	77.3	83.0	83.1	83.6	82.8
Female					
20 and 21 years old...................	60.4	65.4	49.3	23.8	27.3
22 to 24 years old....................	70.5	75.9	70.7	59.5	46.6
25 to 29 years old....................	77.6	82.6	80.9	77.3	68.0
30 to 34 years old....................	80.5	84.9	84.2	82.0	75.0

Source: *1960 Census of Population, Subject Reports, Educational Attainment*, Series PC(2)–5B, table 8. *1950 Census of Population, Special Reports, Education*, Series P-E–5B, tables 4 and 5.

Figure VI–1.—Percent Married Before Age 22 and at Age 28 or Later, for Husband-Wife Families, by Educational Attainment, Head or Wife, and Period of Marriage: 1920 to 1960

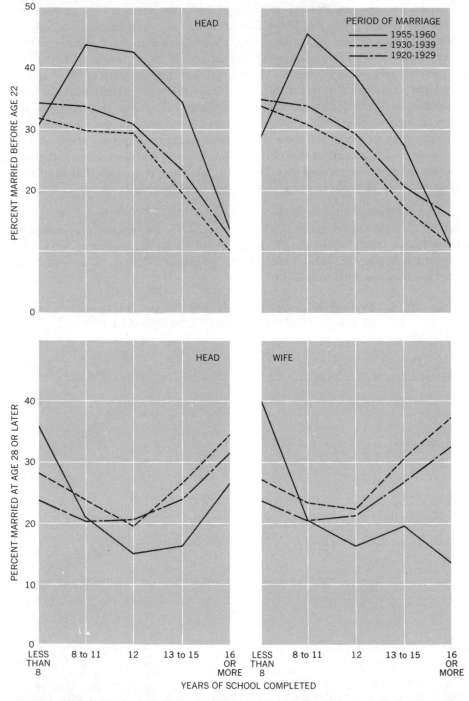

Table VI–16.—Percent of Wives Who Married At and Before the Expected Age for Attaining Selected Levels of Educational Attainment, for Husband-Wife Families in Which Both Husband and Wife are Younger than 35 Years: 1960

Level of educational attainment	Expected age at which attainment level is normally reached	Percent who married—	
		At expected age	Before expected age
High school, 3rd year...................	17 years	26.0	17.3
High school, 4th year...................	18 years	21.0	12.9
College, 1st year.......................	19 years	24.9	18.5
College, 2nd and 3rd years.............	20 and 21 years	[1]22.0	[1]31.8
College, 4th year......................	22 years	22.3	36.4

[1] Estimated from two-years distribution of attainment.

Source: *1960 Census of Population, Subject Reports, Families,* Series PC(2)–4A, table 53.

The decline in average age at marriage after World War II had the least effect on those with little education, and those with 4 or more years of college. While a few girls marry and complete college before age 22, this pattern is uncommon even though the average age at marriage has dropped. Nor has the decline in age at marriage affected those with less than an eighth-grade education; they were less likely to marry early, and more likely to defer marriage until after age 28, in the 1955-1960 period than in the two earlier decades. In the 1955-1960 period the group with less than an eighth-grade education was probably more handicapped economically than the much larger groups of the 1920's and 1930's with the same amount of education. The increasing deferment of marriage among the poorly educated who eventually marry may reflect the greater economic and social handicaps of a limited education in the 1960's than in the 1920's and 1930's. One other marked change revealed by figure VI–1 is the sharp decline in the percent of college-educated women who defer marriage past age 28. Women college graduates of the 1955-1960 period were more likely than graduates of prewar years to marry between the ages of 22 and 27. Consequently, they had lower percentages delaying marriage beyond age 28 than college graduates of the earlier period, and also lower percentages delaying marriage beyond age 28 than any of the less well educated groups who were married between 1955 and 1960.

In summary, educational attainment has a very close relationship with age at marriage because of the tendency, especially among women, to marry in the year they complete their formal education. The level of formal education completed has practically no effect on the percent of men who eventually marry, and very little effect on the comparable percent for women. There have been some substantial changes in the effect of education on the patterns of age at marriage in the 40 years between 1920 and 1960. These changes have tended to increase educational differentials in both the percent of people who marry young, and the percent who delay marriage beyond age 28. Student marriages seem to occur at about the same age as marriages of nonstudents. An estimated one-third of all girls who attend college complete at least part of their college education after marriage; this estimate is not necessarily inconsistent with the 14 percent of women college students who were reported as married at the time of the 1960 Census.

Family patterns of educational attainment

The family is the primary institution for early socialization of children, and shares with the schools the major responsibility for their later educational development. The family and the school are the major settings where educational goals and motivation for scholastic success are developed.

The census provides several kinds of evidence about the ways in which educational experiences are influenced by one's family. One of these, the relation of fathers' and sons' education, was described in part in chapter V, and is also described in two Bureau of the Census *Current Population Reports.*[37]

A second kind of information is provided by census data on educational interrelations within families, both those containing adults of two generations, and those in which all the adults are members of a single generation. There are two principal sources of educational patterns within families: first, educational homogamy (the tendency of persons with similar amounts of education to marry); and second, the persistence of educational levels from generation to generation within the same family. In addition to published census data, there are available special tabulations of the 1-in-1,000 sample of the 1960 Census.

The educational relationships of adults within families, for four different family types, are described in tables VI–17 and VI–18; they reveal the extent of clustering of educational levels within families. Although the data do not cover all families in the country, they do represent 90 percent of them. The differentiation by number of adults within the family enables us to study the effect of family size and type, and the differentiation by number of generations permits study of time differences in the schooling of adult family members.

Clustering of educational levels within families can be observed in such family types. The chances of any adult in a two-adult, one-generation family not having completed high school are 52 out of 100. In those families where at least one of the adults is not a high school graduate the chances of the other adult not being a high school graduate are 76 out of 100, whereas if at least one of the adults had some college education the chances are only 15 out of 100 that the other did not finish high school.

Similarly, the probability that any one of the adults has had some college education is 19 out of 100. If at least one of the adults has had such education the chances of the second adult having been enrolled in college is 56 out of 100, but if at least one of the adults had not completed high school the chances of the second adult having had some college education is only 5 out of 100.

These relative patterns of educational consistency within families are found in each type of family. In families composed of adults from two or more generations, the correlation of educational statuses is less than where all adults are of the same generation, but the clustering pattern still exists.

Table VI–17.—Probability That an Adult Member of a Two-Adult Family Will Have Attained a Given Educational Level, by Educational Level of the Other Adult in the Family: 1960

[Probability range is from .00, which indicates no chance whatsoever, to 1.00 which indicates certainty]

Educational level of other adult	Probability that an adult—		
	Is not a high school graduate	Is a high school graduate, no college	Has had some college
TWO-ADULT, ONE-GENERATION FAMILIES			
Total	.52	.29	.19
Not a high school graduate	.76	.19	.05
High school graduate, no college	.34	.47	.19
Some college	.15	.30	.56
TWO-ADULT, TWO-GENERATION FAMILIES			
Total	.67	.20	.13
Not a high school graduate	.75	.17	.09
High school graduate, no college	.56	.28	.16
Some college	.44	.25	.31

Source: Special tabulations of the 1-in-1,000 samples of the census.

The magnitude of consistency of educational status among family members may be measured by comparing the actual number of families comprised of adults of the same educational level with the number that would be expected if there were no forces operating to produce similar educational attainments of different family members. The expected number, in other words, is that number which would have resulted for a given distribution of individuals among three educational levels, had there been no relation between the educational attainments of members of the same family.

For two-adult, one-generation families in the United States in 1960, we would expect 39 percent of the families to have adults with like educational statuses on the basis of chance, whereas actually 63 percent of the families were so classified. (See table VI–19, footnote 2.) The ratio of the actual to the expected percentages is 1.63, where unity would be expected if there was no tendency toward consistency of educational levels within families. The

Table VI–18.—Probability That an Adult Member of a Three-Adult Family Will Have Attained a Given Educational Level, by Educational Level of the Other Adults in the Family: 1960

[Probability range is from .00, which indicates no chance whatsoever, to 1.00 which indicates certainty]

Family type and educational level of other two adults	Probability that an adult—		
	Is not a high school graduate	Is a high school graduate, no college	Has had some college
ONE-GENERATION FAMILIES			
Total.................................	.66	.24	.10
Neither a high school graduate............	.89	.09	.01
One not a high school graduate............	.72	.23	.05
One a high school graduate...............	.49	.30	.22
Both high school graduates...............	.26	.55	.20
One some college........................	.25	.51	.24
Both some college.......................	.11	.24	.64
TWO-GENERATION FAMILIES			
Total.................................	.58	.28	.14
Neither a high school graduate............	.78	.20	.02
One not a high school graduate............	.56	.36	.08
One a high school graduate...............	.56	.17	.26
Both high school graduates...............	.41	.21	.37
One some college........................	.26	.53	.21
Both some college.......................	.16	.35	.49

Source: Special tabulations of the 1-in-1,000 samples of the census.

ratio is as high as 2.85 for families where both adults have some college, compared with 1.65 and 1.46, respectively, for consistency at the high school graduation level and below the high school level. The ratio is as low as 0.28 for families where one adult has had some college and one has failed to complete high school, indicating the unlikely occurrence of this type of family educational structure.

In two-adult families where the adults are a generation apart the ratios tend to be somewhat closer to unity, but the same kind of pattern persists. Extension of this type of analysis to three-adult, one-generation families reveals similar patterns of clustering (see table VI–19). Such families typically include among their adults a husband and wife and brother or sister of one of the spouses. In three-adult families comprising two or three generations the patterns of consistency of educational statuses within families is similar to that for three-adult, one-generation families. These families are predominantly of the husband-wife-parent and husband-wife-older child types, but also include some of the person-parent-grandparent and husband-wife-aunt-or-uncle types. One notable exception to the general pattern is that there are fewer families than might be expected in which all the adults are only high school graduates. The suggestion here is that in larger, more complex families (in terms of generations), the generational effect will contribute to educational heterogeneity. This idea is supported by the high ratios of actual-to-expected numbers of families where two of the adults are high school-educated and one has had some college, or where two have had some college and one is a high school graduate.

Table VI–19.—ACTUAL AND EXPECTED NUMBERS OF FAMILIES WITH GIVEN EDUCATIONAL LEVELS, BY FAMILY TYPE: 1960

Family type and educational structure[1]	Expected families[2]		Actual families		Ratio of actual to expected
	Number	Percent	Number	Percent	
2-adult, 1-generation........................	32,365	100	32,365	100	1.00
N–N...	8,751	27	12,769	39	1.46
N–H...	9,761	30	6,415	20	0.66
H–H...	2,722	8	4,501	14	1.65
N–C...	6,395	20	1,783	6	0.28
H–C...	3,567	11	3,563	11	1.00
C–C...	1,168	4	3,334	10	2.85
2-adult, 2-generation........................	2,633	100	2,633	100	1.00
N–N...	1,182	45	1,322	50	1.12
N–H...	706	27	592	22	0.84
H–H...	105	4	145	6	1.38
H–C...	459	17	301	11	0.66
N–C...	137	5	168	6	1.23
C–C...	44	2	105	4	2.39
3-adult, 1-generation........................	849	100	849	100	1.00
N–N–N.......................................	244	29	419	49	1.72
N–N–H.......................................	266	31	133	16	0.50
N–H–H.......................................	97	11	72	8	0.74
H–H–H.......................................	12	1	51	6	4.25
N–N–C.......................................	111	13	15	2	0.14
N–H–C.......................................	80	9	48	6	0.60
H–H–C.......................................	15	2	55	6	3.67
N–C–C.......................................	17	2	11	1	0.65
H–C–C.......................................	6	1	24	3	4.00
C–C–C.......................................	1	(z)	21	2	21.00
3-adult, multi-generation....................	4,751	100	4,751	100	1.00
N–N–N.......................................	927	20	1,534	32	1.65
N–N–H.......................................	1,343	28	1,200	25	0.89
N–H–H.......................................	649	14	489	10	0.75
H–H–H.......................................	105	2	84	2	0.80
N–N–C.......................................	671	14	100	2	0.15
N–H–C.......................................	647	14	426	9	0.66
H–H–C.......................................	157	3	438	9	2.79
N–C–C.......................................	162	3	117	2	0.72
H–C–C.......................................	78	2	247	5	3.17
C–C–C.......................................	13	(z)	116	2	8.92

[1] N—not a high school graduate; H—high school graduate only; C—some college.
[2] The expected number is the number of families of a given type that would result if there were no association between the educational statuses of different members of the same family.

Source: Special tabulations of the 1-in-1,000 samples of the census.

To the extent that the adult population is comprised of married couples, the marriage of persons with like educational levels will contribute to the similarity of educational levels within families. The writings of Burgess and Wallin,[38] Landis and Day,[39] Hollingshead,[40] and Glick and Carter[41] reveal a definite tendency for persons of like educational status to marry. All but the last of these writings were based on studies covering restricted populations, and the last was based on a survey of couples in the United States who were married between 1947 and 1954.

The educational patterns of married couples, as might be expected, are very much like those of two-adult, one-generation families who, as indicated before, are principally of the husband-wife type (see table VI–20). The similarity of educational status in two-adult, one-generation families is primarily a function of the extent of educational homogamy, or the attraction of marriage mates with the same educational levels. Presumably, the extent of educational homogamy also accounts for a substantial part of the clustering of educational statuses within three-person families.

Table **VI–20.**—Percent Distribution of Educational Levels of Husbands and Wives, for all Married Couples and for Married Couples With Husband Under 35 Years Old: 1960

Education of husband	Total	Education of wife		
		Not a high school graduate	High school graduate, no college	Some college
ALL MARRIED COUPLES				
Percent by Education of Wife				
Total........................	100	52	33	15
Not a high school graduate..........	100	74	21	5
High school graduate, no college.....	100	30	57	13
Some college.......................	100	14	38	48
Percent by Education of Husband				
Total........................	100	100	100	100
Not a high school graduate..........	58	81	37	19
High school graduate, no college.....	23	14	40	20
Some college.......................	19	5	22	61
MARRIED COUPLES WITH HUSBAND UNDER 35 YEARS OLD				
Percent by Education of Wife				
Total........................	100	38	45	17
Not a high school graduate..........	100	63	33	4
High school graduate, no college.....	100	28	62	10
Some college.......................	100	10	41	49
Percent by Education of Husband				
Total........................	100	100	100	100
Not a high school graduate........	42	70	32	9
High school graduate, no college.....	33	24	46	19
Some college.......................	25	7	23	72

Source: *1960 Census of Population, Subject Reports, Families,* Series PC(2)–4A, tables 25 and 26.

In an effort to discover whether or not the patterns of educational homogamy were changing over time, the data for married couples where the husband was under 35 years of age were examined. As shown in table VI–21, the ratio of actual-to-expected number of couples with like educational levels was slightly higher for the younger couples than for all couples. The ratio was considerably higher among the younger couples at the lowest educational level but somewhat lower (though much above unity) at the high school graduation and college levels. This suggests that as the educational level of the population becomes further upgraded, and particularly as women as well as men attain higher levels, the opportunities of persons of like educational status to marry will increase and the actual-to-expected ratio at these higher education levels will decline. At the same time, a drop in the relative numbers of men and women without a high school education may lead to a further increase in the ratio at that level. On balance, however, it would appear that changes in the pattern of educational consistency among husbands and wives has been gradual, and that educational homogamy will probably continue into the future.

Table VI–21.—ACTUAL AND EXPECTED NUMBER OF MARRIED COUPLES WITH GIVEN EDUCATIONAL LEVELS, BY AGE OF HUSBAND: 1960

Age of husband and educational level of husband and wife	Expected couples		Actual couples		Ratio of actual to expected
	Number	Percent	Number	Percent	
ALL MARRIED COUPLES					
Total..............................	39,659	100	39,659	100	1.00
Husband not a high school graduate:					
Wife: Not a high school graduate.........	11,997	30	16,900	43	1.41
High school graduate................	12,215	31	7,639	19	0.63
Some college.......................	3,109	8	5,226	13	1.68
Husband a high school graduate:					
Wife: High school graduate................	7,416	19	2,227	6	0.30
Some college.......................	3,776	10	4,056	10	1.07
Husband and wife, some college...............	1,146	3	3,611	9	3.15
MARRIED COUPLES WITH HUSBAND UNDER 35 YEARS OLD					
Total..............................	10,567	100	10,567	100	1.00
Husband not a high school graduate:					
Wife: Not a high school graduate..........	1,691	16	2,808	27	1.66
High school graduate................	3,297	31	2,466	23	0.75
Some college.......................	1,607	15	2,153	20	1.34
Husband a high school graduate:					
Wife: High school graduate................	1,775	17	434	4	0.24
Some college.......................	1,731	16	1,422	13	0.82
Husband and wife, some college...............	466	4	1,284	12	2.76

Source: Derived from data in table VI–20.

As pointed out earlier, educational homogamy cannot account for all educational clustering within families. In two-adult, two-generation families, educational homogamy cannot explain the clustering of educational status found; and in larger, more complex families, the same tendency for similar educational attainment of family members must be due to other factors as well. The principal one of these "other factors" is the general persistence of educational levels from generation to generation within the same family.[42] A high proportion of sons exceeded the educational level of their fathers, and a very low proportion had less education than their fathers. This intergenerational educational pattern is partly a function of improved educational opportunities over time. Even if the effect of changes in the relative size of the educational classes at different times is held constant, so that the remaining effect is a measure of the propensity to inherit one's father's educational status apart from improved educational opportunities, there still is a great deal of persistence between generations in educational attainment. Ratios similar to those described earlier can be computed on the basis of the relation of the actual and expected numbers of sons with educational levels the same as their fathers, assuming no necessary association between the education of fathers and sons.

The results of this computation, not shown in the tables, indicate an overall ratio of the actual-to-expected cases of 1.47. Educational consistency of fathers and sons was greater than would be expected by chance at all educational levels, but particularly at the lowest and highest levels (the ratio being 1.72 for those lacking an eighth-grade education and 2.89 for those having had some college education).

The pattern of father-son educational relationships was compared for sons 25 to 34 years old, and 55 to 64 years old, to see if there had been any significant changes over time. (Data not shown.) The younger group had greater upward educational mobility. However, when changing opportunities are taken into account, the ratios of actual-to-expected cases of fathers and sons with like educational levels are not significantly different (1.41 for the older age group, and 1.39 for the younger).

On the whole, the clustering of educational status for fathers and sons, apart from that produced by changing educational opportunities, exists to about the same extent as that for husbands and wives. Moreover, other data, not shown here, indicate a high degree of correlation between the educational levels of men and their brothers.[43]

In summary, while the educational structure of families in the United States varies among the several forms it may possibly take, there is a considerable tendency for family members to have the same educational level. This tendency can be traced both to a high degree of educational homogamy and to a high degree of persistence in the educational levels of different generations within the same family. Improvements in educational opportunities over time contribute to a lesser degree of educational consistency between generations. Those families composed of two or more generations of adults will, therefore, tend to have less clustering of educational status, primarily because of the different educational opportunities for the different generations.

School retardation of children and parents' education

Perhaps the most direct census measure of the effects of the family on educational standards and motivations is the relation of the children's educational progress to the parents' educational attainment. This is shown for families in table VI–22 and was also discussed in chapter II (see table II–13). There is a consistent relationship for all combinations of parents' education; the higher the parents' educational attainment the lower the percent of their children of school age who are retarded in school. When neither parent has attended high school, 30 percent of their children aged 6 to 17 are retarded in school. When both parents are college graduates, only 3 percent of their children are so retarded.

Table VI–22.—PERCENT OF FAMILIES WITH EMPLOYED WIFE AND CHILDREN 6 TO 17 YEARS OLD, AND PERCENT WITH SCHOLASTICALLY RETARDED CHILDREN, BY EMPLOYMENT STATUS OF WIFE, BY EDUCATIONAL ATTAINMENT OF HUSBAND AND WIFE: 1960

Educational attainment of husband and wife	Percent of families with employed wife and with children 6 to 17 years old	Percent of families with scholastically retarded children	
		Mother in labor force	Mother not in labor force
Husband a college graduate:			
Wife: College graduate...............	31.5	3.6	3.0
Some college....................	20.3	3.8	3.2
No college......................	19.1	4.7	4.1
Husband some college:			
Wife: College graduate...............	43.9	3.5	3.6
Some college....................	30.5	4.7	4.1
No college......................	26.6	6.2	5.4
Husband no college:			
Wife: College graduate...............	56.5	4.6	4.5
Some college...:................	39.6	6.5	5.2
No college......................	34.6	7.3	8.8
Husband a high school graduate:			
Wife: High school graduate...........	28.9	5.5	4.9
Some high school................	26.5	8.6	7.6
No high school..................	24.6	13.3	13.0
Husband some high school:			
Wife: High school graduate...........	32.6	7.3	6.5
Some high school................	29.1	11.4	10.7
No high school..................	26.2	17.2	17.8
Husband no high school:			
Wife: High school graduate...........	33.7	10.9	9.8
Some high school................	31.3	17.1	17.1
No high school..................	25.5	27.4	31.2

Note: The group in the table above "Husband no college, wife no college," are in families where some adult in the family has attended college. This differentiates it from the next group "Husband a high school graduate and wife, high school graduate." Numbers in each group are shown in table VI–23.

Source: *1960 Census of Population, Subject Reports, Families,* Series PC(2)–4A, tables 25 and 26.

It might be assumed that more of the poorly educated wives must work outside the home, and that this contributed to the higher level of school retardation among their children. However, as shown in table VI–22, the better educated women are more likely to be working, and whether the mother works or not has little effect on the school retardation of children at any level of parents' education.

Where any adult in the family has attended college, the children are not very likely to be retarded in school; at these higher attainment levels, the father's education has about as much influence as the mother's on the school progress of their children. When none of the adults in the family has attended college, the wife's education has a little closer relationship than the husband's to the school retardation of the children, but the difference is not great. If neither parent has attended high school there is a marked increase in the percent of children retarded in school. As families where neither parent has attended high school comprise nearly 22 percent of all husband-wife families, their school-retarded children make up a substantial part of all children retarded in school.

Since school retardation is a good predictor of early dropouts and non-completion of school, it is clear that the patterns of educational inheritance observed for the generation of fathers and sons who are now adults are likely to be continued for the children who are now in school. We cannot tell from these figures whether educational inheritance will be weaker in the future, but they suggest that it will still be substantial.

Education and labor force participation of the wife

Education is one of the important determinants of whether or not the wife will work outside the home. Since an education helps to equip a person with skills in demand in the job market, we would expect to find more working wives among the better educated women. We might also expect to find more women working in families where the husbands' education is lower, since the wife's contribution to the total family income would be more important. Both of these relationships are found in the data in table VI–23. The presence of children and the educational level of the husband has an effect on the percent of wives who work, but no matter what the husband's education, or what age the children, wives with better education are more likely to be working than wives with less education.

The educational level of the family head has relatively little effect on the percent of wives working unless there are young children in the family. The percentage of working wives with small children declines where the head of the family has had some college education or is a college graduate, compared with heads with lesser education. As might be anticipated, the educational level of the wife, and the presence or absence of small children, has more influence than the education of the husband on the wife's labor force participation. The husband's education is probably influential primarily because it is correlated with family income.

Table VI–23.—Percent of Wives in the Labor Force, by Education of Husband and Wife, and Presence of Children Under 6 Years Old and 6 to 17 Years Old: 1960

Educational attainment of husband and wife	Total wives (thousands)	Percent in labor force			
		Total	With own children under 6 years old	With own children 6 to 17 years old	Without own children
Husband a college graduate:					
Wife: College graduate...........	1,264	35.0	19.0	31.5	53.3
Some college...............	1,103	23.7	12.7	20.4	38.2
No college.................	1,572	21.7	10.4	19.1	32.9
Husband some college:					
Wife: College graduate...........	334	47.6	29.2	44.3	60.6
Some college...............	911	34.4	28.1	30.6	45.4
No college.................	2,402	29.1	16.9	26.6	39.4
Husband no college:					
Wife: College graduate...........	534	56.5	35.2	56.4	62.5
Some college...............	1,764	39.9	25.6	39.6	45.1
No college.................	857	. 31.0	24.9	34.6	29.4
Husband a high school graduate:					
Wife: High school graduate........	5,076	31.1	17.3	29.0	48.7
Some high school............	1,827	26.5	14.0	26.5	37.2
No high school..............	903	24.6	13.3	24.6	28.0
Husband some high school:					
Wife: High school graduate........	2,569	34.6	20.4	32.6	49.2
Some high school............	2,838	29.1	16.3	29.1	35.5
No high school..............	1,619	25.6	15.2	26.3	27.3
Husband no high school:					
Wife: High school graduate........	2,120	34.7	22.0	33.7	40.7
Some high school............	3,066	30.5	18.6	31.4	32.7
No high school..............	8,891	22.2	15.8	25.5	20.9

Source: *1960 Census of Population, Subject Reports, Families,* Series PC(2)–4A, tables 25 and 26.

NOTES

[1] Herman P. Miller, *Income Distribution in the United States,* chapter VI. Washington: U.S. Government Printing Office, 1966.

[2] Seymour Harris, *The Market for College Graduates,* Cambridge, Mass.: Harvard University Press, 1949.

[3] David M. Blank and George J. Stigler, *The Demand and Supply of Scientific Personnel.* New York: National Bureau of Economic Research, 1957.

[4] Robert J. Havighurst, *American Higher Education in the 1960's.* Columbus, Ohio: Ohio State University Press, 1960. Quoted with the permission of Kappa Delta Pi, an Honor Society in Education, owners of the copyright.

[5] The substantial interest in skilled manpower problems has led to the development of a number of techniques for making such analyses and projections of needs. The most useful approach seems to be based on the projection of total economic growth by sectors, and the derivation of the occupational distribution and manpower requirements from these projections. Recent examples of this approach include: U.S. Bureau of Labor Statistics, *The Long-Range Demand for Scientific and Technical Personnel, A Methodological Study,* National Science Foundation Report, No. 61–65; "Employment Projections, by Industry and Occupation, 1960–75, *Monthly Labor Review,* March 1963; and U.S. Department of Labor, *Manpower Report of the President and a Report on Manpower Requirements, Resources, Utilization, and Training.* Washington: U.S. Government Printing Office, March 1963.

[6] Harris, op. cit., p. 64.

NOTES—Continued

[7] Havighurst, op. cit., p. 25.

[8] Martin Trow, "Education and the American Occupational Structure." Paper read as part of a series on "The Impact of the Modern World on Education," sponsored by University Extension, University of California, Berkeley, April 1963, p. 23.

[9] Havighurst, op. cit., pp. 47-48.

[10] Edward E. Denison, "Measuring the Contribution of Education (and the Residual) to Economic Growth," *The Residual Factor and Economic Growth,* Paris: Organization for Economic Cooperation and Development, 1964, p. 37. Denison has also suggested some mechanisms by which education affects the occupational structure: ". . . the availability of better educated labour has led to changes in the whole organization of production as among occupational groups in order to take advantage of a labour supply of higher quality . . . [and] advances in technology have been such as to shift the pattern of demand toward occupations requiring more education . . ." Ibid., p. 38.

[11] U.S. Department of Commerce, Bureau of the Census, *Current Population Reports,* Series P-25, No. 305, "Projections of Educational Attainment in the United States, 1965 to 1985."

[12] David L. Kaplan and M. Claire Casey. Bureau of the Census, Working Paper No. 5, *Occupational Trends in the United States, 1900 to 1950.* Washington: U.S. Department of Commerce, 1958 ; and U.S. Census of Population: 1960, Vol. I, Part 1, *U.S. Summary* Washington: Government Printing Office, 1964, p. 216.

[13] Projections for 1975 are based on unpublished data provided by the U.S. Bureau of Labor Statistics that are consistent with their published projections in the March 1963 *Monthly Labor Review,* pp. 240-250.

[14] Gamma can take values from +1.00 to −1.00. It is necessary that the variables used have ordered distributions. For a discussion of gamma as a measure of association, see Leo A. Goodman and William H. Kruskal, "Measures of Association for Cross Classification," *Journal of the American Statistical Association,* Vol. 49, No. 268, December 1954 , pp. 747-754. Procedures for computing gamma are shown in Morris Zelditch, *Basic Course in Sociological Statistics,* New York: Holt & Company, 1959.

[15] Likewise, different index values probably would be obtained if we included farm occupations, nonwhites, and persons in other age groups. It is doubtful, however, that the degree of association would change a great deal or that the downward trend of the index values would vary significantly.

[16] For somewhat conflicting findings, however, see Duncan and Hodge "Education and Occupational Mobility, a Regression Analysis," *American Journal of Sociology,* Vol. 68 May 1963 , pp. 629, 644, who conclude from regression analysis of more detailed data from a labor mobility survey that education was no less important as a determinant of occupational status in 1950 than in 1940. Our data indicate, however, that the sharpest decline was between 1950 and 1960.

[17] Arnold Katz, "Educational Attainment of Workers, 1959," *Special Labor Force Reports* No. 1, Bureau of Labor Statistics, pp. 121, 122 and table 7.

[18] The distributions were standardized for changes in the size of the group, and the components were computed both with attainment standardization for occupational shifts and occupational shifts standardized for attainment increases. The "interaction" or differences in the two bases of standardization were small, ranging from 2.5 to 4 percent of the total change to be "explained."

[19] Some indirect evidence of the value of more detailed occupational categories is provided by data presented by Otis Dudley Duncan, "Occupational Components of Educational Differences in Income," *Journal of the American Statistical Association,* Vol. 56 December 1961, pp. 783-792, who found that, "The size of the 'between' component

NOTES—Continued

implies that about 57 percent of the gross educational difference in income is accounted for by major occupation groups, and about 73 percent by detailed occupation."

[20] Since this modal deals only with shifts in the structure of the labor force, the possibility that persons with lesser education will be pushed out of the labor force or become unemployed cannot be studied.

[21] A high proportion of professionals have been college graduates for a long time, and the proportion has been fairly stable. This can be inferred by data on median attainment level at different ages in 1960. For example, the median educational attainment for professional men (total U.S. in 1960) was 16.3 for ages 25 to 29, 16.5 for 30 to 34, 16.5 for 35 to 44, 16.3 for 45 to 54, and 16.1 for 55 to 64. Paul Glick makes this point in "Educational Attainment and Occupational Advancement," paper presented at the Second World Congress of the International Sociological Association, Liege, Belgium, August 1953.

[22] For examples of this approach, see Theodore Schultz, "Education and Economic Growth," in Nelson Henry, ed., *Social Forces Influencing American Education,* Part II of the 1961 Yearbook of the National Society for the Study of Education. Chicago: University of Chicago Press, 1961; and Edward Denison, "Measuring the Contribution of Education (and the Residual) to Economic Growth" in *The Residual Factor and Economic Growth.* Paris: Organization for Economic Cooperation and Development, 1964.

[23] For examples of this approach see Paul Glick and Herman P. Miller, "Educational Level and Potential Income," *American Sociological Review,* June 1956; and Herman P. Miller, "Annual and Lifetime Income in Relation to Education, 1939–1959," *American Economic Review,* December 1960.

[24] Herman P. Miller, *Income Distribution in the United States,* chapter VI. Washington: U.S. Government Printing Office, 1966.

[25] Herman P. Miller, "Annual and Lifetime Income in Relation to Education, 1939–1959," op. cit., and Chapter VI, *Income Distribution in the United States,* op. cit.

[26] O. D. Duncan, "Occupational Components of Educational Differences in Income," *Journal of the American Statistical Association,* Vol. 56. December 1961, p. 788.

[27] Don Bogue and Margaret J. Haygood, *Differential Migration in the Corn and Cotton Belts,* Oxford, Ohio: Scripps Foundation Studies of Population Distribution, No. 6, 1953, pp. 45-57. This study also shows the great variability in educational selectivity by age, color, sex, and type of origin and destination.

[28] Henry Shryock and Charles Nam, "Educational Selectivity of Interregional Migration," *Social Forces,* Vol. 43, March 1965, pp. 299-310. See tables 3, 4, and 5. See also Henry Shryock and Hope Eldridge, "Internal Migration in Peace and War," *American Sociological Review,* Vol. 12 (February 1947), pp. 27-39.

[29] C. Horace Hamilton, "Educational Selectivity of Net Migration From the South," *Social Forces,* Vol. 38, October 1959, pp. 33-42.

[30] Dorothy Thomas, *Research Memorandum on Migration Differentials.* New York: Social Science Research Council, Bulletin 43, 1938, p. 111.

[31] There is a substantial overreporting of previous urban residence in the migration statistics; people from rural-farm and rural-nonfarm areas tend to give the name of the nearest urban place for their previous residence; as a consequence, the data substantially understate the amount of rural to urban migration. This type of response error probably is greater among the poorly educated, thus any analysis of educational selectivity of rural-urban migration using census data will be affected by these response errors. The census shortened the time period for reporting migration to one year in 1950, but the response bias still existed; in 1960 the data are not tabulated by rural-urban residence in 1955; the only comparisons that are possible are the metropolitan-nonmetropolitan movement.

NOTES—Continued

[32] Bogue and Hagood, op. cit., figures 9, 10, and 11.

[33] Shryock and Nam, op. cit., p. 309.

[34] Loc. cit.

[35] Daniel O. Price, "The Effects of Migration on Educational Level of Nonwhites in a Southern Area." Paper presented at the 1965 meeting of the Population Association. The East South Central Division contains Mississippi, Alabama, Tennessee, and Kentucky.

[36] Ibid., tables 3–11.

[37] U.S. Dept. of Commerce, Bureau of the Census, *Current Population Reports,* Series P-11, No. 110, July 24, 1961, and P-20, No. 132, September 22, 1964.

[38] Ernest W. Burgess and Paul Wallin, "Homogamy in Social Characteristics," *American Journal of Sociology,* Vol. 44 (September 1943), pp. 109-124.

[39] Paul H. Landis and Katherine H. Day, "Education as a Factor in Mate Selection," *American Sociological Review,* Vol. 10 (August 1945), pp. 558-560.

[40] August B. Hollingshead, "Cultural Factors in the Selection of Marriage Mates," ibid., Vol. 15 (October 1950), pp. 619-627.

[41] Paul C. Glick and Hugh Carter, "Marriage Patterns and Educational Level," ibid., Vol. 23 (June 1958), pp. 294-300.

[42] There is a tendency for other relatives to have similar educational orientations, and thus similar educational attainments. No test of this was made in the analysis reported here.

[43] U.S. Department of Commerce, Bureau of the Census, *Current Population Reports,* Series P-20 No. 132, September 22, 1964.

CHAPTER VII

SUMMARY

The growth of enrollment in America

In 1960 the United States had developed an educational system of great size and complexity. Educational institutions employed about 5 percent of all workers and expended a little more than 5 percent of our gross national product. There were 45 million students enrolled in regular schools, about one-fourth of the total population of the United States.

Education would not have become a major influence in American life if there had not been a strong belief in the values of education on the part of nearly all citizens. The origins of these values and their early influence occurred prior to the collection of the first government statistics about education, but the last 120 years of the Nation's educational development can be traced with increasingly comprehensive and detailed information.

The history of enrollment growth in America can be divided into three general periods which have indistinct boundaries. The first, the development of universal elementary education, had begun in the northeast before the Census of 1840, which provided the first statistical information about education in the United States. Although elementary schooling spread unevenly to different parts of the country and to different classes of the population, some elementary education was received by nearly all segments of the population by 1900. The development of universal secondary education characterized the second period, which began about 1900-1910 and extended to about 1940-1950. Just as with elementary education, this development proceeded at different rates in different segments of the population and in different geographic regions. The same groups that were slow to attain an elementary education were slow to attain a high school education.

The country is now in the early part of a third era of educational growth, the expansion of higher education. Some observers question whether universal higher education will actually develop; if the test is for half or more of our youth to attend college for at least some period of time, we had not reached this point in 1960, although it is possible that it will be achieved by 1970.

The development of universal elementary and secondary education means that nearly all the future enrollment change at those levels will be the result of population change. Population projections indicate a very slow growth of elementary and secondary enrollment from 1965 to 1975; after 1975, elementary enrollment will grow more rapidly again, as a result of the entry into school of the children of the larger number of new families formed during the late 1960's. The anticipated rates of growth in enrollment below college will be much less in the late 1960's and 1970's than was the case between 1950 and 1960. College enrollment, by contrast, is expected to grow rapidly between 1965 and 1970, and more slowly in the subsequent 5-year periods up to 1985.

Events such as wars and depressions have had a temporary influence on school enrollment, but their influence is small compared with the normal spread of education to all groups in American society. Although large educational differences remain between groups at the college level, at the pre-college level the remaining differences are more qualitative than quantitative, and are not revealed in the census statistics. A discussion of these topics is included in chapter I.

Social factors related to school and college enrollment

The extent to which particular persons or groups enroll or persist in school is influenced by many personal, family, community, and societal factors, which at some points in the educational process have an important effect on enrollment rates. At the compulsory attendance ages, nearly all youth attend school and differences in enrollment rates are very small.

Most personal and family characteristics have different effects at different points in the educational continuum. For example, the enrollment rates of boys and girls are about the same at all precollege levels. However, attendance in college, and persistance to graduation, is greater for men than women.

Ethnic differences in enrollment rates are fairly substantial at the school-beginning ages (5 and 6), become quite small at the compulsory attendance ages (7 to 16), and grow large again at the college ages. Chinese and Japanese have the highest enrollment rates, followed by native whites, with Negroes, Indians, and Puerto Ricans having lower enrollment rates.

Rural children have lower enrollment rates than urban children at the school-beginning ages, but at higher educational levels the rural-urban differences that exist can largely be explained by other social and economic factors.

Socioeconomic status, as measured by parents' education, occupation, and income, has a small to moderate independent effect on enrollment rates at all educational levels, but its strongest effect is seen at the point of college entrance.

Scholastic ability, as measured by grades and tests, is a very important determinant of high school graduation, college attendance, and persistence in college. It is less important at the compulsory school ages when children of all ability levels continue in school. Adequate advance plans (which are also measures of motivation) are another very important determinant of who goes to college. Other factors such as financial means and the "social milieu" in which a person is raised also affect entrance into and completion of college.

However large or small the effects of the factors described above, they are additive in the sense that a favorable rating on each factor increases the probability of persistence in school. For example, youths who have high scholastic ability and who come from high-income families are more likely to be in school at any level if their parents are college-educated than if they are not.

Not much information is available from census data to indicate which factors are becoming more important and which less important as determinants of school attendance. The detailed analysis of social factors unfortunately must be done with data from only the most recent censuses and current population surveys. It is clear that most of the future differentiation will occur beyond high school, but we do not have the necessary information to tell, for example, whether the independent effects of socioeconomic background, or ethnic status, or ability, are becoming more or less important as determinants of college entry.

School dropouts are at a disadvantage, relative to high school graduates, in the economic market. They are more likely to be out of the labor force; if in the labor force, they are more likely to be unemployed; and if employed, are more likely to have lower status occupations and lower earnings.

The general pattern of relationships found between social factors and school retention is also found between social factors and the tendency to be retarded in school, that is, at a grade below that expected for one's age.

More than any other nation in the world, the United States offers substantial opportunity for educational advancement to all classes of the population. Further equalization of enrollment rates will occur primarily at the college level, since most young persons now remain in school through the precollege levels. The development of vocational, technical, and business schools, the further development of junior and community colleges, as well as the expansion of baccalaureate and higher degree-granting institutions, will make it important in the future to identify the type of post high school education as well as the mere fact of attendance or nonattendance. Personal and social factors will probably influence the particular type of education beyond high school as much as or more than they will influence the chances of any post high school education.

So long as education beyond high school is voluntary, costs substantially more than high school, and has entry controlled in part by ability and previous achievements, we may expect differential attendance rates for different segments of society. More information on social factors related to enrollment is given in chapter II.

Characteristics of teachers

At the beginning of the 20th century teaching was a poorly paid occupation, greater educational requirements for secondary teaching, made it necessary graduates and who usually remained in teaching for only a few years until they married.

The rapid expansion of elementary and secondary enrollment, and the greater educational requirements for secondary teaching, made it necessary to make teaching more attractive so that a sufficient number of persons would make teaching their career. This was accomplished by improved income (both in terms of purchasing power and relative to alternate occupational opportunities) and by allowing women to combine a career with marriage and a family. Up to 1920 only about 10 percent of women teachers were married; by 1960 this figure had risen to over 70 percent, and this change as well as the higher earnings of teachers made the development of longer teaching careers possible. By 1960, the basic family pattern of women teachers below the college level was marriage, with temporary retirement from teaching when their children were of preschool age, and reentry to teaching when their children were older. These changed career patterns have meant that the average number of years of teaching for women has increased from about 5 years in the period from 1900 to 1910 to about 15 years in 1960. The average age of women teachers has also increased from 29 in 1930 to 44 in 1960.

During each of the last four decades about 80 to 85 percent of the elementary teachers have been women. Since 1920, secondary teaching has been attracting an increasing percentage of men, and by 1960 there were about an equal number of men and women secondary teachers. College teaching has always been predominantly a male occupation, but about 20 to 25 percent of college teachers are women.

The extremely rapid growth in the number of elementary and secondary teachers that characterized the 1950's and early 1960's will be replaced by a slower growth until 1975, when enrollments will again require a rapid expansion of the corps of elementary teachers. At the same time the number of college graduates qualified to teach will expand rapidly in the period 1960 to 1970. This will increase competition for teaching positions, and will probably lead to further upgrading of the educational attainments of teachers and to other changes in teachers' characteristics and in their compensation relative to other occupations.

In the period 1965 to 1970 the number of college teachers employed will probably continue to increase very rapidly, and only between 1970 and 1975 will any substantial change occur in the supply-demand relations for college teachers. The characteristics of college teachers, as revealed in census statistics, have changed less in the last 30 to 40 years than the characteristics of elementary and secondary teachers, and the next decade may see a continuation of these past trends. Further details on the characteristics of teachers are discussed in chapter III.

Trends in illiteracy

The first collection of information about the educational level of the adult population was in 1840, when a question on illiteracy was added to the census. For the next century (through 1930) this was the only census information available about the educational attainment of adults.

Available evidence indicates that one-third to one-half of the adults in the Colonial Period could not read and write. By the time of the Census of 1840, about 25 to 30 percent of adults were illiterate. With the development of the educational system, however, the younger generations nearly all learned to read and write. By 1900 only 11 percent of the population was illiterate. As the older generations containing large numbers of illiterates died, the proportion of illiterates in the population was reduced.

Today about 2 out of 100 Americans outside of institutions lack reading and writing ability, and to these 2½ million persons can be added another ¼ million who are institutionalized (in mental hospitals, homes for the aged, prisons, and the like). Despite these large numbers, the United States already ranks among the countries of the world with the lowest rates of illiteracy.

Illiteracy is relatively low among all groups in the population but is more prevalent in rural than urban areas, among nonwhites than whites, and among the lower than upper social classes. Since literacy is principally determined by the adequacy of early formal schooling, as equalization of school opportunities becomes a reality we may eventually expect these distinctions in literacy rates to disappear.

Merely being able to read and write a simple message in some language does not equip an individual to communicate satisfactorily in a modern, complex world. If literacy is defined as the ability to deal with the English language in a fairly comprehensive manner, the count of illiterates is much larger. Additional information on illiteracy trends will be found in chapter IV.

Trends in years of schooling completed

If educational achievement is measured by the number of years of schooling completed by members of the adult population, an enormous increase in educational attainment has been achieved in the United States over the past half century.

The educational stock, as measured by formal school years completed by the adult population, has risen from 24 out of 100 without as many as 5 years of school in 1910 to only 8 out of 100 in 1960; from 14 out of 100 attaining a complete high school education in 1910 to 41 out of 100 in 1960; and from the average adult in 1910 having received an elementary school certificate to his counterpart in 1960 having attained most of a high school education.

The educational attainment of those 25 to 29 years old at each census date gives a better indication of the educational level of recent products of the school system. Among this age group in 1910, 1 out of 5 had failed to complete the fifth year of school; in 1960, only 1 out of 36 had failed to do so. In 1910, 2 out of 10 were high school graduates, whereas in 1960 there were 6 out of 10; and while the average young adult in 1910 was an elementary school graduate, in 1960 he was a high school graduate.

Projections of future educational attainment levels indicate further steady rises in the educational stock of the Nation. Each succeeding cohort of adults is better educated than the last, and the 25 to 34 year old age group, when compared with the 55 to 64 year old age group of 1960, generally had about twice the proportion of high school graduates and twice the proportion with some college, and less than half the proportion with 5 or fewer years of schooling. The educational upgrading of the population proceeds slowly by this process; by 1980, 61 percent (rather than the 44 percent of 1960) of the male population will be high school graduates, and 32 (rather than 20 percent) of the male population will have attended college for some time.

As would be expected from the review of enrollment differentials, social, personal, and economic factors produce marked differentials in educational attainment. Differences in educational attainment between the sexes are small and are narrowing, especially at the lower attainment levels (which used to contain more men but now contain very few persons of either sex). At the college level, which contains more men than women, the sex differential has not decreased in the past, but appears likely to decrease slowly in the future.

Differences in the attainment level of whites and nonwhites have also decreased slightly in the last 20 years. This has been brought about by a large decrease in the differential among those with less than five years of schooling, and a slight increase in the differential at the high school and college levels, where whites have increased their attendance more rapidly than nonwhites.

Examination of generational differences in the education of fathers and sons reveals a sharp educational upgrading of all sons as compared with fathers, but the upgrading at the levels of high school graduation and college attendance of the sons was much greater for whites than for nonwhites.

Attainment differences in different regions tended to follow the patterns described above, that is geographic differentials narrowed at the lower educational levels, but widened at the high school graduate and college attendance levels. A considerable part of the regional differences could be attributed to rural-urban differences and their unequal distribution among regions.

Educational attainment is more evenly distributed in the population than it used to be, and years of schooling are more evenly distributed than are such other measures as income, net worth, occupational prestige, and value of home. Additional information on trends in educational attainment can be found in chapter V.

Educational attainment, occupation, migration, and family patterns

The amount of education a person received influences in an important way whom he will marry, what kind of job he will obtain, how much money he will earn, how often he moves, and the educational chances of his children. Most of these relationships are quite complex.

The relationship between educational level and occupational level, for males in nonfarm occupations, seems to be getting weaker. The association declined by about a fourth between 1940 and 1960 (from .52 to .39).

Most (85 percent) of the rise in educational attainment between 1940 and 1960 occurred within broad occupational groups (professionals, managers, clerks, craftsmen, etc.) rather than being absorbed by the shifts in the occupational structure (15 percent) which provided more jobs at the upper end of the educational continuum.

About 3 million more male high school graduates, and about 4 million more males who have attended college, will be available in 1975 than would be required to maintain the 1960 educational level of each broad occupational group. To absorb this number of additional educated persons into the occupational structure will require an increase in the 1950-1960 rate of educational upgrading of occupations for college graduates. Additional persons with some college and additional high school graduates will need to be absorbed into the occupational structure at about the same or lower rates than those between 1950 and 1960.

If the additional college graduates of 1960 to 1975 are absorbed into the occupational structure in the same way that graduates in the period 1950 to 1960 were, most will go into the managerial occupations; most of the additional high school graduates will go into blue-collar occupations; craftsmen, operatives, and service workers.

Migration may redistribute the educational resources of the Nation, as people move in search of jobs, better living conditions, or for other reasons. With few exceptions, persons with higher levels of education are more migratory than persons with lower levels of education, and the difference in migration rates between poorly educated and well educated persons increases for longer distance moves.

When areas as large as a State or region are considered, the effects of migration on the educational level of the population at either origin or destination are usually small, because the net change (the difference between the total in-and-out movement) is often small, and because in some areas migrants are similar to the nonmigrants in their educational distribution. The net migration between any two regions has not changed the attainment level in either the area of origin or destination by more than .2 or .3 of a school year in a decade.

There is a strong positive relationship between age at marriage and age of completion of formal education among women; nearly one-fourth of the women marry at the age that corresponds with the typical age for completing their amount of schooling. Although educational attainment exerts a strong influence on the timing of marriage, it exerts very little influence on the proportion who eventually marry.

There is also a strong tendency for families to be made up of members with similar educational attainment. There is a high degree of similarity in the educational level of husbands and wives. The educational level of fathers and sons is also positively associated, and to about the same degree as husbands and wives.

In general, the higher the educational attainment of the wife, the more likely she is to be in the labor force, and the lower the educational level of the husband the more likely he is to have a working wife. The educational level of the wife is more influential than her husband's educational level in determining her labor force participation. These relationships exist whether there are preschool children, school-age children, or no children in the family. Further discussion of some of the relationships involved will be found in chapter VI.

The census has begun to provide in the last three decades, and especially in 1960, data which permit specification of important interrelationships between education, family structure, geographic mobility, income, and the occupational structure. These relationships are changing, and it is the understanding of these changes which will be most important to the assessment of the future role of education in the family and occupational systems. The information presented in this monograph and in the 1960 Census provide a baseline which should facilitate future studies.

EVALUATION OF CENSUS BUREAU STATISTICS ON EDUCATION

Census statistics on education may be evaluated in several ways. Estimates of response and coverage errors are provided by the Census Bureau's special content evaluation program. Another means of evaluation is the comparison of Census statistics with those from independent sources, primarily the U.S. Office of Education. Although the comparison of Census and Office of Education statistics may not give us definite information about which source is "right" when there are differences, the comparison is valuable because both sources of data are widely used, and an understanding of their similarities and differences is important. Another basis for assessment of the quality of census statistics is through the examination of the consistency of data in different parts of the same census, or between different censuses.

1960 Content Evaluation Study

The 1960 Census evaluation program compared responses supplied in the census with responses to a later reinterview of a sample of the population conducted by skilled interviewers, who probed more completely, and presumably obtained better and more accurate answers. The details of this program are described in U.S. Bureau of the Census, *Evaluation and Research Program of the U.S. Censuses of Population and Housing 1960: Accuracy of Data on Population Characteristics as Measured by Reinterviews.* Series ER60, No. 4, Washington, 1964. See also *Background Procedures and Forms,* ER60, No. 1, Washington, 1963.

One measure of the adequacy of the census is the extent to which information on the educational characteristics of the population was collected from everyone who was enumerated. Persons for whom reports of educational attainment or enrollment status were not supplied had these characteristics "allocated" to them, so that the tables on these subjects in the 1960 Census reports do not show nonrespondents separately. School enrollment was reported by 87.8 percent of the respondents, and was one of the characteristics most often omitted by census respondents. It is one of the few census inquiries to have a response rate below 90 percent. A substantial proportion of the

nonrespondents were at the upper end of the college age range and these may
have felt that the enrollment question did not apply to them if they had
been out of school for some time. There was a better response rate for educational attainment with 96.6 percent of the people 25 years old and over
reporting on this item (see table A-1).

Table A-1.—RESPONSE AND NONRESPONSE RATES IN THE CENSUS AND CONTENT
EVALUATION STUDY (CES): 1960

Reporting status	Response rates	
	School enrollment and type of school	Educational attain-ment
Reported in both Census and CES..................	87.8	96.6
Not reported in both Census and CES..............	12.2	3.4
Reported in CES but not Census..................	6.6	2.0
Reported in Census but not CES..................	1.1	1.4
Not reported in either Census or CES...........	4.5	-

—Represents zero.

Source: U.S. Bureau of the Census, *Evaluation and Research Program of the U.S. Censuses
of Population and Housing, 1960: Accuracy of Data on Population Characteristics as Measured
by Reinterviews,* Series ER 60, No. 4, table E.

As the census allocation procedures are designed to impute to respondents
for whom information was lacking the attributes of other census respondents
of similar characteristics for whom information was reported, another important
question is whether or not the census distributions of educational attainment
and enrollment correspond to those obtained in the Content Evaluation Study
reinterviews (CES). The census reported an enrollment of 43,435,000 persons
aged 5 to 34 years; after editing to remove inconsistencies, the total rose to
43,746,000. The reinterview sample, largely because it sought enrollment status
reports from more of the population, yielded an estimated total enrollment of
44,719,000, or 973,000 more than the census returned. This difference is
2.2 percent of the census total enrollment.

A comparison of census and reinterview data for people whose enrollment
status was given showed a *net* increase of 537,000 people (1.2 percent) in
the reinterview sample. Thus a little less than half of the higher enrollment
total reported in the reinterview was due to increased numbers of people
answering the question on enrollment status, and the other half was due to
reclassifying people who had reported on enrollment status.

In terms of the grade in which they were enrolled, 2.0 percent reported a
higher grade in which enrolled in the census than in the reinterviews, and
0.6 percent reported a lower grade, for a net of 1.4 percent overreporting
of grade enrolled.

APPENDIXES 213

Approximately 6.8 million people had an enrollment status allocated to them by census procedures. A high proportion of these were older people who probably had ignored the question, since they were well beyond the usual school-age range; 2.2 million of the 6.8 million were allocated the attribute of being enrolled in school.[1] About 3 percent of elementary enrollment comprised nonresponses for which such an allocation had been made; 4 to 5 percent of high school enrollment other than grade 12, 10 percent of grade 12 enrollment, and about 5 to 7 percent of college enrollment was similarly allocated. For nonwhites the percent of enrolled persons with enrollment status allocated was higher (overall 7.6 percent compared with 5.0 percent for the total). The allocation process should not have introduced biases into the data, but for educational levels like kindergarten, where allocations were 15 percent of enrollment and nonwhite allocations of kindergarten enrollment reached 25 percent, differences must be examined cautiously.

The reporting of educational attainment for persons 25 years old and over in the Census and in the CES reinterviews is shown in table A-2. Differences are largest in elementary grades 5 to 7 and college grades 1 to 3. Of more significance is the apparent upward bias in the census responses on educational attainment; about 9.0 percent more people indicated some college education in the census than in the more careful CES interviews. This kind of bias can affect some kinds of comparisons, such as the relative income advantage of college graduates over high school graduates, but for others it may not be significant.

Table A–2.—DATA ON EDUCATIONAL ATTAINMENT REPORTED IN THE CENSUS AND CONTENT EVALUATION STUDY REINTERVIEW: 1960

[Numbers in thousands. Minus sign (−) denotes decrease]

Educational attainment	Census	Content Evaluation Study	Difference as a percent of Census
No school years completed	1,871	1,884	0.6
Elementary: Grade unknown	37	632	(1)
1 to 4 years	5,022	5,241	4.3
5 to 7 years	12,348	13,527	9.5
8 years	15,598	14,784	-5.2
High school: Grade unknown	71	309	(1)
1 to 3 years	17,771	17,018	-4.2
4 years	24,503	24,927	1.7
College: Grade unknown	20	143	(1)
1 to 3 years	9,221	8,165	-11.4
4 and 5 years	6,773	6,568	-3.1
Total educational attainment reported in both Census and CES	93,235	93,235	

—Represents zero.
[1] Not relevant to the analysis.

Source: U.S. Bureau of the Census, *Evaluation and Research Program of the U.S. Censuses of Population and Housing 1960: Accuracy of Data on Population Characteristics as Measured by Reinterviews*, Series ER 60, No. 4, table 12.

Census-Office of Education enrollment comparisons below the college level

Comparisons between Census enrollment statistics by grade and Office of Education grade enrollment statistics can be made for 1940, 1950, and 1960 (see table A-3). The 1940 Census had only a question on highest grade of school completed, in addition to the question on enrollment, whereas the 1950 and 1960 Censuses contained separate questions on highest grade of school attended, and whether or not the grade was finished. The notes to

Table A-3.—Comparison of the Grade Distribution of Enrollment from Census Data and U.S. Office of Education Enrollment Statistics: 1960, 1950, and 1940

Year of school in which enrolled	1960		1950		1940	
	Census	Office of Education	Census	Office of Education	Census	Office of Education
Total enrolled.............	38,683	39,112	25,912	27,321	24,982	27,323
Percent..................	100.0	100.0	100.0	100.0	100.0	100.0
Elementary:						
1.............................	10.5	11.1	11.7	13.0	6.0	12.3
2.............................	10.2	10.1	10.9	11.0	11.0	9.5
3.............................	9.8	9.9	10.1	10.0	9.8	9.5
4.............................	9.2	9.3	9.4	9.5	9.7	9.5
5.............................	9.1	9.1	8.8	9.1	9.6	9.2
6.............................	9.0	9.0	8.6	8.7	9.2	8.9
7.............................	9.1	9.3	8.1	8.1	9.0	8.6
8.............................	8.0	8.0	7.8	7.2	8.4	6.9
High school:						
9.............................	6.8	6.8	6.7	7.1	7.5	7.9
10.............................	6.4	6.4	6.3	6.2	7.7	6.9
11.............................	6.0	5.9	5.3	5.3	6.3	5.8
12.............................	5.9	5.1	6.2	4.6	6.0	5.0
Median grade..................	5.1	5.1	5.9	5.7	6.4	6.0

Source: *1960 Census of Population,* Vol. I, *Characteristics of the Population,* Part 1, U.S. Summary, table 168; *1950 Census of Population,* Vol. I, U.S. Summary, table 112; *1940 Census of Population,* Vol. IV, *Characteristics by Age,* table 16; U.S. Office of Education, *Biennial Survey of Education, Statistics of State School Systems* 1939-1940, and 1949-1950; and U.S. Office of Education, *Digest of Educational Statistics, 1963.* Nonpublic school enrollment distributed by grade like public school enrollment.

the 1940 Census (Volumes IV, *Characteristics by Age,* Part 1, U.S. Summary) state that "in the tables for those attending school, persons may be assumed to have been attending the grade above the one given as completed." This assumption was a poor one, since many people reported the grade in which they were enrolled, possibly in the belief that they would complete the grade.

The grade distribution of enrollment from census figures has a definite upward bias, and the median grade enrollment of 6.4 was about four-tenths of a year higher in 1940 than the median grade of 6.0 reported by the Office of Education. Inspection of the grade distribution shows that the greatest problem occurred at grade 1, where the Office of Education reported about twice the proportion enrolled as the Census did.

In the 1950 Census, the enrollment question was followed by one on highest grade attended. These questions produced responses that were much more like the Office of Education figures. The median year in which enrolled differed by only .2 of a year, with the Office of Education figure being lower than the Census figure in 1950, as in 1940. The two grade distributions were quite similar in 1950, with the Office of Education distribution being significantly higher only at grade 1, and significantly lower only at grade 12. This may be additional evidence of overstatement of year enrolled, which would tend to cumulate at terminal grades.

If we include enrolled persons whose grade is unknown, Census enrollment totals are only about one-half million, or 2 percent, lower than Office of Education totals. This small difference is surprising, since the Office of Education cumulative figures undoubtedly include some duplicates. If duplicates were excluded from the Office of Education statistics, the Census enrollment figures would probably be higher. The report in the 1940 Census of total number enrolled was probably affected slightly by the one-month period of reference (enrollment from March 1 to April 1) compared with the two-month period for the 1950 and 1960 Censuses and the nine-month period of the Offices of Education statistics.

In summary, when the 1940 data on attainment are used to estimate level of enrollment, by assuming enrollment in the year above the highest attained, a definite upward bias is introduced. A reasonable estimate of this bias would be about one-third of a year (approximately the difference between overreporting in 1940 and 1950 when compared with the Office of Education standard). If this estimate is accurate, it would mean that perhaps half as many enrolled people overreported their school grade in 1940 as reported it correctly.

As the error appears to be so large, and as there is no good way to estimate its magnitude accurately, it does not appear possible to make accurate comparisons of the amount of grade retardation between 1940 and 1950.

There was further reduction in the difference between the Office of Education and Census statistics in 1960. A large part of the reduction appears to be due to the allocation procedures used in the 1960 Census, so that persons with unknown grade had a grade allocated to them. The Office of Education grade report provides information on unduplicated enrollment which should reflect the maximum enrollment during the year. This usually occurs in the fall. For example, the total Office of Education enrollment in grades 1 to 12 in 1959 to 1960 was 39.1 million. The 1959 fall enrollment reported in a Bureau of the Census sample survey taken in October was 39.0 million, and the Census of April 1960 showed 38.7 million. The difference between the

Office of Education series and the Census Bureau's fall enrollment sample survey series is less than .3 of 1 percent, and differences between the Office of Education statistics and the decennial census statistics amount to only 1.1 percent. Considering the differences in time period, the differences in methods of data collection, and the range of error associated with each series, the two seem to be in very close agreement.

These comparisons suggest that current enrollment statistics collected by the Bureau of the Census and by the Office of Education do not have substantial coverage errors (unless these are compensating) nor do the Census statistics on year in which enrolled contain a bias in overreporting large enough to affect the utility of the statistics for most purposes.

It is also possible to compare Census and Office of Education statistics of enrollment in public and private schools from the two sources for 1960—the first time a question on public or private school enrollment was included in the census. As shown in table A-4, the Census Bureau and Office of Education statistics on private school enrollment differ more than do the figures on public school enrollment. Part of the difference may reflect confusion on the part of census respondents about whether a school was public or private, and part may reflect the greater difficulty encountered by the Office of Education in getting private schools to report on their enrollment.

Table A–4.—ENROLLMENT IN PRIVATE SCHOOLS AS REPORTED IN THE 1960 CENSUS OF POPULATION AND IN U.S. OFFICE OF EDUCATION STATISTICS: 1960

Grade level	Census	Office of Education	Percent of Office of Education figure
Total........................	5,552	5,675	97.8
Kindergarten to elementary 8 years...	4,472	4,640	96.4
High school 1 to 4 years.............	1,080	1,035	104.8

Source: *1960 Census of Population,* Vol I, *Characteristics of the Population,* Part 1, U.S. Summary, table 75; U.S. Office of Education, *Digest of Educational Statistics, 1962.*

Census-Office of Education comparison of college enrollment

Comparison of Bureau of the Census and Office of Education statistics at the college level are affected by the difference in time of reporting. Office of Education fall enrollment statistics are quite similar to those collected by the Census Bureau in its *Current Population Survey* (table A-5). The Census *Current Population Survey* yielded an estimate of college enrollment of 3,340,000 in the fall of 1959, and the April 1, 1960 Census figure was 2,935,000, or about 13 percent lower.

A special check of the enumeration of college students in the 1960 Census was made by comparing enumeration forms with lists of enrolled students obtained from the colleges they were attending.   College records were checked against Census records both as to where the student was in fact living (and, hence, where he was supposed to have been counted) and at his parent's home (where he may have been counted).   This study produced several estimates of the percent of college students missed; the most reasonable estimate indicated a net undercount of 2.4 percent, the resultant of 7.4 percent of the students missed and 5.0 percent erroneously included.   Of those counted, about 95 percent were counted at the proper residence location and the remainder were counted elsewhere.

As a check on the 1960 Census enrollment data, we have made a special effort to collect directly from colleges data in a form that would be comparable in definition and time of collection with data collected in the census. A special questionnaire was sent to all higher educational institutions listed in the *Educational Directory* of the Office of Education in 4 States in different parts of the country, namely Florida, New Mexico, Rhode Island, and Wisconsin.   Replies were received from all but one small college, and data for it were estimated by recourse to Office of Education statistics.   One person in each of these States assisted in the collection of the data.[2]

Table A–5.—FALL COLLEGE ENROLLMENT AS REPORTED IN THE BUREAU OF THE CENSUS CURRENT POPULATION SURVEY AND U.S. OFFICE OF EDUCATION: 1959 TO 1963

Year	Census	Office of Education	Percent of Office of Education figure
1959	3,340	3,377	.989
1960	3,570	3,583	.996
1961	3,731	3,861	.966
1962	4,208	4,175	1.008
1963	4,336	4,495	.965

Source: U.S. Bureau of the Census, *Current Population Reports—Population Characteristics,* Series P–20, Nos. 101, 110, 117, 126, and 129; U.S. Office of Education, *Projections of Educational Statistics to 1973-74,* OE–10030 (1964 edition).

The 4 States were chosen because it was felt that a complete response could be obtained from each.   Although these States do not constitute a sample of the United States, they provide useful information for examination of the kinds of errors that may be present in the 1960 Census data.

The responses indicate a fairly close agreement between the institutional reports and the 1960 Census college enrollment figures, with the latter being from 4 to 10 percent lower in the 4 States.   (See table A-6.)   One defect that had been expected, namely an overreporting of year in which enrolled, proved to be minor.   In 3 of the 4 States the institutions reported a slightly

Table A–6.—Comparison of College Reports of Spring Term Enrollment and Census Reports on College Enrollment, for Selected States: 1960

State and category	Institutional reports as a percent of Census figures		
	Total	Male	Female
TOTAL ENROLLMENT			
Florida............................	107.0	104.5	111.3
New Mexico.........................	110.4	110.1	110.9
Rhode Island.......................	105.5	103.6	108.4
Wisconsin..........................	103.8	103.1	104.9
TOTAL UNDERGRADUATE ENROLLMENT			
Florida............................	104.6	104.0	105.6
New Mexico.........................	105.4	107.1	101.6
Rhode Island.......................	101.6	103.0	98.7
Wisconsin..........................	104.2	104.0	104.4
TOTAL 5TH YEAR AND GRADUATE ENROLLMENT			
Florida............................	129.8	107.7	225.8
New Mexico.........................	145.1	127.5	237.5
Rhode Island.......................	143.6	108.3	281.6
Wisconsin..........................	100.9	98.5	114.4

Source: Special survey of institutions in the 4 States listed.

larger percent of freshmen and sophomores and a slightly smaller percent of juniors and seniors than did the census, but this difference was small. (See table A-7). If the institutions had been forced also to allocate special students to grade levels, the discrepancy might disappear or be reversed. The difference between institutional reports and 1960 Census figures ranged from 2 to 5 percent at the undergraduate level; at the graduate level there appears to be a serious undercount, especially of women, in the Census data for 3 of the 4 States.

The part-time enrollment of many teachers possibly explains the very large difference in the reporting of graduate enrollment of women. As most schoolteachers are women, and many enroll for part-time graduate work, and as many of these part-time students were women over 35, they would be eliminated in the editing of the replies to the census enrollment question. The fact that the 1960 Census was largely taken by self-enumeration may also account for some of this difference, as part-time enrollment could be more easily overlooked.

It is hard to explain on this basis why Wisconsin is not similar to the other States. Errors in institutional reporting (so that special graduate students were reported as special undergraduates, for example) may be partly responsible. Only 17 percent of the graduate students reported in the institutional reports in Wisconsin were women; in the 3 other States the percent of women ranged from 25 percent to nearly 40 percent.

Table A–7.—Comparison of Institutional Reports and Census Reports of
Undergraduate College Enrollment: 1960

State and source of data	Total	Percent distribution of reported enrollment			
		Fresh-men	Sopho-mores	Juniors	Seniors
Florida:					
Institutional report........	100	41	28	16	15
Census report..............	100	36	28	17	19
New Mexico:					
Institutional report........	100	36	27	19	18
Census report..............	100	35	26	18	21
Rhode Island:					
Institutional report........	100	31	29	19	21
Census report..............	100	33	28	19	20
Wisconsin:					
Institutional report........	100	37	26	19	18
Census report..............	100	35	27	20	18

Source: *1960 Census of Population,* Vol. I, *Characteristics of the Population,* Part 1, U.S. Summary, table 168, and special survey of the 4 States listed.

On the basis of this comparison, it appears that most of the difference in the reported totals may be explained by the omission in the census of persons over 35 years of age from the enrollment figures.

The college enrollment statistics may be compared further according to whether the enrollment was in a public or private college. (See table A-8.) Although this information was first collected in a decennial census in 1960, it has been collected over a period of years in the Census Bureau's *Current Population Surveys* (CPS) and in the Office of Education fall surveys. The percentage of students in public colleges consistently runs somewhat higher in the CPS than in the Office of Education survey. Because of this difference, a check was made in the 1958 CPS. Respondents were asked, as is generally done in the CPS, whether a college enrollee was in a public or private college and, at another point in the interview, were also asked for the name of the college.

Table A–8.—Public and Private College Enrollment According to the 1960 Census, the 1959 Current Population Survey, and 1959–1960 U.S. Office of Education Biennial Survey

Type of enrollment	1960 Census		1959 CPS		1959-60 OE Survey	
	Number	Percent	Number	Percent	Number	Percent
Total.....................	2,935,446	100.0	3,340,000	100.0	3,402,297	100.0
Public.....................	1,727,789	58.9	2,120,000	63.5	2,002,868	58.9
Private....................	1,207,657	41.1	1,220,000	36.5	1,399,429	41.1

Source: U.S. Bureau of the Census, *Current Population Reports—Population Characteristics,* Series P–20, No. 101, May 22, 1960; *1960 Census of Population,* Vol. I, *Characteristics of the Population,* Part 1, U.S. Summary, table 169; U.S. Office of Education, *Opening Fall Enrollment in Higher Education, 1959.* Circular 606.

Classification of the college names was made by using the Office of Education college directory and comparisons were made on a case-by-case basis with the CPS information. The results are shown in table A–9. If, as seems proper, one accepts the Office of Education classification, the CPS reports which were in error were largely those in which a private college was reported as public. Since many private colleges have place names (for example, the University of Dayton), this type of error is understandable. Further instructions on this point to CPS interviewers in 1959 did not result in improved reporting, as may be seen in table A–8, but the 1960 Census figures matched exactly, percentagewise, with the Office of Education figures. The explanation of the greater accuracy of the census in reporting this item is probably the fact that college students were counted in the census where they attended school, and they tended to report for themselves, whereas in the CPS, unmarried college students were reported by their parents, whose knowledge of the type of control of the college may have been incomplete.

Table A–9.—Enrollment in Public and Private Colleges of College Students Enumerated in the Current Population Survey, According to the Classification of the College in the Current Population Survey and by the U.S. Office of Education: October 1958

Category	Number	Percent
College students in sample......................	2,062	(X)
With name of college not given or incomplete...........	143	(X)
With name of college fully reported...................	1,919	100.0
In colleges having same CPS and OE classification....	1,778	92.7
In colleges having different CPS and OE classification....................................	141	7.3
OE-Public, CPS-Private.......................	26	1.4
OE-Private, CPS-Public.......................	115	6.0
Net number with different classification............	89	4.6

X Not applicable.

Source: Unpublished tabulations from the U.S. Bureau of the Census, *Current Population Survey*, October 1958. See text for description.

Evaluation of Census statistics on educational attainment

Census data on years of school completed are limited for several reasons: (1) Only certain kinds of schooling are included in the definition; (2) the number of school years completed within the Census definition is often misreported; and (3) there is variability among subgroups of the population and among areas of the country in what constitutes a year of schooling. Each of these reasons will be discussed.

Definition of years of schooling. Census educational attainment data refer to scholastic or academic years of formal schooling obtained in public and private (denominational and nondenominational) kindergartens, elementary schools, high schools, colleges, universities, and professional schools. This education may have been obtained in either day or night school and on either a full- or part-time basis. Thus, schooling counted in the census figures may have advanced a person toward an elementary school certificate or high school diploma, or toward a college, university, or professional degree. Schooling not obtained in such a "regular" school and schooling from a tutor or through correspondence courses were counted only if credits which were transferable to a school in a regular school system were obtained.

By this definition, many types of "nonregular" (formal and informal) schooling and training which may contribute substantially to an individual's knowledge and skills are excluded from the census statistics.[3] These include coursework not leading to a diploma or degree, such as courses in technical, trade, or commercial schools or "colleges" outside the regular school or college systems; most adult education courses, sometimes taken within the same buildings used by regular schools but nontheless usually not leading to a diploma or degree; on-the-job training through which knowledge is accumulated that may have wider applicability than to the individual's current job; correspondence courses, lectures, and individual instruction on topics of broad significance or of special concern; and other types of schooling or training, as well as self-instruction at home and in libraries.

The census statistics on educational attainment are restricted to progress in "regular" schools for several reasons: (1) Nearly all persons in the country are required to attend regular schools and to pursue fairly standardized courses of basic study; (2) regular schools tend to be graded schools, with the result that a grade continuum for years of school completed can be shown and statistical comparisons can be effected; (3) "nonregular" types of schooling are varied and are difficult to define and to classify in enumeration. The census statistics, therefore, deal with what is comparable and measurable.

On the whole, then, census data on years of schooling refer to what might be called the hard core of a person's formal education. While it is not likely that in very many cases a more encompassing definition of education received would place an individual in a higher category of educational attainment than the one in which the present definition places him, the Census definitional restrictions do have the effect of understating, to some extent, the amount of schooling, formal and informal, attained by the population.

The quality of census attainment data. Census statistics on educational attainment, like most census data, often tend to be used without regard for their accuracy. Studies completed by the Census Bureau show that there is a good deal of misreporting of years of school completed. Since, however, a high proportion of the misreports are compensating (that is, errors in one direction cancel errors in the opposite direction), the net effect of misreporting on the published statistics is not nearly as great as the gross errors might indicate. But a review of information on quality of data seems in order here because of its effect on the interpretation of trends.

A major source of knowledge about the accuracy of reporting census education data is the postenumeration survey. Such surveys were conducted both after the 1950 Census and after the 1960 Census. Estimates from the latter survey indicated that for about 16 percent of the population 25 years old and over, the reported educational attainment was at least one grade higher in the census than in the survey, whereas for about 10 percent the reported attainment was at least one grade lower in the census than in the survey (see table A–10).

Table A–10.—SUMMARY OF POST-ENUMERATION STUDIES ON MISREPORTING OF YEARS OF SCHOOL COMPLETED, FOR PERSONS 25 YEARS OLD AND OVER: 1960 AND 1950

Subject	1960	1950
Reporting same grade...........................	73.3	62.4
Misreporting by one or more grades:		
Gross....................................	26.7	37.6
Higher in census............................	16.4	21.9
Lower in census............................	10.4	15.8
Net.....................................	6.0	6.1
Net overreporting in census on grades:		
High school 4 years or higher................	0.4	2.0
College 4 years or more.....................	0.2	0.5

Source: Based on *The Post-Enumeration Survey: 1950*, U.S. Bureau of the Census, Technical Paper No. 4, table 4, and U.S. Bureau of the Census, *Evaluation and Research Program of the U.S. Censuses of Population and Housing: 1960*, Series ER 60, table 12.

On balance, if one regards the evaluation survey as the standard for comparison, there was a net overreporting of years of school completed for 6 percent of the population 25 years old and over. Comparison with data from the 1950 postenumeration survey shows that the percentages of gross overreporting and underreporting were lower in 1960 than in 1950, but that the percent of net overreporting (for all grades combined) was about the same in the two censuses. The 1950 data also show that net overreporting tended to be relatively greater at older that at younger years.

There are numerous reasons why years of schooling may be incorrectly reported. Some persons may intentionally overreport their educational attainment because of its obvious prestige and economic value. There may also be a small amount of intentional understatement of education received, for whatever reasons. A great deal of the misreporting is unintentional, however. Problems of recall exist, both for persons reporting their own educational attainment and for those reporting the education of other persons in the household. This is especially true of the older population. Misunderstanding of the census questions and their definitions as well as errors in recording the information contribute to misreporting, as do errors in processing the data.

While the distortion of the distribution of years of school completed which results from misreporting is an impediment to a thorough analysis, the total effect is probably not too severe. In addition to the factor of compensating misreporting, which does not minimize the concern with gross misreporting but does limit the net effect, errors in reporting one-grade differences often are not analytically important. For example, the misreporting of 2 years of elementary schooling for 1 year of schooling has no effect on the computation of the median level of educational attainment, or even on the percentage of the population with, say, less than 5 years of schooling.

As a person's educational level is generally fixed by the time he reaches his late twenties or early thirties, another source of knowledge about the relative accuracy of census data on education comes from the analysis of the consistency of reported education data for the same cohort at successive censuses. (See table A–11.) We find from such an analysis that the statistics for 1960 are distributed more like those for 1940 than those for 1950. For given cohorts, reports on educational attainment tend generally to have been somewhat higher in 1950 than at the earlier or later censuses. Thus, although net overreporting of years of schooling is found in each census and seems to have been at about the same level in 1950 and 1960 for all grades combined, overstatement of

Table A–11.—Percent of Persons Attaining Specified Educational Levels, by Cohort: 1940, 1950, and 1960

[Based on population reporting years of school completed]

Age of cohort (years) in—			Years of school completed								
1940	1950	1960	Less than 5 years			4 years of high school or more			4 years of college or more		
			1940	1950	1960	1940	1950	1960	1940	1950	1960
15 to 19	25 to 29	35 to 39	5.4	4.7	4.0	18.1	52.8	54.7	0.1	7.7	9.5
20 to 24	30 to 34	40 to 44	5.3	5.1	4.7	44.4	47.7	48.4	3.3	7.4	8.1
25 to 29	35 to 39	45 to 49	5.9	6.4	5.9	38.1	40.5	40.6	5.9	7.2	7.4
30 to 34	40 to 44	50 to 54	7.1	7.9	7.5	33.0	35.6	34.9	6.3	7.4	7.3
35 to 39	45 to 49	55 to 59	9.7	10.2	10.4	26.9	30.0	28.5	5.5	6.5	6.1
40 to 44	50 to 54	60 to 64	12.2	12.8	13.2	23.7	26.8	24.6	4.7	5.6	5.0
45 to 49	55 to 59	65 to 69	15.7	16.2	18.2	20.6	23.3	20.7	4.2	4.9	4.1
50 to 54	60 to 64	70 to 74	18.2	19.1	20.9	18.5	21.0	18.6	3.8	4.3	3.6
55 to 59	65 to 69	75 to 79	19.3	22.3	(1)	17.1	18.4	(1)	3.4	3.7	(1)
60 to 64	70 to 74	80 to 84	20.2	22.5	(1)	16.4	17.8	(1)	3.3	3.6	(1)

[1] Data for this cohort in 1960 are not available but figures for the population 75 years old and over show 22.1 percent with less than 5 years of school, 17.7 percent with 4 years or more of high school, and 3.2 percent with 4 years or more of college.

Source: 1950 Census of Population, Vol. II, U.S. Summary, table 115; 1960 Census of Population, Vol. I, Characteristics of the Population, Part 1, U.S. Summary, table 173.

high school and college graduation appears to have been greatest in 1950, and of about the same level in 1940 and 1960. The reasons for this inconsistency are somewhat obscure, but possible contributing factors may include variations in sampling procedures and the different biases introduced by them at the several census dates, variations in enumeration procedures, and differences in the distribution by educational attainment of persons who did not report on this subject at the different dates.

What are the implications of these findings for the interpretation of trends? First, the "true" levels of formal education of the population at all dates are probably slightly lower than they appear to be in published tables. Second, because greater net overstatement of education is estimated for the older population on whom the earlier Census estimates are based, the improvement in years of schooling between 1910 and 1960 was probably slightly greater than is indicated in chapters V and VI. Third, because of the differential pattern of misreporting over the past few censuses, the increase in years of school completed between 1940 and 1950 is somewhat overstated, and that between 1950 and 1960 is somewhat understated. These conclusions should be considered in any use of the statistics.

Other problems in interpreting attainment trends and differentials. A number of other factors related to the census classification of years of school completed should be noted and evaluated. Four of these important factors are distinguished here; there are numerous others which have an effect on the statistics that might also be discussed.

1. Changes and variations in the length of the school year and the school day. Some analysts argue that adjustments of the historical data on years of school completed are needed because the national average number of days spent in school per year and hours spent in school per day have increased greatly. In fact, between 1910 and 1960, the increase in school days per year was about as great as the increase in years of school completed. On this basis a correction factor has sometimes been used to deflate the earlier census figures to make them "equivalent" to the latest census figures.[4] Similarly, at any point in time, including the present, there have been variations among different parts of the country and among different classes of the population—variations in the number of days per year and hours per day spent in school—for which an adjustment might be made. We have not made such corrections or adjustments in this monograph. Information is lacking on the actual effect of changes and variation in the length of the school year and school day on educational attainment. Certainly, we can recognize that days and hours of school are not equal to years of school as meaningful time units of education received. Moreover, much of the school program in the United States today involves repetition and reinforcement of instruction in basic ideas and principles. How much of this is essential to the learning process remains a moot point. An important ques-

tion here is whether or not the amount of fundamental knowledge acquired through the formal school systems has changed over the past 50 or 60 years. and there is no reliable information in this subject.

2. Changes and variations in content and quality of instruction. Over the past several decades, new fields of study have developed, new areas of information in old fields of study have arisen, and the training of teachers to impart this knowledge to students has undergone much change. We do not know how much better prepared scholastically a person may be after completing a given school level today than was his counterpart some decades ago, in terms of assuming his responsibilities in the community and contributing to his own and his family's welfare. Standardized achievement tests have not been administered to large groups of youths for any extended period of time, and no other yardstick is available for gauging time trends in these factors. Nor do we have statistical measures of the variation in types of schools attended, courses taken, and quality of teaching—measures which can be used to reduce to equivalence the reported educational attainment of different population groups.

3. Variations in abilities and learning of persons completing the same school level. Apart from the factors already mentioned, persons with the same number of school years completed may differ in their educational achievements because of differences in their native abilities and in the extent to which they acquired and retained the skills and knowledge afforded by their schooling.

4. Equivalence of different numbers of years of schooling. In interpreting census statistics on years of school completed, it is customary to regard the different years of school as being of equal interval. For example, increases from 9 to 11 years of school and from 10 to 12 years of school are viewed as of generally the same magnitude, even though the latter increase results in the attainment of a critical level of education—namely, high school graduation. In terms of analytical significance, different years of schooling are usually not equivalent, and interpretation of census data on education should take this into account.

In summary, the quality associated with, and the benefits accruing from, a given measure of schooling have probably varied over time and no doubt vary among areas of the country and among subgroups of the population. These differences may be accounted for partly by the relative adequacy of the school systems which persons have attended and the level of training provided, and partly by the individual's cultural, social, and psychological background.

While these variations can have a disturbing effect on the analysis of census data on education, they are probably not so great as to make invalid the direct analysis of the census information, especially when the effects of the variations themselves are considered in making interpretations.

It is also possible to compare statistics on educational attainment compiled by the Bureau of the Census and the Office of Education. Few direct comparisons can be made but it is possible to make some indirect comparisons. For instance, according to the March 1959 *Current Population Survey*, about 6.9 million persons 25 to 29 years old were high school graduates (that is, had completed 4 years of high school or some college); if one sums the number of high school graduates reported each year by the Office of Education for a 5-year period corresponding to the time at which this age group should have completed high school, about 6.0 million persons are recorded as high school graduates. The most obvious reason for this difference is the probable net overreporting of persons completing high school in the CPS. However, it is difficult to match cohorts in the two sets of data, and some persons receive high school equivalent certificates at a late age. It is significant that a special study conducted by the Census Bureau in the fall of 1960, in which information was gathered on the high school status of youths reported as high school seniors in the October 1959 CPS, an estimated 1,803,000 were reported as high school graduates; and this number agreed exactly with the independent estimate made by the Office of Education on the basis of its survey.

When we compare the number of 25-to-29-year-old college graduates, that is, persons of this age who had completed 4 or more years of college, according to the CPS, with the number of college degrees granted (bachelor's and first professional level according to the Office of Education) for the appropriate time period, the CPS figure is found to be slightly lower than the Office of Education figure (about 1.2 million vs. 1.4 million). Quite likely, some net overreporting of college graduates in the CPS was more than compensated for by the fact that the Office of Education data included many persons (perhaps as much as 10 percent of the total with bachelor's or first professional degrees) who received a professional degree after having received a bachelor's degree in the same 5-year period. The difficulty of exactly matching cohorts precludes making any very precise comparisons.

Comparability of Bureau of the Census and Office of Education statistics on teachers

The Office of Education collects data on teachers from local school systems, State departments of education, and collegiate institutions. The Census has collected data from individuals since 1890. There is a possibility of error in each type of collection, in addition to some conceptual differences. The census data refer to principal occupation, so that if teaching is a secondary occupation (which it is fairly frequently for college teachers—nearly one-third of the faculty in degree-granting colleges are part-time teachers), the teacher will be classified in another occupation by the Census Bureau but counted as a teacher by the Office of Education, which is not concerned with *principal* occupation but with the total number of people working in educational institutions. Also, Census data cover teachers in all types of institutions, while the Office of Education has very incomplete returns on private elementary and secondary school teachers.

Census occupational categories include "college teachers" and "teachers, not elsewhere classified." In addition, there are the mixed categories "musicians and music teachers," "artists and art teachers," "sports officials and instructors," each of which includes some teachers. Unless the teachers in these groups can be distinguished and added to the other figures for teachers, the census figures will be too small. A basis for the identification of teachers in the combined occupational categories such as "musicians and music teachers" exists in the detailed cross-classification of occupation by industry of employment. One of the industry classifications is "educational services," and musicians and music teachers who work for an educational institution may be assumed to be teachers. It is not possible to make this assumption for all detailed occupations; in 1950, for example, there were 11,820 nurses in educational services. We cannot assume that they were all teachers in nursing schools. Most of them were probably school nurses, or nurses in college infirmaries. For several groups which have a large percentage and number of teachers, and for whom data were available for the 1900 to 1960 period, an allocation to teaching was made on the basis of the proportion employed in educational services, as shown in table A–12. This included:

> Artists and art teachers
> College presidents, professors, and instructors
> Librarians
> Musicians and music teachers
> Teachers (n.e.c.)

Data for some other occupational groups such as sports officials and instructors were available only in 1950 and 1960 and could not be identified separately in 1940 and earlier years.

Table A–12.—Percent of Selected Professional Groups Employed in Educational Services: 1960 and 1950

Selected professional occupations	Percent in educational services	
	1960	1950
All professionals	31.5	30.6
Artists and art teachers	24.1	19.4
College presidents, professors, and instructors	100.0	100.0
Librarians	80.2	82.5
Musicians and music teachers	63.4	54.2
Teachers (n.e.c.)	77.9	97.2

Source: *1960 Census of Population, Subject Reports, Occupation by Industry,* PC(2)–7C, table 2; *1950 Census of Population,* Vol. IV, *Special Reports, Occupation by Industry.*

The sum of the teachers in these occupations has been called total teaching groups; while these groups do not include all the teachers, they probably contain at least 95 percent of the total, and should be roughly comparable with the Office of Education data. The percent of workers in these detailed occupations who were teachers had to be estimated for 1930 and earlier years, since occupation was not then classified by industry group. Using the 1940 and 1950 data as a basis, we estimated that all "college presidents, professors, and instructors," and "teachers, n.e.c.," both male and female, were teachers. Ten percent of the male and 25 percent of the female "artists and art teachers" were classified as teachers; 30 percent of the male and 75 percent of the female musicians were classified as teachers; and among librarians, 90 percent of both sexes were so classified. This is the basis for the figures on total teaching groups presented in chapter III.

The data for 1930 and earlier years refer to "gainful workers," which category includes both employed and unemployed teachers. Using 1940 and 1950 ratios of employed teachers to total teachers, and estimates (from *Historical Statistics of the United States, Colonial Times to 1957*) for unemployment levels during earlier years, the census statistics from 1900 to 1930 were adjusted to an "employed worker" concept, equivalent to that used by the Office of Education.

The Office of Education data were adjusted by adding estimates of private elementary and secondary school teachers for 1920 and earlier years, and by allocating principals and supervisory teachers, by sex for 1930 and 1950. Private school teachers were estimated from private school enrollment data. The resultant of all these adjustments is shown, by sex, in table A–13.[5]

The relationship between the two series fluctuates quite a bit, and is not consistent for the sexes. Female teachers reported by the Census are consistently more numerous than those reported by the Office of Education. For males, the agreement between the two series is closer except in 1900, when the Office of Education figures were much higher.

The agreement between the Office of Education and Bureau of the Census figures for 1940, 1950, and 1960 is fairly close, although what difference there is might be expected to be in the opposite direction, with the Office of Education figures the larger, because the Census figures omit some teachers, namely those who were not counted at all and those who were listed in other occupation groups rather than as teachers.

Some of the people reported as teachers by the Census would not be counted as teachers by the Office of Education because they do private tutoring, give private music lessons, etc. The number of such persons is impossible to estimate accurately, but it could be as much as 5 percent of the total. The Office of Education figures[6] probably missed some schools, especially private schools, and

Table A–13.—NUMBER OF TEACHERS REPORTED BY THE U.S. OFFICE OF EDUCATION
AND IN EACH CENSUS, BY SEX: 1900 TO 1960

[Numbers in thousands]

Census year and sex	Census data	Office of Education data	
		Number	Percent of Census data
TOTAL			
1960	2,060	1,990	96.6
1950	1,368	1,330	97.2
1940	1,189	1,157	97.3
1930	1,154	1,060	91.8
1920	842	800	95.0
1910	675	602	89.2
1900	480	481	100.2
MALE			
1960	674	780	115.7
1950	405	429	105.9
1940	333	335	100.6
1930	247	232	93.9
1920	153	147	96.1
1910	144	146	101.4
1900	125	153	122.4
FEMALE			
1960	1,386	1,210	87.3
1950	963	901	93.6
1940	856	821	95.9
1930	908	828	91.2
1920	688	653	94.9
1910	531	456	85.9
1900	355	328	92.4

Source: U.S. Office of Education. Elementary and secondary teachers from *Digest of Educational Statistics*, OE–10064 (1964 Edition), table 99, with administration staff sex distribution estimated and added into figures. Higher education total faculty from *Historical Statistics of the United States, Colonial Times to 1957; Continuation to 1962, and Revisions*, Series H 317–H 319. For derivation of census data, see text.

they also contain an undetermined number of duplications of teachers who teach in more than one school during the year. We have only a sketchy way of estimating the number of duplicates, but 1950 Census data indicate that about 10 percent of teachers (9 percent public school and 13.5 percent college) moved from one county to another in 1949. Even if only a third of these are duplicates, the Office of Education figures would be overstated by about 3 percent.

If an allowance of 3 percent is made for duplicate reporting by the Office of Education, it appears that the Office of Education misses at least 5 percent of all the teachers in its statistical compilations; most of this incomplete coverage is probably among private self-employed teachers, and among teachers employed by noneducational institutions.

When Office of Education and Bureau of the Census reports are compared by teaching level (see table A–14), the largest discrepancies are seen at the college level. At the elementary and secondary levels, the comparisons suggest that coverage of private school teachers may be deficient in the Office of Education figures, and that this may have been a greater problem in 1950 and 1940 than in 1960, when the totals were in closer agreement.

Some of the difficulties in determining the size of the college faculty group can be discerned by examining the Office of Education Summary Report (OE-53014) on "Faculty and Other Professional Staff in Institutions of Higher Education, 1959-60." This report indicates a total of 383,000 persons, but the total faculty for resident instruction in degree credit courses with rank of instructor or above is only 244,000, and the full-time faculty for resident instruction (instructor or above) is only 164,000, or 43 percent of the total. Also included in the total are 33,000 administrators, who might or might not have been counted in the census as college professors; some, more likely, would have been counted as accountants, or architects, or engineers, etc.   There are

Table A–14.—Number of Teachers Reported by the U.S. Office of Education and in Each Census, by Level of Teaching: 1940 to 1960

[Numbers in thousands. Census data for 1940 relate only to those working or seeking work, whereas the data for 1950 are for the entire civilian labor force, and the data for 1960 relate to the experienced civilian labor force]

Census year and level of teaching	Census data	Office of Education data	
		Number	Percent of Census data
COLLEGE PRESIDENTS, PROFESSORS, AND INSTRUCTORS			
1960	179	244	.73
1950	124	190	.65
1940	76	117	.65
TEACHERS BELOW COLLEGE LEVEL			
1960	1,682	1,693	.99
1950	1,130	1,045	1.08
1940	1,053	982	1.07
TEACHERS IN 1960 BELOW COLLEGE LEVEL			
Total	1,682	1,693	.99
Teachers (n.e.c.)	150	–	(X)
Elementary	1,011	1,098	1.09
Public	849	943	1.11
Private	162	155	.96
Secondary	521	595	1.14
Public	460	530	1.15
Private	61	65	1.07

—Represents zero.

Source: U.S. Office of Education, *Biennial Survey of Education, 1948-50,* table 7, p. 9; U.S. Office of Education, *Faculty and Other Professional Staff in Institutions of Higher Education, 1959-60* (OE–53014); *1940 Census of Population, The Labor Force,* Part 2, table 1; *1950 Census of Population, Economic Characteristics,* Vol. IV, Part 1B, table 1; *1960 Census of Population,* Vol. I, *Characteristics of the Population,* Part 1, U.S. Summary, table 205.

10,000 librarians, who probably would have been counted in the librarian group. Research and extension staff members number 67,000; many do not teach, and many do not have faculty status. It is hard to say how they would have been classified in the census. There are about 40,000 graduate students who also teach; they might or might not have been reported as teachers in the census. About 10,000 people who are employed by colleges but teaching below the college level would probably have been reported in the elementary and secondary teacher groups. Finally, there are about 80,000 part-time college teachers probably counted in large numbers in other occupations, such as doctors, lawyers, accountants, etc., since for many of them teaching is a secondary occupation.

Considering the large number of conceptual problems involved in developing an occupational classification, it is easy to understand the magnitude of the differences between the Census and Office of Education figures on teachers. These differences should be kept in mind by the user of the figures from either source.

Summary

Census statistics on enrollment, attainment, and teachers are subject to a variety of errors in collection and reporting, and differ conceptually from information about enrollment and teachers compiled in other sources. In general, the magnitude of these errors is relatively small and conceptual differences are of minor importance, although in a few instances they are sufficient to seriously hinder the use and interpretation of the census data. The usefulness of the data is substantially improved, however, by the more comprehensive information available about the quality of the 1950 and 1960 Census statistics on education, and research workers and administrators may more readily use this information to evaluate the statistics.

NOTES

[1] U.S. Department of Commerce, Bureau of the Census; *U.S. Census of Population: 1960,* Vol. II, PC(2)–5A, *School Enrollment,* tables A-1 to A-4 for data on allocated enrollment.

[2] The persons in each State who assisted in data collection had many contacts with all institutions of higher education in the State, all held responsible positions in their States, and were largely responsible for the excellent response obtained.

[3] See Jacob Mincer, "On-the-Job Training: Costs, Returns, and Some Implications," *Journal of Political Economy,* Vol. 70. Supplement, October 1962, pp. 50-79.

[4] Theodore W. Schultz, "Education and Economic Growth," in Nelson B. Henry, ed., *Social Forces Influencing American Education* (the Sixtieth Yearbook of the National Society for the Study of Education, 1961), pp. 66-70; and Edward Denison, "Measuring the Contribution of Education (and the 'Residual') to Economic Growth," in *The*

NOTES—Continued

Residual Factor and Economic Growth. Paris: Organization for Economic Cooperation and Development, 1964, pp. 30-32.

[5] Basic census data from U.S. Department of Commerce, Bureau of the Census, *Occupational Trends in the United States: 1900 to 1950,* Bureau of the Census Working Paper No. 5 , tables 6, 6a, and 6b; *U.S. Census of Population: 1950,* Special Reports PE-1C, *Occupation by Industry,* table 2 and *U.S. Census of Population: 1940,* Series P-14, No. 11, *Occupations of Employed Persons in Each Industry,* March 1953. Basic data from the U.S. Office of Education from the U.S. Bureau of the Census, *Historical Statistics of the United States: Colonial Times to 1957,* Series H-234-240. Washington, D.C., 1960; and from Office of Education Biennial Survey of Education *Statistical Summary 1955-56,* table 7.

[6] There are no adequate studies of coverage and reporting errors in the Office of Education surveys.

APPENDIX B

METHOD OF PREPARING ENROLLMENT PROJECTIONS

In order to provide for a greater increase in enrollment rates at the college level than is inherent in the Bureau of the Census projections of enrollment in *Current Population Reports,* P-25, No. 232, "Illustrative Projections to 1980 of School and College Enrollment in the United States," (June 1961), two new series of projections were prepared for this monograph, utilizing the same basic approach described in P-25, No. 232. The later Bureau of the Census projections published in *Current Population Reports,* P-25, No. 388, "Projections of School and College Enrollment in the United States to 1985," did not become available until May 1966, and hence no account is taken of them here.

The first or high projection series, high series "A," is based on cited population projections of the Census Bureau,[1] and on enrollment rates by single years of age for ages 5 to 24. The enrollment rates are shown in tables B-1 to B-4. For ages 25 to 34, the enrollment has been projected by means of the ratio of enrollment of persons 25 to 34 to the enrollment of the population 18 to 24 years old. Enrollment rates were generally computed as a linear projection of the trend in observed fall enrollment rates between 1950 and 1963, in the annual October *Current Population Survey* of enrollment. This trend was compared with the trend between 1950 and 1960 for the same age specific rates of enrollment in April reported in the census, and the projected trend generally represented an average of the slope of these two trends. For most ages, the CPS and decennial census trends in increase in the percent enrolled were consistent with each other (tables B–1 to B–4).

The second or low projection series utilizes the next to lowest level "C" Census Bureau projection of population, and enrollment rate increases one-half as large as those used for the high series.[2]

After projections of persons enrolled had been made for 1965 through 1985, by single years of age, they were distributed among the elementary, secondary, or college enrollment levels in accordance with the percent of each age group enrolled at each level in 1963. The same percentages were used to produce this distribution for every year of the projection period.

Table **B–1.**—PROJECTED ENROLLMENT RATES BY SINGLE YEARS OF AGE: 1965 TO 1985

[High series projections—males]

Age	1965	1970	1975	1980	1985
5 years old	.700	.750	.800	.825	.850
6 years old	.982	.987	.990	.990	.990
7 years old	.992	.992	.992	.992	.992
8 years old	.994	.994	.994	.994	.994
9 years old	.995	.995	.995	.995	.995
10 years old	.993	.993	.993	.993	.993
11 years old	.993	.993	.993	.993	.993
12 years old	.993	.993	.993	.993	.993
13 years old	.992	.992	.992	.992	.992
14 years old	.990	.990	.990	.990	.990
15 years old	.980	.980	.980	.980	.980
16 years old	.948	.960	.960	.960	.960
17 years old	.841	.881	.910	.910	.910
18 years old	.610	.670	.730	.790	.850
19 years old	.460	.510	.560	.610	.660
20 years old	.369	.404	.439	.474	.509
21 years old	.304	.344	.384	.424	.464
22 years old	.241	.271	.301	.331	.361
23 years old	.186	.196	.206	.216	.226
24 years old	.157	.172	.187	.202	.217

Source: Computations described in the text.

Table **B–2.**—PROJECTED ENROLLMENT RATES BY SINGLE YEARS OF AGE: 1965 TO 1985

[High series projections—females]

Age	1965	1970	1975	1980	1985
5 years old	.691	.741	.791	.825	.850
6 years old	.990	.990	.990	.990	.990
7 years old	.991	.991	.991	.991	.991
8 years old	.996	.996	.996	.996	.996
9 years old	.996	.996	.996	.996	.996
10 years old	.996	.996	.996	.996	.996
11 years old	.996	.996	.996	.996	.996
12 years old	.995	.995	.995	.995	.995
13 years old	.995	.995	.995	.995	.995
14 years old	.990	.990	.990	.990	.990
15 years old	.969	.979	.980	.980	.980
16 years old	.944	.950	.950	.950	.950
17 years old	.778	.818	.850	.850	.850
18 years old	.407	.447	.487	.527	.567
19 years old	.266	.306	.346	.386	.426
20 years old	.200	.230	.260	.290	.320
21 years old	.137	.162	.187	.212	.237
22 years old	.058	.068	.078	.008	.098
23 years old	.004	.054	.064	.074	.084
24 years old	.030	.035	.040	.045	.050

Source: Computations described in the text.

Table B–3.—PROJECTED ENROLLMENT RATES BY SINGLE YEARS OF AGE: 1965 TO 1985

[Low series projections—males]

Age	1965	1970	1975	1980	1985
5 years old	.690	.715	.740	.740	.740
6 years old	.980	.980	.980	.980	.980
7 years old	.992	.992	.992	.992	.992
8 years old	.994	.994	.994	.994	.994
9 years old	.995	.995	.995	.995	.995
10 years old	.993	.993	.993	.993	.993
11 years old	.993	.993	.993	.993	.993
12 years old	.993	.993	.993	.993	.993
13 years old	.992	.992	.992	.992	.992
14 years old	.990	.990	.990	.990	.990
15 years old	.973	.973	.973	.973	.973
16 years old	.939	.950	.950	.950	.950
17 years old	.831	.857	.877	.897	.900
18 years old	.584	.614	.644	.674	.704
19 years old	.440	.465	.490	.515	.540
20 years old	.357	.377	.397	.417	.437
21 years old	.266	.286	.306	.326	.346
22 years old	.229	.244	.259	.274	.299
23 years old	.182	.187	.192	.197	.202
24 years old	.153	.163	.173	.183	.193

Source: Computations described in the text.

Table B–4.—PROJECTED ENROLLMENT RATES BY SINGLE YEARS OF AGE: 1965 TO 1985

[Low series projections—females]

Age	1965	1970	1975	1980	1985
5 years old	.671	.696	.721	.746	.750
6 years old	.985	.985	.985	.985	.985
7 years old	.991	.991	.991	.991	.991
8 years old	.996	.996	.996	.996	.996
9 years old	.996	.996	.996	.996	.996
10 years old	.996	.996	.996	.996	.996
11 years old	.996	.996	.996	.996	.996
12 years old	.995	.995	.995	.995	.995
13 years old	.995	.995	.995	.995	.995
14 years old	.986	.986	.986	.986	.986
15 years old	.965	.970	.975	.980	.980
16 years old	.917	.927	.937	.947	.950
17 years old	.762	.782	.802	.822	.842
18 years old	.391	.411	.431	.451	.471
19 years old	.250	.270	.290	.310	.330
20 years old	.188	.203	.218	.233	.248
21 years old	.125	.135	.145	.155	.165
22 years old	.054	.059	.064	.069	.074
23 years old	.040	.045	.055	.055	.060
24 years old	.030	.035	.044	.045	.050

Source: Computations described in the text.

During the period 1950 to 1963, enrollment rates were increasing at ages 5 and 6; they were high (over 99 percent) and stable at ages 7 to 14; high and increasing at ages 15 and 16; and increasing at all ages above 16. In general, during the decade 1950-1960, enrollment rates at the upper ages increased slightly more for males than for females. Enrollment rates are expected to reach a peak by 1975 and stabilize for all ages between 6 and 17; for age 5, and ages 18 to 34, they are projected to increase at a constant rate during the period 1963-1985, either at the rate observed for the period 1950-1963 for the high projection, or at one-half the observed rate for the low projection.

This projection is lower at the elementary level than is the high census series (II–A) contained in P-25, No. 232, because it utilizes a more recent population projection which takes into account the declining birth rates of the early 1960's. For the same reasons, it is also slightly lower at the high school level in 1980 and 1985.

At the college level, the present projection is lower than the census projection for males in 1970, and about the same for females. For both sexes combined, it is higher by a little more than one-half million in 1980. This projection utilizes a lower enrollment rate than the Census Bureau's rate for ages 25 to 34. An adjusted projection, shown in table B-5, provides the same enrollment rates at ages 25 to 34 as the Census projection presented in P-25, No. 232, II-A (high) series. This revised high projection is about 100,000 lower than the II-A series in 1970, but about 1,400,000 higher in 1980; this is the result of continuing a constant rate of increase in enrollment rates to 1980 and 1985. This revision is included in the figures in tables I–14, I–15, and I–16.

Neither the Census projection nor these projections provide for any increase in the percent of women enrolled in college in 1970 and 1980. There is some evidence in past trends that the percent of women enrolled in college is increasing slowly and might increase by about 3 percent a decade in the future. Women comprise the largest group of able high school graduates who do not go on to college; an increase in the percent of women attending college would be one way of maintaining the ability level of entering students while increasing the total percent in attendance.

An alternate projection which provides for an increase of women in college to 39 percent in 1970 and 42 percent in 1980 is shown in table B–5. To achieve these increases in the percent of women enrolled would require an increase of 500,000 women enrolled by 1970 and an increase of an additional 900,000 by 1980, or a total of 1.4 million over the high projection of enrollment for women in 1980. These alternatives are *not* included in the projections in tables I–15 and I–16. An increase of this magnitude would be hard to achieve, but the assumption of no increase in the percent of women among all college students may also be inaccurate, even though it is the result of extrapolation of enrollment rates of the past decade.

The high and low projections of enrollment differ by about 2 million in 1970, about 13 million in 1980, and about 18 million in 1985. Most of this difference (about 14½ million of the 18 million) is due to the different population projections used; the remainder is due to higher enrollment rates at the college level and, to a limited extent, higher enrollment rates in kindergartens and secondary schools.

Table B–5.—EFFECT OF INDICATED REVISIONS OF HIGH SERIES ENROLLMENT PROJECTIONS: 1970 AND 1980

Type of revision, year, and sex	1970			1980		
	Elementary	Secondary	Higher	Elementary	Secondary	Higher
TOTAL						
Original..	37,030	14,785	6,726	46,065	16,941	9,637
Adjusted for higher enrollment rates at ages 25 to 34..	37,034	14,796	6,924	46,079	16,988	10,450
Adjusted for higher percent of women in total enrollment....................................	37,034	14,796	7,428	46,079	16,988	11,849
MALE						
Original..	19,013	7,556	4,369	23,700	8,733	6,217
Adjusted for higher enrollment rates at ages 25 to 34..	19,016	7,564	4,528	23,712	8,765	6,849
FEMALE						
Original..	18,017	7,229	2,357	22,364	8,208	3,420
Adjusted for higher enrollment rates at ages 25 to 34..	18,018	7,232	2,396	22,367	8,223	3,601
Adjusted for higher percent of women in total enrollment....................................	18,018	7,232	2,900	22,367	8,223	5,000

Source: Computations described in the text.

NOTES

[1] Bureau of the Census, "Projections of the Population of the United States, by Age and Sex: 1964-1985," *Current Population Reports,* P-25, No. 286, (July 1964).

[2] Recent declines in the birth rate suggest that the "B" and "D" series of population projections in P-25, No. 286, might provide a more appropriate range of possibilities for future population growth. If series "B" rather than "A" had been used, by 1985 the high projection of elementary enrollment would have been about 3.9 million lower, the secondary enrollment projection would have been more than 1.5 million lower, and the high projection of college enrollment would have been reduced by over half a million. There would also have been corresponding, but smaller, reductions in the low series had series "D" been substituted for series "C."

APPENDIX C

QUESTION WORDING AND INSTRUCTIONS FOR EDUCATION ITEMS IN DECENNIAL CENSUSES

SCHOOL ENROLLMENT

Census 1840 (June 1, 1840)

Question wording: "Schools, etc., universities or colleges, number of students, academics and grammar schools, number of scholars, primary and common schools, number of scholars of public charge."

Population coverage: Population not specified. Tables indicate that the inquiries were asked of "free inhabitants," white and colored.

Instructions: Not specified.

Census 1850 (June 1, 1850)

Question wording: "Schedule Number 1. Free Inhabitants; Question 11. Attended school within the year."

Population coverage: "Free Inhabitants," white and colored.

Instructions: "Under heading 11, entitled 'at school within the last year.' The marshal should ask what member of this family has been at school within the last year; he is to insert a mark, thus, (1), opposite the names of all those, whether male or female, who have been at educational institutions within that period. Sunday Schools are not to be included."

Census 1860 (June 1, 1860)

Question wording: "Schedule Number 1.—Free Inhabitants; Question 12. Attended school within the year."

Population coverage: "Free Inhabitants," white or colored.

Instructions: Not specified according to Wright's *History and Growth of the United States Census, 1790-1880.* "The eighth census was carried on under the same plans and in accordance with the same methods which governed the seventh census." (That is, as it pertains to the questions on school enrollment.)

Census 1870 (June 1, 1870)

Question wording: "Schedule Number 1.—Inhabitants; Question 15. Attended school in the year."

Population coverage: "Persons 10 years of age and over."

Instructions: "The inquiries in columns numbered . . . 15 . . . are of such a nature that these columns only require to be filled when the answer to the inquiry is 'Yes' . . . if he or she attended school during the year, than an affirmative mark, thus (1), will be drawn in each of the above columns opposite the name."

Census 1880 (June 1, 1880)

Question wording: "Schedule Number 1.—Inhabitants; Question 21. Attended school within the census year."

Population coverage: Persons 10 years of age and over.

Instructions: "Note D.—In making entries in columns . . . , 16 to 23 an affirmative mark only will be used, thus, (1) . . ."

Census 1890 (June 1, 1890)

Question wording: "Schedule Number 1.—Population and Social Statistics; Question 18. Attendance of school (in months) during the census year (June 1, 1889 to May 31, 1890)."

Population coverage: Persons 5 to 17, inclusive.

Instructions: "18. Attendance at school (in months) during the census year June 1, 1889 to May 31, 1900. For all persons between the ages of 5 and 17, inclusive, the attendance of school during the census year should be in all cases stated in months and parts of months. Where a person within the above ages did not attend school at all during the census year write '0' and for all other persons to whom the inquiry is not applicable use the symbol 'X'."

Census 1900 (June 1, 1900)

Question wording: "Schedule Number 1.—Population; Question 21. Attended school (in months)."

Population coverage: Persons of all ages.

Instructions: Par. 224, Column 21. "Attended school (in months). For all persons attending school during the year ending June 1, 1900, enter the number of months (or parts of months) of school attendance, as 9, 8½, etc. If a person of school age did not attend school at all during the year, write '0'. For all other persons to whom the inquiry is not applicable, leave the column blank."

Census 1910 (April 15, 1910)

Question wording: "Schedule Inquiries—25. Attended school any time since September 1, 1909."

Population coverage: Persons of school age 5 to 21 years, inclusive, and persons below or above school age who actually attended school.

Instructions: Par. 185, Column 25. "Attended school any time since September 1, 1909. Write 'Yes' for any person who attended school, college, or any educational institution at any time since September 1, 1909, and 'No' for any person of school age, 5 to 21 years, who has not attended school since that date. For persons below or above school age, leave the column blank, unless they actually attended school."

Census 1920 (January 1, 1920)

Question wording: "Schedule Inquiries—Question 16. Attended school any time since September 1, 1919."

Population coverage: Persons of school age 5 to 21 years, inclusive, and persons below or above school age who actually attended school.

Instructions: Par. 133, Column 16. "Attended school any time since September 1, 1919. Write 'Yes' for a person who attended school, college, or any educational institution at any time since September 1, 1919, and 'No' for any person of school age 5 to 21 years who has not attended school, otherwise leave the column blank."

Census 1930 (April 1, 1930)

Question wording: "Population Schedule—Question 16. Attended school or college any time since September 1, 1929."

Population coverage: Persons of all ages.

Instructions: Par. 162, Column 16. "Attended school or college any time since September 1, 1929—write 'Yes' for a person who attended school, college, or any educational institution at any time since September 1, 1929, and 'No' for any person who has not attended school since that date. Include attendance at night school."

Census 1940 (April 1, 1940)

Question wording: "Schedule Inquiries—Question 13. Attended school or college any time since March 1, 1940? (Yes or No)."

Population coverage: Persons of all ages.

Instructions: Par. 466, Column 13. "Attended school or college any time since March 1, 1940, write 'Yes' for a person who at any time since March 1, 1940, has attended, or been enrolled in, any school, college, university, or educational institution. Enter 'No' for all others. Include attendance at a night school, extension school, or vocational school only if it is a part of the regular school system. Do not include correspondence school work of any kind."

Census 1950 (April 1, 1950)

Question wording: "Schedule Inquiries—Question 28. Has he attended school at any time since February 1st?"

Population coverage: Persons under 30 years of age.

Instructions: Item 28. "Make entry for every sample person.—An entry should be made for each person on a sample line. However, for those persons 30 years old and over it is not necessary to ask the question but merely to check the box '30 or over.' There should be a check in either 'Yes' or 'No' for each person under 30 years of age."

"Regular school.—Check 'Yes' for each person under 30 years of age who has attended or been enrolled in any 'regular' school at any time since February 1, 1950. (See section on Educational Attainment for 1950)."

Enrolled but not attending.—Check "Yes" for persons enrolled in school but who have not actually attended since February 1, 1950 (for example, because of illness).

Kindergarten.—Check "Yes" for persons attending kindergarten.

Tutor.—Check "Yes" for persons under 30 years of age receiving regular instructions at home from a tutor, if the instruction is comparable to that of a regular school or college.

"Nonregular" schools.—Check "No" for persons under 30 years of age who attended "nonregular" schools such as nursery schools, correspondence schools, business colleges, etc., and other schools not part of a regular public or private school system.

Census 1960 (April 1, 1960)

Question wording: "Question 16. Has he attended regular school or college at any time since February 1, 1960?"

Population coverage: All persons 5 to 34 years old.

Instructions: Mark "Yes, regular" school for the following:

a. Persons who have attended or have been enrolled in any "regular" school or college since February 1, 1960 (see section on Educational Attainment for 1960 for complete definitions of "regular" or "nonregular" schools).

b. Persons who have been enrolled in school or college since February 1, 1960, but who have not actually attended, for example, because of illness.

c. Children attending kindergarten.

d. Persons receiving "regular" instructions from a tutor.

Mark "No" for the following:

a. Persons not attending or not enrolled in any type of school since February 1, 1960.

b. Persons who have been enrolled in schools which are not "regular."

c. Children attending only nursery school.

d. Persons who are registered in school but who have not attended school since February 1, 1960, because the school has not been open.

Question wording: "Question 17. Is it a public school or a private school?

Population coverage: Persons reported as enrolled in school or college.

Instructions: Definitions of public and private or parochial schools:

a. *Public school* is any school or college which is controlled and supported *primarily* by a local, State, or Federal government or agency.

b. *Private or parochial school* is any school or college which is controlled and supported *primarily* by private persons or organizations.

EDUCATIONAL ATTAINMENT

Census 1940 (April 1, 1940)

Question wording: "Question 14. Highest grade of school completed."
Population coverage: 5 years of age and over.
Instructions: Column 14. Highest grade of school completed. Enter here, for each person, the last full grade of school completed, that is, the highest full grade that the person has successfully finished or from which he has been graduated. Do not include half years or grades that were not finished.

This question refers only to the education obtained in public, private, or parochial schools, colleges, or universities. Education obtained at vocational schools is not to be considered, unless such school or college was a part of the regular school system. For a person still in school, the last grade completed will be the grade preceding the one in which he is now enrolled. For a person who completed his formal education in an ungraded school or in a foreign country, enter the approximate equivalent grade in the American school system, or, if this cannot readily be determined, the number of years the person attended school. For a person who obtained his entire education in night school, enter the approximate equivalent grade completed. Indicate the grade as follows:

Grade completed	Entry in Column 14
None	0
Elementary school:	
First grade	1
Second grade	2
Third grade	3
Fourth grade	4
Fifth grade	5
Sixth grade	6
Seventh grade	7
Eighth grade	8
High schoool, academy, or equivalent:	
First year (sometimes known as 9th grade)	H-1
Second year (sometimes known as 10th grade)	H-2
Third year (sometimes known as 11th grade)	H-3
Fourth year (sometimes known as 12th grade)	H-4
College, university, or professional school:	
First year	C-1
Second year	C-2
Third year	C-3
Fourth year	C-4
Fifth or subsequent year	C-5

Census 1950 (April 1, 1950)

Question wording: "Question 26. What is the grade of school that he has attended?"

Population coverage: 5 years of age and over.

Instructions: Item 26. Enter highest grade of regular school ever attended.— Enter the highest grade of school that this person has ever attended in a "regular" school. This may be the grade he is now attending.

Enter the highest grade attended regardless of "skipped" or "repeated" grades. If the person reached a given grade or year of school in less time or in more time than is usually required, enter the grade or year of school attended (and not the number of years taken). For example, a child attending the seventh grade after only 5 years in school should be coded "S7" and a person who took 5 years to complete 4 years of college should be coded "C4."

"Regular" school.—The highest grade attended in a regular school refers to formal education obtained in graded public, private, or parochial schools, colleges, or universities, or professional schools, whether day school or night school, and whether attendance was full time or part time. That is, "regular" schooling is that which advances a person toward an elementary or high school diploma, or a college, university, or professional school degree.

"Nonregular" schools.—Do not count education or training received in the following, because they are usually not "regular" schools:

a. Vocational, trade, or business schools outside the "regular" system.— Exclude such schools unless they were graded and considered a part of a regular school system. Examples of schools usually not in the regular school system are barbers' schools, beautician schools, citizenship schools, and all other schools which are not affiliated with a city, county, State, or Federal educational system or with a private educational system.

b. On-the-job training.—Do not include any training obtained in connection with working on a job.

c. Correspondence schools.—Do not include any training received by mail from "correspondence schools." If, however, the correspondence course was given by a regular school, such as a university, and it counted toward promotion in the regular school system, it should be included.

Codes.—Use the following codes to indicate the highest grade attended in item 26:

	Code
None	O
Kindergarten	K

ELEMENTARY AND HIGH SCHOOL SYSTEMS
Elementary School

Grade	**Code**
First	S1

Second	S2
Third	S3
Fourth	S4
Fifth	S5
Sixth	S6
Seventh	S7
Eighth	S8

High School

Year	Code
First (ninth grade)	S9
Second (tenth grade)	S10
Third (eleventh grade)	S11
Fourth (twelfth grade)	S12

ELEMENTARY AND JUNIOR-SENIOR HIGH SCHOOL SYSTEMS

Elementary School

Grade	Code
First	S1
Second	S2
Third	S3
Fourth	S4
Fifth	S5
Sixth	S6

Junior High School

Year	Code
First	S7
Second	S8
Third	S9

Senior High School

Sophomores (first year)	S10
Junior (second year)	S11
Senior (last year)	S12

COLLEGE OR PROFESSIONAL SCHOOLS

First year	C1
Second year	C2
Third year	C3
Fourth year	C4
Graduate or professional school 1 year or more	C5

Nursery schools.—For children who have attended nursery school only, enter "0" as highest grade attended.

Seven-year elementary school system.—In some areas, the school system has or used to have 7 years of elementary school and 4 years of high school. Enter "S7" for persons who attended only the 7 years (that is, no high school). However, for persons who attended some high school, following their 7th grade, use the code "S9," "S10," etc., whichever is applicable. For example, a person who attended the third year of high school following 7 grades of elementary school, should be coded "S11."

Junior high school.—For persons who attended their highest grade in junior high school, do not assume that the correct entries will always be "S7," "S8," or "S9," although in most instances this will be true. In some junior-senior high school systems, the correct junior high codes may start with "S6," or end with "S10."

Post-graduate high school.—Enter "S12" for persons who have attended "post-graduate" high school courses after completing high school, but have not attended regular college.

"Normal" and professional schools.—In some areas a person may attend "normal" school after completing merely elementary school; elsewhere it follows 2 years of high school and in other places it may follow 4 years of high school or even some college. When the respondent answers in terms of "normal" school, attempt to obtain the equivalent in the regular school system.

Also in some areas, persons may attend professional schools (law, medicine, dentistry, nursing, etc.) after less than 4 years of college. When the respondent answers in terms of one of these schools, attempt to obtain the equivalent in college years.

Foreign schools.—For education obtained in foreign schools, enter the approximate grade equivalent in the American school system. If you cannot determine the approximate equivalent grade, determine the number of years the person attended school.

Ungraded schools.—Treat education obtained in ungraded schools in the same way as foreign schools in the above paragraph. Enter the regular school equivalent, or the number of years of attendance. For the person whose level of education was measured by "readers," the first reader is roughly equivalent to the first grade, second reader, to the second grade, etc.

Tutor.—Enter the approximate equivalent in the regular school system for education received from tutor.

Question wording: "Question 27. Was grade finished?"

Population coverage: 5 years of age and over.

Instructions: Item 27. Determine if grade entered in item 26 was completed.—This question refers to the highest grade ever attended, as entered in item 26. Check "Yes" if the person had fully completed the grade or year entered in item 26. Check "No" if the person did not finish the complete grade or year entered in item 26. (For example, he may have completed a half-grade, or he may have failed to "pass" the last grade he attended.)

Never attended school.—Check "No" for each person with an entry of "0" in item 26 without asking the question.

Census 1960 (April 1, 1960)

Question wording: "Question 14. What is the highest grade (or year) of regular school this person has ever attended?"

Population coverage: All persons 5 years old and over.

Instructions: "Item P14. What is the highest grade (or year) of regular school he has ever attended?"

Mark only one circle for this item. Mark "Never attended school" for persons who have never attended a "regular" school. Mark "Kindergarten" for those who have gone to kindergarten but not elementary school. Mark the circle designating the highest grade of school each person has ever attended in a regular school. For persons not attending a regular school, this will be the grade or year they are attending.

Definition of "Regular" school

The highest grade attended in a "regular" school refers to formal education obtained in graded public, private, or parochial schools, colleges, universities, or professional schools, whether day or night school, and whether attendance was full time or part time. That is, "regular" schooling is that which may advance a person toward an elementary or high school diploma, or a college, university, or professional school degree. Schooling in other than "regular" schools should be counted only if the credits obtained are regarded as transferable to a school in the regular school system.

Exclusion

Do *not* count education or training received in the following schools because they are usually not "regular" schools:

a. Nursery schools.—For children who have attended nursery school only, mark "Never attended school."

b. Vocational, trade, or business schools outside the "regular" system.— Exclude such schools unless they were graded and considered a part of a regular school system. Examples of such schools outside the regular system are television repairman's schools, barber's colleges, or typist's training schools.

c. Adult education classes.—Exclude adult education classes unless they will be counted for credit in a regular school system.

d. On-the-job training.—Exclude training obtained in connection with working on a job.

e. Correpondence schools.—In general, exclude training received by mail from correspondence schools. If, however, correspondence courses were given by a regular school, such as a university, and they are counted toward promotion in the regular school system, such schooling should be included.

Report exact code

If the answer is in terms of only the level of school and not the grade, determine the specific grade. For example, an answer of high school is not enough; it is necessary to know the highest year of high school attended.

How to determine highest grade in special situations

When questions arise, apply the following rules to determine the highest grade of school attended:

a. 7-year elementary system—In some areas, the school system has, or used to have, 7 years of elementary school and 4 or 5 years of high school. Mark "7" after "Elementary School" for persons who attended only 7 years in such a system and did not attend high school. For persons who attended some high school following the 7th grade, mark "High School 1" "High School 2," etc., whichever it applicable. For example, for a person who attended the first year of high school following 7 grades of elementary school, mark "High School 1." For persons who attended 5 years of high school under this system, mark "High School 4."

b. Junior high school—If the highest grade of school completed was a junior high school, determine the equivalent in elementary grades (1-8) or high school grades (1-4). Do not assume that junior high grades always consist of "elementary school 7," "elementary school 8," and "high school 1." In a few school systems, junior high starts with "elementary school 6," and in some it ends with "high school 2."

c. Post-graduate high school—For persons who have attended "post-graduate" high school courses after completing high school, but have not attended college, mark "high school 4."

d. Graduate or professional school—For persons who have attended more than 4 years of college, or who have attended professional school (law, medical, dental, etc.) after completion of some years of college, mark the number representing the total number of *full school years* the person attended college and graduate or professional school. If it was 6 years or more, mark "6 or more."

e. Miscellaneous situations—Translate to equivalent grades or years in the *"regular"* American school system any schooling received in foreign schools, ungraded schools, normal schools, or from private tutors. For the person whose level of education was measured by "readers" consider the first reader as equivalent to the first grade, second reader to the second grade, etc.

f. Skipped or repeated grades—For persons who skipped or repeated grades, enter the highest grade attended regardless of the number of years it took to arrive there.

Question wording: "Question 15. Did he finish the highest grade (or year) he attended?"

Population coverage: 5 years old and over.

Instructions: Mark this item "Yes" if the person has *successfully completed* the entire grade (or year) entered in item P14. Mark "No" if the person has *not* finished the entire grade entered in item P14. For example, he may have completed just a half year, or he may have failed to pass the highest grade he attended. For a person currently enrolled in a regular school, mark "No" since the grade has not yet been completed.

LITERACY

Census 1840 (June 1, 1840)

Question wording: "Number of white persons over 20 years of age in each family who cannot read and write."

Population coverage: White persons over 20 years of age who cannot read and write.

Instructions: Not specified.

Census 1850 (June 1, 1850)

Question wording: "Question 12. Persons over 20 years of age who cannot read and write."

Population coverage: "Free Inhabitants," white and colored, over 20 years of age who cannot read and write.

Instructions: Under heading 12, entitled "Persons over 20 years of age who cannot read and write." The marshal should be careful to note all persons in each family, over 20 years of age, who cannot read and write, and opposite the name of each make a mark, thus, (1); the space opposite the names of those who can read and write are to be left blank. If the person can read and write a foreign language, he is to be considered as able to read and write.

Census 1860 (June 1, 1860)

Question wording: "Question 13. Persons over 20 years of age who cannot read and write."

Population coverage: "Free Inhabitants," white and colored, over 20 years of age who cannot read and write.

Instructions: Not specified. According to Wright's *History and Growth of the United States Census, 1790-1880,* "the eighth census was carried on under the same plans and in accordance with the same methods which governed the seventh census." (This comment pertains to the question on literacy.)

Census 1870 (June 1, 1870)

Question wording: Education: "Question 16. Can not read." "Question 17. Can not write."

Population coverage: Persons 10 years of age and over.

Instructions: "The inquiries in columns numbered . . . . 16, 17 . . . . are of such a nature that these columns only require to be filled when the answer to the inquiry is 'Yes.' If he or she can not read or can not write . . . . then an affirmative mark, thus, (1) will be drawn in each of the above columns opposite the name."

"Education—It will not do to assume that, because a person can read, he can therefore write. The inquiries contained in columns 16 and 17 must be made separately. Very many persons will claim to be able to read, though they really do so in the most defective manner, will frankly admit that they can not write. These inquiries will not be asked of children under 10 years of age. In regard to all persons above that age, children or adults, male or female, the information will be obtained."

Census 1880 (June 1, 1880)

Question wording: Education: Question 22. Can not read. Question 23. Can not write.

Population coverage: Persons 10 years of age and over.

Instructions: "Note C.—Question Nos. . . . 22, and 23 are not to be asked in respect to persons under 10 years of age."

"Note D.—In making entries in columns . . . 16 to 23 an affirmative mark only will be used, thus (1), . . ."

Census 1890 (June 1, 1890)

Question wording: "Question 19. Able to read." "Question 20. Able to write."

Population coverage: Persons 10 years of age and over.

Instructions: Inquiries numbered 19 and 20 relate to illiteracy, and are to be made only if or concerning persons 10 years of age and over,

19. Able to read
    Write "Yes" or "No" as the case may be.
20. Able to write
    Write "Yes" or "No" as the case may be.

Census 1900 (June 1, 1900)

Question wording: "Question 22. Can read." "Question 23. Can write."

Population coverage: Persons 10 years of age and over.

Instructions: Paragraph 225.   Column 22.   Can read—Write "Yes" for all persons 10 years of age and over who can read any language, and "No" for all other persons of that age who cannot read in any language.   For persons under 10 years, leave the column blank.

Paragraph 226.   Column 23.   Can write—Write "Yes" for all persons 10 years of age and over who can write any language and "No" for all other persons of that age who cannot write in any language.   For persons under 10 years, leave the column blank.

Paragraph 227.   The inquiries in column 22, and 23 are intended to show the literacy of all persons 10 years of age and over and should be answered according as they are able to read and write the language ordinarily spoken by them.

Census 1910 (April 15, 1910)

Question wording: "Question 23.   Whether able to read."   "Question 24. Whether able to write."

Population coverage: Persons 10 years of age and over.

Instructions: Paragraph 181.   Column 23.   Whether able to read.—Write "Yes" for all persons 10 years of age and over who can read any language, whether English or some other, and "No" for all such persons who cannot read any language.   For persons under 10 years of age, leave the column blank.

Paragraph 183.   Column 24.—Whether able to write.—Write "Yes" for all persons 10 years of age and over who can write any language, whether English or some other, and "No" for all such persons who cannot write any language.   For persons under 10 years of age, leave the column blank.

Census 1920 (January 1, 1920)

Question wording: "Question 17.   Whether able to read."   "Question 18. Whether able to write."

Population coverage: Persons 10 years of age and over.

Instructions: Paragraph 134.   Column 17.   Whether able to read.—Write "Yes" for a person 10 years of age and over who can read any language, whether English or some other, and "No" for such persons who cannot read any language.   For persons 10 years of age, leave the column blank.

Paragraph 136.   Column 18.   Whether able to write.—Write "Yes" for a person 10 years of age and over who can write any language whether English or some other, and "No" for such persons who cannot write any language.   For persons under 10 years of age, leave the column blank.

Census 1930 (April 1, 1930)

Question wording: "Question 17.   Whether able to read and write."

Population coverage: Persons 10 years of age and over.

Instructions: Paragraph 163. Column 17. "Whether able to read and write.—Write 'Yes' for a person 10 years of age or over who can read and write in any language, whether English or some other, and 'No' for such person who cannot both read and write in some language. Do not return any person as able to read and write simply because he can write his own name. For persons under 10 years of age, leave the column blank."

APPENDIX D

GUIDE TO CENSUS DATA
ON EDUCATION

Decennial census statistics on school enrollment, illiteracy, and years of school completed for past years may be found in Census volumes for the years indicated in the guide below. However, since such data are distributed over a large number of tables, even within the volumes for a given census, it is often difficult to determine whether education statistics for a given year were published in certain area detail or in cross-classification with other items. Moreover, census data are sometimes revised after initial publication and more accurate statistics for a given year may be found in Census volumes for later years. For these reasons, and in order to indicate the kinds of historical data available, this guide to census data on education has been prepared.

It is by no means a complete index. For example, greater attention was given to data for the United States as a whole and for regions, than for smaller areas. Furthermore, it is possible that some pertinent references have been omitted. The reader should therefore regard this guide as a research aid, and should consult the original source if his work requires detailed use of census data which might be available.

This guide covers only the education data published in decennial census volumes. The same kinds of data are collected periodically through the Census Bureau's Current Population Survey (CPS) and are published in *Current Population Reports*. These surveys relate principally to the United States as a whole and are shown in cross-classification with other items in limited detail. For reference to CPS sources, and for statements about the comparability of Census and CPS education statistics, see *Current Population Reports,* Series P-20, Nos. 129 and 138.

The guide is presented in a form which groups references for different years according to kinds of cross-classifications and types of areas for which data were published. In order to simplify presentation, references to Census volumes have been abbreviated as follows:
United States Summary, 1960, Vol. I, *Characteristics of the Population;* Part 1.
    Coded as: U.S. '60.

State Summaries, 1960, Vol. I, *Characteristics of the Population;* Parts 2-57.
  Coded as: St. '60.
Subject Reports, 1960
  All coded as S.R., followed by the report number, such as 5A, etc.
Selected Area Reports, 1960

  All coded as A.R., followed by the report number, such as 1D, etc.
United States Summary, 1950, Vol. II, *Characteristics of the Population;*
  Part II.
  Coded as: U.S. '50.

State Summaries, 1950, Vol. II, *Characteristics of the Population;* Parts 3-54.
  Coded as: St. '50.
Special Reports, 1950
  All coded as S.R., followed by the report number, such as 5B, etc.

Sixteenth Census of the United States, 1940, Population; *Internal Migration
  1935-1940, Age and Economic and Social Characteristics.*
  Coded as: 16AES.
Sixteenth Census of the United States, 1940, Population; *Nativity and Parent-
  age of the White Population, General Characteristics.*
  Coded as: 16GC.
Sixteenth Census of the United States, 1940, Population; *Special Report on
  Institutional Population, Fourteen Years Old and Over.*
  Coded as: 16IP.

Sixteenth Census of the United States, 1940, Population; *The Labor Force*
  (Sample Statistics) : *Occupational Characteristics.*
  Coded as: 16OC.
Sixteenth Census of the United States, 1940, Population; *Characteristics of the
  Nonwhite Population by Race.*
  Coded as: 16NW.
Sixteenth Census of the United States, 1940, Population: *Differential Fertility
  1940 and 1910, Women by Number of Children Ever Born.*
  Coded as: 16CB.

Sixteenth Census of the United States, 1940, Population; *Differential Fertility
  1940 and 1910, Fertility by Duration of Marriage.*
  Coded as: 16DM.
Sixteenth Census of the United States, 1940, Population; *The Labor Force,
  Employment and Family Characteristics of Women.*
  Coded as: 16LF.
Sixteenth Census of the United States, 1940, Population and Housing; *Families,
  General Characteristics.*
  Coded as: 16FGC.

Sixteenth Census of the United States, 1940, Population; *Families, Types of Families.*

Coded as: 16FT.

Sixteenth Census of the United States, 1940, Population; *Education, Educational Attainment by Economic Characteristics and Marital Status.*

Coded as: 16 Ed.

Sixteenth Census of the United States, 1940, Population; *Education, Occupation, and Household Relationship of Males 18 to 44 Years Old.*

Coded as: 16EOH.

Sixteenth Census of the United States, 1940, Population; *Education, Educational Attainment of Children by Rental Value of Home.*

Coded as: 16EA.

Sixteenth Census of the United States, 1940, Population, Vol. II; *Characteristics of the Population,* Part I, United States Summary.

Coded as: U.S. '40.

Sixteenth Census of the United States, 1940, Population, Vol. II; *Characteristics of the Population,* Parts I-VII, State summaries.

Coded as: St. '40.

Fifteenth Census of the United States, 1930, Population, Vol. II; *General Report, Statistics by Subjects.* Chapters on School Attendance and on Illiteracy.

Coded as: U.S. '30.

Fifteenth Census of the United States, 1930, Population, Vol. III; Reports by States; *Composition and Characteristics for Counties, Cities, and Townships.*

Coded as: St. '30.

Note: Any table number followed by "S" indicates a summary table presented in the opening pages of the State Volume III. The tables for the individual States are indicated by merely the table number, as usual.

Fourteenth Census of the United States, 1920, Population, Vol. II; *General Report and Analytical Tables.* Chapters 11 and 12 on School Attendance and Illiteracy.

Coded as: U.S. '20.

Fourteenth Census of the United States, 1920, Vol. III, Population; *Composition and Characteristics of the Population by States.*

Coded as: St. '20.

Thirteenth Census of the United States, 1910, Vol. I, Population; *General Report and Analysis.* Chapters 12 and 13 on School Attendance and Illiteracy.

Coded as: U.S. '10, followed by the table number, taking into account the subject indexed and its corresponding chapter.

Thirteenth Census of the United States, 1910, Vol. II, Population; *Reports by States.*

Coded as: St. '10.

Twelfth Census of the United States, 1900, Vol. I, *Population;* Part I.
    Coded as: U.S. '0.
Twelfth Census of the United States, 1900, Vol. II, *Population;* Part II.
    Coded as: U.S. '00.
Report on Population of the United States at the Eleventh Census; 1890; Part
    II, *Population.*
        Coded as: U.S. '89.
    Included as a supplement to this report is the report on education in the
    back of this book, pages 1-141. General tables begin on page 46.
        Coded as: U.S. '89 E, followed by the table number indicating the sup-
        plementary table.
Compendium of the Eleventh Census: 1890, Part II.
    Coded as: C2 '89.
Compendium of the Eleventh Census: 1890, Part III.
    Coded as: C3 '89.

Tenth Census of the United States, 1880, Vol. I, *Population.*
    Coded as: U.S. '88.
Compendium of the Tenth Census: 1880, Part II.
    Coded as: C2 '88.

Ninth Census, Vol. I, 1870, *Population.*
    Coded as: U.S. '87.
Eighth Census, 1860; *Mortality and Miscellaneous Statistics.*
    Coded as: MM '86.

Seventh Census, 1850, Appendix.
    Coded as: U.S. '85.
Sixth Census, 1840, *Population.*
    Coded as: U.S. '84.

ILLITERACY

United States—Total
    1930—U.S.'30; 1,4,6,7,8; St.'30; 115,245.
    1920—U.S.'30; 1,4,7; St. '30; 115,245; U.S.'20; 1-3,21,23.
    1910—U.S.'30; 4,7; U.S.'20; 1,3; U.S.'10; 1-5,11-14,26,27,37.
    1900—U.S.'30; 4,7; U.S.'20; 1,3; U.S.'10; 2-4,14,26; U.S.'00; LXVI,73.
    1890—U.S.'30; 4; U.S.'20; 1; U.S.'10; 2-4,14,26; U.S.'89; 48; C3'89;
        47,54,60; C2'89.
    1880—U.S.'30; 4; U.S.'20; 1; U.S.'10; 2-4; U.S.'88; VII, VIII.
    1870—U.S.'30; 4; U.S.'20; 1.
    1860—MM'86; p. 508.
    1850—U.S.'85; XLIII.

United States—By Age
    1930—U.S.'30; 2-8,26-29; St.'30; 115,245.

1920—U.S.'30; 2,4,5,7; St.'30; 11,245; U.S.'20; 2-4.

1910—16CB; 51-56; U.S.'30, 4,5,7; U.S.'20; 3,4; U.S.'10; 5,6,8-10,12-14.

1900—U.S.'30; 4,5,7; U.S.'20; 3; U.S.'10; 6,8-10,14; U.S.'00; LXVI, 73.

1890—U.S.'30; 4; U.S.'10; 6,9,10,14; U.S.'89; 48; C3'89; 54,55-59,60.

1880—U.S.'30; 4; U.S.'88; VIII.

1870—U.S.'30; 4.

United States—By Sex

1930—U.S.'30; 4-8,26,27; St.'30; 245.

1920—U.S.'30; 4,5,7; St.'30; 245; U.S.'20; 1-4,23.

1910—16CB; 51-56; U.S.'30; 4,5,7; U.S.'20; 1,3,4; U.S.'10; 11-15,25,37.

1900—U.S.'30; 4,5,7; U.S.'20; 1,3; U.S.'10; 14; U.S.'00; LXVI, 73.

1890—U.S.'30; 4; U.S.'20; 1; U.S.'10; 14,26; U.S.'89; 48; C3'89; 48, 49-53,55-59,60; C2'89.

1880—U.S.'30; 4; U.S.'20; 1, U.S.'88; VII, VIII.

1870—U.S.'30; 4; U.S.'20; 1.

1860—MM'86; p. 508.

1850—U.S.'85; XLIII.

United States—By Color

1930—U.S.'30; 1,3-9; St.'30; 245.

1920—U.S.'30; 1,4,5,7; St.'30; 245; U.S.'20; 1-4,23.

1910—16CB; 51-56; U.S.'30; 4,5,7; U.S.'20; 1,3,4; U.S.'10; 1-5,11,12-14, 25,26,37.

1900—U.S.'30; 4,5,7; U.S.'20; 1,3; U.S.'10; 2-4,14,26; U.S.'00; LXVI,73.

1890—U.S.'30; 4; U.S.'20; 1; U.S.'10; 2-4,14,26; U.S.'89; 48; C3'89; 47,60; C2'89.

1880—U.S.'30; 4, U.S.'20; 1; U.S.'10; 2-4; U.S.'88; VII, VIII.

1870—U.S.'30; 4; U.S.'20; 1.

1860—MM'86; p. 508.

1850—U.S.'85; XLIII.

United States—By Residence

1930—U.S.'30; 3,8,9,28,29; St.'30; 245.

1920—St.'30; 245; U.S.'20; 23.

1910—16CB; 54.

United States—By Marital Status

1910—16CB; 51-56.

United States—By Number of Children Ever Born

1910—16CB; 51-56.

United States—By Nativity

1930—U.S.'30; 1,3-7; St.'30; 245.

1920—U.S.'30; 1,4,5,7; St.'30; 245; St.'20; 4.

1910—U.S.'30; 4,5,7; St.'20; 4; U.S.'10; 14,15.

Regions—By Sex
　　1930—U.S.'30; 12,13,16.
　　1920—U.S.'30; 12,13,16; U.S.'20; 7,8,12,13,22.
　　1910—16CB; 113-118; U.S.'30; 12,13; U.S.'20; 7,8,13; U.S.'10; 21,26,
　　　　28,37,38.
　　1900—U.S.'30; 12,13; U.S.'20; 7,8,13; U.S.'10; 26,28; U.S.'00; LV,LVI,
　　　　LXI,LXII,LXIII,LXIV,LXV,57,58-64,65,66-72.
　　1890—U.S.'10; 26; U.S.'00; LV,LVI,LXI,LXII,LXIII,LXIV,LXV;
　　　　U.S.'89; 32,33-39,40,44-47; C3'89; 48,49-53,54,55-59; C2'89.
　　1880—U.S.'00; LV,LVI.

Regions—By Color
　　1930—U.S.'30; 10-16; St.'30; 50S.
　　1920—U.S.'30; 12-16; St.'30; 50S; U.S.'20; 5-12,21,22.
　　1910—16CB; 113-118; U.S.'30; 12,13; U.S.'20; 7-11,21; U.S.'10; 16-19,
　　　　21-24,26-28,30,37.
　　1900—U.S.'30; 12,13; U.S.'20; 7,8; U.S.'10; 26,28,30; U.S.'00; LIX,
　　　　LXIV,LXV,56.
　　1890—U.S.'10, 26; U.S.'00; LIX,LXIV,LXV; U.S.'89; 31; C3'89; 47;
　　　　C2'89.
　　1880—U.S.'00; LIX.

Regions—By Residence
　　1920—U.S.'20; 21,22.
　　1910—16CB; 116-118; U.S.'20; 21; U.S.'10; 22-24.
Regions—By Marital Status
　　1910—16CB; 113-118.
Regions—By Number of Children Ever Born
　　1910—16CB; 113-118.
Regions—By Nativity
　　1930—U.S.'30; 10-16; St.'30; 50S.
　　1920—U.S.'30; 12-16; St.'30; 50S.
　　1910—U.S.'30; 12,13; U.S.'10; 18,19.
　　1900—U.S.'30; 12,13; U.S.'00; LVII,LVIII,LX,LXI,LXII,LXIII,56.
　　1890—U.S.'00; LVII,LVIII,LX,LXI,LXII,LXIII; U.S.'89; 31; C3'89;
　　　　47.
　　1880—U.S.'00; LVII,LVIII.

Regions—By Parentage
　　1910—U.S.'10; 20-24,26-28,30.
　　1900—U.S.'10; 26,28,30.
　　1890—U.S.'10; 26.
Regions—By Nationality
　　1910—U.S.'10; 29,37,38.
　　1900—U.S.'10; 38.

Regions—By Occupation
  1890—C3'89; 83.
Regions—By Degree of Illiteracy
  1900—U.S.'00; 57; 58-64.
  1890—U.S.'89; 32,33-39; C3'89; 48,49-53.

States—Total
  1930—U.S.'30; 10-13,16,17; St.'30; 50S,7.
  1920—U.S.'30; 12,13,16; St.'30; 50S,7; U.S.'20; 5-8,11-13,22; St.'20; 4.
  1910—U.S.'30; 12,13; U.S.'20; 7,8,11,13; St.'20; 4; St.'10; 10,I.
  1900—U.S.'30; 12,13; U.S.'20; 7,8,13; St.'10; 10. U.S.'00; LIV,56,57,65.
  1890—U.S.'00; LIV; U.S.'89; 31,32,40; C3'89; 47,54; C2'89.
  1880—U.S.'00; LIV; U.S.'88; VII,VIII; C2'88; CXXXVII.
  1870—C2'88; CXXXVII; U.S.'87; X.
  1860—C2'88; CXXXVII; MM'86; p. 508.
  1850—U.S.'85; XLIII,IX.
  1840—U.S.'84; summary table.

States—By Age
  1930—U.S.'30; 10-19; St.'30; 50S,7.
  1920—U.S.'30; 12-16; St.'30; 50S, 7; U.S.'20; 9,10,12,22; St.'20; 4.
  1910—U.S.'30; 12,13; U.S.'20; 9,10; St.'20; 4.
  1900—U.S.'30; 12,13; U.S.'00; LXVII, LXVIII, LXIX,65,66-72.
  1890—U.S.'00; LXVII,LXVIII,LXIX; U.S.'89; 40,41-47; C3'89; 54, 55-59.
  1880—U.S.'88; VIII; C2'88; CXXXVII.
  1870—C2'88; CXXXVII; U.S.'87; X.
  1860—C2'88; CXXXVII.

States—By Sex
  1930—U.S.'30; 12,13,16,18,19; St.'30,7.
  1920—U.S.'30; 12,13,16; St.'30; 7; U.S.'20; 7,8,12,13,22; St.'20; 4.
  1910—U.S.'30; 12,13; U.S.'20; 7,8,13; St.'20; 4; St.'10; 10.
  1900—U.S.'30; 12,13; U.S.'20; 7,8,13; St.'10; 10; U.S.'00; LV,LVI, LXI,LXII,LXIII,LXIV,LXV,57,58-64,65,66-72.
  1890—U.S.'00; LV,LVI,LXI,LXII,LXIII,LXIV,LXV; U.S.'89; 32,33-39,40,41-47; C3'89; 48,49-53,54,55-59. C2'89.
  1880—U.S.'00; LV,LVI; U.S.'88; VII,VIII; C2'88; CXXXVII.
  1870—C2'88; CXXXVII; U.S.'87; X.
  1860—C2'88; CXXXVII; MM'86; p. 508.
  1850—U.S.'85; XLIII,IX.

States—By Color
  1930—U.S.'30; 10-19; St.'30; 50.
  1920—U.S.'30; 12-16; St.'30; 50S; U.S.'20; 5-12,22; St.'20; 4.

1910—U.S.'30; 13,21; U.S.'20; 7-11; St.'20; 4; St.'10; 10,I.

1900—U.S.'30; 12,13; U.S.'20; 7,8; St.'10; 10; U.S.'00; LIX,LXIV,LXV, 56; U.S.'0; 68,69.

1890—U.S.'00; LIX,LXIV,LXV; U.S.'89, 31; C3'89; 47; C2'89.

1880—U.S.'00; LIX; U.S.'88; VII,VIII; C2'88; CXXXVII.

1870—C2'88; CXXXVII; U.S.'87; X.

1860—C2'88; CXXXVII; MM'86; p. 508.

1850—U.S.'85; XLIII,IX.

States—By Residence

1930—U.S.'30; 18,19; St.'30; 7.

1920—St.'30; 7; U.S.'20; 22; St.'20; 4.

1910—St.'20; 4; St.'10; 10.

1900—St.'10; 10.

Cities—Total

1930—U.S.'30; 20,21; St.'30; 65S,15,16.

1920—U.S.'30; 20; St.'30; 65S; U.S.'20; 14-20; St.'20; 10,11,13.

1910—U.S.'20; 16,17,20; U.S.'10; 31-36,38; St.'10; II,III,IV,V.

1900—U.S.'20; 16,17,20; U.S.'10; 31,34,35,38; U.S.'00; LXXI,74,79.

1890—U.S.'10; 34; U.S.'89; 49,54; C3'89; 61.

1870—U.S.'87; XI.

1840—U.S.'84; summary table.

Cities—By Age

1930—U.S.'30; 20-25; St.'30; 65S.

1920—U.S.'30; 20; St.'30; 65S; U.S.'20; 18,19; St.'20; 10,11,13.

1910—U.S.'10; 33.

1900—U.S.'00; 79.

1890—U.S.'89; 54,55-58; C3'89; 62.

1870—U.S.'87; XI.

Cities—By Sex

1930—U.S.'30; 20-22,24,25.

1920—U.S.'30; 20; U.S.'20; 16-20; St.'20; 10,11,13.

1910—U.S.'20; 16,17,20; U.S.'10; 32,34,36,39; St.'10.

1900—U.S.'20; 16,17,20; U.S.'10; 34,38,39; U.S.'00; 74,75-78,79,80-83.

1890—U.S.'10; 34; U.S.'89; 49,50-53,54,55-58; C3'89; 61,62.

1870—U.S.'87; XI.

Cities—By Color

1930—U.S.'30; 20-23; St.'30; 65S,15.

1920—U.S.'30; 20; St.'30; 65S; U.S.'20; 14-19; St.'20; 10,11,13.

1910—U.S.'20; 16,17; U.S.'10; 31-36,38,39; St.'10; II,III,IV,V.

1900—U.S.'20; 16,17; U.S.'10; 31,34,35,38,39; U.S.'00; LXXI; U.S.'0; 81.

1890—U.S.'10; 34.
1870—U.S.'87; XI.

Counties—Total
1930—St.'30; 13,14.
1920—St.'20; 9.
1910—St.'10; I.
1900—U.S.'00; 84.
1870—U.S.'87; X.
1850—U.S.'85; IX.
1840—U.S.'84; summary table.

Counties—By Age
1930—St.'30; 13,14.
1920—St.'20; 9.
1870—U.S.'87; X.

Counties—By Sex
1930—St.'30; 14.
1920—St.'20; 9.
1870—U.S.'87; X.
1850—U.S.'85; IX.

Counties—By Color
1930—St.'30; 13.
1920—St.'20; 9.
1910—St.'10; I.
1900—U.S.'00; 84.
1870—U.S.'87; X.
1850—U.S.'85; IX.

YEARS OF SCHOOL COMPLETED

United States—Total
1960—U.S.'60; 76,172-174.
1950—U.S.'50; 114-116; S.R.5B; A-C,E,1-6,8-13; S.R.2E; 5,9,14,19,24,29.
1940—U.S.'50; 114-116; U.S.'40; V,13,31-35; 16EA; I,II; 16GC; VI,26.

United States—By Age
1960—U.S.'60; 172-174.
1950—U.S.'50; 114-116; S.R.5B; A,E,1-6,8-13; S.R.5A; 2; S.R.5C; 20-23, 44,45.
1940—U.S.'50; 114-116; U.S.'40; V,13,31-35; 16GC; VI,16,26,31,60H, 2-6; 16EA; I,II,1,2.

United States—By Sex
1960—U.S.'60; 172-174.
1950—U.S.'50; 114-116; S.R.5B; A,C,E,1-6,8-13; S.R.3A; 9; S.R.5A; 2.

1940—U.S.'50; 114-116; S.R.3A; 9; U.S.'40; X,13,33-35; 16GC; VI,26, 31; 16EOH,2-6; 16EA; I,II,1,2.
United States—By Color
1960—U.S.'60; 76,172-174.
1950—U.S.'50; 114-116; S.R.5B; 1-6,8-13; S.R.2E; 5,9,14,19,24,29; S.R.5C; 20-23,44,45.
1940—U.S.'50; 114,116; U.S.'40; 13; 16GC,26,31; 16EOH; 2.

United States—By Residence
1960—U.S.'60; 76,172,173.
1950—U.S.'50; 114,115; S.R.5B; 1-5,13; S.R.2E; 5,9,14,19,24,29; S.R.5C; 20-23,44,45.
1940—U.S.'40; 13; 16EA; I,II,1,2; 16AES; 9; 16GC; 26,31.
United States—By Employment Status
1960—S.R.5A; 13; S.R.5B; 4,5; S.R.6A; 20.
1950—S.R.5B; 9,10.
1940—16LF; 17-19; 16Ed; 18.

United States—By Occupation
1960—S.R.5A; 13; S.R.5B; 8-10; S.R.7A; 9-11,32; S.R.7B; 1,4; S.R.7D; 4,10; S.R.7E; 7,9.
1950—S.R.1B; 10,11; S.R.5B; 11.
1940—16OC; 3,4; 16Ed; 23,24.

United States—By Income
1960—S.R.4C; 3,6; S.R.5A; 15; S.R.5B; 6,7,9,10; S.R.7A; 32; S.R.7B; 1,4; S.R.7D; 10; S.R.7E; 7,9.
1950—S.R.5B; 12,13.
1940—16Ed; 31,32.

United States—By Family Characteristics
1960—S.R.4A; 10,19-26,28,45,52-54; S.R.4B; 8a,8b,26; S.R.5A; 14.
1950—S.R.2A; 16,17,25.
1940—16FBC; 5; 16FT; 10; 16KOH; 5.
United States—By Fertility
1960—S.R.3A; 25-29,39,40.
1950—S.R.5C; 20-23,44,45.
1940—16CB; 23-32.

United States—For Institutional Population
1960—S.R.8A; 22,25-32.
1950—S.R.2C; 15.
1940—16IP; 6.
United States—By Marital Status
1960—S.R.5B; 4,5.
1950—S.R.5B; 8.

      1940—16Ed; 38-40.

United States—By Duration of Marital Status
      1950—S.R.2E; 5,9,14,19,24,29.
United States—By Nativity and Parentage
      1960—S.R.5A; 11; S.R.5B; 1.
      1950—S.R.3A; 9,10,11,21,22; S.R.5B; 5.
      1940—16GC; 26.
United States—By Race
      1960—S.R.1C; 9-31; 50-54; S.R.5A; 11.
      1950—S.R.3B; 8-14,20-24; S.R.5B; 5.
      1940—16NW; 6,12,18,24,30,36,42.

United States—By Persons of Spanish Surname
      1960—S.R.1B; 3,5,7,10,13,14.
      1950—S.R.3C; 3,6,8,9.
United States—For Puerto Ricans in U.S.
      1960—S.R.1D; 2,4,6,9,12,14.
      1950—S.R.3D; 4,5.

United States—By Mobility Status
      1960—S.R.2B; 6; S.R.2D; 7,8; S.R.5B; 3.
   1950—S.R.4B; 2,15,19,20; S.R.4C; 3,7,8; S.R.4D; 2,4,6,10-12,14; S.R.5B; 7.
      1940—16AES; 7.
United States—By Size of Place
      1960—AR1B; 1,6.
      1950—S.R.5A; 2,2a.
United States—By Value and Tenure of Home
      1940—16EA; 1,2; 16Ed; 5,6,13-16.
United States—By Veteran Status
      1960—S.R.8C; 7,11,12,16.
United States—For Americans Overseas
      1960—AR1C; 2,4,7,9,11,13,14,17.

Regions—Total
      1960—U.S.'60; 102,241.
      1950—U.S.'50; 153,154,172,173; S.R.5B; A,1,2,5,7-13.
      1940—U.S.'40; 31-35; 16EA; 3,4; 16GC; 27,28.
Regions—By Age
      1960—U.S.'60; 241.
      1950—U.S.'50; 153,154,172,173; S.R.5B; 1,2,4,5,7-13.
      1940—U.S.'40; 31-35; 16GC; 27,28,31,32; 16EA; 3,4.
Regions—By Sex
      1960—U.S.'60; 102,241.
      1950—U.S.'50; 153,154,172,173; S.R.5B; A,1,2,4,5,7-13.

1940—U.S.'40; 33-35; 16GC; 27,28,31,32; 16EA; 3,4.

Regions—By Color
1960—U.S.'60; 102,241.
1950—U.S.'50; 153,154; S.R.5B; 1,2,4,5,7-13.
1940—16GC; 27,28,31,32; 16EA; 3,4.

Regions—By Residence
1960—U.S.'60; 104,241.
1950—U.S.'50; 154; S.R.5B; 1,2,4,5.
1940—16EA; 3,4; 16GC; 27,28,31,32.

Regions—By Employment Status
1950—S.R.5B; 9,10.
1940—16LF; 18; 16Ed; 19,20.

Regions—By Occupation
1960—S.R.5B; 8; S.R.7B; 2,3,5,6; S.R.7D; 4.
1950—S.R.5B; 11.
1940—16OC; 3,5; 16Ed; 25-28.

Regions—By Income
1960—S.R.4C; 3; S.R.5B; 6,7; S.R.7B; 2,3,5,6.
1950—S.R.5B; 12,13.
1940—16Ed; 33-36.

Regions—By Family Characteristics
1960—S.R.4A; 10,22,45,53; S.R.4B; 8a,8b.
1940—16FT; 10; 16EOH; 4,6.

Regions—By Fertility
1960—S.R.3A; 25-29,39,40.
1940—16CB; 79-83.

Regions—By Institutional Population
1940—16IP; 10.

Regions—By Marital Status
1950—S.R.5B; 8.
1940—16Ed; 41,42.

Regions—By Nativity and Parentage
1950—S.R.3A; 21; S.R.5B; 5.
1940—16GC; 27,28,31,32.

Regions—By Race
1960—S.R.1C; 9-27.
1950—S.R.3B; 8-14.
1940—16NW; 6.

Regions—By Mobility Status
1960—S.R.2D; 7,8; S.R.5B; 3.
1940—16AES; 14,20,21.

Regions—By Value and Tenure of Home
    1940—16EA; 3, 4.
Regions—For Puerto Ricans in U.S.
    1960—S.R.1D; 4.
    1940—16Ed; 1,2,7-12.
Regions—By Size of Place
    1960—AR1B; 2-5,7.

States—Total
    1960—St.'60; 47,102,103.
    1950—St.'50; 20,64,65.
    1940—St.'50; 20,64,65; U.S.'40; 31-35; St.'40; 13.
States—By Age
    1960—St.'60; 102,103.
    1950—St.'50; 20,64,65.
    1940—St.'50; 64,65; U.S.'40; 31-35; St.'40; 13.
States—By Sex
    1960—St.'60; 47,102,103.
    1950—St.'50; 20,64,65.
    1940—St.'50; 20,64,65; U.S.'40; 33-35; St.'40; 13.
States—By Color
    1960—St.'60; 47,102,103.
    1950—St.'50; 20,64,65.
    1940—St.'50; 20,64,65; St.'40; 13.
States—By Residence
    1960—St.'60; 47,102,103.
    1950—St.'50; 20,64,65.
    1940—St.'40; 13.
States—By Income
    1960—U.S.'60; 223.
States—By Puerto Ricans in U.S.
    1960—S.R.1D; 2,6.
States—By Family Characteristics
    1940—16FGC; 25,39.

States—By Race
    1960—S.R.1C; 9-13,19-23.
    1950—S.R.3B; 20-24.
States—By Persons of Spanish Surname
    1960—S.R.1B; 3,5,7.
    1950—S.R.3C; 3,6,8,9.
States—By Mobility Status
    1950—S.R.4B; 15.
States—By Nativity and Parentage
    1940—16GC; 29,33.

Urban Areas—Total
    1960—St.'60; 34,36,38,64,65; AR1E; 1-6; AR1D; 6a,6b.
    1950—U.S.'50; 181; St.'50; 34,36,38,65.
    1940—St.'40; 30,31,39,48.
Urban Areas—By Age
    1960—St.'60; 64,65; AR1E; 1,3.
    1950—U.S.'50; 181; St.'50; 34,65.
    1940—U.S.'40; 58-63; St.'40; 30,31,39,48.
Urban Areas—By Sex
    1960—St.'60; 34; AR1E; 3,6; AR1D; 6b.
    1950—U.S.'50; 181; St.'50; 34,65.
    1940—U.S.'40; 59,60,62,63; St.'40; 31,39,48.

Urban Areas—By Color
    1960—St.'60; 36,64; AR1E; 1,2,6; AR1D; 6a.
    1950—St.'50; 36.
    1940—St.'40; 38,48.
Urban Areas—By Nativity and Parentage
    1950—S.R.3A; 11,22.
    1940—16GC; 30,34.
Urban Areas—By Race
    1960—S.R.1C; 50-54.
    1950—S.R.3B; 20-24.
    1940—16NW; 12,18,24,30,36,42.
Urban Areas—For Puerto Ricans in U.S.
    1960—S.R.1D; 4,9,12,14.
    1950—S.R.3D; 5.
Urban Areas—By Family Characteristics
    1960—S.R.4A; 21,28.
    1940—16FGC; 50,64; 16FT; 10.
Urban Areas—By Mobility Status
    1960—S.R.2C; 4,5.
    1940—16AEA; 24.
Urban Areas—By Employment Status
    1940—16LF; 18,20; 16Ed; 17.

Urban Areas—By Value and Tenure of Home
    1940—16Ed; 3,4.
Urban Areas—By Occupation
    1940—16Ed; 21,22.
Urban Areas—By Income
    1940—16Ed; 29,30.
Urban Areas—By Marital Status
    1940—16Ed; 37.

Urban Areas—For Persons of Spanish Surname
    1960—S.R.1B; 10,13.

Counties—Total
    1960—St.'60; 83,103.
    1950—St.'50; 42,44,48,49.
    1940—St.'40; 21,26,27.

Counties—By Age
    1960—St.'60; 103.
    1950—St.'50; 42.
    1940—St.'40; 26,27.

Counties—By Sex
    1960—St.'60; 83,103.
    1950—St.'50; 42.

Counties—By Color
    1960—St.'60; 87,103.
    1950—St.'50; 44.

Counties—By Residence
    1960—St.'60; 91,93.
    1950—St.'50; 48,49.
    1940—St.'40; 26,27.

SCHOOL ENROLLMENT

United States—Total
    1960—U.S.'60; 73,74; S.R.5A; 1-16.
    1950—U.S.'50; 42,43,66,111,112,113,119,151,170; S.R.5B; E,1,2,5.
    1940—U.S.'50; 110; U.S.'40; 11,12,30,V.
    1930—U.S.'50; 110; U.S.'40; 11,12; U.S.'30; 4,6; St.'30; 23S.
    1920—U.S.'50; 110; U.S.'40; 12; U.S.'30; 4; St.'30; 23S; U.S.'20; 1,2.
    1910—U.S.'50; 110; U.S.'40; 12; U.S.'30; 4; U.S.'20; 1,2; U.S.'10; 1-4,
        6,12.
    1900—U.S.'40; 12; U.S.'30; 4; U.S.'20; 1; U.S.'10; 12; U.S.'00; LI,LIII,
        48.
    1890—U.S.'40; 12; U.S.'30; 4; U.S.'20; 1; U.S.'89; 24,E:6,7,9,10,14;
        C3'89; 32,33,40; C2'89; 1,2-10.
    1880—U.S.'30; 5; U.S.'20; 1; U.S.'89; E:5,9,10.
    1870—U.S.'30; 5; U.S.'20; 1; U.S.'89; E4; U.S.'87; XII.
    1860—U.S.'30; 5; U.S.'20; 1; U.S.'89; E3; U.S.'87; XII; MM'86; p. 507,
        509,C.
    1850—U.S.'30; 5; U.S.'20; 1; U.S.'89; E2; U.S.'85; XLI,XLII.
    1840—U.S.'89; E1; U.S.'85; XLIV.

United States—By Single Ages
    1960—U.S.'60; 165-168; S.R.5A; 1-16.
    1950—U.S.'50; 110-113,151,170; S.R.5B; 1,2,4.

1940—U.S.'50; 110; U.S.'40; 11.

1930—U.S.'50; 110; U.S.'40; 11; U.S.'30; 1,8,9,29.

1920—U.S.'50; 110; U.S.'30; 1,9; U.S.'20; 3.

1910—U.S.'50; 110; U.S.'30; 9; U.S.'20; 3; U.S.'10; 5,8,10,11.

United States—By Age Groupings

1960—U.S.'60; 73,74.

1950—U.S.'60; 73,74; S.R.5B; 2,3,4,5,6; U.S.'50; 42,43,66,86,109,112,113, 170; S.R.5B; E.

1940—U.S.'60; 74; U.S.'50; 43; U.S.'40; V,11,12,30.

1930—U.S.'60; 74; U.S.'50; 43; U.S.'40; 11,12; U.S.'30; 1,6,7,10,11,29,30; St.'30; 10S,23S.

1920—U.S.'60; 74; U.S.'50; 43; U.S.'40; 12; U.S.'30; 1,7; St.'30; 10S,23S; U.S.'20; 2.

1910—U.S.'60; 74; U.S.'50; 43; U.S.'40; 12; U.S.'30; 7; U.S.'20; 2; U.S.'10; 3,4,6,7,9,11,12,19-22; U.S.'00; LI.

1900—U.S.'40; 12; U.S.'10; 12; U.S.'00; 48.

1890—U.S.'40; 12; U.S.'89; 24; E:16-21; C3'89; 33,40.

United States—By Sex

1960—U.S.'60; 165,166,167; S.R.5A; 3-16.

1950—U.S.'50; 109-113,117,151; S.R.5B; 5,6; S.R.1A; 12.

1940—U.S.'50; 110; U.S.'40; V,11,12,30.

1930—U.S.'40; 11,12; U.S.'30; 1,4,6-11,29,30; St.'30; 10S,23S.

1920—U.S.'40; 12; U.S.'30; 1,4,7,9; St.'30; 10S,23S; U.S.'20; 1,2,3.

1910—U.S.'40; 12; U.S.'30; 4,7,9; U.S.'20; 1-3; U.S.'10; 2,6,9-12.

1900—U.S.'40; 12; U.S.'30; 4; U.S.'20; 1; U.S.'10; 12; U.S.'00; LI,LIII, 48.

1890—U.S.'40; 12; U.S.'30; 4; U.S.'20; 1; U.S.'89; 24,E:16-21; C3'89; 33,40; C2'89; 1,2-10.

1880—U.S.'30; 5; U.S.'20; 1.

1870—U.S.'30; 5; U.S.'20; 1; U.S.'87,XII.

1860—U.S.'30; 5; U.S.'20; 1; U.S.'87; XII; MM'86; p. 507.

1850—U.S.'30; 5; U.S.'20; 1; U.S.'85; XLI.

United States—By Color

1960—U.S.'60; 73,74,165-167; S.R.5A; 3-10,12-16.

1950—U.S.'50; 109-113,117,151; S.R.5B; 1-6; S.R.1A; 12.

1940—U.S.'50; 110; U.S.'40; 11,12.

1930—U.S.'40; 12; U.S.'30; 2-4,6-10,29,30; St.'30; 23S.

1920—U.S.'40; 12; U.S.'30; 4,7,9; St.'30; 23S; U.S.'20; 1,3.

1910—U.S.'40; 12; U.S.'30; 4,7,9; U.S.'20; 1,3; U.S.'10; 1-3,6-10,12,21,22.

1900—U.S.'40; 12; U.S.'30; 4; U.S.'20; 1; U.S.'10; 12; U.S.'00; LI,LIII, 48.

1890—U.S.'40; 12; U.S.'30; 4; U.S.'20; 1; U.S.'89; 24,E:14; C3'89; 32,40; C2'89; 1,2-10.

1880—U.S.'30; 5; U.S.'20; 1.
1870—U.S.'30; 5; U.S.'20; 1.
1860—U.S.'30; 5; U.S.'20; 1; MM'86; p. 507.
1850—U.S.'30; 5; U.S.'20; 1; U.S.'85; XLI.

United States—By Residence
1960—U.S.'60; 73,165,168; S.R.5A; 1-7,11-16.
1950—U.S.'50; 42,109,111,112,117,151; S.R.5B; 1,2,4; S.R.1A; 12.
1940—U.S.'40; 11,12.
1930—U.S.'40; 11,12; U.S.'30; 3,10,11,30; St.'30; 23S.
1920—U.S.'40; 12; St.'30; 23S.
1910—U.S.'40; 12; U.S.'10; 19,20.
1900—U.S.'40; 12.
1890—U.S.'40; 12.

United States—By Employment Status
1960—U.S.'60; 197; S.R. 1C; 32-49,55-59.
1950—S.R.1A;12; S.R. ('60) 6A;10.
United States—By Occupation
1960—S.R.5A; 13; S.R.7A; 11.
United States—By Income
1960—S.R.5A; 10,15.

United States—By Family Characteristics
1960—S.R.4A; 28,54; S.R.4B; 23; S.R.5A; 3-8,14,16.
United States—For Institutional Population
1960—S.R.8A; 21,26,29-32.
1950—S.R.2C; 14.
United States—By Marital Status
1960—S.R.5A; 8,9.

United States—By Nativity and Parentage
1960—S.R.5A; 1,11.
1950—S.R.5B; 2.
1930—U.S.'30; 2-4,7-10,29,30.
1920—U.S.'30; 4,6,7,9.
1910—U.S.'30; 4,7,9; U.S.'10; 3,6,8-10,12.
1900—U.S.'30; 4; U.S.'10; 12; U.S.'00; LI,LIII,48.
1890—U.S.'30;⁴4; U.S.'89; 24; C3'89; 32,40.
1850—U.S.'85; XLI.

United States—By Race
1960—S.R.1C; 32-49,55-59; S.R.5A; 1,11.
1950—S.R.5B; 2,3.

United States—By Persons of Spanish Surname
    1960—S.R.1B; 4,11.
United States—For Puerto Ricans in U.S.
    1960—S.R.1D; 3,10.
United States—For Mobility Status
    1960—S.R.2B; 6,19,20.
    1950—S.R.5B; 4.
United States—By Size of Place
    1960—S.R.5A; 2,12; A.R.1B; 1,6.
United States—By Months of School Attendance
    1900—U.S.'00; 48.
    1890—U.S.'89; 24; C3'89; 40.

Regions—Total
    1960—U.S.'60; 239,240; S.R.5A; 2,12.
    1950—U.S.'50; 66,151,152,170; S.R.5B; 1,2,4,5.
    1940—U.S.'40; 30.
    1930—U.S.'30; 12; St.'30; 495.
    1920—U.S.'30; 121; St.'30; 495; U.S.'20; 4,12.
    1910—U.S.'30; 12; U.S.'20; 4; U.S.'10; 13,15-22,25,27-32.
    1900—U.S.'10; 28-32; U.S.'00; LII,33,34,42.
    1890—U.S.'89; 9,10,18,E:6,7,9-15; C3'89; 32,33,39; C2'89; 1,2-10.
    1880—U.S.'89; E:5,9,10,12.
    1870—U.S.'89; E4.
    1860—U.S.'89; E3.
    1850—U.S.'89; E2.
    1840—U.S.'89; E1; U.S.'85; XLIV.

Regions—By Single Ages
    1960—U.S.'60; 239,240; S.R.5A; 2,12.
    1950—U.S.'50; 150,151,152,170; S.R.5B; 1,2,4.
    1930—U.S.'30; 15.
    1920—U.S.'30; 15; U.S.'20; 13.
    1910—U.S.'30; 15; U.S.'10; 26.

Regions—By Age Groupings
    1950—U.S.'50; 66,151,152,170; S.R.5B; 2,4,5.
    1940—U.S.'40; 30.
    1930—U.S.'30; 12-20; St.'30; 495.
    1920—U.S.'30; 12-17; St.'30; 495; U.S.'20; 4,5,6,9-12,19,20.
    1910—U.S.'30; 12-17; U.S.'20; 4,5,6,9,19; U.S.'10; 13,16,28,29,31,33,34.
    1900—U.S.'10; 28,29,31; U.S.'00; LII,34,35-41,42,43-47.
    1890—U.S.'89; 10,11-17,18,19-23; C3'89; 33,34-38,39.

Regions—By Sex
    1960—U.S.'60; 239,240; S.R.5A; 12.

1950—U.S.'50; 150-152; S.R.5B; 5.
1930—U.S.'30; 13,20.
1920—U.S'30; 13; U.S.'20; 5,10-13,20.
1910—U.S.'30; 13; U.S.'20; 5; U.S.'10; 18,25-28,32,33.
1900—U.S.'10; 28,32; U.S.'00; 34,35-41,42,43-47.
1890—U.S.'89; 10,11-23,E:13,16-21; C3'89; 33-39; C2'89; 1,2-10.
1880—U.S.'89; E:12.

Regions—By Color
1960—U.S.'60; 239,240; S.R.5A; 2,12.
1950—U.S.'50; 150-152; S.R.5B; 1,2,4,5.
1930—U.S.'30; 16-20.
1920—U.S.'30; 16,17; U.S.'20; 7-9,12,13,20.
1910—U.S.'30; 16,17; U.S.'20; 8,9; U.S.'10; 13,15,17,25,26,28,30,31,33.
1900—U.S.'10; 28,30,31; U.S.'00; LII,33.
1890—U.S.'89; 9,E: 11,12,14,16-21; C3'89; 32; C2'89; 1,2-10.

Regions—By Residence
1960—U.S.'60; 104,240; S.R.5A; 2,12.
1950—U.S.'50; 150-152; S.R.5B; 1,2,4.
1920—U.S.'20; 19.
1910—U.S.'20; 19,22; U.S.'10; 33,34.

Regions—By Months of School Attendance
1900—U.S.'00; 42-47.
1890—U.S.'89; 18-23; C3'89; 39.

Regions—By Employment Status
1960—S.R.1C; 32-45.

Regions—By Nativity and Parentage
1950—S.R.5B; 2.
1930—U.S.'30; 16,18,20.
1920—U.S.'30; 16.
1910—U.S.'30; 16.
1900—U.S.'00; LII,33.
1890—U.S.'89; 9; C3'89; 32.

Regions—By Race
1960—S.R.1C; 32-45.
1950—S.R.5B; 2.

Regions—By Mobility Status
1960—S.R.2B; 19,20.
Regions—By Size of Place
1960—S.R.5A; 2,12; A.R.1B; 2-5,7.

States—Total
    1960—St.'60; 44-46.
    1950—St.'50; 18,19,62,63.
    1940—St.'50; 19,62; U.S.'40; 30; St.'40; 11,12.
    1930—St.'50; 19; St.'40; 11,12; U.S.'30; 12; St.'30; 495,6.
    1920—St.'50; 19; St.'40; 12; U.S.'30; 12; St.'30; 495,6; U.S.'20; 4,12;
        St.'20; 2.
    1910—St.'50; 19; St.'40; 12; U.S.'30; 12; U.S.'20; 4; St.'20; 2; St.'10;
        9,I.
    1900—St.'40; 12; U.S.'00; LII,33,34,42.
    1890—St.'40; 12; U.S.'89; 9,10,18,E:6,7,9-15; C3'89; 32,33,39; C2'89;
        1,2-10.
    1880—U.S.'89; E:5,9,10,12.
    1870—U.S.'89; E:4; U.S.'87; IX,X,XII.
    1860—U.S.'89; E:3; U.S.'87; IX,XII,XIII; MM'86; p. 506, p. 507.
    1850—U.S.'89; E:2; U.S.'87; IX; U.S.'85; XLI,XLII,VII,VIII.
    1840—U.S.'89; E:1; U.S.'85; XLIV; U.S.'84; summary table.

States—By Single Ages
    1960—St.'60; 44-46.
    1950—St.'50; 62,63.
    1940—St.'50; 62; St.'40; 11,12.
    1930—St.'40; 11,12; U.S.'30; 15,21,31; St.'30; 6.
    1920—St.'40; 12; U.S.'30; 15; St.'30; 6; U.S.'20; 13; St.'20; 2.
    1910—St.'40; 12; U.S.'30; 15; St.'20; 2; St.'10; 9,I.
    1900—St.'40; 12.
    1890—St.'40; 12.

States—By Age Groupings
    1960—St.'60; 44,45.
    1950—St.'50; 18,19,63.
    1940—St.'50; 19; U.S.'40; 30; St.'40; 11,12.
    1930—St.'50; 19; St.'40; 11,12; U.S.'30; 12-19,22,23,31,32; St.'30; 6.
    1920—St.'50; 19; St.'40; 12; U.S.'30; 12-17; St.'30; 6; U.S.'20; 4,5,6,9-12,
        19,21.
    1910—St.'50; 19; St.'40; 12; U.S.'30;12-17; U.S.'20; 4-6,9,19.
    1900—St.'40; 12; U.S.'00; LII,34-47.
    1890—St.'40; 12; U.S.'89; 10-23; C3'89; 33-39.

States—By Sex
    1960—St.'60; 101.
    1950—St.'50; 61-63.
    1940—St.'50; 62; St.'40; 11,12.
    1930—St.'40; 11-13, 21-23,32; St.'30; 6.
    1920—St.'40; 12,13; St.'30; 6; U.S.'20; 5,10-13; St.'20; 2.

1940—St.'40; 31,38,47.
1930—St.'40; 38; U.S.'30; 24,35; St.'30; 15,64S.
1920—St.'30; 64S; U.S.'20; 18; St.'20; 10,11,13.
1910—U.S.'10; 23,24,35-37; St.'10; II-V.
1900—U.S.'00; 49,55.
1890—U.S.'89; 25,30; E:22; C3'89; 40,41; C2'89; 11.
1870—U.S.'87; XI.
1840—U.S.'84; summary table.

Urban Areas—By Single Ages
1960—St.'60; 101.
1950—U.S.'50; 179,180; St.'50; 62,63.
1940—St.'40; 38,47.
1930—St.'40; 38; U.S.'30; 33,34.
1920—U.S.'20; 18.
1910—U.S.'10; 35.

Urban Areas—By Age Groupings
1960—St.'60; 73.
1950—U.S.'50; 86,93,179,180; St.'50; 34,62,63.
1940—U.S.'40; 57; St.'40; 31, 38, 47.
1930—St.'40; 38; U.S.'30; 25-28,33,34; St.'30; 15,64S,15.
1920—St.'30; 64S; U.S.'20; 14-17; St.'20; 10,11,13.
1910—U.S.'20; 15, 16; U.S.'10; 36,37; St.'10; II.
1900—U.S.'00; 49-55.
1890—U.S.'89; 25-30; C3'89; 41-45.

Urban Areas—By Sex
1960—St.'60; 101.
1950—U.S.'50; 180; St.'50; 62,63.
1940—St.'40; 38,47.
1930—St.'40; 38; U.S.'30; 24-26,28,33,34.
1920—U.S.'20; 17,18.
1910—U.S.'10; 35-37.
1900—U.S.'00; 49-55.
1890—U.S.'89; 25-30; C3'89; 41,42,45,46; C2'89; 11.
1870—U.S.'87; XI.

Urban Areas—By Color
1960—St.'60; 101.
1950—St.'50; 62,63.
1940—St.'40; 38,47.
1930—St.'40; 38; U.S.'30; 24-26.
1920—U.S.'20; 14-18.
1910—U.S.'20; 15,16; U.S.'10; 23,24,35-37; St.'10; II-V.

1890—U.S.'89; E:22; C2'89; II.
1870—U.S.'87; XI.

Urban Areas—By Employment Status
1960—S.R.1C; 55-59.
Urban Areas—By Family Characteristics
1960—S.R.4A; 28.
Urban Areas—By Race
1960—S.R.1C; 55-59.
Urban Areas—For Persons of Spanish Surname
1960—S.R.1B; 11.
Urban Areas—For Puerto Ricans in U.S.
1960—S.R.1D; 10.

Counties—Total
1960—St.'60; 83.
1950—St.'50; 42.
1940—St.'40; 21.
1930—St.'30; 13.
1920—St.'20; 9.
1910—St.'10; I.
1890—U.S.'89; E:8.
1870—U.S.'87; X.
1850—U.S.'85; VII,VIII.
1840—U.S.'84; summary table.

Counties—By Age Groupings
1960—St.'60; 83.
1950—St.'50; 42.
1940—St.'40; 21.
1930—St.'30; 13.
1920—St.'20; 9.
1910—St.'10; I.

Counties—By Sex
1870—U.S.'87; X.
1850—U.S.'85; VIII.

Counties—By Color
1960—St.'60; 87.
1910—St.'10; I.
1870—U.S.'87; X.
1850—U.S.'85; VIII.

INDEX

[The letter *n* after page number indicates reference to note]

W

Wages. *See* Salaries and wages.

Wallin, Paul, 193, 202n38

Wars, 24, 204

Washington, D.C., educational attainment, 183, 185

Webbink, Paul, iv

West (Region), 32n20, 89, 92–94, 98, 117, 152, 153, 155, 185

Western European foreign stock, educational attainment, 150, 151

Western Geographic Division, 3, 4, 16, 18, 20

White-collar workers, 44, 49, 51, 62, 123, 169
Literacy status, 121, 123

Windle, Charles, 129n1

Winston, Sanford, 122, 129n10, 129n11

Wolfle, Dael, 33, 67, 74n1, 75n27

Women
Educational attainment, 142–144, 189, 190
Employment status, 197–199, 210
Teachers, 80–84, 92, 96–98, 206

Work patterns
By high school graduation status, 48–52
College students, 71–73
Work-school patterns, 25
By urban-rural residence, 23

World War II (*see also* GI Bill of Rights, Veterans), 8, 27, 28

Wright, Carroll, 30n1, 30n2, 30n4, 239, 249

Y

Years of school completed (*see also* Educational attainment), 224, 225
Census definitions, 135, 220, 221
Length of school year, 31n6, 224
Median, 132, 136, 143, 145, 146, 170
Misreporting, 221–224

Yugoslavia, literacy data, 129n1

Z

Zarhovic, S. S., 129n1

Zelditch, Morris, 200n14